# STUDIES IN HEBREW AND ARAMAIC SYNTAX

# STUDIES IN SEMITIC LANGUAGES AND LINGUISTICS

EDITED BY

J. H. HOSPERS AND C.H.M. VERSTEEGH

XVII

STUDIES IN HEBREW AND ARAMAIC SYNTAX

Professor J. Hoftijzer.

# STUDIES IN HEBREW AND ARAMAIC SYNTAX

PRESENTED TO

## PROFESSOR J. HOFTIJZER

ON THE OCCASION OF HIS SIXTY-FIFTH BIRTHDAY

EDITED BY

K. JONGELING, H.L. MURRE-VAN DEN BERG AND L. VAN ROMPAY

E.J. BRILL
LEIDEN • NEW YORK • KØBENHAVN • KÖLN
1991

The paper in this book meets the guidelines for permanence and durability of the Committee on Production Guidelines for Book Longevity of the Council on Library Resources.



**Library of Congress Cataloging-in-Publication Data**

Studies in Hebrew and Aramaic syntax : presented to Professor J. Hoftijzer on the occasion of his sixty-fifth birthday / edited by K. Jongeling, H. L. Murre-Van den Berg, and L. van Rompay.
p. cm.—(Studies in Semitic languages and linguistics : 17)
Includes bibliographical references.
ISBN 90-04-09520-9
1. Hebrew language—Syntax. 2. Aramaic language—Syntax. 3. Bible. O.T.—Language, style. I. Jongeling, K. II. Murre-Van den Berg, H. L. III. Rompay, Lucas van. IV. Hoftijzer, J. (Jacob) V. Series.
PJ4514.H64S78 1991
492.4'5—dc20 91-29240
CIP

ISSN 0081-8461
ISBN 90 04 09520 9



PRINTED IN THE NETHERLANDS

# Contents

# Acknowledgements

This volume has been prepared in the Department of Hebrew, Aramaic and Ugaritic Languages and Cultures of the University of Leiden. From its inception the Board of the Department welcomed the idea of the Festschrift and contributed to its progress and completion.

The articles submitted by the authors were converted to a format acceptable for the typesetting program TEX (used with the LATEX system) by dr. K. Jongeling and drs. H.L. Murre - van den Berg.

Dr. W.J. Jaffe kindly allowed us to use the Hebrew font created by him and helped us, moreover, to solve a number of technical problems.

We should like to thank the "Oosters Genootschap in Nederland" for having provided a subvention to defray the costs of publication. We gratefully acknowledge the willingness of the editorial board of "Studies in Semitic Languages and Linguistics" to include the volume in their series. In this way it also benefited from the expertise of the publishing-house E.J. Brill.

Leiden, 17 May 1991. The editors.

# Preface

This volume is dedicated to professor Jacob Hoftijzer on the occasion of his retirement from the chair of "Hebrew Language and Literature, the Israelite Antiquities and Ugaritic" at the State University of Leiden.

There are as many kinds of *Festschriften* as there are types of scholars. The reader will have no difficulty in recognising this volume as a modest tribute by colleagues and fellow scholars —a number of them former students— writing on subjects of Hebrew and Aramaic grammar and linguistics. These lines are therefore not meant as an introduction to the book and its contents. This is, rather, the place to make a few remarks on the scholarly work of the dedicatee, and on the events that determined his career — refraining from a detailed exposition of professor Hoftijzer's personal merits. At the same time these remarks should be regarded as a small tribute from a close colleague, acting as the representative of the Department in which professor Hoftijzer has served for such a long period.

Like many other semitists, professor Hoftijzer began his academic career as a student of Divinity. He chose the study of the Old Testament as his special field of interest and made his entrance in the scholarly world with a dissertation on the promises to the Patriarchs contained in the book of Genesis. This study, appearing in 1956, is a strictly scholarly analysis of the passsages containing God's blessings of Abraham, Isaac and Jacob, and —to the slight amazement even of the author himself— its results fell in line with the dominant Documentary Hypothesis of Pentateuchal criticism.

The plan to complete the dictionary of North-West Semitic inscriptions, started by the French scholar Ch.-F. Jean, the publication of which had stopped at the latter's sudden demise, brought Hoftijzer deeper into the field of Semitic philology. This ambitious and time consuming project was completed in 1965. It is not only a compilation of previous scholarship, but also marks the progress of the research in this specialised field, and it contains many new contributions and insights. It established Hoftijzer's reputation as a dedicated and discerning scholar. In the same period his study on the use of the particle *ʾęt* in Classical Hebrew appeared. This article revealed the linguistic and theoretical side of Hoftijzer's work. Henceforward these two poles characterised his scholarly output: the close analysis of texts —both epigraphical and documentary— by means of sound grammatical reasoning and thorough semantic study of the lexicon on the one hand, and the methodological reassessment of the description of Classical Hebrew on the other.

In the latter category a number of studies may be mentioned. Most important are his "Search for Method", demonstrated on the use and function of the *H-locale* (1981), the study of the imperfect forms with *nun paragogicum* (1985) and a similar study on the short imperfect forms that still awaits its final revision.

During his work on the dictionary of North-West Semitic inscriptions, Hoftijzer had joined the staff of the Department of Hebrew, Aramaic and Ugaritic, at the time headed by professor T. Jansma. In this department he became the ordinarius for "Hebrew Language and Literature, Israelite Antiquities and Ugaritic" in 1973. The interest in matters of methodology and linguistic theory, mentioned above, was confirmed by the subject of his inaugural lecture (1974), dealing with the problems of the verbal system of Classical Hebrew. The same interest was apparent in a long study on the Hebrew nominal clause, published the year before (1973).

The other pole of Hoftijzer's interest, text interpretation, was greatly stimulated by the discovery, in 1967, of large fragments of an ancient plaster text at the excavations in Deir ʿAlla (Jordan) by a team of archeologists from Leiden. The decipherment, interpretation and edition of this text, in which unexpectedly the prophet Balaam was encountered, was entrusted to professor Hoftijzer and, in co-operation with G. van der Kooij, he published the text with ample comments in 1976. The edition is an example of careful and dedicated editing which inspired discussions on a number of linguistic and historical issues. The vividness of these discussions splendidly manifested itself during a symposium on the Deir ʿAlla texts, organised by Hoftijzer and Van der Kooij in the summer of 1989 to evaluate fourteen years of scholarly research.

The latest scholarly enterprise to be mentioned, the results of which are not yet at the disposal of the scholarly world, has engaged professor Hoftijzer for more than ten years now. During this period he has been engaged, in close cooperation with K. Jongeling, in the preparation of a greatly enlarged edition of the Dictionary of North-West Semitic inscriptions. Since the number of texts and the scholarly literature related to them greatly increased during the last decades, the scope and complexity of the dictionary has grown accordingly. At the present moment the text is completed and the final editing of the text will take place in the course of 1991.

The studies presented in this volume are all related to syntactical questions, one of Hoftijzer's main interests. In several of them the authors are found quoting and discussing Hoftijzer's publications in this particular field. A volume like this, therefore, is an appropriate tribute to the *honorandus*. Let it be accompanied by the sincere expression of our gratitude as well as by our best wishes for a successful continuation of the work in which he is engaged.

A. van der Heide,
h.t. chairman of the Department of
Hebrew, Aramaic and Ugaritic
languages and cultures.

# Bibliography of the Works of J. Hoftijzer

This bibliography covers the period 1953-1991. Book reviews have not been included. They have appeared in *Bibliotheca Orientalis*, *Nederlands Theologisch Tijdschrift*, *Orientalistische Literaturzeitung*, *Theologische Literaturzeitung*, *Ugarit-Forschungen* and *Vetus Testamentum*.

1. "A propos d'une interprétation récente de deux passages difficiles: Zach. xii 11 et Zach. xi 13", *Vetus Testamentum* 3 (1953), pp. 407-409.

2. *Die Verheissungen an die drei Erzväter*, Leiden 1956.

3. "Ex. xxi 8", *Vetus Testamentum* 7 (1957), pp. 388-391.

4. "Some Remarks to the Tale of Noah's Drunkenness", *Oudtestamentische Studiën* 12 (1958), pp. 22-27.

5. "Kanttekeningen bij het onderzoek van de Westsemitische epigrafie", *Jaarbericht van het Vooraziatisch-Egyptisch Genootschap Ex Oriente Lux* 15 (1957-1958), pp. 112-125.

6. "Eine Notiz zum punischen Kinderopfer", *Vetus Testamentum* 8 (1958), pp. 288-292.

7. "Notae Aramaicae", *Vetus Testamentum* 9 (1959), pp. 312- 318.

8. "Enige opmerkingen rond het Israëlitische 12-stammensysteem", *Nederlands Theologisch Tijdschrift* 14 (1959/60), pp. 241-263.

9. "Deux inscriptions votives puniques inédites", *Vetus Testamentum* 11 (1961), pp. 343-344.

10. "Notes sur une épitaphe en écriture néopunique", *Vetus Testamentum* 11 (1961), pp. 344-348.

11. "Het zogenoemde Rijksaramees", in: M. de Mey, A. Sieders, R. Zuurmond (edd.), *Theologische Studiën uitgegeven ter gelegenheid van de Dies Natalis LXV van het Collegium Theologicum*

*cui symbolum Concordia Res Parva Crescit*, Leiden 1961, pp. 39-44.

12. "Ein Papyrusfragment aus El-Hibeh", *Vetus Testamentum* 12 (1962), pp. 341-342.

13. (In collaboration with P.W. Pestman), "Hereditary Rights as Laid down in the Marriage Contract Krael. 2", *Bibliotheca Orientalis* 19 (1962), pp. 216-219.

14. (In collaboration with P.H.L. Eggermont), *The Moral Edicts of King Aśoka. Included the Greco-Aramaic Inscription of Kandahar and Further Inscriptions of the Maurian Period* (Textus Minores 29), Leiden 1962.

15. "Deux vases à inscription identique", *Vetus Testamentum* 13 (1963), pp. 337-339.

16. "La nota accusativi *ᵓt* en phénicien", *Le Muséon* 76 (1963), pp. 195-200.

17. "Liste des pierres et moulages à textes phéniciens/puniques du Musée des Antiquités à Leyde", *Oudheidkundige Mededelingen uit het Rijksmuseum van Oudheden te Leiden* 44 (1963), pp. 89-98.

18. "In Memoriam Prof. Dr. G.J. Thierry", *Phœnix* 8 (1962), pp. 124-125.

19. (Based on a manuscript by Ch.-F. Jean), *Dictionnaire des inscriptions sémitiques de l'Ouest*, Leiden 1965.

20. "Remarks concerning the Use of the Particle *ᵓt* in Classical Hebrew", *Oudtestamentische Studiën* 14 (1965), pp. 1-99.

21. "Das sogenannte Feueropfer", in: B. Hartmann e.a. (edd.), *Hebräische Wortforschung. Festschrift zum 80. Geburtstag von Walter Baumgartner* (Supplements to Vetus Testamentum 16), Leiden 1967, pp. 114-134.

22. *Religio Aramaica. Godsdienstige verschijnselen in Aramese teksten* (Mededelingen en Verhandelingen van het Vooraziatisch-Egyptisch Genootschap Ex Oriente Lux 16), Leiden 1968.

23. "De zogenaamde Phoenicische tekst van Parahyba", *Phœnix* 14 (1968), pp. 182-185.

24. "Ontdekten de Foeniciërs Amerika?", *Spiegel Historiael* 4 (1969), pp. 431-432.

25. "Scrolls from the Wilderness of the Dead Sea", *UCLA Librarian* (University of California Library, Los Angeles) 22,3 (1969), pp. 13-14.

26. (In collaboration with J.P. Hayes), "Notae Hermopolitanae", *Vetus Testamentum* 20 (1970), pp. 98-106.

27. "David and the Tekoite Woman", *Vetus Testamentum* 20 (1970), pp. 419-444.

28. "Absalom and Tamar: A Case of Fratriarchy?", in: *Schrift en uitleg. Studies ... aangeboden aan Prof. Dr. W.H. Gispen ter gelegenheid van zijn vijfentwintigjarig ambtsjubileum als hoogleraar aan de Vrije Universiteit te Amsterdam en ter gelegenheid van het bereiken van de zeventigjarige leeftijd*, Kampen 1970, pp. 54-61.

29. "A Note on *ʾiky*", *Ugarit-Forschungen* 3 (1971), p. 360.

30. "A Note on G 1083³: *ʾištʾir* and Related Matters", *Ugarit-Forschungen* 3 (1971), pp. 361-364.

31. "A Peculiar Question: A Note on 2 Sam. xv 27", *Vetus Testamentum* 21 (1971), pp. 606-609.

32. (In collaboration with B. Hartmann), "Ugaritic *hnk-hnkt* and a Punic Formula", *Le Muséon* 84 (1971), pp. 529-535.

33. "Two Notes on the Baʿal Cyclus", *Ugarit-Forschungen* 4 (1972), pp. 155-158.

34. "The Nominal Clause Reconsidered", *Vetus Testamentum* 23 (1973), pp. 446-510.

35. *De ontcijfering van Deir-ʿAlla-teksten* (Oosters Genootschap in Nederland 5), Leiden 1973.

36. *Verbale vragen. Rede uitgesproken bij de aanvaarding van het ambt van gewoon hoogleraar in het Hebreeuws, de Israëlitische Oudheden en het Ugaritisch aan de Rijksuniversiteit te Leiden op 10 mei 1974*, Leiden 1974.

37. "Een opmerking bij II Sam. 15:24 (*wayyaṣṣīqū*)", in: M.S.H.G. Heerma van Voss, Ph.H.J. Houwink ten Cate, N.A. van Uchelen (edd.), *Travels in the World of the Old Testament. Studies Presented to Professor M.A. Beek on the Occasion of his 65th Birthday*, Assen 1974, pp. 91-93.

38. "Opgravingen in Deir ‹Allā en de daar gedane tekstvondst. De teksten", in: *Jaarboek 1973* (Nederlandse Organisatie voor Zuiver-Wetenschappelijk Onderzoek), 's Gravenhage 1974, pp. 121-123.

39. (In collaboration with G. van der Kooij), *Aramaic Texts from Deir ‹Alla* (Documenta et Monumenta Orientis Antiqui 19), Leiden 1976.

40. "The Prophet Balaam in a 6th Century Aramaic Inscription", *Biblical Archaeologist* 39 (1976), pp. 11-17 [= English translation of no. 35].

41. "De Aramese tekst uit Deir ‹Alla", *Phœnix* 22 (1976), pp. 84-91.

42. "Note on a Newly Found Text Fragment on a Bowl from Deir ‹Alla", *Annual of the Department of Antiquities, Amman* 22 (1977/78), pp. 79-80.

43. "Une lettre du roi de Tyr", in: *Festschrift für Claude F.A. Schaeffer zum 80. Geburtstag* [= *Ugarit-Forschungen* 11 (1979)], pp. 383-388.

44. "Hebreeuws en Aramees als Bijbeltalen", in: A.S. van der Woude (ed.), *Bijbels Handboek*, I. *De Wereld van de Bijbel*, Kampen 1981, pp. 173-200.

45. *A Search for Method. A Study in the Syntactic Use of the H-locale in Classical Hebrew* (Studies in Semitic Languages and Linguistics 12), Leiden 1981.

46. "Schaatsen op dun ijs. Linguïstisch onderzoek van beperkt materiaal", *Forum der Letteren* 22 (1981), pp. 195-203.

47. "Quodlibet Ugariticum", in: G. van Driel, Th.J. Krispijn, M. Stol, K.R. Veenhof (edd.), *Zikir Šumim. Assyriological Studies Presented to F.R. Kraus on the Occasion of his Seventieth Birthday*, Leiden 1982, pp. 121-127.

48. "Une lettre du roi hittite", in: W.C. Delsman e.a. (edd.), *Von Kanaan bis Kerala. Festschrift für Prof. Mag. Dr. Dr. J.P.M. van der Ploeg O.P. zum Vollendung des siebzigsten Lebensjahres* (Alter Orient und Altes Testament 211), Neukirchen-Vluyn 1982, pp. 379-387.

49. "Ugaritische brieven uit de tijd van de ondergang van de stad", in: K.R. Veenhof (ed.), *Schrijvend Verleden. Documenten uit het Oude Nabije Oosten vertaald en toegelicht*, Leiden - Zutphen 1983, pp. 94-99.

50. "De Hermopolis-Papyri. Arameese brieven uit Egypte (5e eeuw v.Chr.)", K.R. Veenhof (ed.), *Schrijvend Verleden. Documenten uit het Oude Nabije Oosten vertaald en toegelicht*, Leiden - Zutphen 1983, pp. 107-119.

51. "Enkele opmerkingen over Psalm 139, vss 2 en 4", in: *Feestbundel aangeboden aan Adriaan Cornelis Schuurman*, Den Haag 1984, pp. 46-50.

52. *The Function and Use of the Imperfect Forms with nun paragogicum in Classical Hebrew* (Studia Semitica Neerlandica 21), Assen - Maastricht 1985.

53. "Some Remarks on the Semantics of *lqr*ʾ*t* in Classical Hebrew", *Jaarbericht van het Vooraziatisch-Egyptisch Genootschap Ex Oriente Lux* 28 (1983/84), pp. 103-109.

54. "A Grammatical Note on the Yavne-Yam Ostracon", in: J.W. van Henten, H.J. de Jonge, P.T. van Rooden, J.W. Wesselius (edd.), *Tradition and Re-interpretation in Jewish and Early Christian Literature. Essays in Honour of Jürgen C.H. Lebram* (Studia Post-Biblica 36), Leiden 1986, pp. 1-6.

55. "Frustula epigraphica hebraica", in: H.L.J. Vanstiphout, K. Jongeling, F. Leemhuis and G.J. Reinink (edd.), *Scripta Signa Vocis. Studies about Scripts, Scriptures, Scribes and Languages in the Near East, Presented to J.H. Hospers by his Pupils, Colleagues and Friends*, Groningen 1986, pp. 85-93.

56. "Hebrew and Aramaic as Biblical Languages", in: A.S. van der Woude (ed.), *The World of the Bible. Bible Handbook*, I, Grand Rapids (Mich.) 1986, pp. 121-142 [= Revised Translation of no 44].

57. "Aramäische Prophetien. Die Inschriften von Deir ʿAlla", in: O. Kaiser (ed.), *Texte aus der Umwelt des Alten Testaments*, Band II, Lieferung l, Gütersloh 1986, pp. 138-148.

58. "A Palmyrene Bas-Relief with Inscriptions", *Oudheidkundige Mededelingen uit het Rijksmuseum van Oudheden te Leiden*, 68 (1988), pp. 37-39.

59. "Three Unpublished Punic Votive Texts", *Oudheidkundige Mededelingen uit het Rijksumuseum van Oudheden te Leiden*, 68 (1988), pp. 41-43.

60. "An Unpublished Aramaic Fragment from Elephantine", *Oudheidkundige Mededelingen uit het Rijksmuseum van Oudheden te Leiden*, 68 (1988), pp. 45-48.

61. *Grammatica toch nuttig. Over het nut van grammaticaal onderzoek voor Bijbelstudie, speciaal voor het Oude Testament*, Vierhouten 1988.

62. "Philological-Grammatical Notes on 1 Kings xi 14", in: A.S. van der Woude (ed.), *New Avenues in the Study of the Old Testament. A Collection of Old Testament Studies Published on the Occasion of the Fiftieth Anniversary of the Oudtestamentisch Werkgezelschap and the Retirement of Prof. Dr. M.J. Mulder* [= *Oudtestamentische Studiën* 25 (1989)], pp. 29-37.

63. "Six Shekel and a Half. Notes on Hermopolis Letters 2 and 6", *Studi epigrafici e linguistici* 6 (1989), pp. 117-122.

64. "In Memoriam Prof. Dr. P.A.H. de Boer (1910-1989)", *Phœnix* 36 (1990), pp. 4-6.

65. "What did the Gods Say? Remarks on the First Combination of the Deir ʿAlla-Plaster Texts", in: J. Hoftijzer and G. van der Kooij (edd.), *The Balaam Text from Deir ʿAlla Re-evaluated. Proceedings of the International Symposium held at Leiden 21-24 August 1989*, Leiden 1991, pp. 121-142.

In the press:

66. "Notes on the Keret Legend", in: *Festschrift C.W. Bolle*.

67. "Preliminary Remarks on the Study of the Hebrew Verbal System", in: *Festschrift W. Leslau*.

68. (In collaboration with K. Jongeling), *Dictionary of the North-West Semitic Inscriptions*.

# The Status of the Infinitive in Early Piyyut*

Wout Jac. van Bekkum, Groningen

## I

The purpose of this article is to show some peculiarities in the use of infinitive forms in the poetry of the synagogue, composed during the 6th-8th centuries. This period is known as the period of the Classical Piyyut, also called Early Piyyut. For a long time the language of this poetry was not given due recognition as a separate segment within the evolution of the Hebrew language. Thanks to many recent editions of important piyyut collections from the *Genizah*[1] and modern studies on the language of Classical Piyyut[2] our knowledge of the language and grammar of Classical Piyyut is increasing rapidly.

The role of the infinitive in Hebrew has been the subject of much study. It is generally agreed that the infinitive in the Semitic languages exhibits a certain "neutrality" towards nominal and verbal usage. The infinitive forms express by themselves neither tense nor person, merely action[3]. In Classical Hebrew grammar two types of infinitive forms exist with different functions: the infinitive construct and the infinitive absolute. Both types can appear either as subject or as object and both can function with the meaning of a finite verb as in Jer. 9:12: עָזְבָם - "they have forsaken", and in Jer 3:1: וְשׁוֹב - "and would [you]

* I am indebted to Mrs. S.van Gelder-Ottway for correcting the English text.

[1] We will confine ourselves mainly to the critical editions of paytanim from the 7th and 8th centuries, cf. J. Schirmann, *New Hebrew Poems from the Genizah*, Jerusalem 1965 (Hebr.); Z.M. Rabinowitz, *The Liturgical Poems of Rabbi Yannai according to the Triennial Cycle of the Pentateuch and the Holidays*, Jerusalem 1985-1987 (2 vols., Hebr.); J. Yahalom, *Liturgical Poems of Shim'on bar Megas*, Jerusalem 1984 (Hebr.); N. Weisenstern, *The Liturgical Poems of Johanan ha-Kohen*, Jerusalem 1984 (Hebr., diss.); it is my opinion that also Yehudah can be allotted to the classical period of the Piyyut as can be concluded from his exclusive allusions to the Christian Byzantines in some of his compositions without mentioning the Arabs, cf. W.Jac. van Bekkum, *The Qedushta'ot of Yehudah according to Genizah Manuscripts*, Groningen 1988 (diss.).

[2] Cf. M. Zulay, ʿIyyūnēy lāšōn bĕ-Piyyūṭēy Yannāy, *Yĕdīʿōt ha-Mākōn*, 6, 1946, pp. 161-248; J. Yahalom, *Poetic Language in the Early Piyyut*, Jerusalem 1985 (Hebr).

[3] Cf. J.M. Sola-Solé, *L'Infinitif sémitique, Contribution à l'étude des formes et des fonctions des noms d'action et des infinitifs sémitiques*, Paris 1961.

return?". The infinitive forms in the latest stage of Classical Hebrew and in Rabbinical Hebrew were subject to considerable changes in form and usage[4]. There was a general tendency to substitute both infinitive construct and absolute by finite verb forms and verbal nouns, but on the other hand the occurrence of the infinitive form with the preposition -ל increased.

In the language of the Piyyut the infinitive is characterised morphologically through the influence of Classical Hebrew as well as Rabbinical Hebrew grammar. As to infinitive forms of the verba primae-נ one will easily find לֵישֵׁב next to לָשֶׁבֶת; לֵירֵד next to לָרֶדֶת, etc. Also the verba tertiae-ה display the coexistence of different morphological types like לִבְכֹּה next to לִבְכּוֹת; in the Nif‘al לְהֵעָשֶׂה (next to לְהֵעָשׂוֹת); in Pi‘el לְעַלֵּה (next to לְעַלּוֹת), לְחַכֵּה (next to לְחַכּוֹת ) and in Hitpa‘el לְהִתְכַּלֶּה (next to לְהִתְכַּלּוֹת)[5]. As result of the coalescence of the verba tertiae-ה and the verba tertiae-א in Rabbinical Hebrew additional infinitive forms with the ending ות- come into being such as לְבַטּוֹת (instead of לְבַטֵּא), לְמַלְּאוֹת[6] (instead of לְמַלֵּא) and לִבְרֹאות or לִבְרוֹת (instead of לִבְרֹא). In a liturgical composition for Shabbat מטות (Numb. 30:2) by the paytan Yehudah one finds in the third strophe of the *magen*, the first piyyut of the composition, the following rhyme words: לְהַטּוֹת \ הַחֲרוּטוֹת \ לְבַטּוֹ[ת] \ [הַמַּטּוֹת] [7]. Together with the plur. fem. ending ות- the paytanim created a wealth of possibilities for rhyming infinitives with nouns and participles. Thus the paytanim were able to exploit a wide variety of morphological traits with regard to the infinitive. This phenomenon is intrinsically connected with the syntactical setting of the infinitive in the piyyutic texts. The position of the infinitive within the poetic lines enables us to undertstand its specific employment that is to be discussed here.

## II

Like in Classical Hebrew both infinitive construct and infinitive absolute appear in the language of the Piyyut. The function of the infinitive

[4] Cf. my article "The Origins of the Infinitive in Rabbinical Hebrew", *JSS* 28 1983, pp. 247-272.

[5] Cf. J. Yahalom, *Poetic Language*, p. 175.

[6] Cf. Haneman, *A Morphology of Mishnaic Hebrew*, Tel-Aviv 1980, p. 420; cf. Yannay, ed. Rabinowitz, p. 93, l. 39.

[7] Cf. *The Qedushta'ot*, p.296; Yannay shows the usage of both forms in *běhinnāṭōt / lĕḇaṭṭōt / maṭṭōt / la‘aṭōt* and in *binṭōt / ba‘aṭōt / maṭṭōt / lĕḇaṭṭōt* as against *lĕḇaṭṭē’/ lĕmaṭṭęh / nōṭęh / ḥōṭē’*, cf. Rabinowitz I, p. 255 l. 3-4 with II, p. 236, l. 7-8 and p. 69, l. 53-54.

absolute is clearly restricted to paronomastic constructions, emphasizing or intensifying the verbal expression.

In the poetry of Yannay, however, hardly any form of the infinitive absolute is extant except for a few biblical citations as in a qedushta for מקץ (Gen. 41:1): וְקָם פִּתְרוֹן חֲלוֹם הֲמָלֹךְ - "and < Joseph> fulfilled the interpretation of the dream of 'reigning' ", referring to the expression by Joseph's brothers in Gen. 37:8: הֲמָלֹךְ תִּמְלוֹךְ עָלֵינוּ "are you indeed to reign over us?"[8]. The same can be observed in the second piyyut of a qedushta for ויהי בחצי הלילה (Ex. 12:29): רָפוֹא וְנָגוֹף שָׂמָה שַׂמְתָּ - "healing and smiting did You perform there" according to Is. 19:22: וְנָגַף ה׳ אֶת מִצְרַיִם נָגֹף וְרָפוֹא - "and God will smite Egypt, smiting and healing"[9]. Yannay elaborates these two infinitives in the fifth piyyut as follows:

זַעַף וָנַחַת נִגְלֵיתָ נָגוֹף וְרָפוֹא /
לִבְכוֹרֵי צַד נָגוֹף וְלִבְנָךְ בְּכוֹרְךָ רָפוֹא

"anger and pleasure You revealed in 'smiting' and 'healing' / for the first-borns of the enemy (Egypt) in 'smiting' and for Your first-born son in 'healing' "[10]. Also Johanan ha-Kohen, the only paytan from the Classical Piyyut who survived throughout the ages in standard Jewish prayer books, adopts the paronomastic construction from biblical passages in a "frozen" state. In his lengthy poem for טל (dew) he says: קֵץ יָדוֹעַ תֵּדַע עַל עַם הוּטַּל - "the time of 'you will surely know' has been imposed upon the people", relating to the time of exile as God has told Abraham: יָדֹעַ תֵּדַע כִּי־גֵר יִהְיֶה זַרְעֲךָ בְּאֶרֶץ לֹא לָהֶם - "know of a surety that your descendants will be sojourners in a land that is not theirs" (Gen. 15:13)[11]. Other paytanim, however, use these paronomastic infinitives mainly for filling up the poetic line for the sake of the alphabetic acrostic. Such is the characteristic of Yehudah who appears to make use of the "tautological" status of the paronomastic construction without further concern about its idiomatic implications[12]. Thus we find in his sixth piyyut for כי המצוה הזאת

[8] Ed. Rabinowitz I, p. 230, l. 4.

[9] Ed. Rabinowitz I, p. 298, l. 15.

[10] Ed. Rabinowitz I, p. 301, l. 47.

[11] Cf. diss. Weisenstern, p. 7, l. 105.

[12] Cf. G.Goldenberg, "Tautological Infinitive", *Israel Oriental Studies* 1, 1971, p. 36-85; one interesting example from the poetry of Yehudah is the line: *wĕšiklūl miqdaš har'ēnū lhr'wt* = "and show us indeed the completion of the Temple!". It is unclear whether we are concerned here with an infinitive Hiph'il or Niph'al ("and show us the completion of the Temple to be visible"). The latter seems more plausible in a paronomastic construction, but since we have here an infinitive construct,

(Deut. 30:11): רָחוֹק לֹא תִרְחֲקוּ מֵאִמְרֵי אֲרוּכָּה מֵאֶרֶץ - "you will certainly not keep far from the sayings of her (sc. the Torah) that is longer than the earth (Job 11:9)"[13]; and in the same piyyut: סוֹר אִם תָסוּר מֵאַחֲרֵי אוֹהַבְךָ - "if you indeed depart from the One who loves you"[14]. The negation לֹא and the conjunction אִם precede the finite form and bring about a separation between the infinitive and the rest of the line. The isolated infinitive is thus integrated in the alphabetical acrostic. Nevertheless, the paytan did not introduce this construction. Also in Babylonian Aramaic and in the Syriac literature this way of extraposing the infinitive forms is rather common and the construction is already found in Tĕnakh as well[15]. So it is no surprise that this phenomenon can be detected in the language of the Piyyut as well[16]. Yehudah does not adduce literal citations from the Scriptures, but he rather paraphrases them; for instance, in the sixth piyyut for ואברהם זקן (Gen. 24;1) he states: הָלוֹךְ תֵּלֵךְ לַאֲרַם נַהֲרַיִם - "you will indeed go to Aram-Naharayim" on the basis of Gen.24:10: וַיֵּלֶךְ אֶל־אֲרַם נַהֲרַיִם - "and he went to Mesopotamia"[17], or he "invents" paronomastic constructions like in the *mechayyeh*, the second piyyut of a qedushta for shabbat פנחס (Numb. 25:10): מָצֹא יִמְצָא חַיִּים לְהַאֲרִיךְ יָמָיו "he will certainly find life for living long"[18], or in the sixth piyyut from a qedushta for shabbat האזינו (Deut. 32:1): קָרֵיב אֲקָרֵב קוֹרֵא בַּמִּדְבָּר - "I will indeed come quickly, crying in the wilderness (Is. 40:3)"[19]. Most examples show the appearance of the infinitive absolute at the beginning of the line and therefore it can be concluded that these forms were mainly created for serving the alphabetical acrostic.

## III

The infinitive construct in the language of the Piyyut, while incorporating traditional elements from Classical and Rabbinical Hebrew, employs

the "tautological" position of this form could be stressed, by which means the paytan was able to fill up the rhyme scheme, cf.my diss., p. 273, l. 7.

[13] Cf. my diss. p. 325, l. 39.

[14] Cf. my diss. p. 325, l. 29.

[15] Cf. Joüon §123 g,o.

[16] Cf. G. Goldenberg, "Tautological Infinitive", pp. 44-59; for the comparabale phenomenon in Biblical Hebrew, cf. e.g. Joüon, §123g, o.

[17] Cf. my diss., p. 261, l. 9; Yehudah employs in every fourth line of every strophe a scriptural verse ending, sometimes containing a paranomastic construction, but these instances ought to be left out here.

[18] Cf. my diss., p. 291, l. 1.

[19] Cf. my diss., p. 333, l. 41.

them in novel ways, as demanded by the classical paytanim for their specific poetic aspirations. Certainly, in most instances one would not even notice a difference from the previous stages of Hebrew language and literature. The traditional grammatical functions of the infinitive construct are preserved in the piyyut; most frequent are the infinitives with -לְ for expressing some aim or purpose, either combined with a finite verb or used independently, being the only verbal form within the piyyutic line. Yannay employs a wide variation of final infinitives in his piyyut תְּדַבֵּר לֶאֱסוֹף אֲבֵידָתָךְ ("You will speak in order to remove Your loss")[20]. El'azar ha-Qilir and Johanan ha-Kohen have a special preference for infinitives with final meaning in their works as can be observed from their compositions for טַל in the strophe on the month of Ellul. Johanan versifies:

לָשׂוּם כְּאָז בֶּאֱלוּל חִתּוּלָה
טַ[ל] לְרַוּוֹת נְטוּעָה וּשְׁתוּלָה
לְשַׂמְּחָם בִּמְחוֹל בְּתוּלָה

"to put as of old in Ellul a remedy / dew to water plant and seedling / to give them gladness in the dance of *Virgo*", in comparison with Qilir:

תֵּת לְעוֹלָם חִתּוּלָה
טַל לְנוֹבֵב תְּנוּב שְׁתוּלָה
לְהָגִיל בִּמְשׂוֹשׂ בְּתוּלָה

"to give forever a remedy/ dew to make flourish crop < and> seedling/ to rejoice in the gladness of *Virgo*"[21]. In the latter case we often see that these infinitives adopt the meaning of the finite verb in the imperf. form. However, in combination with verbal forms all syntactical positions within the line are possible. Finite verbs in conjunction with infinitive forms appear at the beginning, within or at the end of the line. Both forms are often separated by specific particles, adverbs or even by subject or object. The infinitive forms sometimes precede the finite verb in every conceivable position within the line. The following example from Yehudah's poetry may suffice: בִּקֵּשׁ כָּל אֶחָד וְאֶחָד תַּאֲוַת נַפְשׁוֹ לְהֵעָשָׂה - "every one desired the wish of his soul to be

---

[20] Cf. Rabinowitz II, p. 307

[21] Cf. diss. Weisenstern, p. 293, p. 10, l. 162-164; in the same composition for *ṭal* infinitive construct with a finite verb in the line: *ṭa[l] pĕdūyẹḵā tānīf lĕhaḥăyẹh* - "the dew of Your redeemed ones You will raise to revive" as against the line: *ṣō'an lārēydẹt ūlĕhiṭṭalṭal* - "Zoan (Egypt - Numb. 13:22) is < destined> to fall down and to be overthrown"; two independent infinitives construct instead of imperf. forms, cf. p. 7, l. 102 and p. 9, l. 141

fulfilled". Subject and object separate the finite verb at the beginning of the line and the infinitive form at the end of the line[22]. The reverse order can be illustrated by the line: בְּכֵן לְנַדֵּב וְלִתְר[וֹ]ם לִשְׁמֹעַ לִי תֶּאֱהָבוּ - "so to donate and to contribute, to obey Me you like"[23].

Other classical paytanim show the same freedom of order like Shimʿon bar Megas in the sixth piyyut of a qedushta for שמות (Ex. 1:1): לְ[הַ]עֲלוֹתָם אֵרֵד בְּתִקְוָ[ה] - "hoping to bring them (Israel) up < from Egypt> I will go down"[24]. This paytan even manages to exploit different functions of the infinitive in one and the same line: כְּרִדְתָּם לַ[עֲ]בֹר לֹא נִפְרָדוּ - "when they (the sons of Israel and their families) went down < to Egypt> , they were not separated in order to disappear". The line opens with the infinitive construct in connection with -כ, expressing a determination of time, followed by an infinitive, serving as a direct object to the finite verb at the end of the line, but both forms are separated by the negation לא [25]. The type of infinitives construct with -ב or - כ are most popular in the works of Yannay. He often employs them with suffixes in combination with a subject or object (without the *nota accusativi* אֶת) in a reverse order within the line, as in the sixth piyyut from a qedushta for ויגש (Gen. 44:18): קוֹלוֹ בְּקָושְׁבָם נִתְעַלְּפוּ - "when they (the brothers of Joseph) heard his voice (Gen. 45:3), they fainted"[26] and in piyyut nine from the same qedushta: שִׂיחָתוֹ כְּשָׁומְעָם דָּאֲגוּ מֵאֵימָתוֹ - "when they (the brothers of Joseph) heard him speaking, they were worried out of fear for him (Joseph)"[27]. Similar appositional constructions can occasionally be separated by other parts of the line as in זֵד עִמָּם בְּהִילָּחֲמוֹ - "when the wicked (Amalek) fought with them", from a qedushta by Yannay for shabbat יתרו (Ex. 18:1)[28].

Returning to the infinitive forms with -ל, by far the most common in the text corpus of Classical Piyyut, their function corresponds largely

---

22 Cf. my diss. p. 260, l. 2

23 Cf. my diss. p. 275, l. 3

24 On the basis of the antonyms *ʿlh / yrd*; ed. Yahalom, p. 156, l. 24

25 Ed. Yahalom, p. 156, l. 27.

26 Ed. Rabinowitz I, p. 242, l. 71; the next line contains the same type of infinitive without prepositions: *rĕʾōtām qarnēy rĕʾēm* - "when they saw the horns of the wild ox (Deut. 33:17)"; also Shimʿon bar Megas: *rĕʾōtām šĕnēy rōʿăṣāw* - "when they saw the two who would smash him (Pharaoh)", ed. Yahalom, p. 173, l. 8

27 Ed Rabinowitz I, p. 245, l 141; the same piyyut contains many similar constructions: *ʾăhūb ʾaḥīm bĕhitwaddĕʿō* - "when the beloved of brothers made himself known"; *zẹh bĕhīwwādĕʿō* - "when this one (Joseph) made himself known"; *ḥay kĕhitwaddĕʿō* - "when the Living (God) will make himself known"; *ṭaʿămō bĕqŏšḇām* - "when they heard his word"; *Yāh bĕšofṭō* - "when God will judge"; l. 134, 137-138.

28 Ed. Rabinowitz I, p. 315, l. 5

to that of finite verbs, representing either imperf. or perf. or imperat., mainly to be inferred from the context. In a comparison between the previously mentioned *shiv'atot* for טַל by El'azar birabbi Qilir and Johanan ha-Kohen this use of the infinitive can be demonstrated explicitly. Whereas Qilir in the strophe on the month of Tishri has: לְהַכְרִיעַ צִדְקָם בְּמֹאזְנַיִם - "to outweigh their justice on *Scales*", Johanan replaces the infinitive by a finite verb: יְוֻכְרַע צִדְקָם [בְּכַף] מֹאזְנַיִם - "their justice will be outweighed [on a scale] of *Scales*"[29]. A *varia lectio* in another line from the same piyyut again reveals the interchange of infinitive and finite verb: טַל רָצוֹן לִבְרָכָה כְּהֵחָשׁוֹר - "when bountiful dew is gathered to blessedness", in other MSS: יֵחָשׁוֹר - "will be gathered"[30]. Certainly not only imperf. froms may be resolved by the infinitive construct; from contiguous verbal forms in the same line or strophe it can be concluded that other tenses and moods are represented as well. For instance in the works of Yehudah the words כְּכוֹכְבֵי שַׁחַק לְהָשִׁית זַרְעוֹ - "like the stars of heaven to put his offspring" establish the second line of a *meshallesh*, the third piyyut in a qedushta for shabbat לך לך (Gen. 12:1). The infinitive form is meant for the past in the context of the lines one and three:

יִקַּרְתִּי אֲבִיכֶם וְחִיזַּקְתִּי זְרוֹעוֹ
מֵעֵבֶר הַנָּהָר לְקַחְתִּיהוּ לְשַׁעְשְׁעוֹ

"I honoured your father and I strengthened his arm // from beyond the river I took him to delight him", and in the context of the verse ending in line four (Josh. 24:3): וָאוֹלֵךְ אוֹתוֹ בְּכָל אֶרֶץ כְּנָעַן וָאַרְבֶּה אֶת זַרְעוֹ - "and I led him through all the land of Canaan, and made his offspring many"[31] the infinitive in כָּל פִּקּוּד דָּת אָזְנַיִם לְהַטּוֹת - "to every commandment of the Torah ears to incline" can be considered as imperative, bearing resemblance to Ps. 17:6: "incline thine ear to me, hear my words"[32].

## IV

As for the infinitive form with -לְ, it is very often connected with a subject or an object, both nominal or pronominal. The rules for their position are relatively strict in Classical Hebrew. In almost all examples subject and object appear after the infinitive form apart from Is. 49:6:

[29] Diss. Weisenstern, p. 293, p. 10, l. 172.
[30] Diss. Weisenstern, p. 8, l. 129.
[31] Cf. my diss., p. 247, l. 1-4.
[32] Cf. my diss., p. 296, l. 11; cf. also l. 6, 9, 12; cf. above n. 7.

וּנְצוּרֵי יִשְׂרָאֵל לְהָשִׁיב - "and to restore the preserved of Israel". Only the infinitive form with subject may be separated by other grammatical parts of the sentence as in Gen. 34:15: לְהִמּוֹל לָכֶם כָּל־זָכָר - "and every male of you be circumcised", Numb. 35:6: אֲשֶׁר תִּתְּנוּ לָנֻס שָׁמָּה הָרֹצֵחַ - "where you shall permit the manslayer to flee", and in connection with both subject and object in Jer. 21:1: בִּשְׁלֹחַ אֵלָיו הַמֶּלֶךְ צִדְקִיָּהוּ אֶת־פַּשְׁחוּר בֶּן־מַלְכִּיָּה וכו׳ - "when king Zedekiah sent to him Pashhur the son of Malchiah etc."[33].

How different is the situation in the language of the Piyyut! Again the paytanim permitted themselves a great deal of freedom in arranging the word order within the poetic lines. The realisation of the alphabetical acrostics and the rhyme schemes obliged them to deviate from the rules of Classical Hebrew syntax, but in the course of piyyutic evolution these changes became in their turn new conventions in their poetic style. Most conspicuous is the disappearance of the particle אֶת as a consistent sign of the definite accusative, apart from its connection with suffixes[34]. In showing this feature the language of the Piyyut seems to go back to a tendency in the archaic poetry of the Scriptures, where the *nota accusativi* hardly occurs[35]. Concerning the infinitive form with object, the usual order is to be found throughout Classical Piyyut and is likely to appear at the beginning, in the middle or at the end of the piyyutic line, but this was practised far less than the reverse order. Yannay is the first paytan to show his awareness of the relation between infinitive and other grammatical entities, striving for a high degree of symmetry between the components of a given line, for instance in a antithetic chiastic construction of infinitive and finite verb with regard to Balaam (Numb. 23:10): יָעַץ לְקַלֵּל וּלְבָרֵךְ עָנָה - "he advised to curse and to bless he replied"[36]. Similarly he juxtaposed objects to infinitive forms according to the structural device of four word-units within a line from the fourth piyyut of his qedushta for וישלח (Gen. 32:1):

---

[33] Cf. W. Gesenius-E. Kautszch, *Hebrew Grammar*, Oxford 1963, pp. 352-355; cf. also A. Bloch, *Vers und Sprache im Altarabischen, Metrische und Syntaktische Untersuchungen*, Acta Tropica, Supplementum 5, Basel 1946, pp. 92-110.

[34] Compare Gen. 48:11: *rĕʾōh pānẹykā lōʾ pillaltī* - "I had not thought to see your face" with Yehudah: *lĕhāʾīr pānẹykā* - "to enlighten your face" instead of *lĕhāʾīr ʾẹt pānẹykā*, cf. my diss., p. 256, l. 11.

[35] As in Ex. 15, Deut. 32 or Jud. 5, but not in the Psalms, cf. J. Hoftijzer, "Remarks concerning the Use of the Particle *ʾt* in Classical Hebrew", *Oudtestamentische Studiën* 1965, pp. 1-99.

[36] Cf. Rabinowitz II, p. 98, l. 5.

דְּרָכָיו לְלַוּוֹת /
אָרְחוֹתָיו לְנַוּוֹת /
וְאוֹתוֹ לְחַוּוֹת /
אֶת פְּנֵי הַוּוֹת

"to accompany < Jacob on> his ways / to embellish his paths / and to inform him / < how to > face trouble (Esau)"[37]. The reason for his arrangement of the line is obvious; thus he creates a rhyme scheme ending with וֹת-. Similar examples are almost always involved in rhyme and only incidentally in the alphabetical acrostic, but serving both poetic devices is also possible as can be shown from the same qedushta by Yannay:

שְׁלוּחִים לְיַשֵּׁר אֶת עָקוֹב /
פְּנֵי עָקוֹב עֲקוּבוֹת לְנְקוֹב

"messengers < were sent> to make level the rugged (Is. 40:4: Esau) / < to> face the deceitful, to undermine < his> cunning". The first infinitive of this line is integrated in the alphabetical acrostic and the second one in the rhyme scheme. The division of the grammatical parts evokes a sublime symmetry in structure and contents[38]. Shim‘on bar Megas follows the same path, when he versifies in a qedushta for איש אשר ישחט (Lev.14:1):

שַׁרְתָּה כִּי עָתִיד מִקְדָּשׁ לְהֵחָרֵב
וְעוֹלוֹת קָרְבָּן אֵין לְקָרֵב
תְּמוּר כִּי אֵין מִזְבֵּחַ לְקָרֵב
תּוֹרָה חִיכֵּנוּ יֵעָרֵב

"< God, > You have seen that the Temple was to be destroyed / and burnt-offerings cannot be sacrificed / instead of an altar on which there is no sacrifice / let our palate be pleased by < the words of the> Torah". Here we see three possibilities of word order: 1. object + infinitive form; 2. object + infinitive form, separated by the negation אין; 3. object + infinitive form, preceded by the negation אין[39].

The object, preceding the infinitive form, is not always a noun. Other grammatical entities can be related to the infinitive construct in the same way like יוֹשֶׁר הַרְשָׁיָּה לוֹ לִיתֵּן- "to give him (Moses) rightly permission"[40], לָהּ לְהַשְׁמִיעַ תְּשׁוּעָה וְשָׁלוֹם - "to proclaim to her

[37] Ed. Rabinowitz I, p. 194, l 36.
[38] Ed. Rabinowitz I, p. 197, l. 72.
[39] Ed. Yahalom, p. 218, l. 17-20.
[40] From the *magen* in Yannay's qedushta for Ex. 4:18: Moses had to ask Jethro for permission to leave for Egypt, ed. Rabinowitz I, p. 275, l. 5.

(Sion) deliverance and peace"[41], טוֹבָתוֹ יְקַיֵּם בָּהּ לְנַחֲמִי - "He will show his favour to comfort me with it"[42], אוֹתָם לְרַחֵימָה - "to have compassion on them"[43], נוֹקְמֵיהֶם מִפְּנֵיהֶם לִכְרוֹת - "to exterminate their enemies before them"[44].

## V

The precedence of subject, object or other related parts of the line to forms of the infinitive construct, in particular at the end of a poetic word-unit or line, exercised a clear influence upon changes in their morphological and semantical characteristics. Such adaptions were mainly connected with the demands of rhyme. Most obvious is the lengthening with the ending ָה in infinitive forms from different stem formations, known from Classical Hebrew, like לְהוֹמֵמָה. לְרַחֵימָה. לְהַאֲכִילָה. לְהִתְהַלְּכָה. לְדַבְּרָה. לְקַלְקְלָה. לְהִתְרוֹמֵמָה, etc.[45]. The functioning of such infinitives with object can be demonstrated from a strophe in the composition for טל by Johanan ha-Kohen:

מֵהָחֵל חֶרְמֵשׁ בַּקָּמָה
טִיכַּסְתָּה אֲיוּמָה
לִנְחוֹל תּוֹרָה תְּמִימָה
יִדּוּעַ שִׁבְעָה שָׁ<בוּעוֹת> לְהָקִימָה
כְּהֶגְיוֹנִי בְּדָת לְקַיְּימָה
לְהַצִּילָה בְּלֹא תְּחַת מֵאוֹתוֹת הַשָּׁמַיְמָה

"from the time one first puts the sickle to the standing grain (from the time of Pesach - Deut. 16:9) / You have adorned the fearsome (Cant. 6:4: Israel) / to inherit a perfect Torah // telling to effectuate < the counting of> seven weeks // in accordance with My word in the Law to perform // to save < Israel> without terror from the signs of heaven". Remarkably enough, apart from the infinitive forms לְהָקִימָה

41 From a *silluq*, the eighth piyyut of a qedushta by Yannay for shabbat *'Anōkī* (Is.52:12), ed. Rabinowitz II, p. 342, l. 8.

42 From a *yozer*-composition by El'azar birabbi Qilir, cf. E. Fleischer, *Hebrew Liturgical Poetry in the Middle Ages*, Jerusalem 1975 (Hebr.), p. 237, l. 11.

43 Yehudah in his qedushta for Ex. 25:1, cf. my diss., p. 271, l. 2.

44 Both object and prepositional part precede the infinitive, cf. the sixth piyyut of a qedushta by Yehudah for shabbat *Mas'ēy* (Numb. 33:1), my diss., p. 309, l. 27.

45 In the poetry of Yehudah, cf. my diss., p. 174; sometimes spelled aleph as in a *Birkat māzōn* for Succoth: *gōhăṣīm lūlībā' / dibrat šīr lĕlabbĕbā'* - " they rejoice with the Lulav / to strengthen the recitation of song< s> , cf. A. Habermann, "Bĕrāḵōt mē'ēyn šālōš ūmē'ēyn 'arba'", *Yĕdī'ōt ha-Māḵōn* 5, 1939, p. 71.

and לְקַיְּמָה at the end of the line the paytan also lengthens the infinitive at the beginning of the last line of the strophe: לְהַצִּילָה[46]. Interesting too is the lengthening of the noun הַשָּׁמַיְמָה without any notion of the ה- locale[47]. As to the contrasting of different stem formations of the root קום a second example can be adduced from Johanan's poetry. In his famous qedushta for Shavu'oth, אַרְקָא הִרְעִישׁ, one strophe runs as follows:

וְנַעֲשָׂה שָׁלִיחַ בֵּינוֹ לְבֵינָם
שׁוֹמֵעַ מִפִּיו וְשָׁב לַהֲבִינָם
בִּינַת עוֹז וְדִיקְדּוּקֶיהָ לְבַיְּנָם
נֶגֶד הָהָר בְּהִתְכַּוְּונָם
מֵאָלֶף וְעַד תָּיו לְבוֹנְנָם
בְּמַאֲמַר קְדוֹשָׁם מהבונם

"and he (Moses) was made messenger between Him (God) and them (Israel) / hearing from his mouth and returning to explain to them, / to make clear to them the understanding of 'strength' (the Torah - Prov. 31:25) / when they were made ready opposite the mountain / to make them understand from *aleph* to *taw* / -in- the word of their Holy One [and their Lord]"[48]. This kind of interaction between stem formations has led to their confusion in the language of the Piyyut, mostly between Qal and Hiph'il, e.g. לְתָמוֹד next to לְהַתְמִיד, לֶאֱזוֹן next to לְהַאֲזִין, לִקְשׁוֹב next to לְהַקְשִׁיב and לְהַמְחִיל next to לִמְחוֹל, etc.[49]. The phonological value of the last syllable in infinitive forms of the Hiph'il is subject to change according to the needs of rhyme from /i/ to /e/ to /a/ as in לְהַזְהִיר, לְהַזְהֵר and לְהַזְהַר. The same applies to the infinitive Pi'el; the last syllable /e/ occasionally changes into /a/: לְבַטַּל next to לְבַטֵּל, לְטַמָּא next to לְטַמֵּא, etc.

One striking morphological change occurs in the infinitives, connected with the pronominal object suffix of the 1st pers. sing. In Classical Hebrew this suffix always appears as נִי-, but due to the influence of spoken Palestinian Aramaic the use of the ending י- is much more popular in the language of the Piyyut, which enables the paytanim to drop

[46] Diss. Weisenstern, p. 18, l. 9-12; the form *lĕhaṣṣīlāh* could also be taken as *lĕhaṣṣīl ʾōtāh*, referring to Israel as *ʾăyummāh* in the first line of the strophe.

[47] Cf. J. Hoftijzer, *A Search for Method. A Study in the Syntactic Use of the H-locale in Classical Hebrew*, Leiden 1981, p. 23, n. 47, also pp. 95-97.

[48] Diss. Weisenstern, p. 58, l. 709-714; Weisenstern suggests reading the last word of the strophe as *wrbwnm*.

[49] For this phenomenon in Rabbinical Hebrew cf. M.Moreshet, "Hip̄ʿīl lĕlōʾ hęḇdēl min ha-Qal bi-lĕšōn Ḥz"l, (bĕ-hašwāʾāh li-lĕšōn ha-Miqrāʾ"), *Bar Ilan* 13, 1976, pp. 249-281; the infinitive forms are to be considered in the context of morphological changes in the froms of the finite verb, cf. J. Yahalom, *Poetic Language*, pp. 86-108.

the distinction between object suffix and subject suffix[50]. Imperf. and imperat. forms are also affected by this characteristic, which enhances rhyming possibilities. In a piyyut for Pesach by Pinhas ha-Kohen we find:

וּבְרוּחַ חָזְרוּ עֲרֵימוֹת לְהַצִּיבִי
נַחַל חוֹבֵט חֵיל מַעֲצִיבִי
לְמוֹלִיךְ חֲבַצֶּלֶת אֲחַלֶּה בְּהִתְיַצְּבִי
וְעָשִׂיתָ מֵרָעָה לְבִלְתִּי עָצְבִּי

"at the blast (Ex. 15:8) piles < of water> returned to stand up / the torrent (Judg. 5:21) beats out the army of my enemy / to Him who led (Ps. 136:16) the rose (Israel - Cant. 2:1) I pray at my appearance / and that You would keep me from harm so that it may not grieve me (I Chr. 4:10)". Object suffix and subject suffix alternate, whereas the first infinitive is lengthened with י- without an explicit meaning[51].

As we have seen so far, the morphological unity of the infinitive with the preposition -ל is almost fully established in the language of the Piyyut. As in Rabbinical Hebrew negations were put before the construction with -ל like בְּלִי ,בִּלְתִּי ,לְבִלְתִּי ,מִבִּלְתִּי and also the preposition מִן with the meaning 'preventing from', developing into a way of negating the infinitive form[52]. The use of מִן or -מִ with infinitive increased considerably in the piyyutim and its equalness with other negations can be proven from the following line in a piyyut for the divisions of the priests in the Temple by Pinhas:

אָנָּא חֵרוּת שְׁלַח לָעָם מִלְּהַעֲבִידוֹ
חַתְּלֵהוּ וּבַגּוֹיִים בְּלִי לְהַאֲבִידוֹ

"please give freedom to the people not to enslave it / bring it healing and among the nations not to let it perish"[53].

---

[50] Cf. J. Yahalom, *Poetic Language*, pp. 132-133.

[51] Cf. M. Zulay, "Lĕ-Tōlĕdōt ha-Piyyūṭ bĕ-ʾęręṣ Yiśrāʾēl", *Yĕdīʿōt ha-Mākōn* 5, 1939, p. 135; the latter type of infinitive occurs incidentally in the Piyyut, e.g. Yannay: *lĕhaqšībī šinnūnīm* - "to tell the instructions (of the Torah)", ed. Rabinowitz II, p. 282, l. 103; in Classsical Hebrew poetry this is known only from participles like *ha-hōpkī* (Ps. 114:8) and *ha-yōšĕbī* (Ps. 123:1).

[52] Cf. J. Yahalom, *Poetic Language*, pp. 149-152; comparable to the use of *mn* in one instance from Classical Hebrew poetry with imperf.: *min yĕqūmūn* - "lest they rise again" (Deut. 33:11).

[53] Cf. M. Zulay, "Lĕ-Tōlĕdōt ha-Piyyūṭ, p. 141; concerning the piyyutim for the *mišmārōt*: E. Fleischer, Ḥadāšōt bĕ-nōśēʾ ha-mišmārōt bĕ-piyyūṭīm, *Sēper Yōbēl lĕ-Dōb Sadān*, Jerusalem 1977, pp. 256-284; in a qedushta for Lev. 15:25 Yannay equates the following forms: *dārĕšāh ṣęmęd ūfištīm, dēy kōaḥ milaʿăṣōr / l[ōʾ] liṭwōt wĕlimṣōr* - "she seeks wool and flax (Prov. 31:13), enough not to stop / not to spin and to beat", ed. Rabinowitz I, p. 238, l. 77.

## VI

Thus far our observations, which show the peculiar status of the infinitive in the language of the Piyyut. The Hebrew infinitive form proves to be a crucial tool for the composition of poetic lines, with or without the accompaniment of finite verbs and in many instances adopting their functions. The syntactical setting of the infinitive has considerably been made subservient to the poetical aspirations of the paytanim, as is often expressed in the reverse order of object/subject and the infinitive form. As a rhyme word the infinitive is very popular. The wide variety of its syntactical possibilities was to exert great influence on later Hebrew poetry, both liturgical and non-liturgical, but the foundations for its exploitation were laid in the period of Early Piyyut.

# The Use and Non-use of the Particle ʾ*et* in Hebrew Inscriptions

G.I. Davies, Cambridge

The possible value of Hebrew inscriptions for the study of classical Hebrew syntax has so far received little attention. It is not mentioned, for example, by A. Lemaire and E. Puech in their reviews of Hebrew epigraphy and its value for Old Testament studies[1]; and even a very recent article by James Barr on the definite article in Hebrew makes no reference to inscriptions, although there is at least one interesting case of the non-use of the article there that might have contributed something to his discussion[2]. Potentially at least inscriptions can offer a valuable supplement to the evidence to be found in the Old Testament, for several reasons. Archaeological and palaeographical dating can now fix the date of writing of an inscription quite closely, normally within half a century, and there are no problems arising from possible editorial or scribal interference after the original writing of the text. The evidence is thus both more firmly attached to a particular point in time and capable of being related to a single writer. Equally valuable is the association that can usually be made with a specific place, though it needs to be borne in mind that the place where a letter is found is not likely to be the place where it was written (unless, as has been suggested in at least one case, it is a draft or copy that was never sent). Some distinction between local variants or dialects of Hebrew may then be possible, comparable to the variations in pronunciation that seem to be implied by different spellings of the same word in "north Israelite" and "Judaean" Hebrew. Another factor which may give the inscriptions special interest is what linguists call "register", the different mannerisms of language which occur in different kinds of situation. Some echoes of different registers no doubt survive in the Old Testament, but it is largely a collection of literary works, and that may well limit its value in

---

1 *Göttingen Congress Volume, SVT* 29 (1978), pp.165-76; *Jerusalem Congress Volume, SVT* 40 (1988), pp. 189-302.

2 " 'Determination' and the Definite Article in Biblical Hebrew", in *JSS* 34 (1989), pp. 307-35. See Arad inscription 40.11 (2.40.11 in the numbering system to be explained below, note 4).

this respect. The inscriptions, on the other hand, include actual letters, commemorative inscriptions, prayers, administrative records and graffiti, and so provide a firmer basis for distinguishing different registers if they exist. In particular we might expect to come closer in at least some inscriptions to the colloquial form of the language at a particular time and place than we do in the Old Testament. In this connection it is perhaps worth adding that, unlike the Old Testament, the inscriptions are only occasionally concerned with specifically religious matters, so that any special characteristics of the religious literature of the Old Testament might be expected to stand out more clearly as a result of a comparison with inscriptions. The main problems still facing the scholar who wishes to bring epigraphic evidence into his discussion are the relatively small extent of the evidence at present available (which makes statistical conclusions very insecure) and the fact that inscriptions are often imperfectly preserved, with the gaps often occurring at precisely the most interesting places. But a beginning can be made on the basis of what has been found so far, with the proviso that future discoveries which can certainly be expected as archaeological excavation continues may well necessitate some revision and refinement of our conclusions.

As far as the particle *ʾet* is concerned, Professor Hoftijzer drew attention to some of its occurrences in inscriptions in his comprehensive treatment of the subject in 1965, where he listed the occurrences (and non-occurrences) in the ostraca from Lachish and Meṣad Ḥashavyahu (Yavneh-Yam)[3]. Subsequent discoveries (especially at Arad) and research have added significantly to this body of material, and there is a need for an up-to-date review of it to see how it fits into the general picture of the usage of the particle as it has been described by Hoftijzer and other scholars. It is a pleasure to dedicate this study to one who has brought a rigorous linguistic approach to bear on several outstanding problems of classical Hebrew syntax.

The instances of the particle *ʾet* in Hebrew inscriptions of the clas-

[3] "Remarks concerning the use of the particle *ʾet* in Classical Hebrew", in *OTS* 14 (1965), pp. 1-99 (see p. 79 n.1). For earlier studies of the particle see p. 1. n.1, to which may now be added R. Meyer, "Bemerkungen zur syntaktischen Funktion der sogenannten Nota Accusativi", in H. Gese and H.P. Rüger (ed.), *Wort und Geschichte*, Festschrift for Karl Elliger (Alter Orient und Altes Testamentes, 18), Neukirchen 1973, pp. 137-42; G.A. Khan, "Object Markers and Agreement Pronouns in Semitic Languages", *Bulletin of the School of Oriental and African Studies* (London) 47 (1984), pp. 468-500; T. Muraoka, *Emphatic Words and Structures in Biblical Hebrew*, Jerusalem 1985, pp. 146-58, and other works mentioned by these scholars. W.R. Garr, *Dialect Geography of Syria-Palestine 1000–586 B.C.E.*, Philadelphia 1985, pp. 193-4 (cf. p. 204 n. 183), gives a fuller account of epigraphic usage which, however, makes no claim to completeness.

sical period are listed below[4]:

Table 1: *Classification of Occurrences of ʾet in Hebrew Inscriptions*

| | | | |
|---|---|---|---|
| 1.2.1-2 | a | p | *yšmʿ̇.yhwh ʾt ʾdny* |
| 1.2.4-5 | a | p | *ky.zkr.ʾdny.ʾt.[ʿ]bdh* |
| 1.2.5-6 | a | p | *ybkr.yhwh ʾt ʾ[dn]y dbr* |
| 1.3.2-3 | a | p | *yšmʿ.yhwh [ʾt] ʾdny* |
| 1.3.4-5 | a | t | *hpqḥ ṅʾ̇[.]ʾṫ ʾzn ʿ̇bdk* |
| 1.3.11-12 | c | t | *ʾm.qrʾty.ʾth* |
| 1.3.16-18 | b | p | *wʾt hwdwyhw...šlḥ* |
| 1.4.1 | a | p | *yšmʿ.yhwh [ʾt] ʾdny* |
| 1.4.7-8 | a | p | *ʾẏṅ[n]ẏ ṧlḥ šmh ʾt hʿ̇[d]* |
| 1.4.12-13 | b | t | *ky lʾ.nrʾh ʾt ʿzqh* |

[4] In the remainder of this essay references to Hebrew inscriptions are given according to the system to be used in my forthcoming publication, *Ancient Hebrew Inscriptions - Corpus and Concordance*. The first number identifies the provenance of a group of inscriptions, the second the number of the inscription within that group, and the remaining number(s) the line(s) in question. An initial '1' indicates the Lachish ostraca, which are numbered according to standard practice (see H. Torczyner et al., *Lachish I: The Lachish Letters*, London 1938); an initial '2' the Arad ostraca (again with the numbering of the original publication: Y. Aharoni, *Ketovot ʿArad*, Jerusalem 1975 (Eng. tr. with additions, 1981)). 3.301 stands for Samaria ostracon C 1101 (J.W. Crowfoot et al., *Samaria-Sebaste III: The Objects from Samaria*, London 1957, p. 11); 4.102 for Ostracon 1 from the Kenyon excavations in Jerusalem (A. Lemaire, *Levant* 10 (1978), pp. 156-58); 4.116 for the Siloam tunnel inscription (D. Diringer, *Le iscrizioni antico-ebraiche palestinesi*, Florence 1934, pp. 81-102); 4.301 and 4.302 for silver plaques I and II from the Ketef Hinnom tombs (G. Barkay, *Cathedra* 52 (1989), pp. 46-59); 4.401 for the Silwan "Royal Steward" inscription (N. Avigad, *IEJ* 3 (1953), pp. 137-52); 7.1 for the letter from Meṣad Ḥashavyahu/Yavneh-Yam (J. Naveh, *IEJ* 10 (1960), pp. 130-36; ibid. 14 (1964), pp. 158-59); 8.17 for the main inscription on Pithos A from Kuntillet ʿAjrud (Z. Meshel, *Kuntillet ʿAjrud: A Religious Centre from the time of the Judaean Monarchy on the border of Sinai* (Israel Museum Catalogue 175), Jerusalem 1978, Inscription E(1)); 8.21 for the blessing on Pithos B from Kuntillet ʿAjrud (Meshel, op.cit., Inscription E(2.2)); 15.5 and 15.6 for Burial Cave inscriptions A and B from Khirbet Beit Lei (Naveh, *IEJ* 13 (1963), pp. 81-86; I follow in the former case the reading of F.M. Cross, in J.A. Sanders (ed.), *Near Eastern Archaeology in the Twentieth Century* (Nelson Glueck Volume), Garden City 1970, pp. 301-302); 25.3 for Tomb inscription 3 from Khirbet el-Qom (W.G. Dever, *HUCA* 40-41 (1969-70), pp. 159-69); 34.1 for the A text of the Wadi Murabaʿat Papyrus (P. Benoit et al., *Discoveries in the Judean Desert, II, Les grottes de Murabaʿat* (Oxford, 1961), pp. 96-97); and 35.1 for the Nimrud Ivory inscription (A.R. Millard, *Iraq* 24 (1962), pp. 45-49). The full text of many of these inscriptions can be found in J.C.L. Gibson, *Textbook of Syrian Semitic Inscriptions*, Volume 1: Hebrew and Moabite Inscriptions, Oxford 1971. The readings given here are those adopted in the forthcoming corpus mentioned above: a dot above a letter indicates that the letter is uncertain, and an asterisk against the reference indicates that the reading cited is not, in my opinion, the most likely, although it is favoured by some scholars.

| | | | |
|---|---|---|---|
| 1.5.1 | a | p | *yšmʿ [yhwh ʾt ʾd]ny* |
| 1.5.4-5 | a | t | *k̇ẏ [šl]ḥ̇t ʾl̇ ʿbdk ʾṫ [h]ṡ[pr]ṁ* |
| 1.6.1-2 | a | p | *yrʾ.yhwh ʾṫ.ʾdny* |
| 1.6.1-2 | a | t | *yrʾ.yhwh ʾṫ.ʾdny ʾṫ ḣʿt hzh* |
| 1.6.3-4 | a | t | *ky.šlḥ.ʾdny ʾ̇[t sp]r hmlk* |
| 1.6.3-4 | a | t | *ky.šlḥ.ʾdny...[wʾt] spry hšr[m]* |
| 1.6.13-14 | a | t | *k[y m]ʾz qrʾ ʿbdk ʾ̇ṫ hsṗṙ[m]* |
| 1.8.1 | a | p | *yšmʿ̇ẏ[hwh] ʾ̇ṫ.ʾ̇ḋ[ny]* |
| 1.9.1-2 | a | p | *yšmʿ yhwh ʾt ʾ̇ḋṅẏ* |
| 1.12.4 | c | t | *q̇[r]ʾty [ʾ]th* |
| 2.3.5-6* | c? | t | *wṣrr.ʾtm.bṣr* |
| 2.5.10-12 | a | t | *y[šlḥ] lk ʾt hmʿ[šr]* |
| 2.12.2-3 | c | t | *wtn.ʾ[tm lqw]sʿnl* |
| 2.12.5-6 | a | t | *wtn [ʾ]t hlḥm* |
| 2.13.1-2 | a? | t | *tš[lḥ ʾt hš]mn hzh* |
| 2.16.4-5 | a | t | *wšlḥty ʾt h[k]sp* |
| 2.16.4-6 | a? | t | *wšlḥty ...wʾt [ ]* |
| 2.16.7-8 | a | t | *whṧ[ ] ʾt ksp [ ]* |
| 2.16.9-10 | b | p | *šlḥ ʾt nḥm* |
| 2.17.5-7 | c | t | *wḥtm.ʾth bḥtmk* |
| 2.24.13 | c | p? | *wšlḥtm.ʾtm.rmt nġ[b]* |
| 2.24.16-17 | a | t | *pn.yqrh.ʾt hʿyr.dbr* |
| 2.40.5-7 | cl? | - | *[wktbt]y ʾl ʾdny [ʾt kl ʾšr r]ṣh hʾyš* |
| 2.40.13-14 | a | ? | *[ky ʾy]nnw.yklm.lšlḥ.ʾt h[ ]* |
| 4.102.7 | a | t | *[ ]ʾṫ.ṅbl [ ]* |
| 4.116.1-2 | a? | t | *bʿwd [hḥṣbm mnpm ʾt] hgrzn* |
| 4.401.2-3 | dem | t | *hʾdṁ ʾšr ypṫḥ̇ʾṫ zʾṫ* |
| 7.1.1-2 | a | t | *ẏšmʿʾdny.hšr ʾt dbr ʿbdh* |
| 7.1.6-7 | a | t | *kʾšr k[l ʿ]ḃdk ʾt qṣr wʾsm kyṁṁ* |
| 7.1.8 | a | t | *wyqḥ.ʾt bgd ʿbdk* |
| 7.1.8-9 | a | t | *kʾšr klt ʾt qṣry* |
| 7.1.9 | a | t | *lqḥ ʾt bgd ʿbdk* |
| 7.1.12 | a? | t | *[hšb nʾʾt] bgdy* |
| 7.1.12-13 | a? | t | *lšr lhš[b ʾt bgd] ʿb[dk]* |
| 7.1.14 | a | t | *[whš]bt ʾt [bgd ʿ]bdk* |
| 8.17.1 | c | p | *brkt.ʾtkm.lyhwh.šmrn.wlʾšrth* |
| 34.1.1 | a | t | *[š]lḥ.šlḥ̇ṫ.ʾt šlm bytk* |
| 35.1.3 | a? | t | *wmḥw[.]ʾ[t hspr hzh]* |

There are five cases where ʾ*et* occurs but its significance is uncertain. In 2.3.5-6 Y. Aharoni read *ṣrrt ʾtm.bṣq*, in which case ʾ*et* is the preposition; but the reading proposed by A. Lemaire presupposes that the particle is present as an "object marker" and I have cited this reading in the table above[5]. I have not included 2.40.15, where most editors restore *[z]ʾt*, although it is theoretically possible that the particle is present[6]; nor 1.13.3, 2.5.7 and 2.111.8, where there is insufficient context to determine what the significance of *ʾet* is. In 8.17.1 (included above) there is no real doubt that *ʾtkm* is an instance of the particle, in view of the parallel combinations in 2.16.2, 2.21.2, 2.40.3(?) and 8.21.1 where the pronominal suffix is used; the spelling *brkt* for the 1st person singular of the perfect is in line with other examples (cf. 7.1.8 and 34.1.1). There are a number of other cases where the presence of the particle is due to partial or even complete restoration, but in most of these cases the restoration is widely accepted and with good reason. The letters in the first column after the reference classify the occurrences of the particle according to a system introduced by Hoftijzer, which I have modified to take account of some exceptional cases which he does not code. In this system 'a' stands for a use with an ordinary noun, 'b' for a use with a proper name, and 'c' for a use with a pronominal suffix. I have added the codings 'cl' for a use before a clause and 'dem' for a use before a demonstrative pronoun. The letters in the next column indicate, where this is clear, whether the following noun or pronominal suffix stands for a person ('p') or a thing ('t').

In nearly every case *ʾet* precedes a clearly definite object of a verb, as in the Old Testament. This is doubted by Hoftijzer at 1.6.1-2 (second occurrence), where he suspects that *ʾet* precedes an adverbial expression denoting time[7]. But there is no objection in principle to the common understanding of it as a second object of the *Hiphil* of *rʾh* and, although no precise parallels for *ʿt* as the object of *rʾh* seem to exist, the verb is often used with an abstract object and the occurrence of *ywm* with *ḥzh* (with *ʿt* in the parallel stich) in Job 24:1 suggests that the idiom is a possible one. There are two more possible exceptions to the general rule. In 1.3.5 there is a growing consensus that the reading *rzm* is incorrect and that *ʾzn* should be read instead. The question is then: what preceded it in the lacuna at the beginning of the line, and how is it connected with *hpqḥ* at the end of the previous line? A reading like that which we print has been adopted by several recent scholars. Some of them regard *ʾt ʾzn* (or *ʿyn*) *ʿbdk* as the object of *hpqḥ*, understood as the *Hiphil* imperative (2nd masc. sing.) of *pqḥ*[8].

[5] See Aharoni, *Ketovot ʿArad*, p. 18; A. Lemaire, *Inscriptions Hébraiques*, Tome I: Les Ostraca (LAPO 9), Paris 1977, p. 165.

[6] Cf. D. Pardee et al., *Handbook of Ancient Hebrew Letters*, Chico 1982, p. 65.

[7] Art.cit. (note 3), p. 79 n.2.

[8] Pardee et al., op.cit., p. 85; and apparently Lemaire, op.cit., p. 102.

But the verb is attested elsewhere in Hebrew of the biblical period only in the *Qal* (eighteen times) and the *Niphal* (three times), and F.M. Cross has argued that it is possible to interpret the sentence within the bounds of this known pattern of usage if *hpqḥ* is regarded as the *Niphal* imperative "with the object of the active construction still subordinated in the accusative with *ʾt*". He translates: "Let be opened, pray, the ear of your servant..."[9] The use of *ʾet* with what is apparently the subject of a passive verb, and occasionally with the subjects of other verbs, is a phenomenon which has been much discussed, but there is no doubt that however it is to be explained it is a well-attested idiom in classical Hebrew[10]. But Cross's analysis of the present passage does not conform to the regular pattern, nor is it easy to see how he gets from a necessarily 2nd person imperative form to the 3rd person jussive translation which he offers. It is, however, possible that his basic insight is correct. *hpqḥ* may be the *Niphal* infinitive absolute, and the infinitive absolute is occasionally used for the jussive[11]. This appears to be the only possible case of *ʾet* as a "subject marker" in the Hebrew inscriptions known at present.

The other problematic case is 7.1.6-7. In the original publication Naveh read *ʾt qṣrw ʾsm*, but the sparse use of word-dividers in this inscription creates uncertainty about the correct division into words. In fact the word-division which we have adopted, which was first proposed by Cross, is to be preferred, as it has been by all recent editors. The use of waw to indicate the 3rd masculine singular suffix of a singular noun would be unique in Hebrew of the period, when *he* was normally used (compare *ʿbdh* in line 2 of this inscription), and the parallel with line 5 indicates that it must be read as the conjunction, with *ʾsm*[12]. The question is then how to explain the use of *ʾet* with an apparently undetermined noun. It may be, as some have thought, that *qṣr* is a careless or deliberately defective spelling, intended to represent *qĕṣīrō*[13]. Alternatively, we may perhaps suppose that *qṣr* is preceded by *ʾet* because it is implicitly determined by the context, as in a few passages in the

[9] "A Literate Soldier: Lachish Letter III", in A. Kort and S. Morschauser (ed.), *Biblical and Related Studies presented to Samuel Iwry*, Winona Lake 1985, pp. 41-47 (see pp. 43,45).

[10] See e.g. GK §121a,b (from which Cross's description is taken). The view that *ʾet* in certain circumstances marks the subject (so Hoftijzer, Meyer and Khan) seems better founded than the claim that all textually sound examples can be regarded as in some sense indications of the object (J. Blau, "Zum angeblichen Gebrauch von *ʾt* vor dem Nominativ", *VT* 4 (1954), pp. 7-19; Muraoka (with some qualifications)): see Khan, art.cit., pp. 496-97, for a possible analogy in non-Semitic languages.

[11] GK §51k (note Jer. 7:9), 113cc.

[12] So Cross, *BASOR* 165 (1962), p. 43 n.31; cf. Gibson, op.cit., p. 28, and Pardee, op.cit., p. 20.

[13] So, respectively, Gibson and Pardee.

Old Testament[14].

Of the 48 occurrences of *ʾet* which are included in the table above 30 belong to type 'a' (with another 6 possible cases), 3 are of type 'b', 6 are of type 'c' (with 1 more possible case), 1 precedes a demonstrative pronoun, and 1 precedes a clause (though the context has been heavily restored). More detailed analysis of the data requires a comparison with those places where *ʾet* is not used, although it might have been expected to be used on the basis of the pattern of usage which is encountered elsewhere. The following are the instances of such "non-use" in the inscriptions so far known:

Table 2: *Classification of "Non-Occurrences of ʾet" in Hebrew Inscriptions*

| | | | |
|---|---|---|---|
| 1.2.6 | f? | t | *dbr.ʾšr lʾ. ydʿth* |
| 1.3.5-6 | f? | t | *lspr.ʾšr.šlḥṫḣ.ʾ̇l ʿ̇ḃḋk̇* |
| 1.3.11-12 | cp | t | *kl sp[r] ʾšr ybʾ.ʾly ʾm.qrʾty.ʾth* |
| 1.3.12-13* | f? | t | *[ʾḥ]ṙ ʾtnnhw ʾ̇l.mʾwṁ[h]* |
| 1.3.16-18 | d | p | *wʾt hwdwyhw...wʾnšw šlḥ.lqḥt.mzh* |
| 1.3.19-21 | cp | t | *wspr.ṭbyhw ʿbd.hmlk...šlḥh.ʿ< b> dk* |
| 1.3.21 | f | t | *šlḥh.ʿ< b> dk* |
| 1.4.6 | cp | p | *wsṁkyhw lqḥh.šmʿyhw* |
| 1.4.6 | f | p | *lqḥh.šmʿyhw* |
| 1.4.6-7 | f | p | *wyʿlhw.hʿyrh* |
| 1.5.6-7 | d | t | *hšb.ʿbdk.hsprm.ʾl ʾdny* |
| 1.5.7-8 | f | p | *yrʾk yhwh ḣqṩṙ* |
| 1.5.7-8 | d | t | *yrʾk yhwh ḣqṩṙ* |
| 1.6.5-6 | d | t | *dbry.[ ] lʾ ṭbm lrṗt ydyk* |
| 1.6.6-7 | d | t | *[lhš]qṭ ydy hʾ[ ]* |
| 1.6.10-12 | d | t | *ḣ[n]h lṁlk̇ [t]ʿšw ḣḋ[b]ṙ ḣżḣ* |
| 1.6.10-11* | f? | t | *[wnq]y šlṁh* |
| 1.13.2 | f | t | *wsmkẏhẇ yḥ̇prhw* |
| 1.16.3 | f? | ? | *[š]lḥh ʿ̇[bdk]* |
| 2.1.3-4 | d | t | *wktb.šm.hym* |
| 2.2.4-5 | d | t | *wmlʾ.hḥmr.yyn* |
| 2.3.2-4 | f | p | *wṣwk.ḥnnyhw.ʿl bʾršbʿ* |
| 2.3.6-7 | d | t | *wspr:hḥṭm* |
| 2.3.6-8 | d | t | *wspr.hḥṭm whlḥm* |
| 2.4.2 | f | t | *wšlḥnw* |
| 2.7.5-6 | f? | t | *[w]ktbth lpnyk* |

[14] Cf. GK §117c-d, and A.M. Wilson, *Hebraica* 6 (1890), pp. 214-15.

| | | | |
|---|---|---|---|
| 2.16.2-3 | f | p | *brktk lyhwh* |
| 2.18.6-8 | f | p | *wldbr.ʾšr.ṣwtny* |
| 2.21.2-3 | f | p | *brktk l̇[yhw]h* |
| 2.24.14-15 | f | p | *whbqydm.ʿl.yd ʾlyšʿ* |
| 2.40.3 | f? | p | *brkt[k lyhw]h* |
| 2.40.4 | d | t | *hṭḣ [ʿ]bdk [l]bh* |
| 2.40.9-10 | d? | t | *whn ydʿth [hmktbm m]ʾdm* |
| 2.40.10 | f | t | *nttm lʾdny* |
| 2.40.12 | d | t | *whʾ.hmktb.bqš* |
| 3.301.2 | f? | p | *hṙʿm* |
| 4.102.4 | d? | ? | *hʿżb.ḥ[ ]* |
| 4.301.4 | d? | t | *[ʾ]hb hbr[yt]* |
| 4.301.15f. | f | p | *[wy]šmrk* |
| 4.301.16ff | d | t | *[y]ʾr yhwh [p]n[yw]* |
| 4.302.5-6 | f | p | *w[y]šmrk* |
| 4.302.7-9 | d | t | *yʾr ? yh[w]ḣ ? pnyẇ [ʾl]yk* |
| 8.21.1-2 | f | p | *brktk.lyhwh tmn wlʾšrth* |
| 8.21.2 | f | p | *wyšmrk* |
| 15.5.1-2* | d? | t | *ʾrṣh ʿrẏ.yhwḣ* |
| 15.5.2* | e? | t | *wġʾl̇ty.yršlm* |
| 15.6.1 | e | t | *hmwrẏh ʾth ḥṅṅṫ* |
| 25.3.1 | f | t | *ʾryhw.hʿ̇šr.ktbh* |

Here again a coding system introduced by Hoftijzer has been followed (and slightly extended) in the second column: a 'd' denotes a determined common noun which is the object of a verb, an 'e' a proper name which is the object, an 'f' a pronominal object suffix attached to the verb, and 'cp' the so-called casus pendens.

Out of 48 instances altogether there are 14 of type 'd' (and 4 more possible cases), 1 of type 'e' (and another possible case), 17 of type 'f' (with 8 more possible cases), and three casus pendentes. The instances of use and "non-use" of *ʾet*, if they are taken as a whole, are thus exactly equal in number. Or to put it differently, for every case where *ʾet* is used there is a case where it is not used, although it could have been. It is important, however, to consider each pair of categories separately. If we do so, we find that in the case of common nouns the use of *ʾet* is about twice as common as its "non-use" (a:d = 30(+6):14(+5)), and that the same is true for the much smaller and statistically quite unreliable number of instances of proper names (b:e = 3:1(+1); whereas for pronominal objects the independent object pronouns formed with *ʾet* are used in only about one-third of the number of cases where an object suffix is attached to the verb (c:f = 6(+1):17(+8). These ratios fall broadly in the middle of the range of those derived from samples of prose texts taken from various parts of the Old Testament[15].

If the material is subdivided according to find-place, the two largest collections, which are the only ones that may be of some statistical significance, have much the same pattern of usage with regard to pronominal objects — the c:f ratio at Lachish is 2:5(+4), while at Arad it is 3:7(+2) — but they differ considerably in the case of nominal objects — the a+b:d+e ratio at Lachish is 18:6(+1), while at Arad it is 7(+2):6(+1). The difference is reduced, but not eliminated, if the three instances of casus pendens (all without *ʾet*) at Lachish (there are none at Arad) are added to the 'd+e' total. At all events the non-use of the casus pendens construction at Arad is a feature that is itself worthy of note.

Another way of sub-dividing the material for a statistical comparison is by date. In discussion of the distribution of *ʾet* in the Old Testament it has often been suggested that there was an increased tendency to use *ʾt* in later texts[16]. The epigraphic material briefly surveyed by Hoftijzer in 1965 all came from the late 7th or early 6th century B.C., but subsequent discoveries have added to the number of inscriptions known from the 8th century, so that a comparison can now be made between earlier and later groups of a size that may give some statistical significance to the results. Of the inscriptions included in our listings the following are now generally thought to be from the 8th century: 2.40, 3.301, 4.116, 4.401, 8.17, 8.21, 15.5, 15.6, 25.3 and 35.1. One (34.1) is dated to the early or mid-7th century, and is left out of account here. The remainder (27 inscriptions in all) come from the late 7th or early 6th century. The numbers of instances of each type for each group are as follows (the figures in brackets, as before, indicate "possible" instances):

| Type | 8th century | late 7th/early 6th century |
|---|---|---|
| a | 1(+2) | 29(+4) |
| d | 1(+2) | 12(+2) |
| b | 0 | 3 |
| e | 1(+1) | 0 |
| c | 1 | 5(+1) |
| f | 4(+2) | 13(+6) |

[15] See Hoftijzer, art.cit., p. 38-42.

[16] Wilson, art.cit., p. 141; Meyer, art.cit., p. 139; Muraoka; op.cit., p. 150. The more detailed statistics compiled by Hoftijzer, however, warn against assuming that the development was straightforward.

Clearly the number of instances of both use of *ʾet* and "non-use" in the 8th-century inscriptions is still too small to warrant any definitive conclusions about a development in the use of the particle. So far as it goes, the evidence now available lends some support to the view that, broadly speaking, there was a growing tendency to use *ʾet* before nouns. Rather surprisingly, in view of the general practice throughout the Old Testament to use *ʾet* before proper names, this seems to be even more true for the latter than for other nouns (compare the b:e ratios for the two groups of inscriptions), though it should be noted that both the 'e' instances from the 8th-century are in what may well be poetic texts, where use of *ʾet* is less common at all periods[17]. In the case of pronominal objects the ratio between the two possible modes of expression (i.e. the c:f ratio) seems to have remained fairly steady through the period under review.

Individual inscriptions do not, with one exception, offer sufficient evidence for us to conclude that the writers were rigidly wedded either to the use or to "non-use" of *ʾet*. The exception is the letter from Meṣad Ḥashavyahu (7.1), in which *ʾet* is used on every occasion that it could have been used (6 certain cases and 2 "possibles", all with ordinary nouns). Some other inscriptions also show a definite tendency to use *ʾet* before nouns wherever possible (1.2, 1.4, 2.16), but the numbers of instances are smaller (three certain instances in each of these cases). The only inscription to show a pronounced avoidance of *ʾet* before nouns (though it is not total) is 2.40 (a:d = 1:2(+1)), and it may be significant that this is dated to the 8th century.

Finally, we shall give brief consideration to the question whether in particular cases the choice between using and not using *ʾet* was influenced by factors on the level of the sentence structure or on the level of meaning or was simply a stylistic variation. The standard grammars of classical Hebrew indicate some situations in which a pronominal object is regularly represented by the independent pronoun formed with *ʾet*[18]. None of the instances of type 'c' in the inscriptions is covered by these "rules", but they do show an interesting regularity in that all of them occur (immediately) after 1st or 2nd person verbs. By contrast 3rd person verbs always (in the inscriptions) have their pronominal objects indicated by a verbal suffix. This is not the case in the Old Testament (e.g. Gen. 12:12, 42:22). The inscriptions do not, however, consistently use the independent pronoun after a 1st or 2nd person verbal form:

---

[17] For the probable poetic character of these inscriptions see P.D. Miller, "Psalms and Inscriptions", in *Vienna Congress Volume, SVT* 32 (1981), pp. 311-32, esp. 320-23, 328-32.

[18] E.g. GK §117 e; P. Joüon, *Grammaire de l'hébreu biblique*, Rome 1923, §125e; R. Meyer, *Hebräische Grammatik*, III: Satzlehre, Berlin 1972, p. 74.

there are places where the pronominal suffix is used (e.g. 2.4.2 and 2.7.5-6), and it is in most cases not clear why the one or the other mode of expression should have been preferred. There is no indication that "emphasis" plays any part. In two instances it is possible to relate the choice of the independent pronoun to a feature of Old Testament usage, namely the tendency to avoid attaching verbal suffixes to 2nd plural perfect forms and not to use 2nd plural object suffixes[19]. 2.24.12 and 8.17.1 are covered by these "rules": in each case the independent pronoun is used. 8.17.1 is particularly interesting, as the contrast with the several instances of the same formula with the 2nd singular object suffix is very clear (2.16.2-3, 2.21.2-3, 2.40.3, 8.21.1-2).

When it comes to nouns, the grammars are silent about any principles that might govern the use and "non-use" of *ʾet* before a definite object. In specialised studies there is a difference of opinion between those who hold that there are no recognisable criteria that were followed by writers of classical Hebrew and those who have sought to identify criteria. A popular view has been that the use of *ʾet* implies a special emphasis on the following noun, but it has recently been severely criticised by T. Muraoka who has, like others before him, drawn attention to pairs of sentences in which the use or non-use of *ʾet* appears to make no difference whatever to the meaning[20]. More complex attempts to specify the conditions in which *ʾet* is used have been made by those who have compiled lists of "rules", such as A.M. Wilson and J. Libni, and, in a recent article, by G.A. Khan, who brings a series of eight "hierarchies" under the general headings of "individuation" and "perceptual salience", that is the degree to which the referent stands out from its background or in the text concerned. In some cases, Khan suggests, *ʾet* is used because the clause in which it occurs is the end-point or climax of a stretch of discourse. He argues, with many examples, that these principles apply also to object-markers in some other Semitic languages and to another semantically redundant feature of these languages, namely agreement pronouns[21]. The general validity of these proposals cannot be discussed here, but it may be noted that what needs to be established if they are to carry conviction is, firstly, that they apply to all or most of the instances which exhibit the features specified, and not just to some of them, and secondly that they do not

[19] J. Libni, "On the study of verbal suffixes and the regulation of their use in attached and separated forms", *Leshonenu* 5 (1932), pp. 225-26. Libni cited three exceptions to the first "rule" and nine to the second.

[20] Meyer is a recent advocate of the emphatic force of *ʾet* (art.cit.). But see Wilson, art.cit., pp. 143-50, Hoftijzer, art.cit., pp. 90-92, and Muraoka, op.cit., pp. 150-51.

[21] Wilson, art.cit., pp. 215-21; Libni, art.cit., pp. 229-30; Khan, art.cit.(see especially the list of "hierarchies" on p. 470).

leave a large number of cases where *ʾet* is used or not used unexplained. A small beginning on this very large task will be made here by means of a few observations on some aspects of the limited sample of instances contained in the inscriptions.

An examination of all these instances suggests that some of the "rules" or "hierarchies" that have been proposed are much more general in their application than others. For example, among Khan's "hierarchies" those which relate to "perceptual salience" are more indicative than those which relate to "individuation". Definite objects whose referents are textually prominent (hierarchy 8) are nearly always preceded by *ʾet*; likewise definite objects whose referents are personal (12 out of 13, compared with 20(+6) cases out of 34(+10) where the referent is inanimate) and those whose referent is inanimate but related to the writer of the inscription, for example by a pronominal suffix (8 cases out of 9), as predicted by hierarchy 7. On the other hand a "qualified" definite object (hierarchy 5) is found nearly as often without *ʾet* as with it (1.6.6-7, 1.6.10-12, 2.1.3-4, 2.40.9-10 and 15.5.1-2 are the counter-examples). Objects which are proper names are preceded by *ʾet* in three cases, but not in two others: however both the latter are in what may be poetic texts, so that the "rule" may hold for epigraphic prose. The rules proposed by Wilson and Libni are mainly based on morphological and syntagmatic features, and the most consistent patterns of usage are found with definite objects followed by a demonstrative and cases where a *Hiphil* verb is followed by two objects: in each situation *ʾet* is present in 4 cases and absent in only one. The "rules" which assert that *ʾet* is not used after an imperative or an infinitive construct or where the object has a pronominal suffix referring back to the subject of the verb each have a proportionally large number of counter-examples (see 2.12.5-6, 2.16.9-10; 1.6.13-14, 2.5.10-12, 2.40.13-14, 7.1.12-13; 1.2.4-5, 7.1.8-9). There are, in addition, a number of cases of both use and "non-use" of *ʾet* where none of the hierarchies or rules seem to apply, or where closely similar expressions are handled differently for no apparent reason. Why, for example, does the writer of 1.5 say *ky [šl]ḥt ʾl ʿbdk ʾt [h]s[pr]m* in ll.4-5, but omit *ʾet* with the same object in ll.6-7: *hšb.ʿbdk.hsprm.ʾl ʾdny*? Again, the treatment of coordinated objects varies considerably, as Hoftijzer pointed out was the case in the Old Testament[22]. Sometimes both objects have *ʾet* (1.6.3-4, 2.16.4-6), sometimes only the first has it (1.3.16-18), sometimes neither does (2.3.6-8). The intermediate case can perhaps be explained. Both components of the object are personal, so that in the light of the general practice in the inscriptions (see above) we should expect both

[22] Art.cit., pp. 21-22. Cf. Wilson, art.cit., pp. 220-21.

to have *ʾet*. But there is a certain subordination of the second to the first, since the suffix on the second noun refers back to the first noun (unlike the other instances) and the *ʾet* may therefore the more easily have extended its force over both nouns. A similar example occurs in 1 Sam. 24:3, but within the Old Testament the pattern is not universal, as in the similar expressions in Gen. 24:59 and 2 Sam. 17:8 both nouns have *ʾet*.

The limited sample of classical Hebrew examined here can only point the way for a much fuller study of all the available evidence. Moreover, it is possible that greater (or less) regularity was observed in "literary" Hebrew than in the ephemeral documents which most of the inscriptions represent. But that in itself would be an interesting discovery to make.

# Die Inkongruenz im Buch Qoheleth

W.C. Delsman, Nijmegen

In seinem Buch *Die Inkongruenz im biblischen Hebräisch*[1] schreibt Jaakov Levi: "Bisher wurde in der Literatur Inkongruenz oft als Sprachfehler angesehen und daraufhin der hebräische Text 'verbessert', aber schon die Statistik zeigt, dass die Inkongruenz nicht selten der Normalfall ist". Wie steht es mit der Inkongruenz, worunter wir das Fehlen der Übereinstimmung syntaktisch verbundener Wörter in Geschlecht, Zahl und Person verstehen, im Buch Qoheleth? In diesem Artikel wird versucht eine vorläufige Antwort auf diese Frage zu geben. Es ist mir eine Ehre ihn dem verehrten Jubilar widmen zu dürfen.

Statt die Fälle der Inkongruenz der Reihefolge nach zu behandeln, haben wir versucht sie zu klassifizieren und dementsprechend zu besprechen.

1) Inkongruenz zwischen dem Subjekt und einem nachfolgenden Prädikat.
Inkongruenz wird meistens als eine Erscheinung der gesprochenen Sprache betrachtet. So hat z.B. Driver[2] die Inkongruenz zwischen Subjekt und Prädikat mal das meist belegte Beispiel der Umgangssprache genannt. Auch Fredericks[3] behandelt in seinem Buch über die Sprache des Buches Qoheleth diese Form der Inkongruenz unter den möglichen umgangssprachlichen Elementen des Buches. Die Beispiele im Buch Qoheleth sind:

a) כבר היה לעלמים אשר היה מלפננו 1:10; "Längst schon ist es dagewesen, in den Zeiten (pl. m.), die vor uns gewesen sind (sg. m.)"[4].

---

[1] Jaakov Levi, *Die Inkongruenz im biblischen Hebräisch*, Wiesbaden 1967, S. 1. Dieses Buch, ursprünglich eine Dissertation der Universität Heidelberg, hätte eine wahre Fundgrube werden können, wäre es durch ein Stellenregister erschlossen.

[2] G.R. Driver, "Colloquialisms in the Old Testament", in D. Cohen (Ed.), *Mélanges M. Cohen* (Janua Linguarum, Series Maior, 27), The Hague - Paris 1970, S. 232-239. S. 234.

[3] Daniel C. Fredericks, *Qoheleth's Language: Re-evaluating its Nature and Date* (Ancient Near Eastern Texts and Studies, 3), Lewiston - Queenston 1988, S. 37.

[4] Soweit nichts anderes angegeben ist, beziehen alle Verweise nach Bibelstellen sich auf das Buch Qoheleth. Die Übersetzungen sind der Zürcher Bibel entnommen. In einigen Fällen war es aber notwendig daran eine eigene, mehr buchstäbliche

Ist Inkongruenz zu einem nachfolgenden Substantiv oft belegt[5], hier steht היה in Inkongruenz zu einem vorangehenden Substantiv. Und das ist ziemlich selten der Fall. Die Grammatik von Gesenius - Kautzsch[6] schreibt darüber: "Die Fälle, in welchen Genus oder Numerus des nachstehenden Prädikats von dem des Subjekts abzuweichen scheint, beruhen teils auf offenbaren Textfehlern ... oder auf besond. Gründen". Koh. 1:10 gehört dann wohl zu der letzten Kategorie. Die meisten Kommentatoren erklären den Singular mit einem Beruf auf die kollektive Bedeutung des Wortes עלמים. Es gibt noch sehr viele andere Beispiele des Singulars bei einem Kollektivum. In einigen Manuskripten steht an unserer Stelle übrigens der erwartete Plural היו, was aber kein Grund zur Textänderung sein darf. Es wäre eine Verschlimmbesserung.

b) ובני בית היה לי 2:7; "zu den im Hause geborenen Sklaven" ["Hausgeborene Diener (pl. m.) gehörten (sg. m.) mir"].

Auch hier steht היה in Inkongruenz zu einem vorangehenden Substantiv. Mit Formen des Verbums "sein" ist dieses Phänomen nach Levi 13x belegt[7], wovon 2x im Buch Qoheleth. Einige der von ihm genannten Fälle der Inkongruenz zwischen היה und seinem Beziehungswort lassen sich dadurch erklären, dass היה als ein erstarrtes Verb empfunden wurde und daher nicht in Kongruenz zu seinem Subjekt konstruiert wurde. Bei erstarrten Formen tritt, wie wir noch sehen werden, oft Inkongruenz auf.

Levis zweiter Beleg der Inkongruenz zwischen היה und seinem Beziehungswort aus dem Buch Qoheleth steht auch in 2:7:

c) גם מקנֶה בקר וצאן הרבה היה לי 2:7; in der Übersetzung von Levi: "Auch Vieh, Rinder und Schafe (oder: Herden von Rindern und Schafen) in Menge besass ich" ["gehörten (sg. m.) mir"].

Es ist aber die Frage, ob hier wohl Inkongruenz vorliegt. בקר וצאן kann man besser auffassen als eine Apposition bei מקנה. Die Übersetzung wird dann: "Auch Viehbesitz (sg. m.), sowohl Rindvieh als auch Kleinvieh, gehörte (sg. m.) mir in Menge". In diesem Fall liegt Kon-

---

Übersetzung [zwischen eckigen Klammern] hinzuzufügen, damit die Inkongruenz deutlich wird.

[5] Vgl. z.B. W. Gesenius - E. Kautzsch, *Hebräische Grammatik*, Leipzig 1909[28], §145o.

[6] GKa, §145u.

[7] Levi, *Inkongruenz*, S. 208. Mit *hyh* 12x (Gen. 15:17 41:53; Jes. 32:14 64:10; Ez. 16:49 21:32 27:19 40:21; Koh. 2:7 (2x); Klgl. 3:47; 2 Chr. 17:13; die oben behandelte Stelle Koh. 1:10 fehlt bei ihm) und mit *hyth* 1x (Ez. 36:2). Die Stelle Ez. 36:2 ist aber mit den Stellen, worin *hyh* wird benutzt, wohl nicht zu vergleichen. In Ez. 36:2 ist der Singular zu erklären durch Attraktion an das danebenstehende *mwršh* oder eventuell durch Ergänzung von *'rṣ* als Beziehungswort.

gruenz vor. מקנה wird neben Koh. 2:7 noch 3x[8] als Subjekt benutzt. Jedesmal wird es mit einem Prädikat im Singular konstruiert.

Vielleicht gibt es noch ein Beispiel der Inkongruenz zwischen einem vorangehenden Subjekt und seinem Prädikat:

d) כשגגה שיֹּצא מלפני השליט 10:5; "wie wenn ein Gewalthaber einen Missgriff tut" ["fürwahr[9] ein (oder: eine Art[10]) Missgriff (sg. f.), der von dem Gewalthaber auszugehen pflegt (sg. m.)"].

Meistens nimmt man an, dass das Verb יצא hier nach Analogie der verba tertiae infirmae (יֹּצָא statt יֹצְאָה oder das normalere יֹצֵאת[11]) konjugiert ist. In diesem Fall liegt keine Inkongruenz vor.

Eine andere, übrigens nicht sehr wahrscheinliche, Möglichkeit aber, u.a. erwähnt von Fredericks[12], ist, dass יֹצָא als ein männliches Partizipium mit Änderung des Vokals (= יֹצָא statt יֹצֵא), wiederum nach Analogie der verba tertiae infirmae, aufgefasst werden muss. In dem Fall liegt wohl Inkongruenz vor.

2) Inkongruenz zwischen dem Subjekt und einem vorangehenden Prädikat.
Nach der Besprechung der Stellen, wo das Verbum "sein" in Inkongruenz zu dem vorangehenden Substantiv benutzt wird, folgt jetzt die einzige Stelle, wo "sein" in Inkongruenz zu dem nachfolgenden Substantiv steht:

a) כי לא תדע מה־יהיה רעה על־הארץ 11:2; "Denn du weisst nicht, was für Unheil (sg. f.) auf Erden kommen mag (sg. m.)".

Vielleicht ist מה יהיה hier schon zu einer erstarrten Form geworden. Der Ausdruck kommt auch noch in 6:12 vor. Ausserdem ist die Redewendung מה שׁ־יהיה 3x belegt (3:22 8:7 10:14). Levi nennt vier Stellen[13], wo יהיה in Inkongruenz zu einem nachfolgenden Substantiv oder einem pronominalen Suffix steht. Bei היה geschieht es nach seiner Angabe fünfundzwanzig Mal[14].

b) ויאבד את־לב מתנה 7:7; "und Bestechung (sg. f.) verderbt (sg. m.) das Herz".

Das Verbum steht bei einem nachfolgenden Subjekt sehr oft in der einfachsten Form des Prädikats: 3 sg. m.[15].

---

[8] Gen. 26:14; Ex. 9:6; Num. 32:1.

[9] Kaph asseverativum.Vgl. R. Gordis, *Koheleth - the man and his world. A Study of Ecclesiastes*, New York 1968, S. 319.

[10] Kaph veritatis.Vgl. GKa, §118x.

[11] Vgl. H. Bauer - P. Leander, *Historische Grammatik der hebräischen Sprache des Alten Testamentes*, Halle 1922, S. 598.

[12] Fredericks, *Language*, S. 163.

[13] Vgl. Levi, *Inkongruenz*, S. 210: Jer. 23:12; Ez. 45:11.17; Koh. 11:2.

[14] Vgl. Levi, *Inkongruenz*, S. 204f.

[15] GKa, §145o.

3) Inkongruenz zwischen einem weiblichen Substantiv und einem pronominalen Suffix.

Im Buch Qoheleth ist Inkongruenz am meisten belegt bei weiblichen Substantiven, die in dem Dual oder in dem Plural stehen, aber mit männlichen Pronominalsuffixen im Plural kongruieren. Diese Art der Inkongruenz, deren Grund vielfach sein kann, kommt, nach dem statistischen Überblick von Levi, in fast allen Büchern der Bibel vor[16]. Die Suffixe ם- und ן- wurden offenbar nicht gut auseinander gehalten. Auch hier mag sich der Einfluss der gesprochenen Sprache auf die Schriftsprache bemerkbar machen. Levi gibt für Qoheleth in seiner Statistik die Zahl "vier" an. Es handelt sich aber um fünf Belegstellen:

a) עשׂיתי לי ברכות מים להשׁקות מהם יער צומח עצים
2:6; "Ich machte mir Wasserteiche (pl. f.), den sprossenden Baumwald daraus (pl. m.) zu tränken".

b) וכל אשׁר שׁאלו עיני לא אצלתי מהם    2:10; "Was irgend meine Augen (du. f.) begehrten (pl. m.), das entzog ich ihnen (pl. m.) nicht".

c) מסיע אבנים יעצב בהם    10:9; "Wer Steine (pl. f.) ausbricht, der kann sich daran (pl. m.) wehe tun".

d) כי אם־שׁנים הרבה יחיה האדם בכלם ישׂמח    11:8; "Ja, wenn der Mensch viele Jahre (pl. f.) lebt, so freue er sich an ihnen (pl. m.) allen".

e) והגיעו שׁנים אשׁר תאמר אין־לי בהם חפץ    12:1; "und die Jahre (pl. f.) sich einstellen, von denen (pl. m.) du sagen wirst: 'Sie gefallen mir nicht'".

Von den angeführten Stellen unterliegt nur 2:6 einigem Zweifel, da es möglich ist, dass מהם (pl. m.) sich auf das Wasser (pl. m.) als dasjenige, womit getränkt wird, bezieht. In 2:10 hat Rendsburg[17] versucht die Inkongruenz zu löschen durch die Endung ם- als eine Dualendung communis generis zu betrachten. Er hat keine Nachfolger gefunden[18]. In 2:10 liegt übrigens noch eine zweite Inkongruenz vor, worauf wir

---

[16] Vgl. Levi, *Inkongruenz*, S. 184. Diese Art der Inkongruenz fehlt, wohl zufällig,bei den kleinen Propheten Obd., Jona, Mi., Nah., Hab., und Mal. Die Aussage von J.L. Crenshaw, *Ecclesiastes*, London 1988 (S. 79) "such lack of agreement ... often occurs in late texts ... occasionally in earlier texts" ist dann auch unrichtig. Vgl. auch die Belegstellen (§14) und der Kommentar dazu (§15) in F.E. König, *Historisch-comparative Syntax der hebräischen Sprache*, Leipzig 1897.

[17] G. Rendsburg, "Personal Pronouns and Dual Verbs in Hebrew" in *Jewish Quarterly Review* 73, 1982/83, S. 38-58. S. 47: "and whatever my eyes desired, I did not keep from them (c. dual)" [S. 43: " the Hebrew third person common dual suffix would be -[h]m].

[18] Zuletzt stellte J. Blau sich gegen ihn in seinem Aufsatz: *klwm nštmrw 'qbwtyw šl hzwgy bthwm hkynwyym whpw'l b'bryt hmqr'*, in *Leshonenu* 52, 5748/1987, S. 165-168.

später zurückkommen werden. In 10:9 11:8 und 12:1 ist der Gebrauch des männlichen Pronominalsuffixes zu erklären als eine Angleichung an die maskuline Pluralendung ים- bei den weiblichen Wörtern אבן und שנה. Levi spricht in so einem Fall über "formale Attraktion"[19].

4) Inkongruenz durch formale Attraktion.
Levi[20] erwähnt als ein mögliches Beispiel:

אמרה קהלת 7:27 12:8 (mit Textkorrektur: אמרה קהלת statt MT אמר הקהלת); "spricht (sg. f.) der Prediger (sg. m.; der Nominalbildung nach weiblich)".

קהלת wäre dann von dem Schreiber als weiblich aufgefasst aufgrund der Endung ת-. Sehr wahrscheinlich ist das aber nicht. Es ist üblich den Text von 7:27 nach 12:8 zu korrigieren.

אסורים ידיה 7:26; "ihre Hände sind Fesseln".

Dazu schreibt Levi[21], die offenbar "ihre Hände (du. f.) sind gefesselt (pl. m.)" übersetzen will: "Ein interessantes Phänomen ist die Tatsache, dass die Mask.-Form des Partizips oft beim Dual Auftritt. Vielleicht liegt der Grund darin, dass diese Formen sowieso mit ים- enden". Insgesamt nennt er zwölf Beispiele[22], wovon sechs Dual-Formen, die Körperteile bezeichnen. Es ist aber die Frage, ob er in bezug auf Koh. 7:26 recht hat. Seine beabsichtigte Übersetzung passt schlecht in dem Kontext. Das ganze Vers lautet: "Da fand ich: Bittrer als der Tod ist das Weib; sie ist ein Fangnetz, ihr Herz ist ein Garn, und ihre Hände sind Fesseln. Wer Gott gefällt, der entrinnt ihr; wer aber sündigt, wird von ihr gefangen". Haben wir es hier wohl mit einem Partizip zu tun? Wahrscheinlich nicht. Die Wörterbücher setzen denn auch kein Partizip an, sondern die Plural von אֱסוּר, einem männlichen Substantiv, das "Fessel" bedeutet. Die Vokalisierung mit Chatef - Patach statt Chatef - Segol in dem Plural fällt auf. Nach Mitteilung in KBL3 gibt es Manuskripten mit der erwarteten Vokalisierung[23].

Wohl auch zu der formalen Attraktion gehören die Fälle, worin Wörter als אדנים, אלהים und קדושים, die morphologisch gesehen Pluralformen sind und, wenn sie singulare Bedeutung haben und sich auf den Gott Israels beziehen, mit dem Singular konstruiert werden, mit einem Pluralsuffix kongruieren. Ein solcher Fall liegt vor in:

---

[19] Levi, *Inkongruenz*, S. 137: "Unter 'formaler Attraktion' verstehen wir die Anziehung in Genus oder Numerus, die ein Satzglied aufgrund der (schriftlichen oder mündlichen) Form auf ein anderes ausübt".

[20] Levi, *Inkongruenz*, S. 138.

[21] Levi, *Inkongruenz*, S. 154.

[22] Ex. 17:12; 1 Sam. 10:18; Jer. 22:14 26:2 29:17; Ez. 41:6; Am. 5:12; Sach. 4:10; Spr. 26:23; Koh. 7:26; Da. 10:5; 2 Chr. 3:13.

[23] Vgl. in bezug auf die Vokalisierung: BLe, S. 473.

בוראיך 12:1; "dein Schöpfer".

GKa[24] schreibt: "Zweifelhaft sind ... eine Reihe von Partizipien im Plural, die als Attribute Gottes die Auffassung als Herschaftsplurale nahe legen". An dieser Stelle will GKa übrigens, genauso wie die Mehrzahl der Codices laut Mitteilung in BHK, statt des Plurals den Singular lesen (בראך).

5) Inkongruenz durch Verlust der weiblichen Formen.
Im Laufe der Zeit sind weibliche Formen, sicher in der Umgangssprache, zugunste der männlichen aufgegeben. Oben erörterten wir Beispiele aus dem pronominalen Bereich. Bei dem Verbum hat sich aber das gleiche ergeben. Im Buch Qoheleth treffen wir davon die folgenden Beispiele an:

a) וכל אשר שאלו עיני לא אצלתי מהם 2:10; "Was irgend meine Augen (du. f.) begehrten (pl. m.), das entzog ich ihnen (pl. m.) nicht". Die weiblichen עיני stehen in Inkongruenz zu dem männlichen Prädikat שאלו.

b) וישחו כל־בנות השיר 12:4; "und alle Töchter (pl. f.) des Gesanges verstummen (pl. m.) ["die Totalität der Töchter"].

Hier steht ein männliches Prädikat in Inkongruenz zu den weiblichen בנות. Obwohl בנותgrammatikalisch gesehen das nomen rectum bei dem nomen regens כל ist, richtet das Prädikat sich in diesen Fällen fast immer[25] nach dem nomen rectum[26] statt nach dem nomen regens. Ein Beispiel davon findet sich auch im Buch Qoheleth:

מכל שהיו לפני בירושלם 2:7; "mehr als alle (sg. m.), die vor mir in Jerusalem gewesen (pl. m.)".

In vielen Manuskripten steht an unserer Stelle, statt des Plurals היו der Singular היה. Das gleiche ist der Fall in 1:16 und 2:9, wo כל ebenfalls das Subjekt ist:

על כל־אשר־היה לפני על־ירושלם 1:16; "mehr als alle (sg. m.), die vor mir über Jerusalem herrschten (sg. m.)".

מכל שהיה לפני בירושלם 2:9; "grösser als alle (sg. m.), die vor mir in Jerusalem gewesen (sg. m.)"

In diesen beiden Fällen steht כל aber nicht in einer status constructus - Verbindung.

6) Das Prädikat richtet sich nach dem nächststehenden Subjekt.

a) עשיתי לי גנות ופרדסים ונטעתי בהם עץ כל־פרי 2:5; "Ich legte mir Gärten (pl. f.) und Lusthaine (pl. m.) an; darein (pl. m.)

---

[24] GKa, §124k.
[25] P. Joüon, *Grammaire de l'hébreu biblique*, Rome 1923. §150: "Les exceptions sont très rares".
[26] GKa, §146c.

pflanzte ich allerlei Fruchtbäume".

In diesem Vers weist בהם sowohl nach גנות (pl. f.) als auch nach פרדסים (pl. m.) zurück. Das Prädikat hat sich in Geschlecht und Zahl nach dem nächststehenden Subjekt פרדסים gerichtet, was sehr oft der Fall ist, vor allem wenn das Prädikat vor dem Subjekt steht[27]. Das gleiche ist in den beiden folgenden Versen der Fall:

b) כי־עת ופגע יקרה את־כלם 9:11; "sondern alle trifft (sg. m.) Zeit (sg. f.) und Zufall (sg. m.)" [ ... Zufall (sg. m.) und Zeit (sg. f.)].

c) עד־אשר לא־תחשך השמש והאור והירח והכוכבים 12:2; "ehe die Sonne (sg. f.) sich verfinstert (sg. f.) und das Licht (sg. m.) und der Mond (sg. m.) und die Sterne (pl. m.)".

Dieser Vers ist weiter noch in sofern interessant, dass das Wort שמש, das meistens männlich, aber manchmal auch weiblich[28] ist, hier weiblich sein muss, da alle anderen Substantive in dem Satz männlich sind und das weibliche Prädikat sonst nicht zu erklären ist. Von den 35 Malen, dass das Wort שמש im Buch Qoheleth belegt ist, ist nur hier und in 1:5 das Geschlecht davon zu bestimmen. An letzter Stelle ist es 2x, beide Male männlich konstruiert, belegt:

וזרח השמש ובא השמש ואל־מקומו שואף זורח הוא שם 1:5; "Die Sonne geht auf (sg. m.), die Sonne geht unter (sg. m.) und strebt zurück (sg. m.) an ihren Ort, wo sie wiederum aufgeht (sg. m.)".

7) Inkongruenz durch einen sachlichen Singular.

a) גם אהבתם גם שנאתם גם קנאתם כבר אבדה 9:6; "Auch ihr Lieben (sg. f.) und Hassen (sg. f.) und Neiden (sg. f.) ist (sg. f.) längst dahin".

Normalerweise würde das Prädikat in diesem Fall in dem Plural stehen. Die Inkongruenz lässt sich dadurch erklären, dass man die drei Begriffe אהבה, שנאה und קנאה, nur in diesem Vers zusammen vorkommend, als *eine* Totalität auffasste und demgemäss das Prädikat demgemäss singularisch kongruierte. Levi[29] nennt insgesamt siebzehn derartige Beispiele, wovon sechs mit einem mehrfachen גם[30].

8) Inkongruenz durch eine distributive Bedeutung.

---

[27] GKa, §146f.

[28] *šmš* ist, ohne Ortsnamen, in der Bibel ingesamt 143x belegt. Nach der Angabe in THAT, Band ii, Sp. 988 ist es, sofern es zu entscheiden ist, 17x weiblich konstruiert. Vgl dazu König, *Syntax*, §248k.

[29] Levi, *Inkongruenz*, S. 54f.

[30] Neben Koh. 9:6 nennt er noch Gen. 24:25 50:9; Ex. 18:18; Ri. 8:22; Zef. 1:18. H. Ewald, *Ausführliches Lehrbuch der hebräischen Sprache des Alten Bundes*, Göttingen 1870[8], schreibt (§359) zu einem mehrfachen *gm*: "Um verschiedenes als in einer rücksicht dennoch zusammenkommend und sich häufend gleichzustellen".

a) גם עיניו [K]לא תשבע עשר 4:8; "und kann des Geldes nicht genug sehen" ["und jedes seiner Auge (du. f.) wird (sg. f.) des Reichtums nicht satt (sg. f.)"].

Es gibt keinen Grund das Ketib anzuzweifeln[31]. Das Qere עינו (sg. f.) wird zwar von vielen Manuskripten und von den versiones antiquae, ausser der Vulgata, die oculi eius übersetzt, unterstützt. Es ist aber die Frage, ob das Qere nicht entstanden ist, weil man die Inkongruenz aufheben möchte. Auch grammatikalisch ist das Ketib zu erklären: Körperteile, die paarweise vorkommen, werden, obwohl selber im Dual stehend, manchmal mit einem weiblichen Singular konstruiert[32]. Meines Erachtens ist das besonders der Fall, wenn der Autor eine distributive Bedeutung beabsichtigt.

Nicht nur ein Substantiv in dem Dual, sondern auch ein Suffix kann übrigens eine distributive Bedeutung haben. Es ist möglich das Ketib an folgender Stelle so aufzufassen:

שמר רגליך [K] 4:17; "sei behutsam" ["achte (imp. sg. m.) auf jeden deiner Füsse ([K] du. f.)"].

Die versiones antiquae und viele Manuskripte lesen das Qere רגלך, eine unnötige Änderung. Gerade bei paarigen Körperteilen steht oft ein Qere in dem Dual mit einem Ketib in dem Singular. Das Ketib רגליך mit dem Qere רגלך ist wohl zu oft belegt um ein Fehler zu sein[33]. Das Qere löscht die Inkongruenz auf. Die Kommentatoren gehen unterschiedliche Wege[34].

b) ושפתות כסיל תבלענו 10:12; "den Toren verderben (sg. f.) seine eignen Lippen (pl. f.)".

Durch das weiter nicht belegte Abstraktum שִׁפְתוּת (sg. f.) statt שְׂפָתוֹת zu lesen hat man wohl versucht die Inkongruenz in diesem Vers auszulöschen. Levi[35] hat das zurecht "unsinnig" genannt. Die status constructus - Form שפתות statt der üblichen Form שפתי ist zwar

[31] Anders: A.Schoors, "Kethibh - Qere in Ecclesiastes", in J. Quaegebeur (Ed.), *Studia Paulo Naster Oblata, II, Orientalia Antiqua*, (Orientalia Lovaniensia Analecta, 13), Louvain 1982, S. 215-222. "The Q reading is undoubtedly superior to K, since it is not only supported by LXX, Syr and Targ, but it is also required by the syntax, the verb *tšbʿ* being singular. Therefore it has been accepted as the original reading by nearly the totality of critics " (S. 215).

[32] Von den Füssen: 1 Kön. 14:6.12; von den Augen: 1 Sam. 4:15; Mi. 4:11. Meistens werden Textänderungen zu den genannten Stellen vorgeschlagen; wohl damit die Inkongruenz verschwindet.

[33] Nach Levi, *Inkongruenz*, S. 232 Anm. 21, 5x (Ex. 3:5; 2 Sam. 11:8; Jer. 38:22; Ez. 21:1 [lege: 2:1]; Koh. 4:17). Ausser in Koh. 4:17 gibt BHS übrigens nirgendwo das von Levi aufgeführte Qere an. Wohl trifft man in den Manuskripten und Versiones sowohl den Dual als den Singular an.

[34] Vgl. Schoors, "Kethibh", S. 216. Er konstatiert dass der Gebrauch des Singulars in diesen Fällen üblicher ist, schliesst aber das Ketib nicht aus.

[35] Levi, *Inkongruenz*, S. 190.

auffällig, aber doch insgesamt 7x belegt[36]. Ausserdem kann die weibliche plurale Form eine kollektive Bedeutung haben und mit einem Singular konstruiert werden. Es gibt mehrere Belege für diese Form der Inkongruenz[37].

c) זבובי מות יבאיש יביע שמן רוקח 10:1; "eine giftige Fliege (pl. m.) macht schlecht (sg. m.) das Öl des Salbenbereiters" ["jede einzelne der giftigen Fliegen (pl. m.) macht schlecht (sg. m.), lässt gären (sg. m.) u.s.w."].

Hier steht in einer distributiven Bedeutung ein Substantiv im Plural vor einem Prädikat im Singular.

d) כי אם יפלו האחד יקים את־חברו 4:10; "Denn fallen sie (pl. m.), so hilft der eine dem andern auf".
Dieser Vers hat den Übersetzern grosse Schwierigkeiten besorgt. Wenn die auch hier gefolgte Übersetzung der Zürcher Bibel stimmt, liegt keine Inkongruenz vor. Die revidierte Fassung der Lutherübersetzung aus 1964 bietet aber: "Fällt (m. pl.) einer (m. sg.) von ihnen, so hilft ihm sein Gesell auf". In diesem Fall liegt wohl Inkongruenz vor. Diese Übersetzung liest aber gegen die masoretische Akzentsetzung (zaqef qaton versetzt nach האחד) und ruft Schwierigkeiten auf durch "sein Gesell" als Subjekt zu nehmen (ein neues Beispiel von את vor dem Subjekt!). Gängig sind auch Übersetzungen wie die von Lauha[38] "Denn wenn zwei fallen, hilft der eine seinem Gefährten auf". Sie beruht auf einer Textänderung (שנים ist hinzugefügt; seine Anmerkung "יפלו erheischt eine Subjektangabe" kann nicht überzeugen).

Stimmt dann doch die Übersetzung der Zürcher Bibel? Vermutlich nicht. Sie ist nicht logisch. Dass beide gleichzeitig fallen, ist zwar möglich, aber doch nicht sehr wahrscheinlich. Man kann besser übersetzen: "Denn wenn einer fällt, so hilft der eine dem anderen auf". In diesem Fall ist der Plural benutzt "zur Bezeichnung eines unbestimmbaren Einzelnen" oder besser, mit König, "Fälle, wo der Plural verwendet wurde, weil die Auswahl unter den einzelnen Vertretern der betreffenden Kategorie dem Leser anheim gestellt werden sollte"[39]. In bezug auf unseren Vers schreibt er[40]: "die Einschränkung auf einen derselben [wird] als natürlich vorausgesetzt: 'wenn bei ihnen ein Fallen vorkommt"'.

9) Inkongruenz durch erstarrte Formen.

---

[36] Neben Koh. 10:12 auch noch in Jes. 59:3; Ps. 45:3 59:8; Hld. 4:3.11 5:13.
[37] Vgl. GKa, §145k.n.
[38] A.Lauha, *Koheleth* (Biblischer Kommentar Altes Testament, XIX), Neukirchen-Vluyn 1978, S. 87.
[39] GKa, §124o; König, *Syntax*, §265c.
[40] König, *Syntax*, §265e.

Oben unter 1) haben wir schon die Frage zur Sprache gebracht, ob Inkongruenz bei dem Verbum "sein" nicht oft der Fall ist, weil bestimmte Formen des Verbums als erstarrte Formen empfunden wurden. Bei erstarrten Formen tritt ja oft Inkongruenz auf. In dem Buch Qoheleth wäre in diesem Rahmen zu nennen:

a) לכה־נא אנסכה בשמחה וראה בטוב 2:1; "Wohlan (imp. sg. m.), versuch's (pi., PK, 1. sg. + sf. 2. sg. m.) einmal mit der Freude und geniesse (imp. sg. m.)". In der Übersetzung von Martin Buber[41]: "Geh doch los, ich will dich mit Freude versuchen, und besieh das Gute!"

לכה, ursprünglich eine Imperativ-Form von הלך, hat sich zu einer erstarrten Form entwickelt. Sie wird hier fortgesetzt mit einer Verbalform in der ersten Person, wobei das Verb נסה metonymisch gebraucht ist. Es schliesst die Folge ein: "eine Probe anstellen","es probieren"[42].

Auch bestimmte Aussagen in Komparativsätzen haben sich im Laufe der Zeit zu erstarrten Ausdrücken entwickelt. In so einem Fall steht ein männliches Adjektivum. Wenn das ihm folgende Substantiv in Geschlecht oder Zahl sich davon unterscheidet, tritt Inkongruenz auf. Im Buch Qoheleth ist das sicherlich bei dem erstarrten Ausdruck טוב מן der Fall:

b) טוב אחרית דבר מראשיתו 7:8; "Besser (sg. m.) der Ausgang (sg. f.) einer Sache als der Anfang"[43].
und vielleicht auch bei und יקר מן:

c) יקר מחכמה מכבוד סכלות מעט 10:1; "so verderbt ein wenig Torheit den Wert der Weisheit" [ein bisschen Torheit (sg. f.) ist wertvoller (sg. m.) als Weisheit und Ehre"][44].

Die Interpretation dieses Verses ist sehr umstritten. Die gebotene Übersetzung bietet in dem Kontext Schwierigkeiten. Oft gibt man darum an יקר hier die weiter nicht belegte Bedeutung "schwer". So übersetzt z.B. S.Wagner in seinem Artikel über יקר "Schwerer als Weisheit, als Ehre wiegt ein wenig Torheit"[45]. Gemeint ist dann, dass die Konsequenzen von ein wenig Torheit sich oft folgenschwerer auswirken als die von Klugheit und Ehre. Im gleichen Sinne übersetzt auch Michel[46]: "schwerer als Weisheit und Ansehen wiegt ein wenig Torheit".

---

[41] M. Buber, *Die Schriftwerke*, Köln - Olten 1962. S. 390.

[42] Die gleiche Konstruktion trifft man auch an in: *kl-zh nsyty bḥkmh* 7:23; "Dies alles habe ich mit der Weisheit versucht".

[43] Andere Beispiele: Ri.8:2; 2 Kön. 5:12; Jes. 56:5; Ps. 119:12; Spr. 15:17 17:1. Vgl. Levi, *Inkongruenz*, S. 97.

[44] Es ist schwierig hier mit Sicherheit zu sprechen, da *yqr mn* weiter nur noch in Spr. 3:15 belegt ist. Hier aber mit Kongruenz: *ḥkmh ... yqrh hyʾ mpnyym* "(3:13) die Weisheit (sg. f.) ... (3:15) ist kostbarer (sg.f.) als Korallen".

[45] ThWAT, Band III, Sp. 860.

[46] D. Michel, *Qohelet* (Erträge der Forschung, 258), Darmstadt 1988, S. 161.

Hiermit ist unser Überblick der Fälle mit Inkongruenz im Buch Qoheleth zu Ende geführt. Es ist schwierig, so nicht unmöglich, Schlussfolgerungen zu ziehen. Die Zahl der Stellen, wo Inkongruenz vorliegt, bleibt auf etwa 25 Fälle beschränkt. Auf 222 Versen ist das noch ziemlich viel. Die Fälle sind aber unterschiedlicher Art. Wir haben sie in neun Kategorien eingeteilt. Wenn wir trotzdem eine Schlussfolgerung ziehen wollen, dann kann man sagen, dass man den Eindruck bekommt, dass das Buch Qoheleth eine Mittelposition zwischen dem klassischen Hebräisch und dem späteren biblischen Hebräisch einnimmt.

a) In bezug auf verbale Inkongruenz kann man sagen, dass es in dem späteren Hebräisch eine Tendenz gibt den Plural zu benutzen in Fällen, wo im klassischen Hebräisch auch der Singular angewandt wird. Polzin[47] nennt als Kennzeichen des späteren biblischen Hebräisch die allgemeine Tendenz der Benutzung des Plurals über die Benutzung des Singulars. So werden z.B. Kollektiva von dem Autor der Chronik fast ausschliesslich mit dem Plural konstruiert, sogar wenn in der Vorlage in den Büchern Samuel und Königen der Singular steht[48].

b) In bezug auf die (pro)nominale Inkongruenz konstatiert man, dass sich in der späteren Sprache die Tendenz nach dem Plural bei dem Numerus des Subjekts und des Substantivums überhaupt durchsetzt[49]. Diese Tendenzen werden sich später in der hebräischen Sprache der Rollen vom Toten Meer[50] und der Mischna[51] noch ausgesprochener durchsetzen.

Beide Erscheinungen sind in der Sprache des Buches Qoheleth anzutreffen. Aber von einer wirklichen Tendenz ist noch nicht die Rede.

---

[47] R. Polzin, *Late Biblical Hebrew. Toward an Historical Typology of Biblical Hebrew Prose* (Harvard Semitic Monographs, 12), Missoula 1976. S. 40-43 + S. 78-79 (die Anmerkungen 19 bis 27).

[48] Vgl. dazu auch: A. Kropat, *Die Syntax des Autors der Chronik verglichen mit der seiner Quellen* (Beiheft zur ZAW, 16), Giessen 1909. S. 28-29.

[49] Kropat, *Syntax*, S. 8-11.

[50] Vgl. E. Qimron, *The Hebrew of the Dead Sea Scrolls* (Harvard Semitic Studies, 29), Atlanta 1986. S. 83-84.

[51] Weniger klar: M.H. Segal, *A Grammar of Mishnaic Hebrew*, Oxford 1927. §448 - 452. Ganz ausgesprochen aber äussert sich A. Bendavid, *lšwn mqrʾ wlšwn ḥkmym* ([Volume I] Tel-Aviv 5731/1971$^2$). S. 70-71.

# Iterative Forms of the Classical Hebrew Verb:

## Exploring the Triangle of Style, Syntax, and Text Grammar

J.P. Fokkelman, Leiden

§1. The house of language is a building with several floors.[1] Traditional grammar was familiar with the first floor only. At this basic level it studied phonology, morphology and sometimes syntax. The phenomena belonging to these three compartments can, in the case of a written text, be said to constitute the texture. The measures taken and devices employed by the speaker or writer to create and assemble the texture are governed, though, by decisions made beforehand that belong to higher levels: levels of structure and composition. Therefore, it can be highly relevant to study the classical Hebrew verb, for example, with a constant awareness of these higher levels. Research of this kind can only be done in a valid and satisfactory way, when the student chooses a text he is thoroughly acquainted with on all levels. In this article I would like to investigate the aspect of the frequentative - or, as I will be calling it from now on, the iterative - in Hebrew narrative prose, and I am going to scan a well-delineated corpus which I can profess to be intimate with after fifteen years of close study.[2] It is that relatively unified composition known as the Books of Samuel, a prose text taking up 114 pages in the standard edition of the Hebrew Bible (the BHS). This work of art features much greater unity, more complexity and a different kind of diversity than has been formulated hitherto.

I have collected the iterative and some adjacent cases into three groups. Under A the reader will find almost exclusively *qtl* and *yqtl* instances from the narrator's text. Under B I offer such cases from characters' texts, and I reserve group C for certain special or seemingly

[1] I dedicate this article to my colleague Prof. Hoftijzer, whose integrity and expertise I could closely watch for more than twenty-five years and greatly admire.

[2] At this point I refer to my tetralogy *Narrative Art and Poetry in the Books of Samuel*, (with the subtitle: A Full Interpretation Based on Stylistic and Structural Analyses) of which the last volume is now being written. The three volumes that are out have the titles *King David* (1981), *The Crossing Fates* (1986), and *Throne and City* (1990). Hereafter I use the abbreviation NAPS.

iterative cases. The main reason for distinguishing between A and B is that in dialogue a character nearly always relates to the unique situation he is part of, whilst the narrator, being omniscient, is able to read minds and survey events and periods. In this way his stance enables him to connect events, discern or create patterns etc.[3] One of the instruments available to him is repetition. In the Hebrew Bible this technique can be found on any text level and its application is amazingly sophisticated most of the time, so that we are only just beginning to understand its many ramifications and effects.[4]

In the following notation a letter (*e.g.* a or f) after a verse number indicates the (first or sixth) clause in that Bible verse; a hyphen means that clauses are connected as regards their iterative meaning; and each particular occurrence is covered by one verse number.[5]

Group **A**. Iterativeness in narrator's text:
First Samuel **1**:3a-4b-5a-6a-7a-7b-7c-7c,
**2**:13b-13c-14a-14b-14b-14c-15a-15b-15c-16a-16d,
**2**:19a-19b-20a-20a-20c, 21b-21b, 22b-22b-22c-23a-25e
**7**:16a-16b-16c-17a, **9**:9a-9c, **13**:19a-20a-21a-22a-22b,
**14**:47c-47c, 52b-52c, **16**:14b, 23a-23b-23b-23c-23c-23d,
**17**:20e, **18**:5b-5b, 30c, **27**:9a-9b-9c-9d-9d-10a-10c-11a-11d-11d-12a.
Second Samuel:
**3**:36c, **8**:6c-6c = 14d-14d, 15b, **12**:16c-16c-16c, 31c-31d,
**13**:18b, 19d, **14**:26b-26b-26c-26c,
**15**:2a-2a-2b-2b-2c-2c-2e-3a-4a-5a-5b-5b-5b-6a-6a, 30d
**16**:6a-13b-13c-13c, 23a-23b-23c, **19**:19a, **20**:12e (and I Kings **1**:1c, 6a).

Group **B**. Iterativeness in character's text:
First Samuel **8**:8a-8b-8b,
**12**:7bc-9bc-9d-10a-10a-11a-11b-11c,
**17**:34c-34c-35a-35a-35a-35b-35c-35c-35c-36a-37b,
**25**:7cd-7cd, 15b-15b-15c-16ab, 21b-21c,
**29**:3f=6e=8c,

---

[3] This does not preclude a character from occasionally having overview; see the cases of direct speech in I 8:8 (God speaking), I 12:7-11 (Samuel surveying the period of the Judges), I 17:34-37 (David talking about his record as a shepherd), and I 29 (king Achish on his vassal's "innocence").

[4] The best treatment of the phenomenon of repetition is that of Meir Sternberg, in the longest chapter, ch.11, of his book *The Poetics of Biblical Narrative*, Bloomington 1985.

[5] This notation with letters standing for the clauses that make up a masoretic verse corresponds with the colometrical presentation of the full Samuel text offered at the back of the NAPS volumes. It would be convenient for the reader to consult these pages of Hebrew text.

and Second Samuel **12**:3c-3c-3c.

Group **C**. Similar or special cases.
First Samuel **1**:10c, 13c, **14**:26c, 39d, **18**:16b-16b, **26**:12-12c-12c
Second Samuel **8**:15b, **15**:12d-12d.

Together groups A and B have a series of 146 cases. The amount can be reduced slightly if we put those verses in brackets that do not use a preformative (*yqtl* and *wyqtl*) or afformative (*qtl* and *wqtl*) verbal form. In I 2:13b we have a temporal clause (or rather a participial phrase, a casus pendens which is the start for v.13c; I am referring to *kol* ʾ*iš zobe*ᵃ*ḥ zebaḥ*) and in 7:17a there is a nominal clause. The main clause of II 16:23, which is v.23c, is also nominal. The same is true of I 27:11d, where the first two words are a nominal clause by the narrator, "such was his behaviour (or: strategy)."[6] If we would leave these four cases aside for a moment, 142 occurrences were still to remain. During the first stage of discussion that I will be devoting to them, we will soon notice that this main collection (groups A + B) cannot be delineated or kept apart absolutely and that some of the bracketed instances, together with most cases under C, have a strong claim to be reinstated in our collection.

The Books of Samuel (and their last Act, I Kings 1-2, which offers David's decision on his succession and Solomon's consolidation) are a literary composition which is ably thought out on every level of texture and structure. Therefore it does not seem advisable to abstract from their literary make-up during the first stage of this investigation into morphosyntactic tissues. I do not wish to start with an atomistic study of isolated details and then work my way upwards; I have decided, on the contrary, to first survey the material in Samuel from a high vantage point that is correlated to the macrostructural levels of the literary units (often stories) and their parts (dialogue by the characters and sequences by the narrator), of Acts (i.e., groups of stories) and sections. Only in the second instance will I be descending to the levels of the smaller units, to pay attention to words and sentences, that is, to the field of traditional grammar.

The Books of Samuel are composed of four sections.[7] There are some

---

[6] In the second volume of my Samuel studies I have pointed out that the first clause starting with *kōh* and being direct speech by informers (verse 11c) has to be carefully distinguished from the second *kōh* sentence; the latter is narrator's text.

[7] The sections are: I Sam.1-12, about Israel's road to kingship; I Sam.13-31 + II Sam.1 on the dialectic of Saul's rejection and David's being chosen; II Sam.2-8 and 21-24 on the civil war and the consolidation of David; and finally II Sam.9-20 & I Kings 1-2 with the Court History. Each one of these sections is dealt with in one of the four volumes of NAPS.

ninety literary units.[8] In NAPS I have made a sustained effort to establish the boundaries and the intrinsic structuring of each Act, and above that to pay attention to the way in which Acts come together into sections of the book.[9] These four levels of composition emerge as highly relevant, as soon as we study the verbal forms of repeated action and develop an overview of their distribution throughout the text.

Initial observation of the iterative forms listed above (under A + B) reveals that about 138 out of the 146 cases - almost 95% of their sum total - occur in clusters or chains. This leads me to the awareness that they should be looked upon and studied for what they are: groups or chains. Taking a look at the hyphens in the list, one can discern eight long chains, six of medium length, and eight short chains.

Here are the *long chains*:

- the eight forms in I 1:3-8 bear and determine the depiction of Elkana's annual visit to the temple of Shiloh and the distress of his barren wife Hannah; they are *wʿlh*, *wntn*, *ytn*, *wkʿsth*, *yʿśh*, *tkʿs*, *wtbkh*, *tʾkl*.

- the eleven verbal forms in I 2:13-16 offer the reader a vivid image of the cultic corruption perpetrated by the aged Eli's sons; (the participle) *zbḥ*, *wbʾ*, *whkh*, *yʿlh*, *yqḥ*, *yʿśh*, *yqṭrwn*, *wbʾ*, *wʾmr*, *wyʾmr*, *wʾmr*.

- a chain of eight forms in the first of several long farewell speeches by the prophet Samuel in I 12, when he fixes the narrow parameters of the monarchy, the new institution requested by the people. In accordance with the Book of Judges (see esp. ch.2) he offers a cyclic view of Israel's history in I Sam.12:7-11; one perfect form (*ʿśh* in v.7c) is followed by six narrative forms that are all unmarked forms of iterativity, *wymkr*, *wylḥmw*, *wyzʿqw*, *wyʾmrw*, *wyšlḥ*, *wyṣl*, *wtšbw*.

- the seven iterative verbal forms of I Sam.16:14b and 23a-d frame and dominate the unit that portrays king Saul's periodic attacks of madness and how David, playing on his lyre, brings healing; *wbʿttw*, *whyh*, *wlqḥ*, *wngn*, *wrwḥ*, *wṭwb*, *wsrh*.

- the eight occurrences which I noted in I 25 can be considered a chain, insofar as they are all direct speech and, moreover, treat the same subject (David's men protecting Nabal's herds in the Judaean hills). There are seven verbal forms in the perfect whose iterative meaning is supported by extensive temporal phrases that encompass a whole

[8] These units are often called scenes in NAPS [but I do not consider this term a very felicitous one] and are grouped in fifteen Acts. For example, the last Act has five units and is to be found, surprisingly, in I Kings 1-2. It is the fourth part of the AB-B'A' composition of the Court History (which in my Samuel studies is called "King David").

[9] For the interpretative reasons and all the considerations of style and structure which led to the division of the entire text into fifteen Acts, I am obliged to refer the reader to the NAPS volumes.

period (v.7d//15c//17b); *hklmnwm* + *nfqd*, *hklmnw* + *pqdnw* + *hth-lknw*, *hyw*, *šmrty*, *nfqd*.

- in I 27:9-11 we find ten forms. They regulate one quasi-individual sequence, into which the narrator compresses the many raids on enemy tribes executed by David, now the vassal of the king of Philistine Gath; *whkh*, *yḥyh*, *wlqḥ*, *wyšb*, *wybʾ*, *wyʾmr*, *wyʾmr*, *yḥyh*, *yšb*, *wyʾmn*.

- the longest chain is in II Sam.15:2-6 and consists of no less than fourteen verbal forms. It is another quasi-individual sequence, which unites many words and deeds of patient canvassing by David's son Absalom in one sketch. The prince is engaged in lengthy preparations for the revolt which was to prove the greatest threat to David's reign, *whškym*, *wʿmd*, *wyhy*, *yhyh*, *wyqrʾ*, *wyʾmr*, *wyʾmr*, *wyʾmr*, *wyʾmr*, *whyh*, *wšlḥ*, *whḥzyq*, *wnšq*, *wyʿś*, *ybʾw*.

Here are the *medium chains*:

- five forms in I 2:19-20, that give a positive picture of the triangle Hannah-Samuel-Eli which is constituted at her yearly return to Shiloh; *tʿśh*, *whʿlth*, *wbrk*, *wʾmr*, *whlkw*.[10]

- another medium-length chain is 2:22-25, again there are five verbal forms. It is an echo of the long chain of vv.13-16; the sons' corruption is mirrored in their father's eyes and condemned by him (in vain); *wšmʿ*, *yʿśwn*, *yškbwn*, *wyʾmr*, *(lʾ) yšmʿw*.

- next we have three verbal clauses in 7:16 which describe Samuel's duty as a Judge in spatial terms; *whlk*, *wsbb*, and *wšpṭ* are followed by an iterative nominal clause in v.17a.

- five verbal forms of iteration bear the picture of I 13:19-22, where the monopoly of forging iron is in Philistine hands. The Hebrews are totally dependent on their craft and weapons are withheld from them; *tmṣʾ*, *wyrdw*, *whyth*, *whyh*, *nmṣʾ*.

- four iterative forms do all the work in the vignette offering Absalom's beauty, II 14:26, *whyh*, *yglḥ*, *wglḥw*, *wšql*.

- the graphic scene of the Saulide Shimei hurling stones, dust and curses at David and his troops during their retreat over the Mount of Olives has four iterative forms which interact with descriptive participles and absolute infinitives, II 16:6a + 13, *wyśql*, *wyqll*, *wyśql*, *wʿpr*.

Here are the *short chains* of iterative forms:

- there is a trio of unmarked forms in I 8:8, when God explains Israel's unfaithfulness to the prophet Samuel; *ʿśw*, *wyʿzbny*, *wyʿbdw*. It is one of the few instances of iterative forms in a speech (in ch.8 by God).

- I see two more trio's in II Sam.12: the first is in direct speech again,

---

[10] This image is immediately followed by the special iterativity of v.21b and its two unmarked *wtqtl* forms: Hannah having five more children, in one sentence.

when the prophet Nathan delivers his famous parable. The axis line v.3c describes the intimacy of the poor man and his ewe lamb, *tʾkl*, *tšth*, *tškb*, in a rapid succession of *X* + *yqtl* forms. The other trio is v.16, where we also find the rapid pace of three verbs in succession (this time of the *wqtl* type) filling one line, *wbʾ-wln-wškb*: David fasting seven days and hoping to save the child Bath-sheba bore to him.

- II 16:23 is a special trio insofar as it begins with a casus pendens plus a relative clause (which has the unmarked perfect *yʿṣ* and a temporal adjunct signifying a whole period of time) and continues with a compound sentence of the "just as.., so .." type. Its main clause, v.24c, is iterative and, interestingly enough, nominal.

- in I 29 there is, in direct speech, a trio that is a sort of broken chain. It is the statement of David's innocence by king Achish, in v.3f, that is repeated by him in v.6e and echoed by David in v.8e; three times a perfect of *mṣʾ* plus an extensive temporal adjunct.

- I have found eight pairs of iterative forms. Line I 2:21b manages to bring five successive acts of deliverance in one sentence (with the formulaic pair of verbs *wthr* + *wtld*). In I 9:9ac we are informed of an early custom in an aside by the narrator (X-*ʾmr*, *yqrʾ*), in 14:47c and 18:5b there are very similar compound sentences on Saul's and David's military successes (*yfnh-ywšyʿ* and *yšlḥnw-yškyl*), and in 14:52bc we meet Saul as organizer (*wrʾh*, *wyʾsphw*). The compound sentence II 8:6c is identical with v.14d. It gives an overview and explains that God's help is the source of David's successful campaigns, *wywšʿ* + *hlk*. In II 12:31 we are told how David treats his many victims at the conclusion of the Ammonite campaign, *whʿbyr* + *yʿśh*.

§2. Pausing to survey the material in the order brought about by recognizing the chains, we notice that eighteen chains occur in First Samuel and only nine (eight short, one long) in Second Samuel. The first of the few isolated cases appear not earlier than I 17 and 18.[11] The chains have their centre of gravity in the first half of First Samuel. The majority of them, thirteen chains, occur in I 1-16. And the fact that the first five chains, which are forged by 31 iterative forms, all occur in the first two chapters of I Sam. catches the eye.

It is now time to match up these data with the higher text-levels or the macro-structural contours of the composition. We then discover that the chains are located at strategic points and we gather that they have an important function in the grand design. The frequency of the iterative chains in I 1-2 marks the beginning of the first Act, the beginning of the first section (i.e., chapters 1-12) and the beginning of

[11] Isolated cases are I 17:20e, 18:30c, II 3:36c, 13:18b and 19d, 15:30d, 19:19a and 20:12e; a total of eight occurrences.

the composition as a whole. In the first two chapters of Sam. there is a very careful alternation of iterative paragraphs about distress and corruption with the single, happy thread of narration telling us about the barren Hannah who becomes a mother and the steadily growing young Samuel. The chains provide the dark backdrop to the career of the prophet. Several of them represent the corruption of the priestly family of the Elides that is to be doomed and substituted by Samuel. One level higher, the first section of Sam. tells us that the institution of judgeship does not work any more after the successful carrying out of that type of leadership by Samuel. In this way the first section is the gloomy background to a national experiment with a new institution, kingship. The sections that follow, presenting Saul's doom (II), the rise of David (II and III) and his moral downfall (IV), are an extended exploration of the monarchy and a test of its legitimacy.

The chain of iterative verbs in I 7:16 (plus the details and the overview of v.17) marks the end of the chapter on Samuel as a Judge and at the same time contributes to the closure of Act II. The overview of the Judges period, given by Samuel in I 12, and the iterative chain supporting it, mark the end of Act III, and, what is more important, they contribute to ch.12 as the exceptional speech closing a whole section. The long chain in ch.16, which as an inclusio stretches from v.14b to the final verse 23 and in this way provides for the closure of a literary unit, offers a picture of Saul's recurring paranoia and the poignant double bind between the healer David and his king who needs treatment. In this way the iterative framework marks the ending of Act IV (chs.13-16: conflicts between king and prophet, and the definitive rejection of Saul's kingship).

Ch. 27 is the start of Act VIII with its highly sophisticated chronology[12] and the contrast between David's victory over the Amalekites and Saul's final defeat by the Philistines. As the domain of another big cluster, this unit offers the durative background for the precision alternation of four David units and the two units about Saul's very last night and day.

We discovered the longest chain in the beginning of II Sam.15. This iterative picture of patiently prepared revolt marks the start of Act XIV, Absalom's Rebellion, which is unique for two reasons: it is the acme of Hebrew narrative art and its length (sixteen units in a concentric pattern revolving around the battlefield that brings the decision)

---

[12] In NAPS II and in JEOL 30 (1987-88) I have worked out the interaction between the explicit time designations in I 27 - II 1 and the hidden dates that can only be computed by the active interpreter. The result is that victory (ch.30) and defeat (ch.31) happened on the very same day. In the text they abut upon one another, on the map they were separated by the distance of a three-day march.

is three times the average.

In fulfilling such vital functions, the chains reveal the inadequacy of studying the micro-levels of words and clauses only, as traditional grammar had done. They prove that we should proceed and incorporate text grammar into an up-to-date linguistics. The chains can only be studied in a satisfactory way when their functions at the higher levels are taken seriously. The writer (or the creative redactor) of the Books of Samuel obviously decided in an early stage of design to place the iterative paragraphs at strategic points in his artistic and narrative composition. Only after so doing did he have the elaboration of the units with the wealth of all their details on his agenda. It was only while shaping the individual stories that he needed to find out how he could or should enform iterativity and which forms of the verb (either marked as iteratives or unmarked) would suit his purposes and where.

Once more I would like to go through all the 143 cases with verbal forms in the perfect or the imperfect. I consider the *wqtl* and the *X* + *yqtl* forms to be marked, and the *X* + *qtl* and *wyqtl* forms to be unmarked as regards iterativity. There are 84 marked forms. Fifty-five of them are *wqtl* cases.

When the *wqtl* form occurs it often alternates with *X* + *yqtl*. However, in the long chains from I 16 and I 17 and in the short ones of I 7:16 and II 12:16c there are only *wqtl* forms.[13]

The combination *X* + *yqtl* occurs 29 times, exclusively so in the pairs in 14:47 and 18:5 which easily admit comparison, and in the beautiful trio of II 12:3c. It appears only nine times in II Sam. The bulk of occurrences is to be found in I Sam., mainly in the long chains of chs.1, 2 and 27, and we can see there that *X* + *yqtl* usually cooperates with the *wqtl* form.

Now for the unmarked forms; there are 56 of them. The combination *X* + *qtl* appears 23 times, mostly cooperating with other forms.[14] The broken chain of I 25 consists exclusively of eight *qtl* forms.

The *wyqtl* form, so often the classical *punctualis*, functions no less than 33 times as an iterative past tense. It can be detected as such, because it is often surrounded or flanked by marked forms of the iterative past. Another forceful indication of its iterative aspect is that its clause either has a plural object or an all-embracing complement referring to time, space or a plurality of persons (e.g. using a collective term like "all the people").

In general the unmarked form can be recognized as an iterative due

---

[13] Here we have one exception in 17:35b, the form *wyqm*, which is changed accordingly by some commentators, but not by me, into *wqm*.

[14] The only cases having an isolated *qtl* are I 18:30c and II 3:36c, with the proviso that the cases in I 29 are a trio.

to the fact that it appears beside a marked and unequivocal form or is put in an envelope of such forms. The very first chain has just one unmarked form (*wtbkh*, 1:7c), and that is exactly the same with the second (*wy›mr* in 2:16a) and the fifth (*wy›mr* in 2:23a). In the chain at the end of I 13 three marked forms (*tmṣ›* of 19a and *whyth* .. *whyh* in 21a-22a) surround the unmarked form *wayyerᵉdū*.[15] The long chain of I 27:9-11 is so composed that four unmarked *wyqtl*-forms in vv.9d-10c are framed by four marked forms.[16]

A clear application of this technique of inclusion is the longest chain, which is to offer the background of Absalom's revolt. Two marked forms (*whškym* and *w‹md* in v.2a) are in initial position and towards the end of the paragraph there is a rapid succession of four more (all in v.5ab: *whyh-wšlḥ-whḥzyq-wnšq*); in between the pair *wyhy* + *yhyh* (i.e. unmarked + marked, v.2b) comes first and then we have a series of five unmarked forms (*wyqr›* once and *wy›mr* four times, vv.2c-4a). To put it another way, the vocal contribution of the subversive prince himself appears in the centre, and around it the narrator reports his location and (the body language of his) activity.

Chains of marked forms only are: the third, I 2:19a-20c (first an *X* + *yqtl*-case, then *wqtl* four times), 7:16abc, the chain of seven *wqtl* cases in I 16, and the four forms of II 14:26bc.[17] The long chain spoken by the shepherd David exhibits a long series of eight wqtl forms, which facilitates calling the *qtl* forms of 17:36a and 37b a kind of iteration.

I would now like to take a closer look at the unmarked forms. The perfect form *qtl* appears each time in an *X* + *qtl* syntax and produces, amongst other things, the next eight instances that can be brought together: *›āmar* 9:9a, *nimṣā›* 13:22b, *šākal* 18:30c, *yāšab* 27:11d, *‹āśāh* II 3:36c, *hālak* 8:6c = 14d, and *yā‹aṣ* 16:23a. These verbal forms have two striking features in common. All of them serve in a sentence that is a survey or summary by the narrator, and that is why almost all of them have (complements with) the word *kol* at their side. In the verses of I 18:30, 27:11, II 3:36, and 8:6c = 14d we get, in one form or another, an overview of David's customs and successes. II 16:23 assesses Ahitophel's importance as the kind of rule that has come about at court, and I 9:9, bearing the specially temporal hallmark of a flashback, as a whole brings a customary expression.[18] The second characteristic of

---

[15] This narrative form has been repunctuated into *wᵉyārᵉdū* by the commentators from the age before text grammars, so e.g. Stoebe ad loc.

[16] These are *whkh*, *yḥyh* and *wlqḥ* of v.9abc and another *yḥyh* in 11a; after this an unmarked and durative *yšb* follows in 11d.

[17] Here I add four minor cases: two sentences, each with a pair of *yqtl* forms, in I 14:47c en 18:5b, the *wqtl* trio of II 12:16c, and the verbal forms of II 12:31c and d.

[18] A similar aspect of overview can be observed in the *qtl* forms spoken by a character in I 8:8a, 12:7b, 17:36a, 37b, 29:3f=6d=8c, and I 25 (the eight cases on

these $X + qtl$ cases is that almost all of them function as a kind of closure.[19] The writer has placed their clauses at the end of a literary unit. This position is well suited to the purpose of providing an overview or summary.

§3. *Lexical or semantic support.*
The 84 cases of verb forms that are marked with regard to the iterative can be studied in their immediate context, which is the clause or sentence they are serving as the predicate. About forty cases appear in sentences without further indications of the iterative. The reader, however, has no problem with identifying the iterative aspect in them, on the simple ground that their verbal forms are marked.

About forty-four cases show lexical, that is semantic, support for the iterative notion. Twenty of them have a noun phrase with the word *kol*.[20] This word is a sign of the narrator being able to survey elements and to accommodate them in one observation or report. (For further information on *kol* see below.) Ten cases have a temporal adjunct that establishes (the period of) iteration explicitly.[21] In eight cases an enumeration - which is a stylistic means of realising the concept of plurality or iteration - is involved in order to show an action being repeated.[22] Another stylistic way to incorporate repetition in a story is to be graphic by offering a description. For this purpose the author likes to use either participles, which have their durative power, in independent or circumstantial clauses, or absolute infinitives functioning descriptively. In Samuel there are seven cases where such paronomasia is applied to underline marked forms of iterativity.[23]

---

David's men and Nabal's sheep).

[19] The verses I 18:30, 27:11, II 3:36c, 8:6c = 14d and *yāʿaṣ* of 16:23a are either at the end of a unit or very near it, preparing for closure. Verse I 9:9 is near a boundary line, marking the transition from the first scene (seeking the asses) to the second (finding the seer, Samuel) in the huge unit 9:1-10:16.

[20] These clauses with *kol* are I 1:4b, 2:14b-14b-14c, 22b-22b, 7:16c, 13:19a-22b, 14:47c-47c, 52ab, 18:5b-5b, II Sam.12:31d, 15:2b-2b-6a, 16:6a and 20:12e.

[21] The cases with such time designations are I 1:3a-7a-7b, 2:15a (*yqtl* after the conjunction *ṭrm*), 2:19b, 7:16a, II 14:26ab (four times in a kind of compound sentence).

[22] The references that exhibit an enumeration are I 2:14a, 7:16b, 13:21a, 17:34c (a short chain: "bear and lion" are almost a hendiadys and stand for more dangerous animals than themselves; that is why David uses the combination three times in his speech), 27:9c and 9b = 11a (both places having the merismus "man and woman"), II 12:31c (following the enumeration immediately preceding in 31b; notice the summarising *kol* in 31d).

[23] Paronomasia illustrating or assisting *wqtl* or $X + yqtl$ is to be found in I 1:6a, 7:16a, II 13:19d, 15:30d (compare 30a!), 16:13b-13c and 19:19a (repeated crossings by Benjaminites?). On the other hand paronomasia can be present in descriptive clauses with unmarked forms: see the sequence on Shimei flinging stones, curses and dust in II 16:6a + 13bc.

What is more exciting is the question as to how the unmarked forms are faring. How can we be sure that the iterative aspect is present? In the cases where *qtl* or *wyqtl* is the predicate, the writer has to resort to other means if he wants to make sure that the component of repetition in his message will be understood. It is now crucial to accommodate unequivocal signs of the iterative in the sentence. I turn to our collection and its 56 unmarked cases. Surveying them we quickly see that the proportion of the verb forms with assistance of the iterative to the unassisted forms is quite different, as is to be expected. The great majority is accompanied and supported by data which explicitly constitute iterativeness.

There are 14 cases where the unmarked form is surrounded by iterative verbal forms belonging to a chain.[24] In this situation the unmarked form is carried off by its marked neigbours to the higher realm of iterativity, so to speak. In 23 cases a complement using *kol* - the word which signals the narrator's overview and omniscience - serves to ensure repetition in the past.[25] Five cases of virtual *kol* can be added.[26] There are thirteen cases where an adjunct signifying a whole period of time cooperates with the verb and in this way ensures the iterative aspect.[27] In five cases something general like a rule or a custom is formulated, or the narrator is offering a conclusion.[28] The readers who adds the figures of the various categories discovers that he gets much more than 56. This can easily be explained by overlap, the clearest manifestation of which is the combination of *kol* with temporal adjuncts; see the occurrences in I 25. This leaves us with the only case where one can find forms, indeed an entire chain of them, which are all unmarked and yet can be considered to be iterative. They appear in the verses 7-11 of Samuel's exceptional speech in I 12. There is no explicit sign of iterativity in this whole paragraph of almost twenty lines, except at the beginning. There the prophet speaks of "*all* the liberating deeds of the Lord" (v.7b) and

---

[24] The cases of unmarked forms in a marked envelope are I 2:16a, 23a, 13:20a, 15:35b, 27:9d-9d-10-10c, II 15:2b-2c-2e-3a-4a-6a.

[25] Cases with *kol* are I 2:16a (because "the man" is identical with "every man" from v.13b), 8:8a, 13:20a-22b, 14:52c (*kol* from 52b being still in operation), 25:7cd (bis) // 15b (bis)-15c-16a (with an additional merismus of time), 25:21b-21c, 27:11d; II Sam.3:36c, 8:6c=14d (four forms), 15:2b-6a, 16:6a, 23a (see 23c).

[26] A virtual *kol* operates in the middle of the longest chain: II 15:2c-2c-2e-3a-4a. Absalom appears to talk to one man, but again this one man is everybody who passes by. His literal answer that he "comes from one of the tribes of Israel" really means to say, and can be rendered as, "from such and such place."

[27] Cases with a temporal adjunct: I 8:8a, 18:30c, 25:7cd//15b (four verbal forms involved), 15a, 16a, 27:11d, 29:3f, 6e, 8c, and II 16:23a.

[28] Cases with a generalizing import are I 2:21b (bis), 9:9a, 27:12a, II 15:6a. Compare the formulating of a rule including a marked form in I 9:9c, 13:21a, II 13:18b, 16:23b.

he places them initially, together with the command of v.7a, as a kind of heading. However, the reader does not, without delay, consider the verbs in vv.9, 10a and 11 to be iterative forms. This comes about only on second thoughts. What happens first is that he/she has to recognize the cyclic pattern which is characteristic of the Book of Judges and its periodisation of history.[29] After this recognition has dawned, the reader notices the enumerations of friends and foes in vv.9 and 11 and becomes aware that a lot of events have been compressed into one line several times.

§4. When we ponder the concept of the iterative, the expectation may soon cross our mind that several other aspects or forms of plurality are close by. Are we perhaps about to observe forms or expressions of the *durative*, the *multiplicative* and the *distributive*? Re-examination of our collection leads to an affirmative answer.

First of all, we ought to realise that there is no watertight partition between the durative and the iterative, in the field of the Hebrew verb. Or rather, this should be formulated in a more positive way: repetition and duration easily coalesce, every now and then. I Sam.25 is illustrative of such a merger. During a certain period of time, which is signified in the text by strikingly extensive and repeated temporal adjuncts (v.7d//15c//16b) and underlined by a repeated *kol*, David's men have been protecting the herds of the rich farmer Nabal. They did this daily and for quite some time, and it would be highly unnatural and forced to try to separate the durative from the iterative. More or less the same can be said of the bad reports Eli got about the corrupt behaviour of his sons, his honest attempts to correct them and their refusal to listen (I 2:22-25). Or compare Achish, the king of Gath, who during a period of more than a year could find no fault with his vassal David (I 29). One can see duration here, but at the same time the text (in ch.27!) had already clarified that his checking of David's exploits took place every time David came back from a raid - which is a case of iteration.

On our guard not to force an artificial division into the durative and the iterative, we are nevertheless able to see considerable differences between the actual occurrences. I envisage a scale which runs from pure iteration at one end through to pure duration at the other. And for practical reasons I propose our dividing this scale into five sections, without attaching too much distinguishing force to the respective boundaries between them. I can identify not only cases of pure dura-

[29] The pattern runs like this: Israel abandons its God - angry, God sends a tyrant or enemy people - in dire straits, Israel cries for help - God has mercy and sends a saviour-Judge.

tion or repetition, but in the middle of the scale good cases of aggregate forms also, and between the middle and each end respectively like to speak of cases which are either mainly durative or mainly iterative.

There are very clear-cut examples of pure iteration. Take the yearly visit to the temple of Shiloh by Eli and his family, which is reported by the very first chain of iteratives, and see the happy sequel in the third chain (2:19-20). Or take proud Absalom who cuts and weighs his beautiful hair "each year" in II 14:26; and there is more.[30] At the other end of the scale there are a few cases of pure duration: I 1:10c, 13c, II 13:19d.[31]

Mainly durative are 15:30d (see the parallel line 30a!), 16:6,[32] and 13c. These three cases occur in graphical-descriptive passages that want to offer a picture and therefore need to leave the flow of *wyqtl* concatenation. Perhaps we could also put I 13:19-22b, 17:20e[33] and II 15:12d into this category. I would call the instance II 12:3c (the expressive trio on the poor man's sheep) mainly iterative. The cases I 18:5 and 30 about David's success as a commander and his growing popularity are perhaps mainly iterative also, but they can be said to function within a durative framework. When a rule, habit or custom is given, they seem to envisage duration more than repetition, although they clearly imply repeated application and derive their validity from it, I 9:9, II 13:18[34] and II 16:23b. These cases using a *yqtl* predicate should of course be

---

[30] Other cases of pure iteration are chain #2 in I 2:13-16, 2:21 (five births in one line!), chain #6 = I 7:16 (Samuel on his round trips as judge), the long chain in I 27, and David failing to correct Adonijah in I Kings 1:6a (*miyyāmāw*).

[31] In King David I have shown that the dramatic four lines of II 13:19 on Tamar's total desolation are a beautiful and precise AB-AB quartet. The remarkable choice of the perfect form *wᵉzāʿāqāh* at the end of line 19d, which seems odd at first sight, is the rhyming and alliterating partner of *qārāʿā* at the end of line 19b. Structural analysis on the square centimeter has proved, then, that a non-iterative, durative *wqtl* form which continues the paronomastic description of the princess's steps is more than permissible: it is correct grammar; against Joüon who called it suspect (§123n).

[32] Notice that the initial verb *waysaqqel* is the immediate continuation of, and shows effective assonance and rhyme with, the last word of v.15, the participle *mᵉqallel*, which is the end of the graphical and expressive lines 15bc. The same construction as in v.5c returns in 13b as an envelope around the Shimei incident; there we find the echo *wayqallel*, immediately followed by another/the same *waysaqqel*. Throwing stones and dust is by nature iterative, but it is offered here in a durative-descriptive framework.

[33] In NAPS II *ad loc.* I maintain the form *whrʿw*, although its position is odd. Notice that it is the continuation of a participle in a circumstantial clause and compare the case in note 31 above as well as II 15:30d.

[34] Some translations render the information that the king's daughters dress themselves in such and such a way in the present. Strictly speaking this cannot be disallowed. But I believe that the *JPS* rendering is to be preferred: "for maiden princesses *were customarily* dressed in such garments." (Italics mine, JF)

distinguished from customs or rules that are followed "until this day", such as Gen.2:24, 32:33 and the like, and also apply the *yqtl* form.

It is possible to locate a group of passages in the middle of the scale, where duration goes hand in hand with the iterative. Some cases where a good mixture can be observed are, as I have already mentioned, the fourth chain (I 2:22b-25e), I 25, especially vv.7 and 15-16, and perhaps I 26:12 (see below). Note how the repeated raids by David in I 27:9-11 are placed within a framework of explicit designations of his Ziklag period (v.7 and 11d). The inclusion and the included do not fuse, but as an instance of effective cooperation they are a good fit.

The dimension of the multiplicative or the distributive can also be conveyed by marked and unmarked forms of iterativity. In several passages the narrator ends an entire sequence (sometimes a chain of iteration) with a summarising or otherwise concluding sentence, using the narrative form *wyqtl*, an unmarked verb thus, which addresses a collective, mostly "the people" or even "all the people". See I 2:14c (and compare 2:22b), 7:16c, 14:52 (multiplication almost literally signified), II 12:31d, 15:6a, and compare the marked form in I 1:7a. Enumerations like I 7:16b, 14:47b,[35] and 27:10d cover the field of the distributive in a natural way. Multiplication is operative in the graphic cases I 2:14a (kinds of vessels) and 27:9c (animals).

The literary skill of the writer reaches a climax where he manages to combine the particular and the general or iterative. There are some remarkable examples of this technique in the books of Samuel; so much so that we are confronted with a splendid paradox to the effect that the numeral "one" comes to mean "many" or "all" and the word "somebody" stands for everybody. An easy and inconspicuous gateway into this matter is offered by the long chain in I 2. The casus pendens which is its beginning (v.13b) says "every man" and refers in v.14c to the same character with "all Israel". This singular which is no single person becomes simply "the man" in v.16a. On the level of words and their meanings this is nothing special. When we survey the whole sequence though, we become aware that this is a meeting between the priests' servant and the average Israelite wanting to offer a sacrifice. One half is solely narrator's text (vv.13-14), the second and climactic half (vv.15-16) is fully shaped as a dialogue. But this single exchange of spoken words stands for countless meetings. One sure sign of the iterative aspect is the enumeration of kinds of pots in v.14a. This line implies that one cult participant is cooking meat in a cauldron, another in a kettle, etc. The narrator has compressed these variations into one line.

[35] Note that the enumeration in 47b offers the evidence for the rule in 47c; for a similar build-up see II 12:31.

A refined application of the technique lending distributive or multiplicative meaning to an enumeration is 27:10. In reply to king Achish's question as to where he has raided "today" (an adjunct appearing to indicate a singular time span!), David answers literally: "Against the Negev of Judah and against the Negev of the Jerachmeelites and against the Negev of the Kenites." The reader quickly realizes that this is again a case of compressing or telescoping different events into one line. The meaning is that David attacked one tribe in this raid, another tribe in the next raid, etc. And of course he gave one name at a time, after returning to his base and his boss. Consequently, today is not today. What is special here is that the narrator has decided to intrude on his character's speech. Such intervention is very rare; direct speech nearly always creates the impression - but this is one of the fictional aspects of narrative art - of quoting the character verbatim. In his quasi-objectivity, the narrator pretends to keep his hands off.

The passage where "one" means "such and such" is the king-sized chain that takes care of the commencement of Absalom's Rebellion. Once more we see a meeting with just one person who is almost everybody. Absalom asks him where he comes from, and the answer is literally: "Your servant is from one of the tribes of Israel." The meaning is, however, "from such and such a tribe", as the *JPS* renders correctly. Preparing a massive revolt, the prince must have conducted hundreds of these exchanges and sealed them with as many kisses. And so, the word "one" ends up covering the content of "everywhere" - an extreme case of compression.

The paradox whereby one merges into all leads to a topic in the description of language which is ignored by traditional grammars. When they treat the negative *ʾayin* or *ʾēn*, they sometimes mention the word yes as its opposite number. This is correct, but not enough. We should explore another close connection of antonymous nature: it is the link between *ʾēn* and *kol*. The passages I 14:26c, 39d and 26:12c (ter) consist of five participial clauses negated by *ʾēn*, and it is easy to see that nobody at all was reaching, answering, waking up, etc. Again the singular covers a multitude. These verses inspired me to check all the references in the Bible where we have *(wᵉ)ʾēn* + participle. I observed some 140 cases of *ʾēn* either denying the existence of a subject or its action (in five of them *ʾayin* follows the participle) and am able to report that none of them resists or prohibits the strong rendering "nobody/none .. at all" and that, moreover, a great many verses require such an idea. Moreover, the strong meaning of the negative is often assisted, prepared for or echoed by a nearby *kol*.

It is necessary and highly relevant to study how frequent and how influential the word *kol* is in the *(w)ʾēn* + participle collection, whether it is present in the clause itself or in the immediate vicinity. It occurs some 16 times in the c. 100 occurrences of *wᵉ ʾēn* + prt., but it occurs 18 times in the 37 places with *ʾēn* + prt. - a frequency of roughly 50%. Many telling examples from both sub-collections could be cited, but there is room for only a few.[36] After Pharaoh has had unsettling dreams, "there is no one to interpret them" and "*all* the magicians of Egypt and *all* its wise men" fail to explain them, Gen.40:8 and 41:8, 15; later on, *one* person does know what they mean, Joseph of course. The interior of Solomon's temple "was all cedar, no stone was exposed", says I Kings 6:18, alternating the opposition *ʾēn* versus *kol* succinctly with two segholates. As a trio, the clauses of the full poetic line in Is.41:26b, "not one foretold, not one announced; no one has heard your utterance!" are a close parallel to I Sam.26:12c, which also reported a surprising intervention by the deity. Hosea 7:7b exhibits the opposition *kol* .. *ʾēn* at the head of its bicola, 7a opens with *kullām*, and alliteration on the roots *ʾkl* and *mlk* tune in. Lam.1:2 reads: "There is none (*ʾēn*) to comfort her / of *all* her friends." In Dan.10:21 we meet the numeral "one" again; this time it heightens the *ʾēn* + prt. construction. Lack of space prevents my going into detail, but what needs to be added is that we may not ignore constructions with negation + *ʾīš* or *lōʾ* .. *mᵉ ʾūmā*.[37] The latter combination is prominent in contexts with *kol* in the books of Samuel: see 25:7-15-21 and 29:3 (with an interesting parallel in 12:5d: Samuel's innocence).

Finally, I annotate the verses from *group C, special cases*.
Neither the standard grammars nor commentaries explain why I 1:10c has *tibkeh* instead of *bākā́tā* or why 1:13c has *yiššāmaʿ* instead of a perfect form. In the first case I notice an expressive-descriptive application of the absolute infinitive before the finite form, which suggests that we have a durative form here: she was weeping "all the while" (according to, correctly, the *JPS*). The context of v.13c is quite revealing. This line not only follows three participial clauses which are notoriously durative and have the obvious function of providing a picture of Hannah's sad condition; but at the head of the series 12b-13a-13b-13c the line on her voice is also preceded by a special semantic-lexical signal of iterativity, the "auxiliary" verb *rbh* in the *hiphʿil*: "As she *kept on* praying before the LORD, .." (once more, correctly, according to the *JPS* rendering, italics mine; see also Driver p. 13). I conclude that as a part of the total

[36] There are two very similar sub-groups of a formulaic nature. Twelve occurrences have the circumstantial clause *wᵉ ʾēn maḥᵃrīd*, and some thirty say: "there was no saviour/helper at all". Mostly the subject is *mōšīᵃʿ* or *maṣṣīl*, a few times it is *ʿōzer*.

[37] Note how the singular *ʾīš* covers a plurality in I 12:4d, II 16:23b or is part of a double rule in I 2:25. It is well-known from the legal portions of the Bible too.

image (instead of the ongoing *wyqtl* concatenation) the imperfect form of v.13c is durative also.

All the participial clauses of I 14:26c, 39d, and 26:12c have the strong negation *ʾēn* and *kol* close by. Each time "all the people", in the sense of the whole army, are involved. Note how the trio "no one saw, no one knew, no one woke up" functions as staccato evidence for the two *kī* clauses that immediately follow, "for all (*kullām*) remained asleep, for a deep sleep from the LORD had fallen upon them." In the case of 14:39d, literally "no one answered him from all the people", there is a striking contrast with the pointedly singular v.37d in all the three parts of the clauses, "but he did not answer him this time." The tense of the verb is changed, the negative had to follow, and even the complement shifts from the broadly general to the precision of the demonstrative pronoun.

The verse I 18:16b is another example in Samuel where the iterative aspect is borne and signified by participles, this time without negation. The whole unit 18:6-16 leads to the concluding verse on David's popularity, and we gather from v.16b that he led many campaigns. The participles in II 15:12d are again the predicate of a clause that summarises an entire unit, but this couple is different. They are durative because they describe a process, which is the gradual increase of support for Absalom. They should be compared with other cases of *hlk* about gradual growth such as II 3:1bc (David growing stronger, the house of Saul weaker) or I 2:26. One step further and we have reached, via the durative, the group of clauses that have the so-called periphrastic construction, i.e. *hyh* plus participle.[38] One example should suffice here. It is II 8:15b, a clause where the durative, the distributive and the iterative are inseparable and which has its connection with the pair v.6c = 14d.

The books of Samuel contain several verses with a *wqtl* form that has no iterative or durative function. This perfect form with a so-called waw copulativum[39] represents a past tense that sometimes can be considered to have a special nuance signalling the start of something special, a resumption or a new sequence.[40] One group consists of five *whyh* cases. Four of them happen to immediately follow speeches with futural *wqtl*

[38] The periphrastic construction occurs in I 2:11b, 4:13c, 7:10a, 18:9a, 14a, 29b (remarkable as a trio), II 3:6b, 17b, 5:2b (note, however, the article; compare the verbs with I 18:16), 7:6b (cf. 7a), 8:15b, 15:32a?, 18:8a, 19:10b, 20:3e.

[39] Cf. Rudolph Meyer, Auffallender Erzählungsstil in einem angeblichen Auszug aus der "Chronik der Könige von Juda", pp. 114-123 in the *Festschrift* for *F. Baumgärtel*, Erlangen 1959.

[40] See P.A. H. de Boer, The Perfect with waw in 2 Samuel 6:16, in the *Festschrift* for *E.A. Nida*, eds. M. Black and W.A. Smalley, 1974, pp. 43-52.

forms, so that the question has been raised[41] as to whether the latter have influenced - if not misled - writer or copyist. This past tense of *whyh* appears in I 1:12a, 10:9a, 17:48a, 25:20, and II 6:16a.[42] The other cases of *wqtl* are I 3:13a (if this *whgdty* is not a performative perfect that wants to convey: "I hereby inform him"), 4:19b,[43] 17:38b, II 6:21d, 13:18d, 16:5a?, 19:18c and 23:20c.[44] All these forms in the past tense do not belong to the field that I have investigated here.[45]

Titles and abbreviations used:

Driver — S.R. Driver, *Notes on the Hebrew Text and the Topography of the Books of Samuel*, 2nd ed. Oxford 1913

Ges-K. — *Wilhelm Gesenius' Hebräische Grammatik, völlig umgearbeitet von E. Kautzsch*, 28th edition, Leipzig 1909

JEOL — *Jaarbericht Ex Oriente Lux*, Leiden

Joüon — Paul Joüon, *Grammaire de l'hébreu biblique*, 2nd ed. Rome 1947

JPSA — *Jewish Publication Society of America* (second version of Tanakh, Philadelphia 1985)

Stoebe — H.J. Stoebe, *Das erste Buch Samuelis*, = *Kommentar zum Alten Testament*, vol. VIII 1, Gütersloh 1973.

---

[41] See S.R. Driver, *Notes* .., p. 13 on *whyh* of I 1:12a. On the other hand Stoebe defends these *wqtl* forms of the masoretic text, in his sections of small print which account philologically for each unit.

[42] More about II 6:16a, 21d (*wśḥqty*) and especially about the series of *wqtl* cases in II 7:9c-11b (which for good reasons should not be taken to be a past tense!) is to be found in the relevant paragraphs of *NAPS III* which has just appeared.

[43] The perfect *wmt* is the continuation of an infin. constr. See also how the forms *wʿbrt* // *whlkt* are the continuation of the infin. constr. *ṣētᵉkā* in I Kings 2:37a//42d.

[44] The latter case, in II 23, is a remarkable example of stylistic considerations guiding the writer. It is impossible to overlook the anaphoral parallelism of the clauses 23:20bc and 21a (the pronoun *hūʾ* plus *hikkā* three times).

[45] Another case to be excluded are the verbs *whlkh* + *whgydh* // *ylkw* + *whgydw* in II 17:17bc. They are not frequentatives; contra Driver p. 324, who wrote that "communication was *regularly* maintained", and against Ges.-K. §112e note 4 and Joüon §119v. When we establish the underlying chronology of Absalom's victorious entry into Jerusalem and David's fleeing across the Jordan the subsequent night, there is no (temporal or textual) space for more than one report or signal being brought to David. Note that the two lines are construed as a parallelism and that their verbs have the pattern ab-ab. Their meaning is primarily modal (jussive) - the same applies to the subsequent *lʾ ywklw* - and they refer to future action: "Jonathan and Ahimaaz were staying at En-rogel, and a slave girl *was to go* and bring them word and they in turn *were to go* and inform King David. For they themselves *dared* not be seen entering the city."(Italics mine, JF)

# Some Remarks on the Use of the Finite Verb Form in the Protasis of Conditional Sentences in Aramaic Texts from the Achaemenid Period*

Margaretha L. Folmer, Leiden

## Introduction

In this contribution I will describe the use of the finite verb form with future time reference in the protasis of conditional sentences introduced by the conjunction *hn* in Aramaic texts from the Achaemenid Period (ca. 550 - 330 B.C.E.).[1]

The Aramaic from this period is often referred to as "Imperial Aramaic".[2] Although this is a problematic term, I will use "Imperial Aramaic" to refer to all the Aramaic linguistic material originating from the Achaemenid Period. One of the pitfalls of the use of "Imperial Aramaic" is that it gives the reader the impression that the Aramaic from

* The abbreviations used in this article are explained at the end. All the readings of legal documents and letters on papyrus have been taken from Porten and Yardeni, unless otherwise stated: B. Porten and A. Yardeni, *Textbook of Aramaic Documents from Ancient Egypt*. Vol. i *Letters*, Jerusalem 1986; vol. ii *Contracts*, Jerusalem 1989. Prof. Porten has been so kind as to give me permission to make use of the new readings in Aḥiqar, which will be published in the third volume of *Textbook of Aramaic Documents from Ancient Egypt* by B. Porten and A. Yardeni.

[1] Other uses of *hn* have been discarded here, namely the use of *hn* in indirect questions (HP 5,9; Ezra 5: 17) and the use of *hn* in oath sentences (Cl G 152 conc. 3.7; see A. Dupont-Sommer, "L'ostracon araméen du sabbat", *Semitica* 2 (1949), p. 31). Cf. also *lmh hn* ("lest") in Cl G 152 conc. 3 and *hn* ... *hn* ("either ... or") in Ezra 7: 26.

[2] E.g. F. Rosenthal, *Die aramaistische Forschung seit Th. Nöldeke's Veröffentlichungen*, Leiden 1939 (reprint 1964). Other names used are "Official Aramaic" (H.L. Ginsberg, "Aramaic Dialect Problems", *American Journal of Semitic Languages* 50 (1933-1934), pp. 1-9 and 52 (1935-1936), pp. 95-103; J.A. Fitzmyer, "Phases of the Aramaic Language", in *idem, A Wandering Aramean. Collected Aramaic Essays*, pp. 57-84, Missoula 1979) and "Standard Aramaic" (Kraeling, *Brooklyn Museum Aramaic Papyri*, p. 6 n.11). The name "Egyptian Aramaic" is sometimes used when referring to the material from Egypt only (P. Leander, *Laut- und Formenlehre des Ägyptisch-Aramäischen*, Göteborg 1928).

this period might be treated as a homogeneous corpus which needs no further differentiation. However, nothing is further from the truth. In recent years some scholars, esp. J.C. Greenfield and the late E.Y. Kutscher, have argued for a wide linguistic diversity in the Aramaic texts from the Persian period.[3] And indeed, closer study of the material has shown that much of the variety of language forms found in the Aramaic from this period can be classified a.o. on the basis of the date of the text, its place of origin, the individual scribe of the text (in the case he is known) and the genre of the text. Since as yet no comprehensive study has been made of all of the material from this period, I will base myself upon the complete corpus and point to variations within the material whenever necessary.

The largest amount of conditional sentences introduced by *hn* is found in the Aramaic legal documents from the isle of Elephantine in Upper Egypt. These legal documents are of a very diverse nature. Among them marriage documents may be found as well as deeds of obligation and conveyances. In these legal documents the rights and responsibilities of the contractal parties have been regulated. All possible kinds of future violations of these regulations have been formulated together with the punishments of those who are to be held liable. The syntactic form which is used in many of these cases is that of the conditional sentence.[4]

Most of the rest of the material is found in letters (papyri and ostraca). The majority of these letters originate from Egypt (Elephantine, Assuan, Migdol, Memphis [Hermopolis letters]). The Arṣham correspondence was written in one of the eastern capitals of the empire. Finally, some conditional sentences can be found in the Aramaic version of the Behistun inscription, in the Aḥiqar text (framework story and proverbs), both found in Elephantine, and in the inscription from Xanthos in Asia Minor. Aramaic texts from other parts of the Persian empire, the Arabian desert, Palestine and the eastern provinces, with the exception of the Arsham correspondence, do not provide us with conditional sentences.

Biblical Aramaic (further BA) has also been included in this overview in order to provide the reader with comparative and often contrasting

[3] For instance, J.C. Greenfield, "Standard Literary Aramaic", in A. Caquot et D. Cohen (eds.), *Actes du premier congrès international de linguistique sémitique et chamito-sémitique*, Paris 16-19 juillet 1969, The Hague - Paris 1974, pp. 280-289; *idem*, "Aramaic in the Achaemenian Period", in I. Gershevitch (ed.), *The Cambridge History of Iran*, vol. ii: *The Median and Achaemenian Periods*, pp. 698-713; E.Y. Kutscher, "Aramaic", in Th. A. Sebeok (ed.), *Current Trends in Linguistics* vol. vi, *Linguistics in South West Asia and North Africa*, The Hague 1970, pp. 347-412.

[4] Additional, but often damaged material comes from the recently published contracts from Saqqara (Segal, *Aramaic Texts from North Saqqâra*).

material. Although BA is different in many respects from the epigraphic texts in Imperial Aramaic, it may not be completely discarded in any discussion of Imperial Aramaic, since their relationship is still under discussion and has not exactly been defined. At the present most scholars agree that the official documents in Ezra have their origin in the Achaemenid Period. The final form of the book is from a later date. The final redactor of Ezra adapted the orthography of the original documents to the orthography of his own time. The book of Daniel may have attained its final form in the Hellenistic Period, two or three centuries after the book of Ezra. The Aramaic found in Daniel differs in many respects from the Aramaic of Ezra. Moreover, the book of Daniel is said to have a more literary character.[5]

Among conditional sentences a distinction is usually made between the realis and the irrealis. The realis, in the present Aramaic corpus of texts the most common one, is a conditional sentence in which the statement in the main clause (apodosis) is dependent on the truth of the condition made in the subordinate clause (protasis). In the irrealis the content of the subordinate clause is false. It is therefore counterfactual. The irrealis occurs only once in the Aramaic texts from this period (C 37,8).

In Imperial Aramaic the conditional sentence is usually introduced by a conjunction which is typical of conditional sentences. Thus the realis is normally introduced by *hn* and the irrealis by *hnlw*. But conditional relationships in the realis may also be expressed in other ways, for example by coordinating two sentences[6] or by using the form of the indefinite free relative clause[7] as in the sentence "Whoever sues you will pay you 2 shekels". In this sentence the person who has to pay the indemnity is not defined, in contrast with X in the following sentence: "If X sues you, he will pay you 2 shekels". In this study I will limit myself to sentences introduced by *hn* and containing a finite verb form with *future time reference* in the protasis.[8]

---

[5] For a discussion concerning the relation of BA with Imperial Aramaic see J. Hoftijzer, "Hebreeuws en Aramees als bijbeltalen", in A.S. van der Woude, M.J. Mulder *et.al.*, *Bijbels Handboek* vol. i, Kampen 1981, p. 188ff. and Greenfield, "Standard Literary Aramaic", p. 284ff.

[6] With P. Joüon, "Notes grammaticales, lexicographiques et philologiques sur les papyrus araméens d'Égypte", *Mélanges de l'Université Saint Joseph de Beyrouth* 18 (1934), p. 22. E.g. C 8,22 *wʾhk bdyn wlʾ ʾṣdq*; C 10,19 *ʾp yhkwn bdyn wlʾ yṣdqwn*; K 10,15 *wyhk bdn wlʾ yṣdq*; Ah pr l.114 *ʾyš zʿyr wyrbh.*

[7] For the terminology used see C.L. Baker, *English Syntax*, Cambridge, Massachusetts 1989, chapter 7.

[8] In letters it is often difficult to decide whether a given form of the sf. conj. in the protasis has future time reference (future or future perfect) or present time reference (present perfect). E.g. C 42,7 *hn hškḥt ksp [ḥ]t lʿbq* "If you will find / will have found / have found silver, [come] down immediately ..." (M.F.).

## 1. Verbal protasis[9]

The finite verb form in the protasis of conditional sentences introduced by *hn* may be either a suffix conjugation or a prefix conjugation, a situation which is found in other Northwest Semitic languages as well.[10] Both verb forms may have future time reference in the protasis and the question which arises is if there is a difference in meaning between the use of the two forms.[11] Several efforts have been made to determine the different values of the sf. conj. and the pref. conj. in these subordinate clauses, taking into account an aspectual difference between the two forms. The use of the sf. conj. in the protasis has been explained as referring to a situation that is viewed by the speaker as preceding the situation in the apodosis.[12] The explanation is only partially successful because the use of either the sf. conj. or the pref. conj. cannot be predicted from it. The problem posed by the use of the two forms has been formulated by B.T. Waltke and M. O' Connor, when discussing the conditional sentence in Classical Hebrew: "We may presume that the suffixconjugation in a conditional sentence has a perfective value even though that value is not obvious. ... It seems unlikely that the

[9] The verbal clause is understood here as a clause which contains a finite verb form, a nominal clause as a clause which does not contain a finite verb form. Because of the limitations of this contribution the structure of clauses which are dependent on the finite verb form in the protasis, namely those which are a direct speech (K 5,13; K 7,25; K 10,10; C 8,20; C 9,14; C 15,33; C 42,5) and those which are marked by *zy* (K 1,5; C 30,27 (*ʿd zy*); C 31,27 (*zy ʿd*); D 8,3f. and Ah pr l.149), has not been taken into consideration here.

[10] For Ugaritic see S. Segert, *A Basic Grammar of the Ugaritic Language*, Berkeley-Los Angeles 1984, p. 120f. and D. Pardee, *Les textes hippiatriques*, Paris 1985, pp. 17-18 and pp. 41-42; for Biblical Hebrew see P. Joüon, *Grammaire de l'hébreu biblique*, Rome 1923, §167 g; for Syriac see Th. Nöldeke, *Kurzgefasste Syrische Grammatik*, Leipzig 1898, §258 (sf. conj.) and §265 (pref. conj.). In South Semitic languages the sf. conj. is very common in the protasis of the realis. For Ethiopian see A. Dillman, *Grammatik der Äthiopischen Sprache*, 2nd improved edition by C. Bezold, Leipzig 1899, §205; for Arabic see e.g. C. Brockelmann, *Arabische Grammatik*, Leipzig 1953, §155 and E. Wagner, *Syntax der Mehri-Sprache unter Berücksichtigung auch der anderen neusüdarabischen Sprachen*, Berlin 1953, §321.

[11] The nominal form of the protasis in many instances has no future time reference but present time reference. Therefore, the nominal protasis as such does not occur in the legal documents. However, it is very common in letters and in the proverbs of Aḥiqar. The apodosis of conditional sentences with a verbal protasis can be verbal (with pref. conj. or imperative) or nominal, regardless of the form used in the protasis.

[12] E.g. Joüon, "Notes grammaticales", p. 21: "Dans tous ces exemples le contexte est le même, et la différence de la forme temporelle dans la protase ne crée pas de différence réelle de sens; seulement le *qetal* représente l'action de la protase comme antérieure à l'action de l'apodose, ce qui a pu être senti comme une finesse". Cf. also R. Degen, *Altaramäische Grammatik der Inschriften des 10.-8. Jh. v. Chr.*, Wiesbaden 1969, §92 dd) p. 131 and Segert, *Altaramäische Grammatik*, p. 431 (7.5.4.3.2) and p. 432 (7.5.4.4.1).

conjugations otherwise distinct, became confused in this one class of sentences, though that is possible".[13]

My point will become clear by comparing the following conditional sentences, all to be found in legal documents from Elephantine. For the sake of the argument only forms of the pref. conj. and the sf. conj. of one and the same root are compared, forms which moreover are found in one document.

Minimal pairs of the root *gry* in K 3 (scribe Haggai bar Shemaiah; 437 B.C.E.)[14]:
K 3,14 *hn grynk dyn wdbb wgryn 15. lbr bbrh lk wlmn zy ṣbyt lmntn ʾnḥn nntn lk ...* (sf. conj.)
"If we institute against you suit or process or institute (suit) 15. against son in/with (scribal error for: or) daughter of yours or (anyone) to whom you desire to give (it), we shall give you ..."[15]

K 3,18 *hn grwk wgrw lbr wbrh lk yntnwn lk ...* (sf. conj.)
"If they institute (suit) against you or institute suit against son or daughter of yours, they shall give you ..."

K 3,19 *whn gbr ʾḥrn ygrnk wygrh 20. lbr wbrh lk ʾnḥn nqwm wnpṣl wnntn lk ...* (pref. conj.)
"And if another person institute (suit) against you or institute (suit) against son or daughter of yours, we shall stand up and cleanse (it) and give (it) to you ..."

Minimal pair of the root *mwt* in K 4 (scribe Mauwziah bar Nathan; 434)[16]:
K 4,16. *lhn 17. hn mytty brt šnn 100 bny zy yldty ly hmw šlyṭn bh ʾḥr 18. mwtky* (sf. conj.)
"But 17. if you die at the age of 100 years, it is my children whom you bore me (that) have right to it after 18. your death".

K 4,18 *wʾp hn ʾnh ʿnny ʾmwt br šnn 10 plṭy wyhwyšmʿ kl 2 bny hmw šlyṭn bḥlqy ʾḥrnʾ ʾnh ʿnny* (pref. conj.)

[13] K.B. Waltke and M. O' Connor, *Biblical Hebrew Syntax*, Winnona Lake 1990, p. 493.

[14] The sf. conj. of *gry* is also found in K 1,8, K 4,14 and C 14,8f. The pref. conj. is found in K 4,16.

[15] Here and in the following the translations of passages in contracts, letters on papyrus and the Aḥiqar proverbs have been derived from Porten and Yardeni, *Textbook* vols. i, ii and iii (unpublished), unless reference has been made to another translation. The English translation of the passages in BA has been taken from *The Revised English Bible*, Oxford 1989. For all other translations see the references in the footnotes.

[16] The pref. conj. of *mwt* is also found in K 6,18 and K 7,28.34. The sf. conj. of this root is found in K 11,8 (*mʾtt* !), C 5,8 and C 10,14.

"And moreover, if I, Anani, die at the age of 100 years, it is Pilti and Jehoishma, all (told) 2, my children, (who) 19. have right to my other portion, I, Anani".

Minimal pair of the root *ršy* in C 25 (scribe Mauwziah bar Nathan; 416):
C 25,12 *whn ʾnh ydnyh ršytkm wrškm 13. br ly wbrh ʾnth wʾyš bšmy wbšm bny šṭr mn br wbrh zy yznyh br ʾwryh 14. wyršwn lbr wbrh wʾnth wʾyš lkm ʾw gbrn zy tzbnwn lh ʾw zy brḥmn tntnw lh 15. bytʾ zk wzy yrškm dyn yntn lkm ʾbygrnʾ zy ksp ...*
"And if I, Jedaniah, bring (suit) against you, or 13. son of mine or daughter, woman or man 12. bring (suit) against you 13. in my name or in the name of my children excluding son or daughter of Jezaniah son of Uriah -14. or they bring (suit) against son or daughter, or woman or man of yours, or persons to whom you sell or to whom you give 15. that house 14. in affection -15. and whoever shall bring suit against you shall give you the penalty of silver ..."

Minimal pair of the root *ršy* in C 28 (scribe Nabutukulti bar Nabuzeribni; 410):
C 28,9 *hn ršynk dynʾ ʿlʾ ʾnḥnh mḥsyh wbny ʾw nršh lbr 10. wbrh lk wlʾnš zylk ʿldbr pṭwsyry ʿbdʾ zk zy mṭʾk bḥlq ʾḥr nntn lk ʾbygrnʾ ksp 11. ṣryp ...*
"If we bring suit against you about it we, Mahseiah or my children — or bring (suit) against son 10. or daughter of yours or against an individual who is yours on account of Petosiri, that slave who came to you as a portion, then we shall give you the penalty (of) 11. pure 10. silver ..."

It should be noted that both C 25 and C 28 attest to an interesting change from the sf. conj. into the pref. conj.[17] (see below sub 4.).

Given these examples, especially those in C 25 and C 28, it is hard to maintain that there is a real difference in meaning between the use of the sf. conj. and the use of the pref. conj. At least in the legal documents such a difference is not to be found. Although a future perfect translation of the sf. conj. often will fit the context it can by no means be justified in every single instance (see also n.8).

In the following an effort will be made to show that the use of a certain finite verb form is primarily connected with the word order in the protasis. Word order itself depends on many other factors, which are often very difficult to grasp. The Old Aramaic VSO order is absent in many Aramaic texts from the Achaemenid period. In certain texts, often those with an eastern origin, the influence of other languages, like

[17] The pref. conj. of *ršy* is also found in C 8, 20.26; C 9,13 and C 20,13.

Akkadian or Iranian, may be responsible for positions of the verb other than initial[18], in other texts the SV / OV order may be explained as the means through which emphasis may be given to certain elements in the sentence (subject, object etc.).

It is impossible, however, to explain the use of all finite verb forms through word order. Apparently there is also a tendency towards the use of specific finite verb forms in a given period.

## 2. Sf. conj. in the subordinate clause[19]

The sf. conj. with future time reference is very frequent in the subordinate clause (protasis) of the conditional sentence in Imperial Aramaic. In Old Aramaic it is attested only once in Sfire III 20.[20] In later Aramaic dialects the use of the sf. conj. seems to become less and less frequent in favour of the use of the pref. conj. in the protasis, although the sf. conj. was never completely ousted in the protasis of conditional sentences.[21] In accordance with this tendency the pref. conj. is usually found in the protasis of conditional sentences in BA. The sf. conj. occurs only once in BA in a conditional sentence in which *lhn* (< *lʾ hn*) is best translated with "unless" (< "if not"):

Dan. 6: 6 *ʾdyn gbryʾ ʾlk ʾmryn dy lʾ nhškḥ ldnyʾl dnh kl ʿlʾ lhn hškḥnh ʿlwhy bdt ʾlhh*

"... they said, 'We shall not find any ground for bringing a charge against this Daniel unless it is connected with his religion'".

In this sentence, too, the *hn* clause describes the condition on which the truth of the rest of the sentence depends.[22]

---

[18] See the discussion by Kaufman about the origin of the SOV order (S.A. Kaufman, *The Akkadian Influences on Aramaic*, Chicago-London 1974, p. 132f.).

[19] In some instances it is impossible to choose between a passive participle or a form of the peʿil sf. conj. (Saq P 1,5 (*hn X zk šʾyl*); Saq P 23, conv.2 (*whn qm qd[m]*); pap. Berlin 23000,7 (6. *hn ʿbw[rʾ zk] 7. qym bydk[m]*). In Ah pr l.103 the interpretation of *pqyd* as a participle is more probable than the interpretation as a sf. conj. form (*hn lk pqyd*). See below sub 6.

[20] *hn hšb zy ly ʾhšb [zy lh]* (Gibson ii nr.9): "If he gives back what is mine, I will give back [what is his]" (M.F.). Cf. Degen, *Altaramäische Grammatik*, §92 dd) p. 131: "Das Perf. im Vordersatz konstatiert ein Faktum, dessen Eintritt Voraussetzung für die Handlung des Nachsatzes ist".

[21] In Syriac both the sf. conj. and the pref. conj. occur in the protasis of conditional sentences introduced by the conditional conjunction *ʾen / hen*. See Nöldeke, *Syrische Grammatik*, §258 (sf. conj.) and §265 (pref. conj.). In the oldest Syriac inscriptions from Edessa only forms of the pref. conj. have been found. See H.J.W Drijvers, *Old-Syriac (Edessean) Inscriptions*, *Semitic Studies Series* vol iii, Leiden 1972 (nrs. 24, 8; P, 12.17).

[22] This use of *lhn* ("if not" > "unless") may be compared with the use of *ky ʾm* ("but if" > "unless") in Hebrew, with the difference that *ky ʾm* is not combined with a negation. Although the semantic development has been different for both combinations, the outcome is similar. Both *lhn* and *ky ʾm* follow a preceding

The situation in Imperial Aramaic is not easy to comprehend. Some texts exclusively use the sf. conj., others the pref. conj. and some use both. Is there a development in time from the use of the sf. conj. towards a more favoured use of the pref. conj. in the protasis or is the choice of the sf. conj. or pref. conj. in the protasis determined by rules of syntax? Probably both explanations hold some truth.

The sf. conj. is mostly found where the verb form immediately follows the conjunction *hn* or *hn l'*. This has been recognized for the first time by Kutscher in an article commenting on the Aramaic papyri published by Kraeling.[23]

*hn (l')* immediately followed by the sf. conj. is found in the following texts (in chronological order[24]):

Legal documents:
Makkibanit bar Nargi: BM 10 (*hn l'*) (515)
Gemariah bar Ahio: C 11,7 (*hn l'*) (488/487)
Pelatiah bar Ahio: C 5,7.8.13 (471)
Nathan bar Ananiah: C 15,35 (458 or 445); C 10,6.7.14.15f.(*hn l'*) (456); K 2,14 (449)
Bunni bar Mannuki: K 1,5.8 (451)
Peteisi bar Nabunathan: C 14,8 (440)
Mauwziah bar Nathan: K 4,17 (434)
Haggai bar Shemaiah: K 3,14.18.20 (*hn l'*) (437); K 5,13 (*'nḥn hn qmn*) (427)
Shaweram bar Eshemram: K 11,5 (*hn l'*).8.9 (*hn l'*) (402)
Nabutukulti bar Nabuzeribni: C 28,9 (410) (for *ršynk* → *nršh* see below sub 4.)
unknown scribes: C 45,7 (*hn l'*) (413); C 7,10 (*hn [l]'*) (401) and probably C 35,6 (*hn l' [šlmt] wyhbt)* (400)

Letters:

---

negated sentence when used this way (Joüon, *Grammaire de l'hébreu biblique*, §173b [proposition exceptive]). In the related meaning "except" *lhn* may be preceded by an affirmative or negative statement (see also E. Vogt, *Lexicon Linguae Aramaicae Veteris Testamenti Documentis Antiquis Illustratum*, Roma 1971, s.v. *lhn*).

[23] E.Y. Kutscher, "New Aramaic Texts", *Journal of the American Oriental Society* 74 (1954), p. 234: "In these aramaic texts *hn* usually takes the perfect like Arabic *'in*. But this holds good only if the verb follows directly upon *hn*; the further it is removed the more the verb tends to be in the imperfect. And this may happen even if the verb follows immediately. But the converse never occurs; that is to say, if the verb is removed from *hn* it never appears in the perfect". This statement has been repeated in the confusing passage of his article "Aramaic" from 1971 in which twice a reference mistakenly has been made to the "imperfect" instead of the "perfect" (Kutscher, "Aramaic", p. 365 and p. 369).

[24] The dates are those given by Porten and Yardeni in *Textbook* vol ii.

papyri: C 42,5 (*hn l*ʾ).7.8 (*hn l*ʾ).10 (*hn l*ʾ).11 (or active part.?); pap. Berlin 23000,5; HP 3,6; HP 4,5.9 and perhaps HP 2,8.9.10.16
ostraca: Cl G 44 conv. 1 (*hn l*ʾ)[25]; *RES* 1793 conv. 1[26]; *CIS* ii 137[27]; for *CIS* ii 138 A2 see n.40.

examples:
BM 10 *[w]hn l*ʾ *qmt 11. wnqt wntnt lk* ʾ*tnnhy lk m[n ]ḥqly lmlk mn 12. bl*ʿ*dy mlt mlk*
"[And] if I do not stand up 11. and cleanse and give (it) to you, I shall give it to you fr[om] my portion from the king, ex12.cept for a word of the king".

K 1,5 *hn qblt 6.* ʿ*lyk dyn wmr*ʾ *bšm hyr*ʾ *[z]nh zy qblt* ʿ*lyk bgw wyhbt l[y] dmwhy ksp šqln [4]+1 wrḥqt mnk* ʾ*ntn lk ksp ...*
"If I complain 6. against you (before) judge or lord in the name of (=regarding) [t]his *hyr*ʾ — (about) which I complained against you 7. herein and you gave m[e] its payment, silver [4+]1 (=5) shekels and I withdrew from you — 8. I shall give you silver ..."

K 2,14 *whn hnṣlth mnk* ʾ*ntn l*ʿ*nny ksp kršn 5*
"And if I do reclaim him from you, I shall give Anani silver, 5 karsh".

HP 4,9 *wk*ʿ*t* ʾ*n* ʾ*škḥt* ʾ*š mhymn 10.* ʾ*th lkn md*ʿ*m*
"And now, if I find a trustworthy person, 10. I shall bring (=dispatch) something to you".

C 42,7 *hn hškḥt ksp [ḥ]t l*ʿ*bq*
"If you find silver, [come] down immediately, ..."

A word should be said here about the fourfold occurrence of *yhb* in conditional sentences in letter 2 of the Hermopolis papyri (end sixth or beginning fifth century B.C.E.). The texts read the following:
HP 2,8 *wk*ʿ*t hn yhb lky nqyh wgzth šlḥy ly*
HP 2,9 *whn yhb lky* ʿ*mrh zy* ʿ*l mky šlḥy ly*
HP 2,10 *whlh yhb lky šlḥy ly w*ʾ*qbl* ʿ*lyhn tnh*
HP 2,16 *whn yhb lky r*ʿ*yh* ʿ*mr šlḥy ly*
From the spelling alone one cannot decide whether the occurrences of *yhb* are forms of the sf. conj. or participles. However, other conditional

[25] A. Dupont-Sommer, "Un ostracon araméen inédit d'Éléphantine (collection Clermont-Ganneau 44)", in D.W. Thomas and W.D. Mc Hardy (eds.), *Hebrew and Semitic Studies Presented to G.R. Driver*, Oxford 1963, pp. 53-58.

[26] For a conditional interpretation of the sentence see P. Grelot, *Documents araméens d'Égypte*, Paris 1972, p. 376.

[27] Following Dupont-Sommer, "Ostraca araméens", p. 120. For another reading and interpretation of these lines see B. Levine, "Notes on an Aramaic Dream Text from Egypt", *Journal of the American Oriental Society* 84 (1964), p. 21.

sentences in the Hermopolis papyri, HP 3,6 and HP 4,5.9, suggest that the occurrences of *yhb* in HP 2 should be interpreted as forms of the sf. conj. This interpretation will prove to be in accordance with other texts from the beginning of the Achaemenid period (see below sub 6.). It is more difficult to decide whether the active or the passive voice has been used. In HP 2,16 only an active explanation of *yhb* is possible, which brings about disagreement in gender between the subject (f. personal name) and the verb form (m.):

HP 2,16 *whn yhb lky r'yh 'mr šlḥy ly*

"And if r'yh (f.) gives you wool, send (word) to me". (M.F.[28])

The same interpretation may be correct for the other occurrences of *yhb* in HP 2. The subject of the other occurrences of *yhb* must then be the woman tby from l.7, an interpretation which also implies an disagreement in gender between the subject (f.) and the verb form (m.).[29]

The conditional sentences in HP 2 may be compared with a conditional sentence in another letter in which *yhb* in all likelihood is a form of the sf. conj.[30]

C 42,10 *whn l' yhb hmw lk [š]lḥ 'ly*

"And if he does not give them to you, [s]end (word) to me". (on the negation see below sub 5.)

Rarely the sf. conj. form is preceded by another sentence constituent. If so, the element which precedes is a subject or an adverbial adjunct.[31]

### Sf. conj. preceded by the subject (SV)

Twice the subject precedes the sf. conj. (K 4,14 and C 25,12). Once the subject is an indep. pers. pron. (K 4,14) and once an indep. pers. pron. with a personal name in apposition (C 25,12)[32]:

K 4,14 *whn 'nh grytky dyn bšm byt' zk 'nh 'ḥwb 15. w'ntn lky ksp kršn 5 hw ḥmšh b'bny mlk' ksp r 2 lkrš 1 wl' dyn*

[28] Porten and Yardeni translate: "And if the shepherd (OR: Reia) gives you wool, ..." (Porten and Yardeni, *Textbook* i, p. 12).

[29] Bresciani and Kamil have given the same interpretation to *yhb* in HP 2,8.9.10 (Bresciani and Kamil, "Le lettere aramaiche di Hermopoli", p. 387).

[30] *yhb* parallels the finite verb form *yntn* in the preceding sentence. In all other conditional sentences found in this letter the sf. conj., not the pref. conj., is used in the protasis (ll. 5 (*[yh]bw* and *zbnw*).7 (*hškḥt*).8 (*hškḥt*) and probably l.11 (*nḥt*).

[31] A SOV order may be attested in C 29,6: *whn ['nh ]ksp' znh krš ḥd šqln 'rb['h l' š]lmt yhbt lk 7 byn yrḥ[ pḥns* ("And if [I do not p]ay (and) give you this silver, one karsh ..."). However, the context is too much damaged to gain certainty.

[32] Perhaps a subject precedes the sf. conj. in Saq P 1,5 : *hn 'sw/pšn zk š'yl wpt[gm' y'mr]* (reading Porten and Yardeni, *Textbook* ii, p.166). However, *š'yl* may also be interpreted as a passive participle. The context, moreover, is completely obscure.

"And if I institute (suit) against you in the name of (= regarding) that house, I shall be 15. liable and I shall give you silver ..."

C 25,12 *whn ʾnh ydnyh ršytkm wrškm 13. br ly wbrh ʾnth wʾyš bšmy wbšm bny šṭr mn br wbrh zy yznyh br ʾwryh 14. wyršwn lbr wbrh wʾnth wʾyš lkm ʾw gbrn zy tzbnwn lh ʾw zy brḥmn tntnw lh 15. bytʾ zk wzy yrškm dyn yntn lkm ʾbygrnʾ zy ksp kršn ʿšrh ...*
(for a translation see above sub 1.)

Both documents were written by the scribe Mauwziah bar Nathan and we will see that the writs of this scribe have more particularities (K 4 434; C 25 416).

When the protasis contains a form of the sf. conj., the subject, if made explicit, in most instances immediately follows the sf. conj. (legal documents: K 1,8; K 3,20; C 5,8; C 10,6.7 and perhaps K 3,20 (?); letters: HP 3,6; C 42,11). However, in the documents written by the Aramean or Akkadian scribes Shaweram bar Eshemram (K 11) and Nabutukulti bar Nabuzeribni (C 28) the subject is separated from the sf. conj. by the indirect object (K 11,9 [V-IO-S]) and by the object and an adverbial adjunct (C 28,9 [V-O-adv. adj.-S]).

SF. CONJ. PRECEDED BY THE ADVERBIAL ADJUNCT

In C 30, the petition of the Jews of Elephantine concerning the rebuilding of their temple, the sf. conj. is preceded by *kn* (C 30,27), but in the second, altered draft of the petition (C 31) the pref. conj *tʿbd* is used instead of the sf. conj. *ʿbdw*. A possible explanation is that the change was meant as a correction. Both the conjugation and the person and number of the verb form have been changed. This could mean either that the use of the sf. conj. after an adverb was felt to be incorrect or that by the time this document was written (407 B.C.E.) there was already an increasing preference for the use of the pref. conj. over the use of the sf. conj.

C 30,27 *hn kn ʿbdw ʿd zy ʾgwrʾ zk ytbnh wṣdqh yhwh lk qdm yhw ʾlh 28. šmyʾ mn gbr zy yqrb lh ʿlwh wdbḥn dmn kdmy ksp knkryn /lp wʿl zhb*
"If they do thus until that Temple be (re)built, you will have a merit before YHW the God of 28. Heaven more than a person who offers him holocaust and sacrifices (whose) worth is as the worth of silver, 1 thousand talents and [[about]] gold".

C 31,26 *hn kn tʿbd zy ʿd ʾgwrʾ zk ytb[nh wṣdqh yhwh lk qdm yhw ʾlh] 27. šmyʾ mn gbr zy yqrb lh ʿlwh wdbḥn dmy ksp knkrn ʾlp*
"If you do thus until that Temple be (re)bu[ilt ..."

### Coordination of forms of the sf. conj. in the protasis

The conjunction *hn* is suppressed before the coordinated verb form.

### Coordination of two forms of the sf. conj.[33]

Two forms of the sf. conj. may be coordinated by *w*. Examples may be found in K 3,14 (*hn grynk ... wgryn*), K 3,18 (*hn grwk wgrw*), C 14,8f. (*hn grytky ... wgrky*), K 11,5 (*hn lʾ šlmt wyhbt*), C 10,7 (*whn mṭʾ... wlʾ šlmtk*), C 10,14 (*hn mytt wlʾ šlmtk*) (legal documents) and in B 23000,5 (*h[n] zbntwn ... wybltwn*) (letter on papyrus).[34] Cf. also C 28,9 *ršynk ... ʾw nršh* where a form of the sf. conj. and a form of the pref. are coordinated by *ʾw* ("or").

### Coordination of three forms of the sf. conj.

Also a few instances of three coordinated sf. conj. forms are attested. The conjunction *w* is repeated before the third verb form. Examples may be found in BM 10f. (*[w]hn lʾ qmt wnqt wntnt*) and in K 11,8 (*hn mytt wlʿd šlmt wyhbt*). Cf. also C 25,12 (*whn ... ršytkm wrškm ... wyršwn*).

In K 11,8 the compound *lʿd* indicates that the situations referred to by *šlmt* and *yhbt* precede the one referred to by *mytt* (*hn mytt wlʿd šlmt wyhbt*). Compare this with C 10,7 (*whn mṭʾ...wlʾ šlmtk*) and C 10,14 (*hn mytt wlʾ šlmtk*) where the second verb also refers to a (omitted) preceding action.

## 3. Pref. conj. in the protasis

In the remaining texts a pref. conj. form is found where in the protasis the finite verb form refers to future time. Very often the pref. conj. is used when another element precedes the verb form. Thus the complements subject and/or object may precede the pref. conj. In many instances an adverbial complement precedes the pref. conj., sometimes on its own, sometimes in juxtaposition with another preceding element.

However, the use of the pref. conj. is not restricted in its use as the sf. conj. is. Many instances may be found in which the pref. conj. is not preceded by another element and immediately follows *hn* or *hn lʾ* (see below). The pref. conj. is also found immediately following the sf. conj.

### Pref. conj. preceded by the subject (SV)

This order is found in the following texts:
Legal documents:

---

[33] In C 29,6 perhaps, the second form of the sf. conj. is not coordinated by the conjunction *w*. See above n.31.

[34] And probably in the following damaged passages: C 42,4f. *whn lʾ [yhbw] ... wlʾ [yh]bw*; C 35,6f. *hn lʾ [šlmt ]wyhbt*.

Haggai bar Shemaiah: K 3,19 (*gbr ʾḥrn* "another man") (437)
Mauwziah bar Nathan: K 4,16 (*gbr ʾḥrn*); K 4,18 (*ʾnh ʿnny "I Anani"*); C 20,12f. (*ʾnḥnh wbnyn wbntn wʾyš zyln wbny šlwmm br ʿzryh* "we and our sons and daughters and somebody who belongs to us and the sons of Shelomam bar Azaria"); K 7,24 (*yhwyšm[ʿ]* "Yehoyishma") (K 4 434; C 20 420; K 7 420)

Literary texts:
Ah pr 1.124 (*lḥyh* "something good")

BA:
Ezra 4: 13.16 (*qrytʾ dk "that city"*).

In some instances the pref. conj. is not only preceded by a subject but by an adverbial adjunct as well:
Xanthos 19 *ʾp 20. hn ʾyš mtwm yhnṣl 21. mn kndwṣ ʾlhʾ ʾw mn 22. kmrʾ nhwy< alef> mn kndws 23. ʾlhʾ wknwth mhnṣl*[35] (S + adv. adj. + V)
"En outre, si jamais quelqu'un enlève (quelque chose) au Roi le Dieu ou au prêtre (alȯrs) existant, (que ce quelqu'un), par le Roi le Dieu et (par) son Compagnon, (soit) enlevé"!

C 8,26 *hn mḥr ʾw ywm ʾḥrn drgmn ʾw br zylh yršh 27. ʿl bytʾ zk sprʾ zk hnpqy wlqblh dyn ʿbdy ʿmh* (adv. adj. + S + V)
(for a translation see above sub 3.)

In most of the instances in epigraphic texts in which the subject precedes the pref. conj. form the result is a certain opposition between the subject of that conditional sentence and the one of a/the preceding sentence. Examples may be found in K 3,19; K 4,16; K 4,18; C 7,24; C 20,12; Ah pr 1.124. All these sentences are introduced by *whn* (and *wʾp hn*), but it should be noted that *whn* in itself is not indicative of a SV order (cf. C 8,26).
examples:
K 4,16. *lhn 17. hn mytty brt šnn 100 bny zy yldty ly hmw šlyṭn bh ʾḥr 18. mwtky wʾp hn ʾnh ʿnny ʾmwt br šnn 10 plṭy wyhwyšmʿ kl 2 bny hmw šlyṭn bḥlqy ʾḥrnʾ ʾnh ʿnny*
"But 17. if you die at the age of 100 years, it is my children whom you bore me (that) have right to it after 18. your death. And moreover, if I, Anani, die at the age of 100 years, it is Pilti and Jehoishma, all (told) 2, my children, (who) 19. have right to my other portion, I, Anani".

[35] Text and translation have been taken from A. Dupont-Sommer, "L'inscription araméenne", in H. Metzger *et al.* (eds.), *Fouilles de Xanthos*, Tome vi ("La stèle trilingue du Létôon"), troisième partie. Institut français d'études anatoliennes, Paris 1979, pp. 131-169.

Ah pr 1.123. *hn npqh ṭbh mn pm ʾ[nšʾ ṭb] 124. whn lḥyh tnpq m[n] pmhm ʾlhn ʾlḥwn lhm*
123. "If good goes out from the mouth of [the] individual [good]; 124. and if bad goes out fr[om] their mouth, gods will make (it) bad for them".

In one instance the subject and the pref. conj. form are preceded by a prepositional phrase:
D 7,8 *mn grdʾ ʾw mn nksyʾ ʾḥrnn zyly mndʿm ksntw yhwh 9. wmn ʾtr ʾḥrn lʾ tbʿwn wlʾ thwspwn ʿl bytʾ zyly ḥsyn tštʾlwn ...*
"If there be any decrease in the domestic staff or in my other goods 9. and from elsewhere you do not seek and you do not add to my estate, you will be strictly called to account ..."

PREF. CONJ. IS PRECEDED BY THE OBJECT (OV)
This order can be found in the following texts:

Legal documents:
Attarshuri bar Nabuzeribni: C 9,8 (*ʾrqʾ zk*) (460/459)

BA: Dan. 2: 6 (*ḥlmʾ wpšrh*); Dan. 2: 9 (*ḥlmʾ*)

examples:
C 9,8 *hn mḥr ʾw ywm ʾḥrn ʾrqʾ zk tbnh ʾḥr brty tšnʾnk 9. wtnpq mnk* ... (adv. adj. + O + V)
"If tomorrow or the next day you build up that plot (and) then my daughter hate you 9. and go out from you ..."

Dan. 2: 6 *whn ḥlmʾ wpšrh thḥwn mtnn wnbzbh wyqr šgyʾ tqblwn mn qdmy* (O + V)
"But if you tell me the dream and its interpretation, you will be richly rewarded by me and loaded with honours".

PREF. CONJ. IS PRECEDED BY SUBJECT AND OBJECT (SOV)
This order is only found in D 4,3: *hn psmš[k] ʾḥr qblt mnk yšlḥ ʿly ḥsn tštʾl wkst ptgm 4. ytʿbd lk* (S + adv. adj. + O + V)
"If Psamshe[k] later sends me a complaint against you, you will be strictly called to account and a harsh word 4. will be directed at you".

Note that the (S)OV order only occurs in texts generally considered to have an "eastern" signature (D, C 9, Daniel).

PREF. CONJ. IS PRECEDED BY AN ADVERBIAL ADJUNCT ONLY
This order is found in C 8,20 (*mḥr ʾw ywm ʾḥrn*), in C 9,13 (*mḥr ʾw ywm ʾḥrn*) and in C 31,26 (*kn*). Both C 8 and C 9 were written by the scribe Attarshuri bar Nabuzeribni in the year 460/459.

example:
C 31,26 *hn kn tʿbd zy ʿd ʾgwrʾ zk ytb[nh wṣdqh yhwh lk qdm yhw ʾlh] 27. šmyʾ mn gbr zy yqrb lh ʿlwh wdbḥn dmy ksp knkrn ʾlp*

The earlier draft of the text in C 30 has a form of the sf. conj. (see above sub 2.).

Finally a passage must be mentioned where an Iranian loan word (*hndyz*) precedes the pref. conj.:
C 27,6 *ʾyty bʾr ḥdh zy bnyh 7. bg[w] b[y]rtʾ wmyn lʾ ḥsrh lhšqyʾ ḥylʾ kzy hn hndyz yhwwn 8. bbrʾ [z]k myʾ štyn*
"There is a well which was built 7. with[in] the f[or]tress and (which) did not lack water to give the garrison drink so that whenever they would be garrisoned (there) 8. they would drink the water in [th]at well".

NO OTHER ELEMENT PRECEDES THE PREF. CONJ.
In the following instances the pref. conj. is not preceded by another element and immediately follows *hn (lʾ)*. In some of these instances no other sentence element is extant apart from the verb form.

Legal documents:
Attarshuri bar Nabuzeribni: C 9,10 (460/459)
Nathan bar Ananiah: C 15,33 (√*ʾmr* followed by a direct speech) (458 or 445)
Mauwziah bar Nathan: K 7,28.33.34.37.38f.(*hn lʾ*).40 (*hn lʾ*).42 (420); C 18,8 (undated)
Haggai bar Shemaiah: K 10,10 (√*ʾmr* followed by a direct speech) (402)
scribe unknown: K 6,18 (420); Saq P 15,3

Letters:
papyri: HP 5,5 (√*ykl* with another pref. conj. as complement); D 6,6; perhaps Pad 1,6 (the passage is damaged)
ostraca: Cl G 16 conv. 2f.; Cambridge ostracon conc.7[36]; *RES* 1792 A4.B2 [*hn*] (√*ykl* with another pref. conj. as complement); *APO* 63,1 conv.1 (*hn lʾ*)

Literary texts:
Ah pr ll.82 (twice).130.171.192[37].

[36] A. Cowley, "Two Aramaic Ostraca", *Journal of the Royal Asiatic Society* 61 (1929), p. 108.
[37] Note the energic forms in l.82 (*ʾšbqn*) and l.171 (*yʾḥdn*)

Other texts:
Bh ll.71 (=C 1.57)(*[hn] l*ʾ)[38].72 (=C 1.58)

BA:
Dan. 2: 5 (*hn l*ʾ); Dan 3: 15 (*hn l*ʾ); Dan. 4: 24; Dan. 5: 16

examples:
K 7,28 *wh[n] ymwt* ʿ*nnyh wbr zkr 29. wnqbh l*ʾ*yty lh mn [y]hw[y]šm*ʿ ʾ*ntth* ...
"And i[f] Ananiah die 29. not having 28. a child, male 29. or female, by [Je]ho[i]shma his wife, ..."
Cl G 16 conv. 1. ʾ*pq ly tly 2. wktwn 1 hn 3. y*ʿ*drn wtpq 4.* ʾ*ḥṭb*ʿ*mr 5. 1 pwlpl 6. H*
"And if they pick (beans?), let then Aḥuṭab bring 1 omer of beans(?)". (M.F.)[39]

Ah pr l.130 ʾ*p [h]n tzp zpt*ʾ *šlyn lnpšk* ʾ*l tšym* ʿ*d 131.[tšlm z]pt*ʾ ...
"Moreover, [i]f you take the loan, rest to your soul do not put(=give) until 131. [you repay] the [l]oan ..."

The many instances in the legal documents K 7 and C 18 are striking. Again the scribe is Mauwziah bar Nathan. In the Aḥiqar proverbs and in the texts from BA many additional examples can be found.

A word should be said about the pref. conj. forms of *ykl* (HP 5,5 and *RES* 1792 A4 and B2) and of ʾ*mr* (C 15,33; K 10,10). Only the pref. conj. of the root *ykl* is known in Aramaic texts from the Achaemenid period. The use of the pref. conj. of *ykl* in the protasis of conditional sentences has to be ascribed to the limited grammatical distribution of this root. When a finite verb form of the root ʾ*mr* is used in the protasis of conditional sentences, it is always the pref. conj.[40] The systematic use of the pref. conj. of *'mr* in the protasis may be lexically determined.

---

[38] The reading is by B. Porten and J.C. Greenfield, *The Bisitun Inscription*, p. 48ff. The conjunction *hn*, which is filled in in l.71, is clear from the parallel in l.72.

[39] Reading A. Dupont-Sommer, "Ostraca araméens d'Éléphantine", *Annales du Service des Antiquités de l'Égypte* 48 (1948), p. 112. Unlike Dupont-Sommer I prefer to connect *wtpq* with what precedes it, thus interpreting it as the apodosis of the conditional sentence, with the conjunction *w* introducing the apodosis (cf. also C 30,27; C 20,14 and C 25,14). According to Dupont-Sommer this conditional sentence has the unusual order apodosis - protasis.

[40] The context of ostracon *CIS* ii 138 A2 is completely lost. Degen reads *whn* ʾ*mrw s[* (R. Degen, "Zum Ostrakon CIS ii 138", *Neue Ephemeris für semitische Epigraphik* 1 (1972), p. 27). However, his translation "Und wenn sie sagen" (p. 33) is uncertain since *hn* may as well introduce an indirect question here.

COORDINATION OF TWO FORMS OF THE PREF. CONJ.
Two forms of the pref. conj. can be coordinated by *w*. Examples can be found in K 3,19 (*ygrnk wygrh*); K 7,24 (*tšn*ʾ... *wt*ʾ*mr*); C 8,20 (ʾ*ršnky* ... *w*ʾ*mr*); C 9,13 ʾ*ršnk* ... *w*ʾ*mr* and C 20,12 (*yršwnkm wyršwn*).[41]

COORDINATION OF THREE FORMS OF THE PREF. CONJ.
Three forms of the pref. conj. may be coordinated. In one instance the conjunction *w* is repeated before the second and third form (D 7,8f. *yhwh w....l*ʾ *tb*ʿ*wn wl*ʾ *thwspwn*). In another instance only the third form is coordinated by *w* (C 9,8 *tbnh* ʾ*ḥr tšn*ʾ*nk wtnpq*). Note that the word ʾ*ḥr* ("then") in the protasis of this sentence defines the sequence of events.

4. CHANGE FROM SF. CONJ. TO PREF. CONJ. IN PROTASIS

An instructive shift from a sf. conj. to a pref. conj. is found in the protasis of two conditional sentences, C 25, 12f. and C 28,9.
C 25,12 *whn* ʾ*nh ydnyh ršytkm wrškm 13. br ly wbrh* ʾ*nth w*ʾ*yš bšmy wbšm bny šṭr mn br wbrh zy yznyh br* ʾ*wryh 14. wyršwn lbr wbrh w*ʾ*nth w*ʾ*yš lkm* ʾ*w gbrn zy tzbnwn lh* ʾ*w zy brḥmn tntnw lh 15. byt*ʾ *zk wzy yrškm dyn yntn lkm* ʾ*bygrn*ʾ *zy ksp ...*
(for a translation see above sub 1.)

C 28,9 *hn ršynk dyn*ʾ ʿ*l*ʾ ʾ*nḥnh mḥsyh wbny* ʾ*w nršh lbr 10. wbrh lk wl*ʾ*nš zylk* ʿ*ldbr pṭwsyry* ʿ*bd*ʾ *zk zy mṭ*ʾ*k bḥlq* ʾ*ḥr nntn lk* ʾ*bygrn*ʾ *ksp 11. ṣryp ...*
(for a translation see above sub 1.)

This change from sf. conj. to pref. conj. may be occasioned by the place of the subject. Note that the form of the sf. conj. in C 28,9 immediately follows (*hn ršynk*). The second form in C 25 follows a suppressed *hn (rškm).* In both cases the subject follows later in the sentence. However, the first form of the sf. conj. in C 25 (*ršytkm*) is preceded by a subject composed of a pronoun and personal name. This is also found in K 4,14, another document written by the same scribe Mauwziah bar Nathan (see above sub 2.). The use of the pref. conj. (*yršwn* and *nršh*) in both instances may be occasioned by the place of the subject. In both cases the subject serves both the sf. conj. (which it follows) and the pref. conj. (which it precedes). Thus *yršwn* is preceded by the subject *br ly wbrh* ʾ*nth w*ʾ*yš bšmy wbšm bny šṭr mn br wbrh zy yznyh br* ʾ*wryh* and *nršh* by the subject ʾ*nḥnh mḥsyh wbny*.

[41] In the protasis a verbal clause with a form of the pref. conj. and a nominal clause may be coordinated by *w* (K 7,28.34 and perhaps Pad 1,6f.). This nominal clause is circumstantial.

## 5. Negation verbal protasis

The verbal protasis may be negated by the negation *l*ʾ. In that case *l*ʾ immediately follows the conjunction *hn*, thus giving *hn l*ʾ.[42] Rarely another element is standing in-between. In Dan. 2: 9 the negation is preceded once by the object:

Dan. 2: 9 *hn ḥlmʾ lʾ thwdʿnny* ...

"If you do not make the dream known to me ..."

In all other instances the negation *l*ʾ immediately follows *hn*. In most cases the sf. conj. follows *l*ʾ (13 instances cited above sub 2.). In only a very few cases the pref. conj. follows (K 7,38.40; ostracon *APO* 63,1 conv.1 and probably Bh 1.71 (=C 1.57); Dan. 2: 5; Dan. 3: 15).

The preference for *hn l*ʾ followed by the sf. conj. should be seen in the light of the general tendency in Aramaic texts from this period to use the sf. conj. when the verb form immediately follows *hn*. In texts from a later period the pref. conj. is found more and more instead of the sf. conj. Accordingly, in BA, where the pref. conj. is the usual finite verb form in the protasis of conditional sententes, it may be negated by *l*ʾ (Dan. 2: 5; Dan. 3: 15).

In view of the preceding, the form *yhb* in HP 2,10 is by preference to be interpreted as a form of the sf. conj. (see also above sub 2.):

*whlh yhb lky šlhy ly wʾqbl ʿlyhn tnh*

"And if she (Tby) does not give to you, send to me (a message) and I will lodge a complaint". (M.F.)

## 6. Evaluation of the use of finite verb forms in the protasis

We have found by now that the choice of the finite verb form in many instances is determined by its place in the sentence. However, many forms remain unexplained. An additional aspect may be relevant for the interpretation of the use of finite verb forms in the protasis of conditional sentences. It is the aspect of time and linguistic change.

Legal documents:

The use of the sf. conj. in the protasis of the conditional sentence can be found in legal documents throughout the Achaemenid Period. Nevertheless, one cannot avoid the impression that its frequency decreases in the course of time. At the end of the sixth century and in the first half of the fifth century, until about 440, the sf. conj. is found almost without exception in dated legal documents (BM (515), C 11 (488/487), C 5 (471), C 15 (458/445), C 10 (456), K 1 (551), K 2 (449), C 14 (440)).

[42] Once *hlh* (< **hn lh*) in HP 2,10. On *lhn* in Dan. 6: 6 see n.22.

Some of the early attestations of the pref. conj. involve forms of the root *ʾmr* (C 8,20; C 9,13; C 15,33). These forms have been explained above in terms of lexical determination (*ʾmr*) (see above sub 3.). The other attestations of the pref. conj. in the first half of the fifth century are found in the conditional sentences written by the Aramean or Akkadian scribe Attarshuri bar Nabuzeribni (C 8,20 (*ʾršnky ... wʾmr*); C 8,26 (*yršh*); C 9,8 (*tbnh ... tšnʾnk wtnpq*); C 9,10 (*thnṣl*); C 9,13 (*ʾršnk ... wʾmr*).[43] Elsewhere forms of the sf. conj. of the root *ršy* are frequently found (see above sub 1. and 2.). Both documents, C 8 and C 9, are from the year 460/459. The use of forms of the pref. conj. in these documents remains unexplained.

With the activities of the scribes Haggai bar Shemaiah and Mauwziah bar Nathan, both working in Elephantine from the mid-thirties (5th century) onwards, divergencies in the use of the verb form among the different scribes and texts become clear. It appears that both verb forms are possible. The sf. conj. can be used under certain restrictions while the pref. conj. enjoys a freer use. While the scribe Haggai bar Shemaiah still made use of the sf. conj., his colleague and contemporary Mauwziah bar Nathan clearly preferred the use of the pref. conj.

From this period onwards most of the texts show a preference for the use of the pref. conj., although the use of the sf. conj. still occurs. It is remarkable that when the sf. conj. is found in a text, the pref. conj. does not occur (e.g. K 11 written by the Aramean scribe Shaweram bar ʾEshemram bar ʾEshemshezib in 402).

Letters on papyrus:
In the Hermopolis papyri (end 6th, early 5th century) the sf. conj. is used in the protasis of conditional sentences (on the interpretation of *yhb* see above sub 2.). The only form of the pref. conj. in the protasis, *tkln* in HP 5,5, may be explained in terms of limited grammatical distribution of the root *ykl* (see above sub 3.).

The finite verb form found in the protasis of conditional sentences in the official Arsham correspondence (end 5th century) is always the pref. conj. In the official correspondence belonging to the Yedaniah archive (end 5th century) the pref. conj. is used in C 27 and C 31. The sf. conj. is used in C 30, the first draft of the petition (and in the protasis of the one and only irrealis in Imperial Aramaic, C 37,8). However, in C 42 (end 5th century) and in Berlin 23000 (end 5th / early 4th century), the sf. conj. systematically occurs in the protasis of conditional sentences. It may be remarked that the scribe of Berlin 23000 has a Persian name (*spndt br prwrtpt*). The scribe of C 42 is Hosea.

[43] Note that the forms of the root *ršy* are all preceded by the adverbial phrase *mḥr ʾw ywm ʾḥrn*.

Letters on ostraca:
In the ostraca both forms are found. It may be noted that with one exception (*RES* 1792) all these ostraca occur in Naveh's list of ostraca which on the basis of palaeographical evidence may have been written by one scribe in Assuan around 475 B.C.E. (*CIS* ii 137; *CIS* ii 138; Cl G 44; *APO* 63,1 conv.1; Cl G 16; Cambridge; *RES* 1793).[44]

Aḥiqar proverbs:
The finite verb form found in the protasis of conditional sentences in the Aḥiqar proverbs (copy end 5th century[45]) is always the pref. conj.[46]

Behistun inscription:
The finite verb form found in the protasis of the conditional sentence in the Behistun inscription (copy ca. 420) is the pref. conj.

Asia Minor:
In the inscription from Xanthos (probably mid 4th century) a form of the pref. conj. is found in the protasis of the conditional sentence in l.20.

In BA the preference for the pref. conj. in the protasis of conditional sentences is very clear. In Nabataean and Palmyrene the pref. conj. is in common use in the protasis.[47] Also in the Aramaic texts from Qumran and Wadi Murabbaʿat the general tendency is to use the pref. conj., although the sf. conj. still occurs.[48] In later texts in Jewish Palestinian Aramaic the pref. conj. and the sf. conj. both remain possible options

[44] J. Naveh, *The Development of the Aramaic Script*, Jerusalem 1970, p. 37f.

[45] Dating of the manuscript. However, the proverbs "may represent Aramean wisdom traditions fixed in writing as early as the seventh century, possibly even earlier" (J.M. Lindenberger, *The Aramaic Proverbs of Aḥiqar*, Baltimore 1983, p. 20).

[46] In agreement with these findings I think that the restoration of *hn* in Ah pr l. 128 is unlikely. E.g. *[hn d]rgt* (Cowley, *Aramaic Papyri*, p. 216; Porten and Yardeni, *Textbook* vol. iii) and *[hn n]gt* (Lindenberger, *Aramaic Proverbs of Aḥiqar*, p. 117).

[47] For references see *DISO* s.v. *hn*.

[48] *Sf.* conj.: 11 Q Tg. Job col. 18,5 *hn ʾtqṣrt bdyn ʿb[dy*; 11 Q Tg. Job col. 22,4 *[h]n ʿwlyn hškḥ* (reading M. Sokoloff, *The Targum to Job from Qumran Cave XI*, Ramat Gan 1974) and perhaps Pap Mur. 33,3 *hn lʾ ʾtybt* (reading K. Beyer, *Die aramäischen Texten vom Toten Meer*, Göttingen 1984, p. 317); pref. conj.: 1 Q Dan. col. 2,6 *hn lʾ thwd[ʿwnny]* (reading J.A. Fitzmyer and D.J. Harrington, *A Manual of Palestinian Aramaic Texts*, Rome 1978); Pap Mur 18,7 *whn kn lʾ ʾʿbd*; Pap Mur 20,7 *[h]n lbyt ʿlmʾ thk*; Pap Mur 21,9 *[h]n ʾpt[rnk*; Pap Mur 21,12 *[wh]n ʾnt l[byt ʿlmʾ t]hk*; Pap Mur 21,14 *[h]n ʾnh ʾhk lbyt[ʾ] dk* (reading J.T. Milik, *Discoveries in the Judean Desert II. Les grottes de Murabbaʿât*, Oxford 1961); 11 Q Tg. Job col. 10,10 *hn yml[ln]*; 11 Q Tg. Job col. 27,5 *hn yšmʿwn wyʿb[dwn bṭb ymhwn wšnyhwn*; 11 Q Tg. Job col. 27,4 *hn ytybwn mbʾyšthwn*; 11 Q Tg. Job col. 26,9 *hn tʾmr[* ; 11 Q Tg. Job col. 22,1 *hn ḥrgty lʾ ts[* (reading Sokoloff, *The Targum to Job*).

in the protasis of the conditional sentence.[49] The sf. conj. was never completely ousted by the pref. conj.

How is the evidence in Aramaic texts from the Achaemenid Period to be combined with the situation found in Old Aramaic? As we have seen the sf. conj. occurs only once in Old Aramaic (see above 2.). In all other texts the pref. conj. is found (thirteen certain instances in Sfire).[50] However, even one single occurrence of the sf. conj. demonstrates that the two forms, pref. conj. and sf. conj., could be used in the protasis of the conditional sentence in Old Aramaic. One cannot exclude that the lack of more evidence for the use of the sf. conj. is due to the scantiness of the material. Note also that almost all the evidence from Old Aramaic comes from one single source, the Sfire inscriptions.[51]

Lipiński has recognized an unnoticed conditional sentence on an Aramaic docket from the Neo Assyrian period (Tell Halaf 6th century).[52] The verb form used in this sentence is the sf. conj. and this matches the frequent use of *šumma* followed by the preterite (*iprus*) in Akkadian. In Neo Assyrian deeds the preterite is used almost without exception when *šumma* is followed by the negation.[53] Many scholars nowadays are of the opinion that the formulary of the Neo Assyrian deeds has exerted a considerable amount of influence on the formulary of the Aramaic legal documents.[54] Although I am aware of the pitfalls of comparing

---

[49] See the new dictionary by Sokoloff s.v. *ʾn* (M. Sokoloff, *A Dictionary of Jewish Palestinian Aramaic of the Byzantine Period*, Ramat-Gan 1990). No figures have been given.

[50] Sfire I B 20-23*[hn]*, I B 25-28 *[hn]*, I B 31-33, I B 38, II B 17/18, III 6/7, III 14-17, III 19, III 22/23. The apodosis in all preceding instances has *šqrt/tm*; I B 23-25 *[hn]*, I B 28/29, II B 4, II B 5/6, III 4-6, III 6, III 9-12. Sfire III 18 has been excluded (read *[l]hn* with J. W. Wesselius, "A New Reading in Sfire III,18", *Bibliotheca Orientalis* 41 (1984), p. 590).

[51] The texts in the Samalian dialect of Old Aramaic are not of much help since in the conditional sentence, in which probably a verb form occurs, the verb form is damaged in such a way that it cannot be decided whether a form of the pref. conj. or of the sf. conj. was written (Hadad l. 29 *hn[ ]ʾ ydyh*, according to Dion *whn[w yš]ʾ ydyh* or *whn[w mṭ]ʾ ydyh* "S'(il lèv)e ses mains" (P.E. Dion, *La langue de Yaʾudi*, Waterloo, Ontario 1974, p. 34). The interpretation of Hadad ll. 31-32 is so complicated that I leave it out of the discussion here.

[52] Tell Halaf nr. 1 obv. 4. *hn lh ntn šʿryʾ 5. z bʾdrʾ 6. šʿr[yʾ y] 7. rb[wn]* and translates "If he does not give (back) that barley on the threshing-floor, the barley will increase" (reading and translation by E. Lipiński, *Studies in Aramaic Inscriptions and Onomastics I*, Leuven 1975, p. 118). The use of the sf. conj. of *ntn*, instead of *yhb*, in this period is not surprising, since it is also found in the earliest documents from the Achaemenid period (BM 2.11.12 (515); C 11,1 (488/487); C 3,12 (483)). The spelling *lh* at this time, if indeed interpreted as the negation, instead of *lʾ*, is unlikely (in the Achaemenid period it is only found in the Hermopolis papyri).

[53] See J.N. Postgate, *Fifty Neo-Assyrian Legal Documents*, Warminster 1976 (index) and W. v. Soden, *Akkadisches Handwörterbuch* vol. iii, Wiesbaden 1981, p. 1272b (*šumma*).

[54] Cf. Y. Muffs *Studies in the Aramaic Legal Papyri from Elephantine*, Leiden

two historically unrelated forms (pref. conj. *iprus* and sf. conj. *qtl*), it is very tempting to see Akkadian *iprus* as the source of the frequent use of the sf. conj. in the protasis of conditional sentences of Aramaic texts from the Achaemenid period, especially in the legal documents.[55] In a later period, perhaps owing to the declining influence of Akkadian, the pref. conj. once again became more commonly used.[56]

It is interesting that one of the Neirab inscriptions (mid 6th century), contemporary with the above-mentioned docket from Tell Halaf, has a form of the pref. conj. in the protasis.[57] These religious texts obviously have nothing in common with legal formulary.

In conclusion I think that the history of the use of the sf. conj. and the pref. conj. in the protasis of conditional sentences may be viewed as a continuing competition between on the one hand the sf. conj., the use of which probably represents an older stage of the language, and on the other hand the pref., which represents relative younger usage.[58] Since the pref. conj. is already found in Old Aramaic in the vast majority of instances, the temporary popular use of the sf. conj. in Aramaic texts from the Achaemenid period, especially so in legal documents, may be due to a strong external impulse, perhaps from Akkadian legal formulary.

I am glad to have the opportunity to express with this contribution my gratitude to Professor Hoftijzer for his stimulating lectures and for his sound and generous guidance during the past fifteen years.

Abbreviations

adv. adj. = adverbial adjunct

*APO* = E. Sachau, *Aramäische Papyrus und Ostraka aus einer jüdischen Militär-Kolonie zu Elephantine. Altorientalische Sprachdenkmäler des 5. Jahrhunderts vor Chr.*, Leipzig 1911.

1969, p. 186: "In all probability, it was from Neo-Assyrian models that the Aramaic formulary was derived".

55 For the functional overlap see D. Cohen, *La phrase nominale et l'évolution du système verbal en sémitique. Études de syntaxe historique*, Leuven - Paris 1984, p. 63: the Akkadian *iprus* :: *iparras* opposition is "analogue fonctionnellement dans une grande mesure à l'opposition ≪ accompli≫ : ≪ inaccompli≫ de l'Ouest".

56 It may be remarked that the systematic use of the pref. conj. in the protasis of the conditional sentences in the Aḥiqar proverbs confirms the conclusion reached by Lindenberger that the proverbs are free from Akkadianisms (Lindenberger, *Aramaic Proverbs of Aḥiqar*, p. 20 and p. 290).

57 Neirab i ll.11-13 (= Gibson ii nr. 18: *whn 12. tnṣr ṣlmʾ wʾrṣth zʾ 13. ʾḥrh ynṣr 14. zy lk* "But if 12. you guard this picture and grave, 13/14. in the future may yours be guarded!" (translation Gibson ii).

58 Cf. also F. Rundgren, "Das Altsyrische Verbalsystem", *Språkvetenskapliga Sällskapets i Uppsala Forhändlingar*, 1958–1960, p. 58.

Ah pr = Proverbs of Aḥiqar
Ah fr = Aḥiqar framework story
BA = Biblical Aramaic
Bh = Behistun inscription, B. Porten and J.C. Greenfield, *The Bisitun Inscription of Darius the Great. Aramaic Version. Corpus Inscriptionum Iranicarum*, part I: *Inscriptions of Ancient Iran*, vol. v: *The Aramaic Versions of the Achaemenian Inscriptions etc.*, London 1982.
C = Cowley papyri, A. Cowley, *Aramaic Papyri of the Fifth Century B.C.*, Oxford 1923.
*CIS* = *Corpus Inscriptionum Semiticarum ii*, Paris 1889 ff.
Cl G = Clermont-Ganneau Ostraca (published by Dupont-Sommer)
D = Arsham correspondence, published by G.R. Driver, *Aramaic Documents of the Fifth Century B.C.*, Oxford 1957.
*DISO* = Ch.F. Jean and J. Hoftijzer, *Dictionnaire des inscriptions sémitiques de l'ouest*, Leiden 1965.
Gibson ii = J.C.L. Gibson, *Textbook of Syrian Semitic Inscriptions*, vol. ii: *Aramaic Inscriptions*, Oxford 1975 (reprint 1985).
HP = Hermopolis Papyri (letters), published by E. Bresciani & M. Kamil, "Le lettere aramaiche di Hermopoli", in *Atti della Accademia Nazionale dei Lincei, Memorie, classe di Scienze morali, storiche e filologiche*, ser. VIII, Vol. xii, fasc. 5 (1966), pp. 361-428.
K = papyri published by E. Kraeling, *The Brooklyn Museum Aramaic Papyri*, New Haven 1953.
O = object
Pad = Padua papyri (letters), published by E. Bresciani, "Papiri aramaici egiziani di epoca persiana presso il Museo Civico di Padova", *Revista degli studi orientali*, 35 (1960), pp. 11-24.
pref. conj. = prefix conjugation
*RES* = *Répertoire d'épigraphie sémitique, publié par la commission du Corpus Inscriptionum Semiticarum* (Paris).
S = subject
Saq P = Saqqara papyri, published by J.B. Segal, *Aramaic Texts from North Saqqâra, with Some Fragments in Phoenician*, London 1983.
sf. conj. = suffix conjugation
V = finite verb form.

# On Direct Speech and the Hebrew Bible

Gideon Goldenberg, Jerusalem

Forms of direct and indirect speech and related constructions are of such prevalence and central importance in all levels of verbal expression that they command closer examination and fuller treatment than what most syntactical descriptions usually offer.[1] It has long been recognized that the logically-ideal distinction between direct and indirect speech is not always clearly discernible, and that some mingling of the two structures appears often to occur, and that in many cases (in some languages more than in others) the use of direct speech forms is extended far beyond the presentation of any real or suppositious speech.[2] After much discussion, mainly in the first decades of the present century, three "styles" are generally distinguished, all of which most usually form complement clauses of some *verbum dicendi* or *sentiendi*, viz. (1) Direct speech, *oratio recta* — speech (or thought &c.) apparently quoted [by 'reporter'] literally as created [by 'speaker'], naturally keeping its deictic markers[3] [as of the original 'speaker'], and asyndetically positioned (i.e. not marked formally as being syntactically substantivized, thus seemingly "independent"); (2) Indirect speech, *oratio obliqua*, reported speech,[4] berichtete/referierte Rede — proposition [worded by 'reporter'] expressing, with deictic markers duly shifted, the content of what is/was said &c. [by 'speaker'], which syntactically will be marked as a substantive-clause, commonly by a conjunction; (3) A third kind, described as independent form of indirect discourse, style indirect libre, otherwise characterized by terms like erlebte Rede, verschleierte

[1] In no few introductions to linguistics and treatises of syntax direct or reported speech and their implications are strangely left altogether unmentioned. A very brief review of the subject with a two-page bibliography will be found in Coulmas *Reported Speech*; cf. below.

[2] "Internal speech", thought, epistemic judgement, any "cerebration" or the like will be understood as included in this description.

[3] Deictic (or "exophoric") markers that may be relevant in this connexion are mostly personal pronouns, possessives, demonstratives, adverbials, tenses or moods.

[4] In Jespersen *MEG* IV (1931) 151, §11.1(1), "reported speech" is suggested for naming the "style indirect libre" (= style 3), replacing "represented speech" which Jespersen *PG* (1924) 290 used in the same sense. "Reported speech" is also used in the most general sense, irrespective of type or "style".

Rede, *oratio tecta*,[5] represented speech, gedachte Rede, objektivierte Rede (or 'pseudo-objektiv'), inner monologue or the like — independent asyndetic representation of "speech", or rather "inner speech", with person markers and sometimes other deictics shifted as in indirect discourse, but with some other deictic markers still disclosing characteristic features of direct quotation. *"Yes", he decided, "she will be my wife"* is with direct speech (1); *He decided that she would be his wife* has the indirect speech (2); and *"Yes", (he decided,) "she will be his wife"* is in the "style indirect libre" (3). What is presented as direct speech (1) like *She asked herself, "Why am I here?"* could thus be reported, in indirect speech (2), as *She asked herself why she was there*, and expressed in the "style indirect libre" (3) as *(She asked herself,) "Why was she here?"* (or: *"Why was she there?"*). It was the third type (3), widely known as the "style indirect libre", that was especially the subject of many discussions, linguistic, literary and psychological. Rather than being due to mingling of direct and indirect discourse, it has mostly been recognized as a special structure and regarded as being, in the first place, a literary phenomenon, embracing most of the relevant forms that are not (1) or (2), and often considered to be necessarily connected with some kind of inner monologue.[6] Notwithstanding the many variant forms purported to represent "speech" &c., which are commonly known to exist,[7] the division of the modes of discourse in the above-mentioned three categories — (1) direct speech, (2) indirect speech and (3) "the third kind" — is the most widely accepted.[8]

The present study is intended to examine forms and uses of direct speech and related structure patterns in Biblical Hebrew and in some

[5] The term *oratio tecta* (to match esp. *or. recta)*, or in Danish "dækket Tale", seems to have been suggested by Brøndum-Nielsen, whose book *Dækning* (1953) is out of my reach; cf. Diderichsen *Dansk Gramm.* 124, 268, 300 & 305. All these Danish references I owe to H. J. Polotsky.

[6] "Historique des recherches sur le style indirect libre" down to 1926, bibliographically well documented, will be found in Lips *Style indir. libre* 220-236. For the most important literature on the subject until 1986 see Coulmas *Reported Speech* 6-10, SprwWb I 827-828. As already noted in Jespersen *PG* 291 fn. 1, "Independent form of indirect discourse" is the title given to the same construction in Curme *German* 245-247 (§172) [=p. 248 ff. in the 1904 1st edition], thus preceding in eight years Bally's better known practically-identical term "style indirect libre"; the origin of the other terms employed is mentioned in the literature.

[7] Some studies in which a larger variety of relevant patterns is taken into consideration will be mentioned in the sequel.

[8] Suffice it to refer to TzNL (1974) 363, HdL (1975) 353 and Coulmas *Reported Speech* 6; cf. SprwWb I 633 (1977) and 827-828 (1986). We may here disregard the differentiation once made between two variants of (3), viz. (3a) the construction where speech of "the third kind" is directly presented by a *verbum dicendi*, defined as "uneigentlich indirekte Rede", and (3b) the one without such verb, "uneigentlich direkte Rede"; see Lerch *Uneigentlich*.

other languages, with the hope of contributing to the better understanding of such constructions as being "syntactical figures", direct and indirect speech being not always formally differentiated, with "style indirect libre" not necessarily being a literary phenomenon connected with "erlebte Rede" or inner speech and the like but rather forming in natural language the syntactical opposite of a "discours direct lié".[9] Further examples will also be considered of direct-speech formation in extended usage — as pseudo-speech which may also be animistic or onomatopoeic — and the grammaticalization of such usage. Some few Biblical passages will come out more naturally construed if the possible varieties of quotative clauses are properly recognized rather than being regarded as carelessly formed.

A re-examination of the true nature of all forms of direct, indirect and "semi-indirect" speech &c. and of the terminologies involved may also be called for.

I."Independent Form of Indirect Discourse"

As a syntactical phenomenon, the occurrence of speech &c. that is shifted as to become (pronominally) "indirect" but still presented "directly" within the matrix sentence is most probably due to natural linguistic process rather than to elaborate literary artifice. Whether or no the skilful use of such constructions is "partout un procédé de la langue littéraire" (Lips *Style indir. libre* 216) and employed for the expression of "experienced" or "veiled speech" or "interior monologue" or the like, the "independent form of indirect speech", or, as Marcel Cohen called it, the "discours semi-indirect",[10] is a more general syntactic stucture and will also be employed for reporting actual speech. The following are examples in English and in French of such "style semi-indirect", which represent in this special way actually-expressed sentences where nothing is "veiled" or internal: *Lucy left a little note in French asking for advice. Could they get a good doctor at Salvapedente, or must she send to Orvieto?*[11] / *Brigitte ouvrit la porte du petit salon et nous appela : Ne voulions-nous pas un peu de thé ? Cela nous réchaufferait après cette course.*[12]

In Biblical Hebrew, the "semi-indirect" presentation may be not

[9] The term "discours direct lié" is quoted (from H. Jacquier) in SprwWb I 633.

[10] This was Marcel Cohen's term for the identical construction, which is found "relativement souvent" in Amharic; v. Cohen *Traité* 366 (ch. X, §31) & Cohen *NE* 350-351 (ch. VIII,F,*f-g*).

[11] This example is quoted (from H. Ward) in G. Wendt *Syntax*, ap. Lips *Style indir. libre* 211. As other examples may show, the fact that a French note is here quoted in English is irrelevant; even in genuine direct speech repetition is not necessarily literal. See below.

[12] From Fr. Mauriac, ap. Grevisse *Bon usage* 1107 (§1057).

only "independent" but also marked explicitly as if it were a direct quotation (by *lēmōr* "saying, —", "so to say, —", or by some other form of *ʾāmar* "say", which from all the *verba dicendi* is the one that normally requires, and is required by, direct speech):

Gen. xli 15 *waʾănī šāmaʿtī ʿālǣkā lēmōr tišmaʿ ḥălōm liptōr ʾōṯō* "and I have heard of thee, saying, Thou canst hear a dream to interpret it" [AV "and I have heard say of thee that thou canst understand a dream to interpret it"]. Direct speech (of what had been said in the absence of Joseph) should have been *yišmaʿ* ... "He would hear &c.".

Gen. xii 13 *ʾimrī-nā ʾăḥōṯī ʾātt* "Say, I pray thee, Thou art my sister". Genuine direct speech (as in the same context ibid., verses 12, 18, 19) must have been *ʾăḥōṯō ʾānī* "I am his sister" (as in the Septuagint).

Neh. vi 6 *baggōyīm nišmaʿ wGašmū ʾōmēr ʾattā whayyhūḏīm ḥošḇīm limrōḏ* "[he sent to me a letter, wherein was written,] It is heard among the heathen and Gashmu saith, Thou and the Jews think to rebel". The letter should actually have said "Nehemiah and the Jews &c.".

Job xxxv 14 *ʾap̱ kī-ṯōmar lō ṯšūrænnū* "although thou sayest, Thou seest him not". In fully-direct speech it must have been *lō ʾăšūrænnū* in the 1st person.

Hos. vii 2 *uḇal-yōmrū lilḇāḇām kol-rāʿāṯām zākārtī* "and they say not in their hearts, I remember all their wickedness". What they could in fact "say to their hearts" would be *kol rāʿāṯēnū zāḵār* "He remembers all our wickedness".

Ezek. xxxiii 13-14 *bʾomrī laṣṣaddīq ḥāyō yiḥyæ* ... *uḇʾomrī lārāšāʿ mōṯ tāmūṯ* ... "when I say to the righteous, He shall surely live ... and when I say unto the wicked, Thou shalt surely die ...". Of these parallel clauses the former has the "style indirect libre" and the latter a genuine direct speech.

Ps. x 11 & 13 *[rāšāʿ ] ʾāmar blibbō šāḵaḥ ʾēl* ... *ʿal-mǣ niʾēṣ rāšāʿ ʾælōhīm ʾāmar blibbō lō ṯiḏrōš* "He [the wicked] hath said in his heart, God hath forgotten ... Wherefore doth the wicked contemn God? he hath said in his heart, Thou wilt not require it". In verse 11 the words that the wicked is supposed to have said in his heart are quoted in direct speech form; in the parallel verse 13 the words of the wicked in his heart are in the "style indirect libre", which in direct speech would have been *lō yiḏrōš* "he will not require".

II Chron. xxv 19 *ʾāmartā hinnē hikkīṯā ʾæṯ-ʾæ̆ḏōm unśāʾăḵā libbḵā lhaḵbīḏ* "thou [Amaziah] sayest, Lo, thou hast smitten the Edomites, and thine heart lifteth thee up to boast" (AV). If what Amaziah was supposed to have said (in his heart) had been presented in direct-speech form, it must have been *hinnē hikkēṯī ʾæṯ-ʾæ̆ḏōm* "Lo, I have smitten the Edomites", as this verse had in fact been rendered in the Septuagint and elsewhere.[13]

Ps. ix 21 *yēḏʿū gōyīm ʾĕnōš hēmmā* "that the nations may know, They are but men".

Two examples are here added just to show that the "semi-indirect" construction in Hebrew is not limited to the language of the Bible:

Babylonian Talmud Brakot 10b *ʾăpillū baʿal haḥălōmōṯ ʾōmēr lō lʾāḏām lmāḥār hū mēṯ ʾal yimnaʿ ʿaṣmō min hāraḥămīm* "even if the Angel of Dreams says to a man, 'On the morrow he will die', he should not despair of mercy (and cease to pray)" (Quoted in Segal *Mishnaic*[2] §422).

Modern colloquial Heb. *kšealax lkeva i nišara lagur im imo. šaalti ota lama la, omeret: ma ixpat la? oevet et Musa, vebeod šnatayim u betax xozer* "when he went to the standing army she remained living with his mother. I asked her why need she. She says, What does she care? she loves M. and within two years he will certainly come back".[14]

In some of the instances here adduced it is real speech that the "style indirect libre" presents; in some others it is thought &c. or what people "said in their hearts", so that as a linguistic phenomenon the "discours semi-indirect" should not be regarded as necessarily implying interior monologue or the like. From what angle and in what respect it could be connected with anything "propre à un procédé européen" (Lips *Style indir. libre* 219) is not fully clear to me; I understand that in studying "the independent form of indirect discourse" as a feature of literary style, one might also wish to examine the meaning and development of its use in European literatures, but as a syntactical phenomenon it is not limited to literary art and certainly not to European languages.

## II. "Style direct lié"

The subordination which commonly characterizes indirect discourse marks the proposition which represents speech &c. as being syntactically substantivized. In such cases where "*that*"-clauses are called for, the conjunction "*that*" is a substantivizing "translatif",[15] and the

---

[13] The New Amer. Bible reads here "You are thinking, 'See, I have beaten Edom!', and thus ambition makes you proud". From the text-critical point of view it appears that the original form of the verse was most probably closer to the II Kings xiv 10 parallel, viz. *hakkē hikkīṯā ʾæṯ-ʾĕḏōm*, where nothing at all is expressed in terms of "saying".

[14] Recorded in the early 1960's and given in broad phonetic transcription.

[15] The pronominal or demonstrative origin from which "*that*"-conjunctions in various languages have historically developed is not directly relevant to their actual analysis, though it may account for some of the difficulties in distinguishing between direct and reported speech (see below). The availability of morphological substantivization, or "clause conversion" (v. Beeston *Arabic* 92), parallel to "*that*"-clauses will further demonstrate their substantival status.

substantival clause formed by such transposition may assume, like any substantive form, the function of (a) subject, (b) predicate, (c) object, or (d) apposition, e.g. (a) *that you should think so is quite natural* / (b)*my opinion is that he is mistaken* / (c) *I think (that) you are mistaken* / (d) *the fact that he is a foreigner does not excuse him* (cf. Sweet *NEG* I 171, §497). The idea of superficially defining *that*-clause as "Complement" and the conjunction as "Complementizer" is therefore misconceived and injudicious. It will be noticed that in languages like English or German, where the conjunction may also be dispensed with, this will only occur, with restrictions, where the substantival clause is in object position (c).[16] Such cases could consequently be analysed as having a zero-variant of the conjunction; their structure differs essentially from the typically asyndetic construction of direct speech and of the so-called "style indirect libre".

In the common form of direct speech, the fact that the quotation would normally not be presented by a conjunction *"that"*, i.e. not formed into a substantival clause, is prima facie not surprising; it would no longer be a literal quotation if it were syntactically or otherwise transposed. And yet, *"that"* beginning direct speech is not unknown in various languages. The existence of apparently subordinate direct speech (which has been termed, as already mentioned above, "style direct lié"), besides indirect speech that is placed 'in included position' asyndetically, will show even more convincingly that the assumed proportional opposition

direct speech : indirect speech = asyndeton indep. : *"that"*-clause

is far from being universal; or should the variety of relations between deictic marking and syntactic frame require revised definitions of what direct and indirect speech really are.

In Biblical Hebrew, content-clauses are mostly introduced by *kī*. Presented by *verba sentiendi* like "see", "hear", "know", "be known", "remember", "believe" such clauses beginning with *kī* belong to the common type of indirect discourse.[17] With a *verbum dicendi*, it has been

[16] On English substantival clauses without *that* see Fowler *Usage* 623b-624a, where tentative lists are given of *verba dicendi & sentiendi* which (i) prefer object clauses with *that* expressed, (ii) prefer object clauses with *that* omitted, and (iii) vary according to the tone of the context.

[17] Examples: (a) with "see" – Gen. xvi 4 *wattēræ kī hārāṯa* "she saw that she had conceived" / Esther iii 5 *wayyar(ʾ) Hāmān kī-ʾēn Mordḵay kōrēaʿ umištaḥăwǣ lō* "Haman saw that Mordecai bowed not, nor did him reverence"; (b) with "hear" – Gen. xiv 14 *wayyišmaʿ ʾAbrām kī nišbā ʾāḥīw* "Abram heard that his brother was taken captive" / Neh. iii 33 *kaʾăšær šāmaʿ Sanballaṭ kī-ʾănaḥnū ḇōnīm ʾæṯ-haḥōmā* "when Sanballat heard that we builded the wall"; (c) with "know" – Josh. ii 9 *yāḏaʿtī kī-nāṯan Yhwh lāḵæm ʾæṯ-hāʾāræṣ* "I know that the Lord hath given you the land" / Job v 24 *wyāḏaʿtā kī-šālōm ʾohŏlæḵā* "thou shalt know that thy tabernacle shall be in peace"; (d) with "be known" – Exod. xxxiii 16 *uḇammǣ yiwwāḏaʿ ʾēp̱ō kī-māṣāṯi*

stated that *kī* "that" will introduce not only indirect speech, as could most normally be expected, but also sometimes, or often, direct speech, like the analogous Greek usage with the so-called *ὅτι recitativum*.[18] Such interpretation, however, of *kī*-clauses as "style direct lié" has been controverted, implying that in all the instances adduced of *kī* + direct speech the *kī* employed is not to be understood as the same conjunction "that" which presents reported speech, but should rather be taken to belong to the quotation itself, representing the other uses and senses of *kī*, typically figuring in direct speech, introducing reason or cause ("for, because, since"), or time ("when"), or the explanation of a proper name, or the fact sworn of, or expressing distinct affirmation ("yea, surely"); v. Esh *Opening-Words* 48-52.

In fact, neither this nor that is the case. The differentiation between direct and indirect speech lies not in the conjunction, but in the *verbum dicendi* that is selected.

The verb *higgīḏ* "tell" would frequently occur with *kī*-clauses, always presenting indirect speech, as in Gen. xii 18 *lāmmā lō-higgaḏtā llī kī ʾištḵā hī* "why didst thou not tell me that she was thy wife?" / Gen. xxix 12 *wayyaggēḏ Yaʿăqōḇ lRāḥēl kī ʾăḥī ʾāḇīhā hū wḵī ḇæn-Riḇqā hū* "and Jacob told Rachel that he was her father's brother, and that he was Rebekah's son" / Judg. xiv 9 *wlō-higgīḏ lāhæm kī miggwiyaṯ hāʾaryē rāḏā haddḇāš* "but he told not them that he had taken the honey out of the carcase of the lion" / II Sam. xix 7 *higgaḏtā hayyōm kī ʾēn lḵā śārīm waʿăḇāḏīm* "thou hast declared this day that thou hast [lit.] neither princes nor servants".

The verb *ʾāmar* "say", on the other hand, with *kī* the same as with asyndetically included clauses, will always introduce direct speech (about *ʾāmar* and the "style indirect libre" see below). It can be said that (a) *ʾāmar* "say" will normally define clauses as representing direct speech, and that (b) direct speech clauses will, of all *verba dicendi*, require ordinarily *ʾāmar* "say" for their presentation in a matrix sentence.

Direct speech instances with *ʾāmar kī* are numerous, like Gen. xxxvii 35 *waymāʾēn lhitnaḥēm wayyōmær kī-ʾērēḏ ʾæl-bnī ʾāḇēl šʾōlā* "he refused to be comforted and said *kī* I will go down into the grave unto

*ḥēn bʿēnǣḵā* "for wherein shall it be known that I have found grace in thy sight?" / I Kings xviii 36 *hayyōm yiwwāḏaʿkī-ʾattā ʾǣlōhīm bYiśrāʾēl* "let it be known this day that thou art God in Israel"; (e) with "remember" – Judg. ix 2 *uzḵartæm kī ʿaṣmḵæm uḇśarḵæm ʾānī* "remember that I am your bone and your flesh"; (f) with "believe" – Exod. iv 5 *lmaʿan yaʾămīnū kī-nirʾā ʾēlǣḵā Yhwh ʾǣlōhē ʾăḇōṯām* "that they may believe that the Lord God of their fathers hath appeared unto thee".

[18] Suffice it to refer here to Gesenius *Grammar* §157*b*, Brown-Driver-Briggs *Lexicon* 471b; Gesenius *Handwörterbuch*[17] 342a, Joüon *Grammaire* 480 (§157*c*), and Baumgartner *Lexikon* 449a (s.v. *kī*, 5 & 7).

my son mourning" / Josh. ii 24 *wayyōmrū ʾæl-Yhōšūaʿkī-nāṯan Yhwh byāḏēnū ʾæṯ-kol-hāʾāræṣ* "and they said unto Joshua *kī* the Lord hath delivered into our hands all the land" / Judg. vi 16 *wayyōmær ʾēlāw Yhwh kī ʾæhyǣ ʿimmāḵ whikkīṯā ʾæṯ-Miḏyān kʾīš ʾæḥāḏ* "and the Lord said unto him *kī* I will be with thee and thou shalt smite the Midianites as one man" / II Sam. xi 23 *wayyōmær hammalʾāḵ ʾæl-Dāwīḏ kī-gāḇrū ʿālēnū haʾănāšīm wayyēṣʾū ʾēlēnū haśśāḏǣ* "and the messenger said unto David *kī* the men prevailed against us and came out unto us into the field" / I Kings i 13 *hălō ʾattā ʾăḏōnī hammælæḵ nišbaʿtā laʾămāṯḵā lēmōr kī-Šlōmō ḇnēḵ yimlōḵ ʾaḥăray* "didst not thou, my Lord O king, swear unto thine handmaid saying *kī* Solomon thy son shall reign after me" / Ruth i 10 *wattōmarnā lāh kī-ʾittāḵ nāšūḇ lʿammēḵ* "and they said unto her *kī* we will return with thee unto thy people".

If *ʾāmar* occurs in one verse or two with a *kī*-clause of indirect speech, it will be found that in those cases *ʾāmar* does not mean "say", but "command" or "think": Job xxxvi 10 *wayyigæl ʾoznām lammūsār wayyōmær kī-yšūḇūn mēʾāwæn* "he openeth also their ear to discipline and commandeth that they return from inquity" (cf. esp. Brown-Driver-Briggs *Lexicon* $56b_{12}$ & $471b_{27-28}$); Judg. xv 2 *wayyōmær ʾāḇīhā ʾāmōr ʾāmartī kī-śānō śnēṯāh* "and her father said, I verily thought that thou hadst utterly hated her".[19]

That direct speech requires *ʾāmar* "say" and would not be presented by any other *verbum dicendi* is evident from the fact that some form of *ʾāmar*, esp. the inf. *lēmōr*, is called for to be added, as a rule, "after another verb of saying, introducing thing said" (Brown-Driver-Briggs *Lexicon* $56a_{28-38}$ and elsewhere). The few ocurrences of direct quotations introduced directly by verbs of saying other than *ʾāmar* are obviously rare exceptions: II Sam. xix 43 *wayyaʿan kol-ʾīš Yhūḏā ʿal-ʾīš Yiśrāʾēl kī-qārōḇ hammælæḵ ʾēlay* "and all the men of Judah answered the men of Israel, Because *(kī)* the king is near of kin to us" (in the parallel next verse — *wayyaʿan ... wayyōmær)* / I Kings xxi 5-6 *wattḏabbēr ʾēlāw ma-zzǣ rūḥăḵā sārā ... wayḏabbēr ʾēlæhā kī-ʾăḏabbēr ʾæl-Nāḇōṯ &c.* "and she said unto him, Why is thy spirit so sad ... ? and he said unto her, Because I spake unto Naboth &c.".[20]

[19] A partly relevant comparison is the syntax of Arabic *qāla*, which reqires an object-clause with *ʾinna* when it means "say", but admits obj.-cl. with *ʾanna* when having the sense of "think, presume".

[20] Such instances may be regarded as special cases of ellipsis where the verb *ʾāmar* that is required by the construction is omitted, analogous to some other cases where direct-speech expressions are inserted with no *ʾāmar* (nor any other verb of saying) to present them explicitly, as in Isa. iii 6 *kī-yitpōś ʾīš bʾāḥīw bēṯ-ʾāḇīw śimlā lḵā qāṣīn tihyǣ-llānū* "when a man shall take hold of his brother of the house of his father [sc. saying], Thou hast clothing, be thou our ruler" / Nahum ii 9 *whēmmā nāsīm*

If *ʾāmar kī* necessarily implies direct speech, and *higgīḏ kī* ... is always "said that ..." which goes with the indirect, then it is certainly not the semantic niceties of *kī* that make the difference in the first place, and the question whether *kī* that introduces direct speech is the same *kī* "that" which makes substantival clauses may not have a simple answer. The well-recognized etymological connexion may not be pertinent, but the fact that *ʾāmar ʾăšær* and *ʾāmar šæ-* as well, in biblical and post-biblical usage, will introduce direct speech (parallel to *higgid ʾasær* with the indirect, Esther iii 4) shows clearly that the various senses of *kī*, when following *ʾāmar*, cannot easily be divorced from each other to mark separate syntactical structures. For *ʾāmar ʾăšær* see I Sam. xv 20 *wayyōmær Šāʾūl ʾæl-Šmūʾēl ʾăšær šāmaʿtī bqōl Yhwh wāʾēlēḵ baddæræḵ ʾăšær-šlāḥanī Yhwh* "and Saul said unto Samuel *ʾăšær* I have obeyed the voice of the Lord and have gone the way which the Lord sent me" (v. Ewald *Lehrb. Hebr.* 831, §338b and elsewhere). Eccl. viii 14 *ʾāmartī šæggam-zǣ hāḇæl* "I said *šæ-* this also is vanity" will also be understood as direct speech in the light of the former example and post-biblical usage of *ʾāmar šæ-* + dir. speech.[21] Well-known parallels to such employment of identical constructions (with the same conjunctions, or "opening-words") for direct and indirect discourse are the Aramaic with *d-/di*, the Arabic with *ʾan* or *ʾinna* and the Greek with ὅτι.

## III. Between Direct and Indirect

After seeing that the syntactical frame cannot serve as a reliable criterion in defining direct and indirect discourse, because each of the two types may be found included in a matrix sentence either asyndetically or syndetically, and because substantivizing conjunctions are not easily distinguishable from the homonymous demonstratives to which they are historically related, there still remain the deictic markers by which the formal distinction can be drawn. Deixis as a criterion of indirect discourse is thoroughly examined in Frank Palmer's study of mood and modality, where some other enlightening observations on reported speech are also made which are not found elsewhere (see esp. Palmer *Mood* 134-138, §§4.1.4 & 4.2.1, and ibid. 163-167, §4.6). It is well recognized that "the most regular and most important marker of an indirect speech clause is found in the deictic markers it contains", or rather in the "switch from the deictics used by the original speaker to those appropriate to the actual speaker now reporting what was or might have

---

*ʿimḏū ʿămōḏū wʾēn mapnǣ* "they shall flee away. Stand, stand! [sc. shall they cry]; but none shall look back".

[21] In post-biblical Hebrew usage *ʾāmar šæ-*, and also *kāṯaḇ šæ-*, will be followed by direct speech; see Epstein *Notes II* 382-3, Epstein *Introduction* p. 1265, Segal *Mishnaic*[1] 205 (§424), Segal *Mishnaic*[2] 229 (§435), Esh *Opening-Words* 52-53.

been said" (Palmer *Mood* 163). All will agree that "the pronouns are the most consistently used markers of indirect speech" (ibid.). And yet, as Palmer has noted, pronoun systems are not always of the familiar type identifying speaker, hearer and 'third' persons. He refers, inter alia, to the Hopi language, where a shift from 'proximate' to 'obviate' person markers is involved in accomodating the speaker's deictic reference, with no switch from 2nd to 3rd person &c. as in forming direct into indirect speech in our commonly known languages; also mentioned is Navaho, with another type of deictic switch (using 4th pers. prons.). And if there is deictic switch, it can consequently be argued that there is indirect speech (Palmer *Mood* 164).[22]

We often find that only some of the deictic markers are shifted in indirect speech, but whereas it is rather usual for tenses, e.g., to be left unchanged,[23] switched pronouns will mostly be regarded as the core of the indirect construction, and even in Palmer's examples from Hopi the distinction between 'proximate' and 'obviate' is connected with personal markers. The question, however, remains whether the construction discussed in ch. I above may lawfully be regarded as "independent form of indirect discourse", "style indirect libre", or "discours semi-indirect" for the only reason that it contains switched personal pronouns, in spite of the fact that all other deictic markers are still those which would have been appropriate to the original speaker in direct speech. "Dækket direkte Tale" (Diderichsen *Dansk Gramm.* 124) implies that it is anyway direct speech which is here "covered" or "veiled". The question appears rather weighty with regard to such constructions in Biblical Hebrew as have been quoted above (ch. I), where the use of the verb *ʾāmar* for directly presenting such clauses makes them strongly marked as belonging (notwithstanding the switched pers. prons.) together with direct speech. If "indirect speech lies half way between direct speech, which ignores the actual speaker's [i.e the reporter's] deictic system, and main clauses, which wholly use the system of the speaker" (Palmer *Mood* 164), then "the third kind" clearly lies half way (more or less) between direct speech and indirect speech.

## IV. Direct Speech Unspoken and Unsusceptible of Being Spoken

Direct-quote expressions appearing to evoke real or imaginary speech can (in some languages more than in others) be grammaticalized so

---

[22] If Palmer is right, then the statement made by Li, mentioning Navaho and Amharic as being "other known examples of languages without indirect speech" (Li *Direct & Indirect* 39) is at least shallow in regard to Navaho; saying the same about Amharic reflects sheer ignorance.

[23] A special section on "Indirect speech in English and Russian" with regard to tenses will be found in Comrie *Tense* 107-117 (§5.3).

that, notwithstanding the syntactical construction, connexion with anything spoken or susceptible of being spoken may altogether be missing or out of the question. An exact boundary line between (a) direct speech in figurative usage and (b) syntactical compounds of { "say" + quotation} that disclose no sense of quotable speech is often hard to draw. The former is extended use of direct speech, or pseudo-speech, which may also be attributed to inanimate and inert objects and may also have onomatopoeic sounds quoted as being "said"; the latter can express in formal terms of direct speech meanings where any form of real or imaginary speech or sound is untraceable and unthinkable. Direct speech form should thus be regarded as a syntactical figure whose use may range from actual quotation of real speech to purely formal means of expression.

Recognition of the full extent to which direct-speech construction can be used has crept rather slowly into modern general-linguistic literature;[24] but it had well been known, e.g., in Turkish and in North-East African languages. For the Turkish, reference can be made, of all grammatical literature, to Kononov *Gramm. tureck.* 540-544 (§§1081-1088), where some special studies on the subject are also quoted. For illustrating the wide range of possible uses of direct-speech constructions, the following examples in Amharic may be adduced:[25]

(1) Real direct speech: *mäṭäṭṭ amč̣! alat, ṭämqähallĕnĕ? aläčäw* "he said to her, 'Bring drink!'; she said to him, 'Have you brewed (any)?'". Thing directly said is introduced by the verb *alä* "say", also as complement to another verb of saying (or writing): *bĕrhanun qän bĕlo ṭärraw* "He called the light (saying) 'Day'" / *'—' bĕla näggäräččĕw* "she told him saying '—'" / *alawqĕm silu setyowa mälläsu* "the woman answered saying 'I do not know'" / *aṣe Yohannĕsĕn kĕfu nĕgus näbbäru yämmiṣĕfĕbbaččäw* "who writes against King John saying 'He was a bad king'".

(2) Direct quotation expressing unspoken thought, feeling or inten-

[24] Expressions like "say 'yes' " for "agree", "say 'it is true' " for "believe", "he called her saying 'N' " for "he called her N", "he came having said 'I will go' " in the sense of "he came because he wanted to go" &c. in a language of New Guinea were described in 1964 in a special article (Healy *Teleéfoól Quotative*) without mentioning parallels in any other language. This reference to quotative clauses with "saying" was presented as "fascinating facts concerning an illocutionary marker in a New Guinea language" in the volume on syntax of the "Penguin Modern Linguistics Readings" where that article was reprinted in 1972 (Householder *Syntactic Theory* 149). It was only in 1986 that the phenomenon was reasonably discussed in its general context (Palmer *Mood* 135), mentioning Amharic, languages of Australia, New Guinea and Brazil.

[25] Reference to the typological affinity between the grammaticalized uses of direct speech in Amharic and in Turkish will be found in Polotsky *Synt. amharique & turque 118* [Polotsky *Coll. Pap.*4].

tion and the like: *agäñalläh$^w$ bĕlo g$^w$agg$^w$a* ("he yearned, saying 'I shall find' ") "he yearned to find" / *wädä kätäma lĕhid bĕlo tänästo täg$^w$azä* ("he got up and set off saying 'Let me go to town"') "he left for town" / *yĕhĕnnĕnu yadärrägäw man yĕhon bĕyye assĕb näbbär* ("I was thinking, saying 'who might do this?'") "I was wondering who had done this".

(3) Direct speech with switched personal pronouns ("semi-indirect", or "indirect libre"): *bäqĕrb qän wĕsṭ lĕttĕddari näw malätĕn sämĕčče* "I have heard saying, 'You are going to get married soon'" (AB $34_{11-12}$).

(4) Expression constructed as imaginary speech addressed to inanimate: *admasu därräsnĕbbĕh silut ĕyyäšäššä yĕhedall* "the horizon, when [people] say to it 'We reached you' it runs away" (LTA $93_{8-9}$).

(5) Imaginary speech attributed to inanimate: *mašĕllaw... yäsäw qumät alfo bämäsälal wäṭṭačč$h^w$ quräṭuññ alä* "the durra surpassed the stature of a man and said 'mount a ladder and cut me!' " [= a ladder was needed to cut it] (GMB $21_{12-14}$) / *gänzäb agäñalläh$^w$ alĕssäbässäb aläññ* "I get money (but) it says to me 'I will not accumulate!'" [= it would not accumulate] (Fables $27_3$).

(6) Expression phrased as imaginary speech addressed by a person to some part of his body: *ĕgre awç̣ĕññ bĕläw šäššu* "they fled away saying 'My feet, get me off!' " [= they took to their heels, они бросились было бежать] (Dubr.$15_9$).

(7) Construction of speech addressed to a person by some part of his body: *ǧorow dänquro alsäma aläw* "[Beethoven] his ear became deaf and said to him ' I will not hear!'" (IMS $144_{18-19}$).

(8) Lexicalized verbal compounds, or quasi-compounds, made of "say" + quoted interjection: *ĕšši alä* "he said 'All right!'", "he agreed" / *ĕmbi alä* "he said 'I won't!'", "he refused" / *ayzoh aläčĕw* "she said to him 'Cheer up!'", "she encouraged him".

(9) Verbal compounds of "say" + onomatopoeic complement, which present no real speech but may still be regarded as having in a way some sense of "saying": *ĕffoy alä* ("he said 'ĕffoy!' ") "he sighed" / *kwa-kwa alä* ("said 'Kwa-kwa' ") "clattered, rustled" / *dub-dubb alä, ṭäb-ṭäbb alä* ("said 'Dub-dubb' or 'Ṭäb-ṭäbb' ") "dripped (drop by drop)" / *futt alä* ("he said 'Futt' ") "he sipped".

(10) Verbal compounds of "say" + primary base as purely formal elements, where "say" has no sense of saying and the base has no independent use of its own: *däss aläw* ("it said to him 'Däss'") "he rejoiced" / *käff alä* ("he said 'Käff'") "he was high" / *qäss alä* ("he said 'Qäss'") "he went slow, was careful" / *zĕmm alä* ("he said 'Zĕmm' ") "he kept silent, said nothing".

(11) Verbal compounds of "say" + bases in special forms derived from ordinary verbal roots, just expressing various degrees of intensity

with no connexion to any idea of saying, as from *säbbärä* "break": *säbärr alä* "être quelque peu cassé", *säbärbärr alä* "être quelque peu fracassé", *sĕbbĕrr alä* "être tout à fait cassé", *sĕbĕrbĕrr alä* "être tout à fait fraccassé".[26]

The extended uses of direct-speech constructions that are brought forward in Healy *Teleéfoól Quotative* are mainly of the varieties listed here under (1), (2) and (8). Amharic in this respect exhibits an areal feature common to Ethiopian Semitic and Cushitic, Nubian, and perhaps some other languages. A brief comparative description of the extended uses of direct speech in North-East African languages will be found in Armbruster *Dong. Nubian* 29-33 (§§209-253), where these languages are even shown to have similar verbal compounds of {"say" + X} for expressing the same meanings.

Sporadic, and much more restricted, use of lexicalized direct-speech expressions is also well known in other languages. Cf., e.g., Hebrew *ʾāmar hæʾāḥ*, as in Job xxxix 25 *bḏē šōp̱ār yōmar hæʾāḥ* "(the horse) saith among the trumpets,'Ha, ha' ";*ʾāmar nōʾāš* (approx.) "said 'There is no hope' ", "lost hope" (Biblical, as in Isa. lvii 10, and later); *ʾāmar hōn* "said 'enough!' "(?), "was satisfied" (after Prov. xxx 15); *ʾōmēr doršēnī* "says 'Explain me!', "calls for explanation" (medieval and later); *ʾāmar hēn* "said 'Yes' ", "agreed", *ʾōmrē hēn* "yes-men" (late Hebrew). The Babylonian-Aramaic expression said of a coin in a vessel that it *qiš-qiš* (or *kiš-kiš*) *qarya* "calls 'Kish-Kish', rattles" is very similar to the Amharic *koš-košš alä* (lit."said 'Koš-košš'") "produisit un bruit métallique (ex. des thalers dans un sac)" (Baet. 724). For the use of imaginary direct speech (involving inanimate beings) in the formation of vivid descriptive expressions cf., e.g., the two following examples, similar to each other, in (1) Arabic and in (2) Neo-Aramaic: (1) *ʿindahū sitt banāt kull wāḥidah taqūl lilqamar qūm waʾanā ʾaqʿud maḥallak* "he had six daughters each (of whom) would say to the moon, 'Stand up and I shall sit in your stead'", "he had six daughters 'fair as the moon'" (Mawsim $86_{12}$); (2) *ba-šrata mara: la nhur, ana nahran!* "(she is so beautiful that) she may say to the lamp, 'Stop shining, let me shine!'(Azer. $209_{9-10}$).

V. Conclusion

The formation and status of direct-speech constructions, the problem of differentiating between direct and indirect, the possible combinations

[26] These approximate translations are taken from Cohen *Traité* 267. For the whole range of Amharic phrasal verb-forms with "say" as auxiliary see Ullendorff *Animistic Expressions*; cf. Goldenberg *Amh. Tense-System* 140 (§142), with further bibliographical references ibid. The causative forms of compounds with "say" in Amharic, with the interesting alternation of *assäññä* (the suppletive causative of *alä* "say") with *adärrägä* "do, make", will not concern us here.

of direct and indirect elements in various proportions, and the practical meanings of 'quotatives' in language use, as we have seen them, do not leave much sense in sticking to the simplistic description of two categories, the one of a direct-literal-asyndetic quotation and the other of an indirect, deictically-switched and syntactically-transposed embedding, even if these are supplemented with a third category of "semi-indirect", half-switched and asyndetic "veiled" speech.

Quotation as a syntactical figure can be examined from several viewpoints:

(1) As to the syntactic frame, it may be set up (a) asyndetically, as an independent grammatical structure, which is the most commonly known form of direct speech; or (b) presented by a particle or a conjunction identical with the substantivizing *"that"*, as in Hebrew with *kī* or with *ʾăšær* or *šæ-*, or in Aramaic with *d-*, or in Arabic with *ʾinna*; see ch. II above. (c) In the latter case, the syntactic constructions of direct and indirect speech are neutralized, as they necessarily are in no few languages in the case of direct/indirect questions, and in other cases where it would not be possible to distinguish direct and indirect speech.[27]

(2) Personal markers in direct quotations are (a) mostly those seemingly used by the original speaker. (b) There is, however, the "semi-indirect" style, with personal forms switched to those appropriate to the actual speaker of the matrix sentence, but whose all other traits are those which typically mark a direct quotation (cf. ch. I and ch. III above). Here the evidence of Hebrew is of great interest, as it employs in such cases the verb *ʾāmar*, which markedly presents direct speech. (c) In many cases, the combination of persons involved would not enable us to distinguish direct and indirect personal markers (see footnote 27).

(3) Tenses and moods in direct speech are naturally those of the supposed original speaker, but in reported speech in various languages they will either (a) remain unchanged, or (b) be fully or partly switched to reflect the situation and involvement of the actual speaker (the 'reporter'); (c) mixture or neutralization of the two structures are not uncommon.

(4) The actual meaning conveyed by the syntactical figure of direct speech is found, as we have seen, to range from (a) real quotation of actual speech, through (b) figurative or imaginary speech, (c) onomatopoeic sounds "quoted" in grammaticalized descriptive expressions, to (d) lexicalized verbal compounds in the form of { *"say"* + base} where the construction is purely formal.

[27] Compare, e.g., in English *I say 'I am coming'* with *I say I am coming.* "Here the conventions of writing, the punctuation, make the distinction, but in the spoken language there would be no such features" (Palmer *Mood* 134).

With respect to the functions of quoted and reported speech forms, the evidence of Biblical Hebrew is particularly worth notice for the distinction it makes between the most typical uses of direct and indirect speech by employing differentially the various *verba dicendi* (ch. II), and for the "direct" characterization of the "semi-indirect" construction.

References

AB — Azzannaw Aläme, *Adduña bĕlaš*. Lĕbb wälläd drama (Addis Ababa, Täsfa, 1949 E.C.).

Armbruster *Dong. Nubian* — Charles Hubert Armbruster, *Dongolese Nubian. A Grammar* (Cambridge 1960).

Azer. — Irene Garbell, *The Jewish Neo-Aramaic Dialect of Persian Azerbaijan*. Linguistic analysis and folkloristic texts [Janua Linguarum, series practica 3] (The Hague 1965).

Baet. — J. Baeteman, *Dictionnaire amarigna-français suivi d'un vocabulaire français-amarigna* (Dire-Daoua 1929).

Baumgartner *Lexikon* — *Hebräisches und aramäisches Lexikon zum Alten Testament* von Ludwig Koehler und Walter Baumgartner. Dritte Auflage neu bearbeitet von Walter Baumgartner (Leiden 1967- ) [Lief. II, 1974].

Beeston *Arabic* — A. F. L. Beeston, *The Arabic Language Today* (London 1970).

Brown-Driver-Briggs *Lexicon* — *A Hebrew and English Lexicon of the Old Testament*, based on the lexicon of William Gesenius as translated by Edward Robinson. Edited by Francis Brown, S. R. Driver and Charles A. Briggs (Cambridge 1907 [1951]).

Cohen *NE* — Marcel Cohen, *Nouvelles études d'éthiopien méridional* [Bibliothèque de l'École des Hautes Études, n° 275] (Paris 1939).

Cohen *Traité* — Marcel Cohen, *Traité de langue amharique* [Université de Paris. Travaux et Mémoires de l'Institut d'Ethnologie.- XXIV] (Paris 1936).

Comrie *Tense* — Bernard Comrie, *Tense* [Cambridge Textbooks in Linguistics] (Cambridge U. P. 1985).

Coulmas *Reported Speech* — Florian Coulmas, "Reported Speech: Some general issues", in: *Direct and Indirect Speech*, edited by Florian Coulmas [Trends in Linguistics: Studies and monographs, 31] (Berlin, New York & Amsterdam 1986) 1-28.

Curme *German* — George O. Curme, *A Grammar of the German Language*. Second Revised Edition (New York 1922).

Diderichsen *Dansk Gramm.* — Paul Diderichsen, *Elementær Dansk Grammatik.* 3. Udgave, 2. Oplag (København 1966).

Dubr. — Alexander Pushkin, *Dubrovskiy* [in Amharic], transl. Yohannĕs Gäbrä-Maryam (Moscow, Progress, 1960).

Epstein *Introduction* — J. N. Epstein, *Māḇō lnusaḥ hammišna* [Introduction to the Text of the Mishna]. 2 vols. (Jerusalem & Tel-Aviv 1948).

Epstein *Notes II* — J. N. Epstein, "Notes on Post-Talmudic-Aramaic Lexicography II", *The Jewish Quarterly Rewiew*, New Series, 12 (1921-1922) 299-390.

Esh *Opening-Words* — Shaul Esh, "ʿAl millōt-ptīḥā lip̱nē dibbūr yāšār bʿIḇrīt" [On Opening-Words before direct speech in Hebrew], *Lĕšonénu* 22,1 (1957) 48-53.

Ewald *Lehrb. Hebr.* — Heinrich Ewald, *Ausführliches lehrbuch der Hebräischen sprache des Alten Bundes.* 8. ausgabe (Göttingen 1870).

Fables — *Cent fables amhariques*, mises en écrit par le dabtara Kenfé, traduites et annotées par M. M. Moreno [Cahiers de la Société Asiatique XI] (Paris 1947).

Fowler *Usage* — H. W. Fowler, *A Dictionary of Modern English Usage.* Second edition, revised by Sir Ernest Gowers (Oxford 1965).

Gesenius *Gramm.* — Gesenius' *Hebrew Grammar*, as edited and enlarged by E. Kautzsch. Second English edition revised by A. E. Cowley (Oxford 1910).

Gesenius *Handwörterbuch*$^{17}$ — Wilhelm Gesenius' *Hebräisches und Aramäisches Handwörterbuch über das Alte Testament*, bearbeitet von Franz Buhl. Siebzehnte Auflage (Leipzig 1921).

Gesenius *Handwörterbuch*$^{18}$ — Wilhelm Gesenius' *Hebräisches und Aramäisches Handwörterbuch über das Alte Testament*, unter verantwortlicher Mitarbeit von Udo Rüterswörden bearbeitet und herausgegeben von Rudolf Meyer und Herbert Donner. 18. Auflage [1. Lief.] (Berlin & Heidelberg, New York &c., Springer-Verlag, 1987).

GMB — Alämayyäh$^w$ Mogäs, *Gäbrä Mäsqäl bariyaw.* Tarikawi lĕbb wälläd (Addis Ababa, Bĕrhanĕnna Sälam, 1955 E.C.).

Goldenberg *Amh. Tense-System* — Gideon Goldenberg, *The Amharic Tense-System.* Diss. (Jerusalem 1966).

Grevisse *Bon usage* — Maurice Grevisse, *Le bon usage. Grammaire française avec des remarques sur la langue française d'aujourd'hui.* 8ème édition revue (Gembloux 1964).

HdL — *Handbuch der Linguistik* ... zusammengestellt von Harro Stammerjohann (München 1975).

Healy *Teleéfoól Quotative* — P. Healy, "Teleéfoól Quotative Clauses", *Linguistic Circle of Canberra Occasional Papers* III (1964) 25-34. Reprinted in: Householder *Syntactic Theory* (1972) 215-222.

Householder *Syntactic Theory* — *Syntactic Theory 1 : Structuralist.* Selected Readings, edited by Fred W. Householder [Penguin Modern Linguistics Readings] (Harmondsworth, Middlesex, 1972).

IMS — Käbbädä Mikael, *Ityopĕyanna mĕĕrabawi sĕlĕṭṭane/ L'Éthiopie et la civilisation occidentale* (Addis Ababa, Bĕrhanĕnna Sälam, 1941 E.C. [= 1949]).

Jean-Hoftijzer *DISO* — Charles-F. Jean & Jacob Hoftijzer, *Dictionnaire des inscriptions sémitiques de l'Ouest* (Leiden 1965).

Jespersen *MEG* — Otto Jespersen, *A Modern English Grammar on Historical Principles.* 7 vols. (London & Copenhagen 1909-1949).

Jespersen *PG* — Otto Jespersen, *The Philosophy of Grammar* (London 1924).

Joüon *Grammaire* — Paul Joüon, *Grammaire de l'hébreu biblique* (Rome 1923).

Kononov *Gramm. tureck.* — A. N. Kononov, *Grammatika sovremennogo tureckogo literaturnogo jazyka* (Moskva & Leningrad 1956).

Lerch *Uneigentlich* — Gertraud Lerch, "Die uneigentlich direkte Rede", in: *Idealistische Neuphilologie.* Festschrift für Karl Vossler zum 6. September 1922, hrsg. von Victor Klemperer & Eugen Lerch [Sammlung romanischer Elementar- und Handbücher hrsg. v. W. Meyer-Lübke V,5] (Heidelberg 1922) 107-119.

Li *Direct & Indirect* — Charles N. Li, "Direct Speech and Indirect Speech: A Functional Study", in: *Direct and Indirect Speech*, edited by Florian Coulmas [Trends in Linguistics: Studies and monographs, 31] (Berlin, New York & Amsterdam 1986) 29-45.

Lips *Style indir. libre* — Marguerite Lips, *Le style indirect libre* [Université de Genève, Faculté des Lettres - Thèse N° 51] (Paris 1926).

LTA — Bäĕmnät Gäbrä Amlak, *Lĕğĕnnät tämällĕso aymäṭamm* (Addis Ababa, Bĕrhanĕnna Sälam, 1949 E.C.).

Mawsim — Al-Ṭayyib Ṣāliḥ, *Mawsim al-hiğrah ʾilà l-šamāl* (Beirut 1969).

New Amer. Bible — *The New American Bible* (1970) *With Revised New Testament* (1986) of the Confraternity of Christian Doctrine (Catholic Biblical Association).

Palmer *Mood* — Frank R. Palmer, *Mood and Modality* [Cambridge Textbooks in Linguistics] (Cambridge U. P. 1986).

Polotsky *Coll. Pap.* — H. J. Polotsky, *Collected Papers* (Jerusalem 1971).

Polotsky *Synt. amharique & turque* — H. J. Polotsky, "Syntaxe amharique et syntaxe turque", in: *Atti del Convegno Internazionale di Studi Etiopici (1959)* [Accademia Nazionale dei Lincei, anno CCCLVII-1960 / Problemi Attuali di Scienza e di Cultura, Quaderno N. 48] (Roma 1960) 117-121 [= Polotsky *Coll. Pap.* 3-7].

Praetorius *Tña* — Franz Praetorius, *Grammatik der Tigriñasprache in Abessinien hauptsächlich in der Gegend von Aksum und Adoa* (Halle 1871).

Segal *Mishnaic*[1] — M. H. Segal, *A Grammar of Mishnaic Hebrew* (Oxford 1927).

Segal *Mishnaic*[2] — M. H. Segal, *Diqdūq lšon hammišna* (Tel-Aviv 1936).

SprwWb — *Sprachwissenschaftliches Wörterbuch*, hrsg. von Johann Knobloch I (Heidelberg [1961-]1986).

Sweet *NEG* — Henry Sweet, *A New English Grammar Logical and Historical.* 2 vols. (Oxford 1891-1898).

TzNL — *Terminologie zur neueren Linguistik,* zusammengestellt von Werner Abraham (Tübingen 1974).

Ullendorff *Animistic Expressions* — Edward Ullendorff, "Animistic Expressions and Some Other Aspects of Direct Speech in Amharic", in: *IV Congresso Internazionale di Studi Etiopici* (1972) [Accademia Nazionale dei Lincei, anno CCCLXXI-1974 / Problemi Attuali di Scienza e di Cultura, Quaderno N. 191, 2 vols.] (Roma 1974) II 269-274.

Wendt *Syntax* — G. Wendt, *Syntax des heutigen Englisch* (Heidelberg 1914).

# Some Remarks about the So-called Imperative Use of the Infinitive Absolute (Infinitivus pro Imperativo) in Classical Hebrew*

J.H. Hospers, Groningen

It is my pleasure to offer this article to Professor Hoftijzer, on the occasion of his retirement, as an expression of my gratitude for the cordial collegiality that we have enjoyed for more than a quarter of a century. It was Prof. Hoftijzer himself who remarked in an inaugural lecture a few years ago that too many people go on using as a matter of course the terms that they learnt previously or have found in grammar after grammar[1].

This is certainly true, as is evident when one considers how certain linguistic phenomena of Classical Hebrew are still being described. This is the case notably with respect to syntax, for as far as morphology is concerned it has gradually become clear that various traditional terms, derived as they are from Latin grammar, cannot be called adequate, and may even be confusing. Awareness of this has led to the coining of new terms such as SC (Suffix Conjugation) and PC (Prefix Conjugation) instead of "Perfect" and "Imperfect", respectively.

Also the study of syntax of Classical Hebrew has to some extent changed for the better. In the past the study of syntax closely followed morphological classification, as if it was merely a list of syntactic instructions relating to the various units – and so observing the same order – at the end of the textbook. This formerly usual method was abandoned more and more, especially since the appearance of Brockelmann's *Hebräische Syntax*[2]. Nowadays it is generally recognized that when dealing with syntax one should take as a starting point not the isolated units of morphology but the relationships present in the sen-

---

* Translation from the Dutch: Sheila van Gelder-Ottway & Geert Jan van Gelder.

[1] J. Hoftijzer, *Grammatica toch nuttig. Over het nut van grammaticaal onderzoek voor bijbelstudie, speciaal voor het Oude Testament*, Vierhouten 1988, p. 13.

[2] C. Brockelmann, *Hebräische Syntax*, Neukirchen 1956.

tence, and beyond that in the discourse as a whole, of Classical Hebrew texts.

Yet what in my opinion is still very unsatisfactory in the description of syntax of Classical Hebrew is the way in which the material is presented in other respects. All too often classifications are made that suggest a division into apparently distinct functions with an independent existence, whereas in fact this is nothing more than a projection of the classificatory structure of the describer's own language. After all, every language has its own way of organizing the linguistic means at its disposal in the surface structure. Such classifications, which, moreover, often employ a Latin-based terminology, do not necessarily always correspond to the syntactical functioning of Classical Hebrew itself. Apparently, one never stops to think that such categorizations, and their concomitant terminologies, would look very different again if these projections were to be made, not from an Indo-Germanic language and Latin grammatical tradition, but from the viewpoint of another language family. When categorizing the several syntactical functions one's starting-point is still too often how a particular Classical Hebrew form could best be *translated* in a certain manner. Thus problems of translation are not rarely confused with those of linguistic description[3]: the structures of one's own language are made to play as it were a normative role in the description of another language. In doing this, however, one runs the risk of taking for granted such categorizations foisted from outside, as if syntactical functioning would be sufficiently described by them. One is unaware that this method obstructs further research, because what is really at stake in the language to be described is no longer taken into consideration. In order to illustrate the above I shall discuss the way in which the phenomenon of the infinitive absolute is still being dealt with in descriptions of Classical Hebrew syntax.

This infinitive absolute, a form that, among the Semitic languages, had an especially important function in Classical Hebrew[4], is characterized by the pattern *qāṭōl* in *qal*[5], and is clearly related formally to

[3] Elsewhere I have pointed out, in another connection, that such categorizations become manifest only from the possibilities for translation that present themselves in other languages. They have, however, no proper foundation in the essential unity of the Classical Hebrew form. In teaching, of course, they may be useful to some extent, since the demands of teaching, particularly its initial stages, differ from those of linguistic description. See J. H. Hospers, "Das Problem der sogenannten semantischen Polarität im Althebräischen", in *Zeitschrift für Althebraistik* 1 (1988), pp. 32-39, 37.

[4] Apart from Classical Hebrew the only other evidence for this form is found in Ugaritic (see C. H. Gordon, *Ugaritic Textbook. Grammar*, Roma 1965, p. 79) and in Phoenician (J. Friedrich & W. Röllig, *Phönizisch-Punische Grammatik*, Roma 1970, p. 135).

[5] The other *binyanim* too have special forms for the infinitive absolute, but these

the Akkadian infinitive pattern *CaCāCu(m)*[6]. Its basis, it seems, was a proto-Semitic abstracting *nomen verbale* of the pattern *qabāru* which served "zur Hervorhebung des Verbalbegriffs *in abstracto*[7] and which expressed neither person nor tense but merely an act or a state; this much is commonly acknowledged[8]. This form has been very productive for centuries in Classical Hebrew, where at an early stage it must have lost its nominal regimen (a special pre-genitive form and the possible affixation of pronominal suffixes) - if it ever possessed it at all. There existed, on the other hand, a verbal regimen by means of the accusative particle or prepositions. In later Hebrew however the form became gradually less productive, finally disappearing altogether[9].

Whereas on the level of morphology the description of the infinitive absolute may not present any difficulties, one is frequently confronted with the unsatisfactory method described above as regards the level of syntax. Both in those parts of current Classical Hebrew grammar books that deal with syntax[10] and in some specialized syntactical studies[11] one still finds a more or less detailed subdivision into different functions of the infinitive absolute. Invariably one finds mention of the emphasizing paronomastic employment of the *figura etymologica*, the adverbial use and the *infinitivus pro imperativo*, examples being taken from *Tĕnak̲*.

Here I shall restrict myself to this *infinitivus pro imperativo*. It is al-

---

are clearly secondary, formed on the analogy of the infinitive absolute of *qal* or the imperative of the *binyan* concerned.

[6] See W. von Soden, *Grundriss der Akkadischen Grammatik*, Roma 1969, p. 202-204.

[7] W. Gesenius, *Hebräische Grammatik*, 28. Aufl., völlig umgearbeitet von E. Kautzsch, Leipzig 1909, p. 353.

[8] Cf. J. M. Solá-Solé, *L'infinitif sémitique. Contribution à l'étude des formes et des fonctions des noms d'action et des infinitives sémitiques*, Paris 1961.

[9] See W. J. van Bekkum, *The Status of the Infinitive in Early Piyyut* in this festschrift.

[10] See, e.g., Gesenius, *Hebräische Grammatik*, pp. 353-61; E. Kautzsch (ed.), *Gesenius' Hebrew Grammar*, translated by A. E. Cowley, 2nd ed., Oxford 1970, corresponding passage; G. Bergsträsser, *Hebräische Grammatik. Mit Benutzung der von E. Kautzsch bearbeiteten 28. Auflage von Wilhelm Gesenius' hebräische Grammatik*, Hildesheim 1962, II (= Leipzig 1929), pp. 61-67; P. Joüon, *Grammaire de l'Hébreu biblique*, 2me éd., Rome 1947, pp. 347-58; R. Meyer, *Hebräische Grammatik: III Satzlehre*, Berlin 1972, pp. 61-65; W. Schneider, *Grammatik des Biblischen Hebräisch*, München 1974, pp. 211, 218-20; J. P. Lettinga, *Grammatica van het Bijbels Hebreeuws*, 8e dr., Leiden 1976, pp. 173-75; E. Jenni, *Lehrbuch der Hebräischen Sprache des Alten Testaments*, Basel & Stuttgart 1978, pp. 117-18; W. Richter, *Grundlagen einer althebräischen Grammatik*, I, St. Ottilien 1978, pp. 169-71, II, 1979, pp. 64, 69, III, 1980, p. 168; J. Körner, *Hebräische Studiengrammatik*, Leipzig 1988, pp. 277-79.

[11] Brockelmann, *Hebräische Syntax*, pp. 1-2, 47-48, 82-85; Solá-Solé, *L'infinitif sémitique*, pp. 79-102; R. J. Williams, *Hebrew Syntax: An Outline*, 2nd ed., Toronto & Buffalo 1976, pp. 37-39.

ways stated that this infinitive can replace the imperative as its equivalent. Thus it is erroneously suggested that in Classical Hebrew the choice of expressing a command by means of the infinive absolute or by the imperative form is a rather arbitrary one. It is true that occasionally reference is made to the emphatic character of such a command represented by an infinitive absolute, and that Jenni remarks quite rightly that such a substitution is something "wobei der Zusammenhang über den genaueren Sinn entscheidet"[12], but any further discussion is lacking. Thus this infinitive absolute is commonly translated as an imperative, as if it were its exact equivalent[13].

It seems to me now that such infinitive absolute forms can be more appropriately described if one does not limit oneself to the abovementioned qualifications, which may be of some use in teaching when used by way of elucidation, but which do not do full justice to the phenomenon linguistically.

A good starting-point for an approach from within Classical Hebrew itself is offered by a recently published study by Th. J. Finley[14], who bases himself on the contrast between surface and deep structure. In this way the author attempts to develop a model for a concept that he calls "proposal", which is employed whenever there is "a situation where a speaker communicates a desire for something to a listener, with the speaker having some degree of expectation that the listener will fulfill that desire"[15]. In the treatment of the several surface structures for the "proposal", attention is also given, under the heading of "Forms without a personal marker", to the infinitive absolute, that could form a "substitute in proposals that would often be formed with imperatives"[16].

One has to agree with the author that there are some distinct advantages involved in "this type of approach over traditional studies which concentrate rather on the various functions of individual forms (imperative, jussive, cohortative, etc.)"[17], but his remark that almost all of the examples of an infinitive absolute as proposal that he has studied "can be described as commands"[18], still does not make clear why in some surface structures precisely this form was chosen, while in others an imperative form, or a second person form of a PC, or an

[12] Jenni, *Lehrbuch der Hebräischen Sprache*, p. 117.

[13] That this view is an ancient one is shown by the imperative form *leḵ* in I Chron. 21: 10, the parallel text of II Sam. 24: 12, where the infinitive absolute *hālōḵ* occurs.

[14] Th. J. Finley, "The Proposal in Biblical Hebrew: Preliminary Studies using a Deep Structure Model", in *Zeitschrift für Althebraistik* 2 (1989), pp. 1-13.

[15] Finley, "The Proposal", p. 3.

[16] Finley, "The Proposal", p. 5.

[17] Finley, "The Proposal", p. 13.

[18] Finley, "The Proposal", p. 9.

SC preceded by *wĕ*, was thought sufficient. These were, after all, the prime linguistic means for expressing commands that were available in Classical Hebrew. This question is not raised by the author, let alone answered, even though he points in the right direction, I believe, when he remarks that in commands the infinitive absolute "often occurs at the head of a series of commands"[19], something that had been observed already by Joüon[20].

It seems to me now that the infinitive absolute in the so-called *infinitivus pro imperativo* construction never – and certainly not primarily – had the character of an imperative. Therefore, when Finley, in his discussion of the construction of *hālōḵ*, states that this form usually occurs "followed by *another* command" [my italics][21], this must be called incorrect in my view.

In my opinion the point of departure ought to be the description of the infinitive absolute as given already by Gesenius-Kautzsch: a verbal noun that serves "zur Hervorhebung des Verbalbegriffs *in abstracto*"[22]. This form was eminently suitable for being fronted as a *casus pendens* by way of rubric for a new section in a series of laws. Well-known passages such as Ex. 20: 8 and Deut. 5: 12 could serve to elucidate this. Taken literally, *zākōr* and *šāmōr* could be rendered here as "Remembering / keeping the sabbath day. < This is done> by sanctifying it", after which more explication and instructions follow. "Keeping the sabbath day" could then be seen as the heading of a new law section. Had one wished to express a straightforward command, surely one would have employed the imperative form, like e.g. Deut. 9: 7, where we find *zĕḵor*.

The infinitive absolute at the beginning of Ex. 13: 3 could be explained in a similar fashion. Here, however, the rubric is supplemented with a relative clause and the further elaboration only starts with *wĕ lo᾽ yē᾽āḵēl* at the end of vs. 3. Perhaps it were best translated by means of a *casus pendens*, for instance: "As for remembering this day, in which ye came out from Egypt, out of the house of bondage – for by strength of hand the Lord brought you out from this place – < this implies> there shall no leavened bread be eaten". A similar description could be given of other occurrences of the infinitive absolute in the *Tĕnaḵ* where it precedes a further instruction; thus e.g. Deut. 1: 16 and 15: 2. Then it may turn out that the imperative character is not implied in the infinitive absolute concerned, but only in what follows.

Special attention remains to be given to the infinitive absolute *hālōḵ* which occurs frequently in such constructions. Here too, in my opinion,

[19] Finley, "The Proposal", p. 9.
[20] Joüon, *Grammaire de l'Hébreu*, p. 356.
[21] Finley, "The Proposal", p. 9.
[22] Gesenius, *Hebräische Grammatik*, p. 353.

there is no question of a mere substitute for an imperative form[23]. When one reads e.g. in Isa. 38: 5: *hālōḵ wĕ ʾāmartā* one could think of an underlying sense: "As for going, you should < not only go but> speak", the command proper being contained only in the form *wĕ ʾāmartā*. Something similar is the case in II Kgs. 5: 10, where it is said to Naaman: *hālōḵ wĕ rāḥaṣtā*; but here the infinitive absolute of *hālaḵ* is to some extent worn down already to a kind of interjection ("Come on", "Now then!") which serves to give a certain emphasis to the command to wash.

It has been my intention to suggest that such infinitives absolute should no longer be characterized so readily as arbitrary substitutes for imperatives or other verbal forms that could express a command. As Williams has noted before, we are dealing here with emphasis [24]. In the past twenty years modern linguistics has been speaking in this connection of "focus"[25]. During this period several definitions of this concept have been proposed[26], which were reviewed recently in a lucid and interesting article by C. H. J. van der Merwe, who applies the concept to Classical Hebrew as well[27]. The infinitive absolute *pro imperativo*, then, is not an example of arbitrary substitution but of focusing, for which this form was one of the principal linguistic means in Classical Hebrew, just as in Dutch or English we employ cleft sentences and intonation for the same purpose – even though the latter would surely have been available to Classical Hebrew too[28].

---

[23] As Finley believes ("The Proposal", p. 9).

[24] Williams, *Hebrew Syntax*, p. 37.

[25] See R. Jackendoff, *Semantic Interpretation in a Generative Grammar*, Cambridge, Mass. 1972.

[26] See J. M. Y. Simpson, *A First Course in Linguistics*, Edinburgh 1979, pp. 232-36.

[27] C. H. J. van der Merwe, "The Vague Term 'Emphasis'", in *Journal for Semitics* 1 (1989), pp. 118-32. It is not clear to me why this author does not want to classify the function of the so-called *infinitivus pro imperativo*, as discussed by me, under the heading of parts of the sentence in focus (p. 130, note 44), because he does not provide arguments to support his point of view.

[28] In my opinion the paronomastic use of the infinitive absolute also involves focusing; this, however falls outside the scope of this article.

# On the VSO Character of Hebrew*

K. Jongeling, Leiden

Many grammars of classical Hebrew insist in their syntactical remarks upon the VSO[1]-character of the language, cf. e.g Gesenius-Kautzsch[2]: "In the verbal-clause proper the principal emphasis rests upon the action which proceeds from (or is experienced by) the subject, and accordingly the verb naturally precedes (*necessarily* so when it is in the perf. consec. or imperf. consec.)"[3]. The same notion, but without the psychological explanation, is to be found with R. Meyer[4]: "Der einfache Verbalsatz besteht aus dem Subjekt und dem Verbum finitum als Prädikat ... Die Wortfolge ist meist Prädikat – Subjekt; sie erklärt sich daraus, dass das Verbum finitum bereits einen geschlossenen Satz einfachster Bauart mit pronominalen Subjekt darstellt .., dass also das Subjekt nur erläuternd hinzutritt"[5]. The explanation in this case is based upon the character of the verbal form. Like others Meyer also points to the VSO character of related languages like Phoenician and Arabic. Without an explanation the same is supposed by R.J. Williams in his Hebrew Syntax[6]. Most apparent, of course, are the many sentences beginning with a narrative form of which nothing need be said here. It is inherent to the specific verbal form that it should be at the beginning of the sentence. As great parts of the biblical text are narrative compositions it is clear that the reader gets the impression that most of the classical Hebrew sentences are VSO. This, however, has not restrained Joüon to remark[7]: "L'ordre des mots dans la proposition verbale ... est normalement: Sujet – Verbe".

---

* Dedicated to professor dr. J. Hoftijzer.

1 Verbum-Subject-Object order.

2 A.E. Cowley (ed.), *Gesenius' Hebrew Grammar as edited .. by E. Kautzsch*, Oxford 1910², §142a.

3 Cf. in the same vein A.B. Davidson, *Hebrew Syntax*, Edinburgh 1901³, §105: "In the verbal sent. the idea expressed by the verb is the emphatic element, and in ordinary calm discourse the order is – pred., subj.".

4 *Hebräische Grammatik*, Band iii, Berlin 1972, §91

5 This is, of course, already a classical explanation, cf. e.g. H. Ewald, *Grammatik der Hebräischen Sprache des Alten Testaments*, Leipzig 1838³, p. 345, §554.

6 R.J. Williams, *Hebrew Syntax, An Outline*, Toronto 1967, p. 96.

7 P. Joüon, *Grammaire de l'Hébreu Biblique*, Rome 1923, §155 k.

| | chapter i | | ii | | iii | | iv | | total | |
|---|---|---|---|---|---|---|---|---|---|---|
| INITIAL VERB | | | | | | | | | | |
| ImpfCons | 16 | 34 | 15 | 44 | 4 | 31 | 10 | 27 | 45 | 136 |
| PfCons | - | 1 | - | 11 | 2 | 11 | - | 1 | 2 | 24 |
| Impf | 2 | 2 | 11 | 11 | 1 | 1 | 4 | 4 | 18 | 18 |
| Pf | 1 | 1 | - | - | - | 1 | 2 | 3 | 3 | 5 |
| Imper | - | 8 | - | 2 | - | 5 | - | 10 | - | 25 |
| | | | | total | | | | | 68 | 208 |
| VERB PRECEDED BY PREVERBALIA OR INTERROGATIVA | | | | | | | | | | |
| *ky / ʾšr / gm* | 3 | 15 | 1 | 13 | 6 | 15 | 4 | 8 | 14 | 51 |
| Interrogative | - | 4 | - | 1 | - | - | - | - | - | 5 |
| Negation | - | 2 | 1 | 9 | 1 | 7 | 1 | 5 | 3 | 23 |
| InfAbs | - | - | - | 1 | - | - | - | - | - | 1 |
| | | | | total | | | | | 17 | 80 |
| VERB PRECEDED BY OTHER ELEMENTS | | | | | | | | | | |
| Subject | 5 | 5 | 2 | 2 | 2 | 2 | 14 | 14 | 23 | 23 |
| Object | - | - | - | - | 1 | 4 | - | - | 1 | 4 |
| Adverb | 3 | 5 | - | 4 | 1 | 1 | - | - | 4 | 10 |
| Prep Phrase | - | 4 | - | 2 | - | - | - | 1 | - | 7 |
| | | | | total | | | | | 28 | 44 |
| Nominal Sentence | 13 | | 14 | | 11 | | 10 | | 48 | |

Table 1: Sentence types in the book of Ruth.

The difference between these two opinions is possibly related to the difference of the starting-points these scholars have chosen. Gesenius-Kautzsch-Cowley as well as R. Meyer are working from a historical-comparative outlook, but Joüon gives as far as possible a synchrone description of classical Hebrew.

From a typological viewpoint it may be interesting to give a more definite answer to the question whether Hebrew is a VSO language or rather SVO as Joüon maintains, although most typologists are inclined to characterise the basic word order only in terms of verb versus object, with exclusion of the subject[8]. The answer to the question may influence our understanding of the Hebrew sentence and the relationship of several syntactical constructions on the one hand and the description of complex sentences on the other.

[8] We do not concern ourselves further with this opinion; for Welsh cf. R. Sproat, *Welsh Syntax and VSO Structure*, Natural Language and Linguistic Theory, ii 1985, pp. 173-216, who maintains that Welsh is best described as a language of which the deep structure is SVO.

In the first place it may be worth while to count the word order in a short but typical classical Hebrew text, although mere numbers may not be conclusive in this respect[9]. For this count we chose the book of Ruth, see table 1 (in the first column for each chapter the number of examples where the subject is expressed, the second column giving the complete number of examples).

In the second table we collected the same material, as far as it is contained in direct discourse.

| | chapter | | | | | | | | | |
|---|---|---|---|---|---|---|---|---|---|---|
| | i | | ii | | iii | | iv | | total | |
| INITIAL VERB | | | | | | | | | | |
| ImpfCons | - | - | 1 | 5 | - | 1 | - | 1 | 1 | 7 |
| PfCons | 1 | 1 | - | 8 | 1 | 11 | - | 1 | 2 | 21 |
| Impf | 2 | 2 | 3 | 11 | - | 1 | 2 | 4 | 7 | 18 |
| Pf | 1 | 1 | - | - | - | 1 | 1 | 1 | 2 | 3 |
| Imper | - | 8 | - | 2 | - | 5 | - | 10 | - | 25 |
| | | | | total | | | | | 12 | 74 |
| VERB PRECEDED BY PREVERBALIA OR INTERROGATIVA | | | | | | | | | | |
| *ky / ʾšr / gm* | 2 | 12 | 1 | 9 | 2 | 12 | 3 | 7 | 8 | 40 |
| Interrogative | - | 4 | - | 1 | - | - | - | - | - | 5 |
| Negation | - | 2 | - | 9 | - | 7 | - | 5 | - | 23 |
| InfAbs | - | - | - | 1 | - | - | - | - | - | 1 |
| | | | | total | | | | | 8 | 69 |
| VERB PRECEDED BY OTHER ELEMENTS | | | | | | | | | | |
| Subject | 3 | 3 | 3 | 3 | 2 | 2 | 3 | 3 | 9 | 9 |
| Object | - | - | - | - | - | 3 | - | - | - | 3 |
| Adverb | 2 | 4 | - | 4 | 1 | 1 | - | - | 3 | 9 |
| Prep Phrase | - | 4 | - | 2 | - | - | - | 1 | - | 7 |
| | | | | total | | | | | 12 | 28 |
| Nominal Sentence | 5 | | 11 | | 10 | | 5 | | 31 | |

Table 2: Sentence types in the book of Ruth, direct speech.

From the first table we see that sentences with an initial verb or with one of the preverbalia together account for 87% of the verbal sentences. As the subject is not expressed in many sentences it is, however, more to the point to consider only those instances where the subject is expressed. Then we find the verb in initial position, or only preceded by one of the preverbalia, in 75% of the verbal sentences, whereas subject-initial sentences form only 7% of all verbal sentences or 20% of the

[9] Cf. e.g. R.S. Tomlin, *Basic Word Order, Functional Principles*, London etc. 1986, p. 34.

sentences in which the subject is expressed as a separate entity. So it is clear that, although not the only order, the VSO order is best considered to be the basic order of classical Hebrew. The situation would change of course when we would not consider the representatives of the second group in the table as forming part of the verb-initial sentence type. For this point of view one may compare the situation in a Celtic language like Welsh, that is also considered to be a VSO language[10], cf. e.g. D.S. Evans in his grammar of Middle Welsh, who in the section on the verb includes a large section on pre-verbal particles[11].

The question is now, whether it is more appropriate to describe the verb-initial sentence as the standard, describing the environment in which deviations from this standard occur or to take another sentence-type as a starting-point, e.g. the SVO type, as is done by Joüon. Taking economy as a criterium a description starting from the VSO viewpoint is the most appropriate, because the SVO sentences are more easily described as deviations from a VSO order than the other way round.

From a typological point of view the difference is thought to be less important. It has been demonstrated that the organisation of sentences and of sentence constituents are related to one another. In typical VSO and SVO languages the normal order of elements is: modifiers following the modified expression. In both Hebrew and Welsh this phenomenon can be observed (both languages share the order noun-adjective, noun-relative, noun-genetive, noun-demonstrative, adjective-adverb)[12]. This observation combined with the results mentioned in table 1 & 2 make it probable that Hebrew is best counted among the VSO languages. As this language type is attested in several language families there seems to be no need for the psychological explanation of Gesenius-Kautszch and the formal reasoning of Meyer, both probably suggested by a desire to explain this striking difference between several well known European languages and the West-Semitic ones. In the descriptions of Welsh grammar this type of reasoning is only to be found in some very old textbooks, whereas modern grammarians contend themselves with the description of the linguistic facts.

To show to what extent Hebrew and Welsh are comparable on the point of word order, we give a few examples (Hebrew compared to

[10] Cf. e.g. D. Simon Evans, *The Sentence in Early Modern Welsh*, Bulletin of the Board of Celtic Studies, 22 1968, pp. 311-337.

[11] D. Simon Evans, *A Grammar of Middle Welsh*, Dublin 1964, pp. 166-179: Preverbal Particles (Affirmative, Negative, Interrogative).

[12] On these combinations cf. e.g. R.S.Tomlin, *Basic Word Order, Functional Principles*, London etc. 1986, G. Ineichen, *Allgemeine Sprachtypologie*, Darmstadt 1979, pp. 130ff., G. Mallinson - B.J. Blake, *Language Typology, Cross-linguistic Studies in Syntax*, Amsterdam etc. 1981.

Welsh from the new bible translation of 1988[13]):
Basic word order
*w-yb› ywsp ›t-dbtm r‹h ›l-›byhm* (Gen. 37:2)
and Josef brought an ill report of them to their father
a chariodd Joseff straeon drwg amdanynt i'w tad.
and brought Josef stories bad about-them to their father

Order substantive - adjective - adverb
*›yš bry› m›d* (Judges 3:17)
a very fat man
(yn) ddyn tew iawn
[PART] man fat very

Order noun - demonstrative[14]
*h-n‹rh h-z›t* (Ruth 2:5)
this girl
y llances hon
[ART] girl this

Order noun - noun complement
*mzbḥ ›dmh* (Ex. 20:4)
an altar made of earth
allor pridd
altar earth

These are all examples of the principle that the modifier follows the expression that is modified. Deviations from this principle are also comparable in both languages, such as the order subject - verb for emphasis or contrast, as a result of the possibilities extant in a VSO language[15]. Other correspondences cannot easily be connected to this principle. These comprise phenomena like the use of the nominal sentence type[16], the construction of the compound nominal sentence, reinforcement of a suffixed pronoun[17] by means of a separate pronoun, the

[13] *Y Beibl Cymraeg Newydd*, Cymdeithas y Beibl, Swindon 1988.

[14] Note the remark by S.J. Williams, *A Welsh Grammar*, Caerdydd 1980, p. 57, where he is treating the demonstrative pronouns in his chapter on pronouns: "These pronouns can be used as substantives and as adjectives" and cf. Joüon, o.c., §36c: "Le pronom démonstratif .... devient adjectif démonstratif ..".

[15] For Hebrew cf. e.g Gesenius-Kautzsch-Cowley, *o.c.*, § 142f., for Welsh cf. e.g. S.J. Williams, *o.c.*, § 246, 247.

[16] For the nominal sentence in Welsh cf. e.g. D. Simon Evans, *Nominal constructions in Early Modern Welsh*, Bulletin of the Board of Celtic Studies, 24 1971, pp. 138-176.

[17] The existence of suffixed pronouns, a phenomenon in line with the order: modifier following - modified element, constitutes another striking similarity between Welsh and Hebrew.

use of a marker of relativity rather than a relative pronoun. Compare the following examples:
Compound nominal sentence
*w-ʾny zʾt bryty ʾtm* (Jes. 59:21)
this is my covenant with them

a minnau, dyma fy nghyfamod â hwynt
and I this my covenant with them

Reinforcement of suffix pronoun
*by ʾny* (i Sam 25:24)
upon me

arnaf fi
upon-me me

Nominal sentence alongside with sentences construed with a form of a verb 'TO BE'
*ʾmt hyh h-dbr // ʾmt h-dbr* (i Kings 10:6 // ii Chron. 9:5)
the report is true
(these sentences have not been differentiated in the Welsh bible translation, but cf.[18]:)

hir yw pob aros // hir pob aros
long is all waiting

Marker of relativity
*šm h-ʾyš ʾšr ʿśyty ʿmw h-ywm bʿz* (Ruth 2:19)
the name of the man with whom I worked today is Boaz

Enw y gwr y gweithiais gydag ef heddiw yw Boaz
Name [ART] man[REL] I-worked with him today is Boaz

Antecedent depending on a noun in the relative clause
*ʾlhy yśrʾl ʾšr bʾt lḥ swt tḥt knpyw* (Ruth 2:12)
the God of Israel under whose wings you have come to take refuge

Duw Israel y daethost i geisio nodded dan ei adain
God Israel [REL] you-came to seek refuge under his wing

Absence of a marker of relativity
*ʾlhym lʾ ydʿwm* (Dt. 32:17)
gods they did not know

i dduwiau nid adwaenent
to gods not they-knew

---

[18] The two proverbs are quoted from resp. S.J. Williams, *o.c.*, p. 164 and H.M. Evans, *Llwybrau'r Iaith*, Llandybie 1985[3], p. 69.

These correspondences clarify the many references in traditional descriptions of Welsh grammar to a relationship with Hebrew[19]. This relationship was formerly understood as a genetic one and against this opinion serious objections have been raised[20]. In the beginning of this century the typological correspondences between Welsh and Afro-Asiatic induced Morris Jones to the postulation of an Afro-Asiatic substratum in the Celtic languages of the British Isles[21]; these ideas were taken up again by J. Pokorny[22] and by H. Wagner in his substantial study on the Celtic verbal system[23].

In terms of language universals it would be highly interesting to know whether more of these correspondences should be connected into a system of dependent features related to the VSO character of these languages. One may ask, e.g., whether these correspondences may be adduced when describing the SVO sentence in Hebrew. Gesenius-Kautzsch-Cowley describe these sentences as representing the SVO order, in earlier versions of the grammar[24], however, the solution of the classic Arabian grammarians was preferred, who explained this sentence type as a compound nominal sentence in which the predicate consists of a verbal sentence[25]. This explanation would be more or less comparable to the description given of the sentences in Welsh in the so called mixed order. In this sentence type the emphasized element precedes the verbal

[19] As one of the older examples, cf. e.g. dr. Joan. Davies, *Antiquae Linguae Britannicae .... et Linguae Latinae, Dictionarium Duplex*, London, 1632; compare also his remarks on the Welsh Bible translation in his *Antiquae Linguae Britannicae ... Rudimenta ...*, London 1621 (in the introduction); on John Davies compare Rh. Ff. Roberts, *Dr. John Davies o Fallwyd*, Llên Cymru, ii, 1952, and also W. Rowlands, Cambrian Bibliography, Llanidloes, 1869 (reprint Amsterdam, 1970), pp. 98-102 and 112-118.

[20] Cf. e.g. G.J. Williams, *The History of Welsh Scholarship*, Studia Celtica 8-9, 1973-1974, p. 195-219.

[21] J.Morris Jones, *Pre-Aryan Syntax in Insular Celtic*, appendix in: J. Rhŷs & D. Brynmor Jones, *The Welsh People*, London 1900, pp. 617-641; Rhŷs and Jones also postulated a substratum language to explain the differences between continental and insular Celtic, cf. ibid. p. 27.

[22] Cf.e.g. J. Pokorny, *Das nicht-indogermanische Substrat im Inselkeltischen*, Zeitschrift für Celtische Philologie 16, 1927, pp. 95-144, 231-266, 363-394, ibid. 17, 1928, pp. 373-388, ibid. 18, 1930, pp. 233-248; also elsewhere he defended this position, cf. lastly *Zur Anfangsstellung des Inselkeltischen Verbums*, Münchener Studien zur Sprachwissenschaft 16, 1964, pp. 75-80.

[23] H. Wagner, *Das Verbum in den Sprachen der Britischen Inseln*, Tübingen, 1959.

[24] E.Kautzsch, *Wilhelm Gesenius' Hebräische Grammatik*, Leipzig $1896^{26}$, §140f.: Den arab. Grammatikern gilt jeder mit einem selbständ. Subjekt beginnende Satz als Nominalsatz .... diese früher (§144a der 22.-24. Aufl. dieser Gramm.) von uns aufgenommene Definition der Satzarten ...

[25] Cf. e.g. W. Wright, *A Grammar of the Arabic Language*, vol. ii, Cambridge $1898^{3}$, §113.

sentence, which is normally connected by means of a relative particle[26], cf.

Prynodd y dyn geffyl
Bought [ART] man horse
ceffyl a brynodd y dyn
horse [REL] bought [ART] man.

In older texts, however, it is normal that the extraposed element is preceded by a form of the copula. So in Welsh at least the extraposed element is the subject of another sentence than the following verbal one[27]. Perhaps there is something to be said for the view of the classical Arabian grammarians after all.

On at least one important point, however, Hebrew and Welsh do not agree. In both languages there seems to a be tendency towards a SVO structure, at least in some instances, but the way in which this tendency is implemented is rather different in both languages. In Hebrew the SVO structure has become the normal one in those sentences where the participle is used in its function of praesens. This use of the participle, that has changed the character of the Hebrew verbal system shortly after the classical period, has been ascribed to Aramaic influence. If Tomlin is correct in his surmise that the SVO order in itself is more appropriate to convey information than the VSO order[28], the Aramaic influence was perhaps enhanced by this inherent principle. We are, however, not convinced of the validity of his reasoning[29]. In Welsh there is a strong tendency for the finite verbal forms to fall into disuse, and to use an auxiliary verb followed by an infinitive, the infinitive taking its place after the subject[30]. This leaves us with the question whether we have to describe the typological similarities shared

---

[26] Cf. e.g. S.J. Williams, *o.c.*, §246, D.S. Evans, *A Grammar of Middle Welsh*, Dublin 1964, §146.

[27] For Hebrew cf. sentences like Numb. 1:20: *wyhyw bny-rʾwbn bkr yśrʾl twldtm* .. (compared to ibid. 22: *lbny šmʿwn twldtm* .. ); Gen. 31:40: *hyyty bywm ʾklny ḥrb* .... (compared to Ruth 1:21: *ʾny mlʾh hlkty* ...); cf. on these sentences also G. Khan, *Studies in Semitic Syntax*, London Oriental Series vol. 38, Oxford 1988, p. 68.

[28] Tomlin, *o.c.*, passim.

[29] The most important objection being that Tomlin does not explain why there are still VSO languages left; modern Hebrew, however, might be adduced in favour of this supposition, cf. L. Glinert, *The Grammar of Modern Hebrew*, Cambridge 1989, p. 413: "Basic word order in all registers is: Subject + Verb/Adjective + Object.

[30] This is the normal way to express the present and past tense, cf. "y maent yn rhedeg" = [PART] they-are [PREP] run = they run /are running; "y maent wedi rhedeg" = [PART] they-are [PREP after] run = they ran/have run; cf. on this account R. Raney, *VSO and SVO order in Welsh and Breton, Papers and Studies in Contrastive Linguistics 18*, Poznań, 1984, pp. 47-54, who remarks (p. 51): ... note that Welsh is syntactically a VSO language, but semantically often SVO.

by Classical Hebrew and Welsh as a result of a chance convergence of two different developments, or as the result of a typological probability that has been broken up in the two languages as a result of different influences into two diverging developments.

# *Qal/Pe‘al* as the Passive of *Hif‘il/Af‘el* in Mishnaic Hebrew and Middle Aramaic

C. Meehan, Jerusalem

1.0 As is generally recognized, there is a radical reduction in the use of internal passives and their corresponding verbal stems *pu‘‘al*[1] and *hof‘al* in Mishnaic Hebrew (= MH) and Middle Aramaic (= MA). In MH *pu‘‘al* has been replaced for the most part by *nitpa‘‘al*, which serves as the passive-reflexive of *pi‘‘el*. Thus קידש /*qiddeš*/ "he sanctified, betrothed (a woman)" contrasts with נתקדש(ה) /*nitqaddaš*/ "it was, got sanctified (she was, got betrothed)"[2]. Only the present participle *mĕfu‘‘al*[3] remains intact but is now chiefly used to indicate a result or state, i.e. מקודש(ת) "sanctified, betrothed". It is true that *hof‘al* is still attested in all tenses of the verb but there are definite signs of its receding in the "past" (*qaṭal*) and especially in the "future" (*yiqṭol*)[4] and its relationship with *hif‘il* in no way parallels the close symmetry existing between *pi‘‘el* and *nitpa‘‘al*, as there are many *hif‘il* forms with no corresponding *hof‘al*[5]. The participle once again denotes a result or state but has no counterpart indicating an occurence, like the relationship between *mitpa‘‘* el and *mĕfu‘‘al*[6].

These trends in MH are usually attributed to the influence of Ara-

---

[1] Although *pu‘‘al* is not attested for early Aramaic, its existence, at least as far as the participle is concerned, may be assumed from the fact that it appears in the Yemenite tradition of Biblical and Babylonian Aramaic and in most dialects of Eastern Neo-Aramaic (at least as a reflex). Cf. Sh. Morag, "A Babylonian-Yemenite Manuscript of the Book of Daniel" in the *Henoch Yalon Memorial Volume*, Jerusalem, 1974, p. 258-9 [Hebrew].

[2] Cf. S. Sharvit, "The Tense System of Mishnaic Hebrew" in G. Sarfatti, P. Artzi, J. Greenfield, M. Kaddari (ed.), *Studies in Hebrew and Semitic Languages*, Ramat-Gan 1980, p. 110–125 [Hebrew].

[3] For a thorough discussion of this form, cf. R. Mirkin, "*Mĕfu‘‘al* Forms", in *Leshonenu 32* (1967-1968), p. 140-152.

[4] The Concordance for Tannaitic Hebrew of the Academy of the Hebrew Language, Jerusalem lists 936 occurences of *hof‘al* in the Mishna for 81 different roots but only 5 occurences distributed over 4 roots (*’gd, ndḥ, ntṣ, pqd*) for *yiqṭol*. There are 144 occurences (33 roots) for *qaṭal* and the remaining are for the participle (787 x).

[5] Cf. section 8.1 and note 46.

[6] Cf. section 8.1.

maic but it is still a moot question whether we have to do here with direct influence or simply with a parallel morphosyntactic drift in both languages[7]. If the system of verbal stems in MH does in fact reflect Aramaic influence, then the adstratum of Aramaic in question must have been a much earlier phase of the language than that represented by any known MA dialect. In Biblical Aramaic *hofʿal* is still very much alive; there are ten examples for a comparatively limited corpus (only ten chapters of the Bible), whereas several centuries later in the Aramaic of Qumran it has for all practical purposes disappeared[8]. Thus the situation in MH in which *hofʿal* is on the wane reflects a stage in the development of Aramaic posterior to Biblical Aramaic but prior to late Qumran Aramaic.

The usual assumption among Semitists is that during the period of Old and Imperial Aramaic both *hofʿal* and *ittafʿal* (or rather the T-stem of the causative) existed side by side[9]. There are several difficulties inherent in such a supposition:

1. Aramaic is the only branch of the Semitic languages (excluding a few Aramaic calques in MH; cf. below, section 8.1) which derives a T-stem from a H/ʾ causative (in spite of what Brockelmann seems to imply for Arabic in note 9) and consequently this phenomenon should most likely be considered an innovation rather than an inherited diachronic feature[10].

2. There are no more than two words in the entire corpus of Old, Imperial and Qumran Aramaic which can be legitimately interpreted as T–H/ʾstems of regular verbs and even in these two cases there is disagreement among scholars.

---

[7] Cf. E.Y. Kutscher, *A History of the Hebrew Language*, Jerusalem, Leiden 1982, p. 119-120, 131-2.

[8] We must distinguish here between the Book(s) of Enoch and later Qumran compositions such as Targum Job and the Genesis Apocryphon. *Hofʿal/ofʿal* forms are still attested in Enoch for, e.g. *ybl* (3x) and *ḥzʾ* (4 or 5x), (cf. J.T. Milik, *The Books of Enoch*, Oxford 1976, p. 376, 378 and references) whereas they have disappeared in the later works. The two sections of the Books of Enoch attested in Qumran "must have been composed by the third century at the latest". (M.E. Stone, *Scriptures, Sects and Visions*, New York, etc. 1980, p. 31.) Targum Job has been dated to c. 100 B.C.E. by its editors and Kutscher places the Genesis Apocryphon in the first century B.C.E. (Cf. M. Sokoloff, *The Targum to Job from Qumran Cave XI*, Ramat-Gan 1974, p. 9 and note 4 for a summary and references.)

[9] Cf. C. Brockelmann, *Grundriss der vergleichenden Grammatik der semitischen Sprachen*, Berlin 1908, Vol. I, p. 540: "Das im Altarab. und *Aram.* rein erhalten System der Verbalstämme — Grundstamm, Intensiv- (Ziel-), *Kausativstamm* mit je einem *Passiv* und einem *Reflexiv* —..."

[10] Cf. M.H. Goshen-Gottstein, "The System of Verbal Stems in the Classical Semitic Languages", in the *Proceedings of the International Conference on Semitic Studies 1965*, Jerusalem 1969, p. 88 and especially note 85.

3. There are no attestations of *ettafʿal* forms for *regular* verbs in early Syriac literature, i.e. the Peshitta of the Hebrew Bible, etc, and consequently *ettafʿal* can hardly be considered an integral part of the basic verbal *system* of Syriac at this period[11].

If *hofʿal* had already fallen into disuse and *ittafʿal* had not yet come into its own, how did early MA express the passive of *afʿel*? The intention of this article is to show that *qal/peʿal* forms frequently served this purpose in MA and MH[12], especially in verbs of motion, the only constraint being that the agent be not explicitly stated[13]; in this latter case transitive *hifʿil/afʿel* forms were most likely used instead.

I shall discuss the following basic Hebrew verbs of motion (roots) plus their Aramaic counterparts: בוא (נכנס) / אתא, עלל "come, enter"; הלך / אזל "go"; יבל / יבל "lead"; יצא / נפק "go out"; ירד / נחת "go down, descend"; ישב / / יתב "sit (down)"; עלה / סלק "go up, ascend"; עבר / עבר "pass, go by"; עמד, קום / קום "stand (up)"; קרב / קרב "approach"[14].

2.0 In the story of Judah and Tamar in Genesis 38, after discovering what Tamar had done, Judah orders her in verse 24 "to be brought out and burned", and in verse 25 we read: "But as she *was being brought out*, she sent word to her father-in-law...". The Masoretic text (=MT) employs a *hofʿal* form here. Note the various translations proffered by the ancient versions[15]:

---

[11] I intend to deal with these questions and the development of *ittafʿal* in general in a separate article.

[12] This usage has already been posited for MH by M. Mishor, cf. section 8.1.

[13] We might term such forms "anti-causatives"; as such they exhibit many features of ergativity. Cf. J. Lyons, *Introduction to Theoretical Linguistics*, Cambridge 1968, p. 350-371. I have limited my inquiry to MH and MA but similar forms are attested in other Semitic languages. Cf. A. Dillmann, *Ethiopic Grammar*, London 1907, §76, p. 143. Fore-runners are found already in BH, cf. note 24.

[14] I excluded the verbal root *npl* "fall" from my discussion in this article for lack of space — most of the examples I discovered were from this root. It also presents several syntactic complications; it is my intention to devote a separate article to this root.

[15] In this article I have consulted the following editions of texts:

Targum Onqelos and Jonathan to the Prophets: ed. A.Sperber, *The Bible in Aramaic*, Vols. I-III, Leiden 1959-1962.

The Palestinian Targum: a) Geniza Fragments: ed. M.L. Klein, *Geniza Manuscripts of Palestinian Targum to the Pentateuch*, Cincinnati 1986. (G = Geniza plus the siglum of Ms. in parentheses). b) Ms. Neophyti: ed. A. Díez Macho, *Neophyti 1*, Vols. 1-5, Madrid-Barcelona 1968-1978. c) Fragment-Targums: ed. M.L. Klein, *The Fragment-Targums of the Pentateuch*, Rome 1980 (P = Ms. Paris 110; V = Ms. Vatican 440).

Targum Pseudo-Jonathan: ed. E.G. Clarke, *Targum Pseudo-Jonathan of the Pen-*

MT והוא מוצאת והיא שלחה אל־חמיה .
Targum Onqelos (=Onq) מתפקא
= Targum Pseudo-Jonathan (= PsJ) מתאפקא
Palestinian Targum (= PT) G(E) נפקת + למתוקדה
= Ms Neophyti (=Neoph) = V ≈ P
G(D) הות נפקא [למתו] קדה
Samaritan Targum (= Sam T) Ms J נפקת B מפקה
E אתפקת A נפיקה
The Peshitta (= Pesh) *wkd hnwn mpqyn lh.*
The Septuagint (LXX) ἀγομένη
= The Syro-Hexapla (=Syr H) *mttyty*ʾ.
The Vulgate: cum duceretur ad poenam.

Onq and Ps J translate literally, i.e. they both employ the *ittafʿal* present participle of נפק, corresponding exactly to the *hofʿal* participle of יצא. Similarly the LXX is a fairly straightforward rendering, using the present passive participle i.e. "being led (out)", which in turn is translated faithfully by the Syr H's *ittafʿal* participle of אתא. The Vulgate likewise has a passive form: "when she was being led to punishment".

The PT and the principle manuscript of the Sam T, on the other hand, employ *active peʿal* forms of נפק to translate the *hofʿal*, i.e. G(E), Neoph, V and P: "(when) she went out te be burned (by fire)" which corresponds to SamT Ms J "she went out", G(D) has "she was

*tateuch*, Hoboken, New Jersey 1984.

Samaritan Targum: ed. A. Tal, *The Samaritan Targum of the Pentateuch*, Parts I-II, Tel-Aviv 1980-1981.

The Peshiṭta: ed. Peshiṭta Institute, Leiden, *The Old Testament in Syriac according to the Peshiṭta Version*, Leiden 1972 sqq. (where available — otherwise ed. Urmia 1852).

Septuagint: ed. Göttingen, *Vetus Testamentum Graecum Auctoritate Societatis Litterarum Gottingensis editum*, Göttingen 1931 sqq. (where available — otherwise ed. A. Rahlfs, *Septuaginta*, Stuttgart$^5$ 1952).

Vulgate: *Biblia Sacra juxta Vulgatam versionem*, Stuttgart $^2$1975.

Syro-Hexapla: 1) ed. A. Vööbus, *The Pentateuch in the Version of the Syro-Hexapla*, Louvain 1975. 2) ed. P. de Lagarde, *Bibliothecae Syriacae quae ad philologiam sacram pertinent*, Göttingen 1892.

NT, Greek: ed. K. Aland, etc., *Novum Testamentum Graece* (Nestle-Aland), Stuttgart$^{26}$ 1979.

NT, Old Syriac: ed. A.S. Lewis, *The Old Syriac Gospels or Evangelion da-Mepharreshē*, London 1910.

CPA texts are quoted according to the sources indicated in the Scriptural Index to F. Schulthess, *Lexicon Syropalaestinum*, Berlin 1903, p. vii-xvi. Rabbinic texts are quoted according to the texts in the data bank of the Academy of the Hebrew Language, Jerusalem.

going out to be burned"[16]. Note that I use an active form in my English translation, but this simply serves as a gloss of the original. A far more accurate rendering would be "(when) she was brought out, etc.", for as will be made abundantly clear in the course of this article the *pe‘al* form functions here as the counterpart of the *hof‘al* form in the Biblical text, i.e. as an anti-causative.

Note that the Pesh likewise has difficulty in translating the *hof‘al* form and prefers to render it with the active *af‘el* participle plus pronominal object pronoun: "and while they were bringing her out". This contrasts strikingly with the use of the *ettaf‘al* by the Syr H and as we shall see, this is not simply coincidental; as pointed out above, the use of *ettaf‘al* was still quite restricted in the early stages of Syriac. As regards the basic verbs of motion I could find no attestations for *ettaf‘al* in the entire corpus of the Pesh of the Hebrew Bible[17].

3.0 To make all this adequately clear, let us consider some of the renderings of *hof‘al* in the Aramaic versions of the Bible. Let us start with the Aramaic portions of Daniel and Ezra and their equivalents in the Pesh.

There are ten examples of *hof‘al* in the Aramaic portions of Daniel and Ezra, six instances with verbs of motion and four others.

3.1 In four of the six cases from the first category the Pesh circumvents the problem by using active *af‘el* forms, e.g.:

3.11 Dan. 3:13 באדין גבריא אלך הֵיתָיו קדם מלכא, "then these men *were brought* before the king". Pesh: *w’ytyw ’nwn*, "and they *brought* them" and likewise in Dan. 6:18.

3.12 Dan. 6:24 וְהֻסַּק דניאל מִן־גבא, "and Daniel was *taken up* from the den". Pesh: *w’sqwhy ldny’yl*, "and they *took* Daniel *up*" and similarly in Dan. 5:15 for the root עלל. Note that in all four instances (as in all ten as a matter of fact) the agent is not explicitly mentioned.

3.2 In the last two cases, however, the Pesh employs a *pe‘al* form to render the *hof‘al*.

[16] See also Genesis Rabba (ed. J. Theodor-Ch. Albeck, *Midrash Bereshit Rabba*, Jerusalem ²1965, p. 1045): *’mr r’ hwn’. hy’ mwṣ’t ’tmh’. hy’ whw’ ṣrykyn lṣ’t.* "R. Huna said 'She was being brought out'? Both *she* and *he* should have been brought out (lit. to go out)". Likewise in the Midrash Haggadol, Genesis (ed. M. Margulies, Jerusalem 1975, p. 650, line 11): *hyh r’wy lmqr’ lwmr hy’ yṣ’t*, "The Scripture should have stated: 'She was brought out (lit. went out)'". For the past form cf. the principal readings in the PT and Ms. J in the Sam T.

[17] Except for the verb *’ttwtb* "settle, sojourn", which appears in all the Targums (cf. Gen. 19:9, Onq, Ps-J., Neoph, Sam T and Pesh) and which is traditionally considered as the *ittaf‘al* of *ytb* but which is possibly better understood as a denominative of *twtb* "sojourner, resident".

3.21 Dan. 5:20 הָנְחַת מִן־כָּרְסֵא מַלְכוּתֵהּ, "he *was deposed* (brought down) from his royal throne". Pesh: *nḥt* lit. "he *descended*" = "he *was deposed*".

3.22 Dan. 5:13 בֵּאדַיִן דָּנִיֵּאל הֻעַל קֳדָם מַלְכָּא, "then Daniel *was brought in* before the king". Pesh: *hydyn dny᾽yl ‘l qdm mlk᾽*, lit. "then Daniel *went in* before the king" = "he *was made to enter* , *brought in*".

3.3 The four remaining examples (other than verbs of motion) are equally noteworthy:

3.31 Dan. 7:11 וְהוּבַד גֶּשְׁמַהּ, "and its body *was destroyed*". Pesh: *w᾽bd gwšmh*, "and its body *perished* (= *was destroyed*)". Note once again the *pe‘al* form to render the *hof‘al*.

3.32 Ezra 4:15 עַל־דְּנָה קִרְיְתָא דָךְ הָחָרְבַת, "because of this that city *was laid waste*". Pesh: *mṭl hn᾽ mdynt᾽ hy dḥrbt*, "because of this it was the city that *became waste* (= *was laid waste*)", again substituting a *pe‘al* and adding a further syntactical reinterpretation.

3.33 And last but not least the two examples from Dan 4:33 ועל מַלְכוּתִי הָתְקְנַת (variant = הָתְקְנֵת) ורבו יתירה הוּסְפַת־לִי, "and I *was established* (= variant) in my kingdom and surpassing greatness *was added* to me". Pesh: *w‘l mlkwty tqnt wrbwt᾽ ytyrt᾽ ᾽ttwspt ly*, which corresponds to the English translation above with the sole exception that the first verb is rendered by *pe‘al*. The rendering for the second verb is quite astonishing. After employing every trick at its disposal, so to speak, to circumvent the first nine cases of *hof‘al* in the Biblical text, the Pesh suddenly does an about-face and uses a *bona fide ettaf‘al* form of *ysp* to render the *hof‘al* of this same root. Can it be just a coincidence that this is the only root for which an *ittaf‘al* is attested in Tannaitic MH (cf. below, section 8.1)? I do not wish to dwell on this question here but I might point out that *ittaf‘al* forms of first-yod verbs seem to play a central role in the development of this verbal stem in MA.

4.0 Now a similar tendency to substitute *qal* for *hof‘al* forms in verbs of motion can be detected in the Isaiah scroll from Qumran. E.Y. Kutscher characterized this text as a popular version of the book of Isaiah, that "modernized" and updated the MT to fit the linguistic situation prevailing in Palestine during the last centuries B.C.E. and many of whose features prefigure linguistic traits found later in MH[18]. Although the material is somewhat limited in scope, it is sufficient to point up the general drift away from the use of *hof‘al* which took place in Hebrew during this period.

[18] E.Y. Kutscher, *The Language and Linguistic Background of the Isaiah Scroll (1QIsa$^a$)*, Leiden 1974, p. 73-77, 363-4.

4.1 *Hofʿal* forms appear in Isaiah (MT) for the following verbs of motion: יבל, ירד, ישׁב.

4.11 יבל — In two out of the three occurences, i.e. Is. 18:7 and 53:7 the scroll has the same *ktiv* as the MT, namely יובל; but for Is. 55:12 ובשׁלום תובלון, "and in peace you shall be led" the Isaiah scroll reads: ובשׁלום תלכו, "and in peace you shall go" which agrees with the reading of the Pesh: t'zlwn[19]. In other words the *hofʿal* form has been replaced by *qal*[20].

4.12 ישׁב

4.121 Is. 5:8 והושׁבתם לבדכם בקרב הארץ, "and you *will be made to dwell* alone in the midst of the land". The scroll reads here ושׁתים [21] (= ותבשׁם ?), "and you will dwell" = Pesh wttbwn, LXX μὴ οἰκήσετε, "shall you dwell?" = Vulgate: Numquid habitabitis; and compare the Targum reading: ומדמן דיתבון, "imagining that they will dwell".

4.122 Is. 44:26 האמר לירושׁלם תושׁב, "who says to Jerusalem: she shall be inhabited". The scroll reads: תשׁב. "she shall inhabit".

4.13 ירד — The *hofʿal* forms of this root present no difficulty, on the surface. For Is. 14:15 the scroll reads תורד as in MT and for the MT reading הורד in Is. 14:11, it is defective: הר [ ], which should probably be restored as הורד in accordance with MT (the right side of the *he* is clearly visible on the photograph) and not ירד, the reading reflected in the LXX[22].

5.0 The Targums and Other Versions of the Torah

The Jewish Targums and that of the Samaritans often render *hofʿal* of verbs of motion with a matching *ittafʿal* but there is considerable discrepancy in usage and frequency in this matter between the PT and

---

[19] Of course the Pesh reading is ambiguous and could reflect either MT or the scroll. Cf. M.H. Gottstein, "Die Jesaia-Rolle im Lichte von Peschitta und Targum", *Biblica 35* (1954), p. 63.

[20] It would seem that the *qal* of *hlk* (*peʿal* of *'zl*) serves to supplete the *hofʿal* (*afʿel*) of *ybl* here since in BH *ybl* appears only in *hofʿal* and *hifʿil* but never in *qal*. There are only 7 occurences of *hifʿil* as against 11 for *hofʿal* - a clearly lop-sided ratio considering the rarity of *hofʿal*. On the other hand, *hwlyk*, the *hifʿil* of *hlk*, appears 46 times in the Bible, whereas there is not a single occurence of *hofʿal*. Observe also that in the Targums *'wbl* frequently translates *hwlyk* (cf. Num. 17:11, 2 Kings 6:19, etc.).

[21] Cf. Kutscher, *Isaiah Scroll*, p. 246 - probably a scribal error for *wyšbtm*.

[22] LXX: κατέβη; the Pesh reads *nḥt*, which could reflect either the *qal* or *hofʿal* form as usual. This is not the place to discuss whether the LXX here reflects a different Vorlage or is simply an interpretation on the translational level. Cf. the note to Is. 5:8 in the edition of Isaiah of the Hebrew University Bible Project: "difficulty in rendering *hofʿal*, hardly *hyšbtm*".

the Sam T, on the one hand, and Onq and Ps J, on the other. The latter employ *ittafʿal* forms as a rule, whereas the PT, similar to the Pesh, frequently circumvents *hofʿal* by using active *afʿel* forms and even *peʿal* in a few cases. This is also true to some extent for the Sam T but neither the PT not the Sam T are as consistent in this matter as the Pesh, which employs *peʿal* and *afʿel* transformations as a matter of course since early Syriac apparently possessed no *ettafʿal* for verbs of motion; only when lexically feasible does it employ an occasional *etpeʿel/etpaʿʿal* form[23].

5.1.Onqelos

Although I discovered no examples of *peʿal* functioning as an anti-causative in Onq, it should nevertheless be pointed out that this Targum does in fact interpret *qal* forms of verbs of motion in the MT as the passive of *hifʿil* in three places: i.e. Ex. 22:5 תצא : יתפק; Lev. 2:12 יעלו[24]: יתסקון [25]; Num. 31:23 אשר יבא: דמתעל [26].

5.2 The Palestinian Targum

The use of *ittafʿal* for verbs of motion is considerably more restricted in the PT than in Onq. In Onq it is attested for the following roots: אתא, נחת, נפק, סלק, עלל and קום [27], whereas in the PT we only find forms for נחת and עלל [28], i.e. אתוחת - G(E) Gen. 39:1 (MT

[23] E.g. *ʾtdbr* "he was led", the *etpeʿel* of the *peʿal dbr* "he led", to render the *hofʿal* of *ybl* in Is. 53:7; Jer. 11:19 and Job 21:30 and in the NT as a rendering of the passive of ἄγω "lead"and its compounds. Cf. Romans 8:14, I Corinth. 12:2 and 2 Timothy 3:6.

[24] The use of the *qal* of *ʿlh* as an anti-causative seems to be quite widespread even in BH. Cf. 1 Kings 18:29, 2 Kings 3:20, Is. 60:7 and the other examples cited in the dictionary of Brown, Driver and Briggs, p. 748b, §6. Observe also the use of *hšb* in Gen. 43:18 as against *hmwšb* in verse 12. Note that most of the ancient versions translate both verbs with the same rendering; the LXX, Onq, PT G(D) and Neoph all render both as passives whereas the Pesh has *peʿal* twice (again ambiguous). The Samaritan version reads *hmwšb* in both verses!!

[25] Cf. also Sam T, Ms. J and LXX.

[26] Cf. also Sam T, Ms. J.

[27] The *hofʿal* of *ybl*, *ʿbr*, *ʿlh* and *yšb* do not appear in the Torah and that of *hlk* and *npl* not at all in BH or MH. In regard to the "*ittafʿal*" of *ytb* cf. note 17.

[28] Klein (*Geniza Manuscripts*, p. 303-305) includes a fragment of Ex. 40 under the siglum G(D), which has an *ittafʿal* of *qwm* for verse 17 as in Onq but a careful perusal of this text will show that it is a fragment of Onq and not of the PT.

Although much of the language usage of this fragment is common to both Onq and PT there are *absolutely no* readings which are typical of PT. On the other hand, there are a significant number of readings which *are* typical of Onq. Note the typically Onq pronominal suffix *-why* (as against *-wy* in PT) in vss. 9, 10, 14, 18, 19, 23, 27 and the conjunction *kmʾ d(y)* (PT = *hyk mh d-*) in vss. 15, 21, 23, 25; *wyhy* (PT = *wyhwy*) in vss. 9, 10. With regard to lexemes and translational equivalents cf. *ʿbrwhy* vs. 18 (= MT *bryḥyw*) (PT = *ngrwy*); *šydʾ* vss. 22, 24 (= MT *yrk*(PT = *špwlwy, sṭrwy*); *[w]ʾdlyq* vs. 25 (= MT *wyʿl*) (PT = *sdr*); *[wʾ]qṭr* vs. 27 (MT = *wyqṭr*)

הורד )[29] and מתעלין .... אתעלו G(D), Neoph Gen 43:18 (MT מובאים ... הובאו ) (Cf. likewise Neoph Lev. 6:23; 10:18; 11:32) and אתועל [30] - Neoph Lev. 16:27; (Cf. also Neoph Margin (=M) Lev. 6:23; 11:32; 13:9 and 14:2) - all renderings of the *hof‘al* of בוא . In a considerable number of cases the PT (i.e. Ms Neoph) renders the *hof‘al* passive with active *af‘el* forms and in many instances it is difficult to decide whether this reflects a different underlying Vorlage or simply an interpretation on the translational level [31].

Besides the one discussed in section 2.0 there are five other examples of anti-causatives in the PT, all from Ms. Neoph.

5.21 Lev. 13:2,9; 14:2 והובא אל־(אהרן) הכהן, "and he shall be *brought* to (Aaron) the priest".

Neoph: וייתי (3x) = Sam T, MB (3x) = LXX 13:9 ἥξει "he shall come"; Neoph M 13:2 ותיעול [32].

5.22 Num. 10:17 והורד המשכן, "(whenever) the tabernacle *was taken down*". Neoph M נחת "came down"; Neoph: מתפרק = Onq "was dismantled".

5.3 The Samaritan Targum

Besides Gen. 38:25 there are six further occurences in the Sam T in which *pe‘al* renders Hebrew *hof‘al* in verbs of motion:

5.31 Gen. 39:1 הורד — Sam T, A נחת

5.32 Gen. 43:18 מובאים — Sam T, A עללין

5.33 Lev. 11:32 יובא — Sam T, VNMCB ייעל

5.34 Lev. 13:2,9; 14:2 והובא— Sam T, MB (V 14:2) וייתי(cf. 5.21).

---

(PT = *sdr*); *ḥwp*’*h* vs. 19 (= MT *mksh*) (PT = *ḥpyy, ḥpwy*). These considerations render Klein's typically PT restorations, such as *l[šymwš* ‘*lm ldryhwn]*in vs. 15 and *ḥwmrw]hy* in vs. 18 highly suspect. (The entries ’*ytqm* (p.481) and ‘*br* "bar, bolt" (p. 394) should be deleted from Sokoloff's new dictionary (note 53); Sokoloff correctly lists neither *šyd*’, ’*qṭr* not *ḥwp*’*h*.)

[29] In Gen. 39:1 Neoph reads *hwnḥt*, apparently a borrowing from Dan. 5:20.

[30] Note the first-yod forms for both verbs; cf. section 3.33.

[31] In Ex. 27:7 MT reads *whwb*’ and the Samaritan version *whb*’*t*; LXX, Vulgate, Onq, Neoph and Pesh have the equivalent of the Samaritan reading; likewise for Gen. 33:11 (MT = *hb*’*t*, Samaritan = *hb*’*ty* but here Onq = MT) and Lev. 16:10 (MT = *y*‘*md*, Samaritan = *y*‘*myd*); LXX, Vulgate and Neoph interpret as *y*‘*mydhw* (Onq and Pesh = MT). In these cases it is very difficult to ascertain whether we have simply an interpretation on the translational level or the reflex of a diachronically real but secondary variant that has survived on the interpretative level. On the other hand, the *af*‘*el* construction in Neoph for Ex. 40:17 is patently interpretational.

[32] One would expect the masc. form *wyy*‘*wl*; this reading may in fact be an error for *wytw*‘*l*. Cf. Neoph M Lev. 13:9: 14:2. Cf. also the discussion of J. Yahalom (*Leshonenu* 45 (1980), pp. 27-28; see also note 69) of Lev. 14:2 and Ex. 40:17 in Midrash Tanḥuma where the *hof*‘*als* of these verses are interpreted as *qal* anti-causatives.

5.4 The Peshitta

The Pesh employs *pe‘al* to render *hof‘al* of verbs of motion in the following verses:

5.41 MT = *hof‘al* of בוא // Pesh = *pe‘al* of עלל : Lev. 6:23; 10:18 and 16:27.

5.42 MT = hof‘al of עמד // Pesh = *pe‘al* of קום : Lev. 16:10

5.43 MT = *hof‘al* of קום // Pesh = *pe‘al* of קום : Ex. 40:17.

5.44 MT = *hof‘al* of שוב // Pesh = *pe‘al* of הפך : Gen. 43:12.

5.5 The Syro-Hexapla

Since the Syr H version of the LXX is relatively late (early 7th century)[33], one would naturally expect a notable increase in the use of *ettaf‘al* forms, comparable with what we find in the Harklean version of the NT (cf. 7.1). As a matter of fact the only *ettaf‘al* form for verbs of motion that is extensively attested is *’ttyty* (< *’t’*); cf. Gen. 38:25; Lev. 13:2 and Ez. 30:18[34]. For κατήχθη in Gen. 39:1 (MT הורד we find *’tnḥt* (vocalised as *etpa‘‘al* in the Ms.) and *’t‘ll* (vocalised as *etpe‘el* or *etpa‘‘al*?) frequently serves as the passive of εἰσάγω and εἰσφέρω "lead in, bring in"[35] (both are renderings of the *hof‘al* of בוא). What is surprising, however, is the fact that we still encounter a fair number of *pe‘al* forms which render the passive of Greek causative verbs:

5.51 הפך — Gen. 43:12,18.

5.52 עלל — Lev. 6:23; 10:18; 16:27.

5.53 קום — Ex. 40:17; Num. 9:15.

Notice that in all seven cases the Pesh also has *pe‘al* of the same root; are we to attribute the occurences in the Syr H to the influence of the Pesh?

6.0 Syriac and Christian Palestinian Aramaic (= CPA) renderings of non-Pentateuchal portions of the Hebrew Bible and Septuagint[36].

6.1 בוא

6.11 = עלל

The Pesh renders the *hof‘al* of בוא with the *pe‘al* of עלל in the following non-Pentateuchal verses: 2 Kings 12:5,10,14,17; 22:4; 2 Chron. 34:9,14 in contrast with the *ittaf‘al* form for all these verses in the Targum.

---

33 Cf. Vööbus, *Syro-Hexapla*, p. 10-13.

34 See also the examples listed by Payne-Smith, p. 416-7 and likewise p. 2806 - Amos 3:12 *ntt‘dwn* "be snatched away" (< *‘d’* "pass") but this question warrants further study.

35 Gen. 43:18 (twice); 2 Kings 12:14,17; 22:4 (but *pe‘al* in 2 Kings 12:5 = Pesh; cf. below 6.11).

36 For further examples from the Pesh cf. above section 4.0 - 4.13.

6.12 = אתא

The *pe'al* of אתא serves in this function for Jer. 10:9; Ez. 23:42; 30:11 and 40:4. Observe that the Targum likewise has *pe'al* for Ez. 23:42 and 30:11.

6.13 = אזל

In Jer. 27:22 the Pesh renders יובאו with *n'zlwn*; the Targum has the *ittaf'al* of יבל here.

6.2 יבל

The Pesh likewise employs the *pe'al* of אזל to render the *hof'al* of יבל. Cf. Is. 55:12 (above 4.11); Ps. 45:15,16 and Job 21:32. The last three verses are of special interest since the CPA translation for them is extant.

6.21 Ps. 45:15-16

לרקמות תובל למלך בתלות אחריה רעותיה
מובאות לך:
תובלנה בשׂמחת וגיל תבאינה בהיכל מלך:

"In embroidered garments she *is led* into the king; maids in her train, her companions, *are brought* to you. (vs.16) With gladness and joy they *are led in*; they enter the king's palace".

The Pesh renders the two *hof'als* of *ybl* with the *pe'al* of *'zl*[37]; the four verbs are translated as follows: *t'zl* ... *wnwblwn* ... *n'zln* ... *wn'lwn*.

6.211 The LXX (= Ps. 44) renders the first three verbs with the future passive of ἀποφέρω "carry back, off" and the last with the future passive of ἄγω "lead".

The CPA[38] has for the first three verbs the *pe'al* of אזל and for the last the *pe'al* of אתא, four successive instances of an anti-causative, i.e.: *wy'zlyn* ... *yzlyn* ... *y'zlyn* ..*wy'twn*

6.22 Job 21:32 והוא לקברות יובל "and he is borne to the grave". Pesh: *'āzel* (part) = CPA (the latter rendering LXX ἀπηνέχθη, the aorist passive of ἀποφέρω again) [39].

6.3 ירד

The Pesh renders the *hof'al* of ירד with the *pe'al* of נחת in Is. 14:11,15 and Ez. 31:18. Similarly the LXX renders the two verses in Isaiah as if they were *qal* forms and for Ez. 31 has a double reading:

---

[37] Cf. note 20.

[38] The CPA version is of course a translation based on the LXX.

[39] Note also that in Is. 53:7 the CPA renders LXX ἤχθη (MT *ywbl*) with *'t'* the *pe'al* participle. Cf. also v. 8.

κατάβηθι καὶ καταβιβάσθητι "descend and be brought down" for MT והורדת.

6.4 יצא
In Jer. 38:22 מוצאות is rendered *npqn* in the Pesh.

6.5 עלה
In Nahum 2:8 the Pesh renders the *hof'al* form with the *pe'al* of סלק and agrees with the LXX which has an intransitive form.

6.6 שוב
The Pesh renders מושבים in Jer. 27:16 as *hpkyn*, the *pe'al* of הפך "return".

6.7 In 1 Kings 22:35 the Pesh translates the *hof'al* participle of עמד with the *pe'al* active participle of *qwm*; a similar rendering appears in the Targum.

7.0 Syriac and CPA — the Translations of the New Testament (= NT)

The following are examples for our usage which I found in the Old Syriac, Pesh and CPA translations of the NT[40]:

7.1 אתא
2 Peter 1:21 οὐ γὰρ θελήματι ἀνθρώπου ἠνέχθη προφητεία ποτέ, "for no prophesy *was* ever *produced, uttered* (lit. brought) through human will". Pesh: *ʾtt*, lit. "came". Note that the Harclean version of the NT in Syriac has *ettaf'al* here: *ʾttytyt*[41]. Similarly in vss 17 and 18 of this same chapter the text speaks of a "voice produced", employing once again the aorist passive of φέρω. In both instances the Pesh translates *ʾtʾ lh*.

7.2 נפק
7.21 Math. 8:12 οἱ δὲ υἱοὶ τῆς βασιλείας ἐκβληθήσονται εἰς τὸ σκότος τὸ ἐξώτερον, "but the children of the kingdom *shall be cast out* into

---

[40] For the latest discussion of the relation between the Old Syriac and Pesh of the NT, see J. Joosten, *The Syriac Language of the Peshitta and Old Syriac Versions of Matthew*, doctoral dissertation, The Hebrew University of Jerusalem 1988. He dates the Old Syriac version to the third century and the Pesh to the end of the fourth (both hypothetical, p. 16). Cf. also B. Metzger, *The Early Versions of the New Testament*, Oxford 1977, p. 3-4.

[41] Cf. Payne-Smith p. 416. This version dates from the beginning of the seventh century (cf. Metzger, *Early Versions*, p. 69) and is therefore considerably more recent than the Old Syriac and Pesh. (Note that a good number of Payne-Smith's examples for *ettaf'al* of this and other roots are culled from either the Syr H or the Harclean version, both relatively late Syriac works.)

the darkness outside". Old Syriac: *npqwn* = Pesh ≈ CPA *ypqwn* (variant = *ypwqwn*) — all *pe῾al* forms. The Harclean version has *ettaf῾al* again: *nttpqwn*[42].

7.22 Luke 13:28 ὑμᾶς δὲ ἐκβαλλομένους ἔξω, "while you *are cast out*". CPA: *w᾽twn npqyn lbr*; using the *pe῾al* active participle.

7.23 Math. 9:25 ὅτε δὲ ἐξεβλήθη ὁ ὄχλος, "and when the crowd *had been put out*". CPA: *npq*, lit. "went out"[43].

7.3 סלק - I have but one example:
Luke 24:51 καὶ ἀνεφέρετο εἰς τὸν οὐρανόν, "and he was taken up to heaven". Pesh: *wslq lšmy᾽*[44].

Non Translational Material

8.0 Mishnaic Hebrew, Galilean Aramaic and Babylonian Aramaic

8.1 M. Mishor has already drawn attention to this phenomenon in MH in his doctoral dissertation[45]. On pp. 204-206 (paragraph 4.05) he points out that the *hof῾al*[46] participle in MH usually has a perfective meaning denoting a state or the result of an action. The other two passive participles, the *qal* and the *pu῾῾al* have complementary forms, i.e. the *nif῾al* and *nitpa῾῾al* participles, indicating an occurence or entrance into a state, i.e. the dynamic aspect of the activity involved. Thus כתוב "is, has been written" is paralleled by נכתב "is being, shall be written" and מקובל "is, has been accepted, received" is balanced by מתקבל "is being, shall be accepted, received"[47]. As a counterpart to the stative *muf῾al* one would accordingly expect a form such as *mittaf῾al*, the participle of *nittaf῾al*, corresponding analogically to the symmetrical relation between *maf῾al/mittaf῾al* in MA dialects[48].

[42] Notice however that there is a variant reading here: ἐξελεύσονται "will go out". Might this be a Semiticism in NT Greek? For the Harclean reading see Payne-Smith, p. 2424.

[43] One might add here the use in CPA of the *pe῾al* of *npq* to render ἀποσυνάγωγος "be expelled or excommunicated from the synagogue" in John 9:22; 12:42.

[44] The phrase is lacking in most Mss. of the NT and in the Old Syriac. The CPA employs the *etpa῾῾al* of *slq* here.

[45] M. Mishor, *The Tense System in Tannaitic Hebrew*, doctoral dissertation, The Hebrew University of Jerusalem, 1983 [Hebrew].

[46] According to the Concordance for Tannaitic Hebrew of the Academy of the Hebrew Language, Jerusalem, *hof῾al* is not attested for the following verbs of motion: *hlk, yrd, yšb, npl, ῾lh, ῾md, ῾br* and seems to be limited to participles serving as *termini technici* for *bw᾽, yṣ᾽, kns* and biblicisms (*qwm*).

[47] These are my own theoretical examples, quoted out of context for the sake of illustration.

[48] This is of course what is taken for granted in most of the standard grammars. I maintain that this correspondence did not hold for MA of the early period (1st

He then notes that the only undisputed example of this verbal stem in Tannaitic MH is in fact נתוסף /*nittōsaf*/ from the root יסף, which, he rightly points out, replaces not a BH *hofʿal* (which does not exist for this root in BH) but rather a *nifʿal* — נוסף, the passive of הוסף in BH. He concludes that in fact the function of the passive of *hifʿil* in Tannaitic MH is fulfilled for the most part by either 1) the *qal* or 2) the *nifʿal*, but chiefly by the latter[49].

8.2 Mishor lists the following occurences for the use of *qal* in this function, illustrating each one with a counter-example with *hifʿil*.

8.21 הלך

Mishna Nazir IV:4 דמי חטאת ילכו לים המלח, "Money intended for the sin-offering *must be taken, conveyed* (lit. — must go) to the Dead Sea (and be thrown in)" as opposed to:

Mishna Aboda Zara III:3 המוציא כלים ועליהם צורת החמה ... יוליכם לים המלח, "One who finds utensils on which there is an image of the sun .... *must take, convey them* to the Dead Sea (and throw them in)".

8.22 יצא

Mishna Zebaḥim XII:4 מימיי לא ראיתי עור יוצא לבית השריפה, "I have never seen a hide *taken out* (lit. : go out) to the place of burning", which contrasts with:

Idem XIII:1 אף השוחט בפנים והמעלה בחוץ כיוון שהוציאו פסלו, "Even one who slaughters inside and offers up outside, once he *has carried it out*, has rendered it unfit".

8.23 בוא

In footnote 176, page 206 he furthermore mentions a passage from Genesis Rabba (ed. *Theodor–Albeck*, p. 295): והבאים זכר ונקבה וגו׳. אמר ליה: קניגי אנה? אמר ליה: אכפת לך? מובאים אין כת אלא הבאים מאיליהן [50], "'And those who entered, male and female', etc. (Gen. 7:16). He said to Him: 'Am I a huntsman (that I

- 3rd century C.E.). Observe that the Pesh uses the *afʿel* passive participle *mpqyn* in Ez. 14:22 and Luke 13:28 but has no matching *ettafʿal* form. As we have shown, the *peʿal* assumes this function. Cf. also Samaritan Aramaic: *Tibat Marqe* (ed. Z. Ben-Ḥayyim, Jerusalem 1988, p. 77, line 632) *wmplyn ḥršyh* "and the magicians are felled".

[49] Similarly in Syriac the *etpeʿel* (the verbal stem corresponding to MH *nifʿal*) together with the *etpaʿʿal* seems to be one of the chief ways of expressing the passive of *afʿel*. Cf. T. Muraoka, *Classical Syriac for Hebraists*, Wiesbaden 1987, §34, p. 27. I found no grammar, however, which mentions *peʿal* in this function.

[50] MH uses this expression (lit.: from their power — < *ʾyl* "strength, power") and *mʿṣmw/n* (lit.: by itself, themselves) to mark the *qal* of verbs of motion as indicating their basic meaning in contradistinction to their function as anti-causatives. Cf. Mishna Baba Metsia VII:9 and Shabbat XXII:1.

could tell the difference)?' 'Should you care?' 'Those who were brought in' is not written (here) but rather 'Those who entered' — *of their own accord*". The purpose of the Midrash here is to prevent one from interpreting the active participle as the passive of *hif'il* and therefore categorically states that it does not have this connotation.

8.3 To these examples I would like to add a few of my own.

8.31 נפק / יצא

8.311 Gittin III:4 היוצא להרג, "he who *is led out* (lit.: goes out) to be executed"[51] and in Galilean Aramaic we find a calque of this expression:

8.312 Cf. the Jerusalem Talmud, Sanhedrin 23b (bottom), (VI,5)[52]: מי נפק מקטליניה ( למיתקטלא = Ms. Leiden), "upon *being taken out* to be executed" with the *pe'al* of נפק.

Note that in a similar passage in the Jerusalem Talmud, Gittin 48a, line 48 (VI,7) the *ittaf'al* form is used: אתאפק לקטלא / למקטלא [53].

8.313 A similar expression appears in Gittin VI:5 and Tebul Yom IV:5: היוצא בקולר "one who *is led forth* in fetters".

8.314 In the Babylonian Talmud (=bT), Moed Qatan 27a, we find the following *Baraita*: מאימתי כופין את המטות? משיצא מפתח ביתו. דברי רבי אליעזר ... מעשה כשמת רבן גמליאל הזקן וכיון שיצא מפתח ביתו ... "From what time does one overturn the bed? From the time he (the dead man, the corpse) *is taken out* (lit.: goes out, leaves) of the door of the house: these are the words of Rabbi Eliezer. ... It happened that when Raban Gamaliel the Elder died and as soon as he *was taken out* of the door of his house ...".

8.3141 Note that in Halakhot Pesuqot, an early Gaonic halachic treatise[54], the *ittaf'al* of נפק is used when discussing a similar situa-

---

[51] Similarly Arakhin I:3,4; this expression seems to lay behind the interpretation of the *hof'al* discussed above in Gen. 38:25 (section 2.0). Cf. also Hosea 9:13 *lhwṣy' 'l-hwrg bnyw*.

[52] According to a manuscript published by M. Assis in *Tarbiz* 46 (1977), p. 74-75.

[53] The use of *ittaf'al* for verbs of motion (and *ittaf'al* in general??) is quite limited in Galilean Aramaic (excluding the Targums, of course). Cf. the concordance for Jewish Palestinian Aramaic, compiled by M. Sokoloff, which he kindly placed at the disposal of the Academy of the Hebrew Language and his recently published *Dictionary of Jewish Palestinian Aramaic*, Ramat-Gan, Israel 1990. The form *'t'pq* cited above is the only case of *ittaf'al* for a verb of *real motion* that I found in the entire corpus of Galilean Aramaic. It is true we do find the verb *'yttb(t)*, the passive of *'tyb* in the technical sense "answer, refute an objection", 18 times in the Jerusalem Talmud. In light of a similar substitution of *'t'p'q* in Gaonic literature for the *pe'al* form in earlier Rabbinic Hebrew mentioned below (8.3141), one is tempted to question the originality of this reading (see also note 56).

[54] Attributed to Rav Jehudai Gaon (eighth century); ed. S. Sasoon, Jerusalem

tion: והיכא דשכיב קודים הרגל ואיתפק חדא שעתא [55], "and (in the case) where he passed away a short time before a major festival and *was brought out* (to be buried)...".

It should be noted that I have not discovered a single *ittafʿal* form for verbs of real motion in the entire corpus of the Babylonian Talmud[56]; it is therefore somewhat surprising that we find them in post-talmudic literature. This diachronic development would seem to parallel the similar one in Syriac noted above (7.1, note 41) and warrants further study.

8.315 Mishna Shabbat ch. V treats of which articles domestic animals are allowed to carry when being led out into the public domain on the Sabbath: במה בהמה יוצא ובמה אינה יוצא?, "With what may an animal *be let out* (lit.: go out) and with what may it not *be let out*?" The verb here obviously serves as an anti-causative for if it had its basic meaning, i.e. if an animal accidentally got out ( מאיליה ), the owner would not be liable halachically and there would therefore be no reason for the Mishna to treat this case in the first place.

8.32 ירד

In its midrashic portion the Passover Haggadah relates of Israel's going down to Egypt[57]: וירד מצרימה אנוס על פי הדבר, "'And he *was brought down* (lit.: went down) to Egypt'— *compelled* by the word (of the Lord)". The midrash teaches us that we are not to take these words at face value. Israel did not go down to Egypt of his own accord ( מאיליו ) but rather that the Lord brought him down there according to His own plan (cf. Gen. 15:13-14).

8.33 עלה

---

1951, p. 166, line 1.

[55] Cf. also *Halakhot Gedolot*, ed. E. Hildesheimer, Vol. I, Jerusalem 1971, p. 427, line 1 and especially the reading of Ms. Berlin: *wʾtʾpʾq*. Note also the form *mtpqʾ* which J.N. Epstein lists in his *Grammar of Babylonian Aramaic* (Jerusalem 1960, p. 77 [Hebrew]) from a Gaonic responsum. Elsewhere in his grammar he records further examples of *ittafʿal* forms culled from Gaonic literature yet not found in the corpus of the Babylonian Talmud.

[56] I exclude from my discussion quotations from the Scroll of Fasting in the Babylonian Talmud (*ʾtwqm*, *ʾtwtb*) and the citation from Targum Isaiah 62:5 in Mo'ed Qatan 2a; (note that most Mss. of the Targum have the *itpaʿʿal* and not the *ittafʿal* of *ytb* here; ed. Sperber, Leiden 1962, p.123 [see also note 17]). Again we do find *ittafʿal* in the *termini technici* of talmudic discussion, i.e. *ʾytwtb*, the passive of *ʾwtyb*, "to be answered, refuted" (cf. note 53) and *mtwqmʾ*, the passive of *ʾwqym*, "be maintained, upheld (as referring to)" (predicated usually of a Mishna or a scriptural quotation) which are found 11 and 9 times respectively, according to the Concordance of Kasowsky (Jerusalem 1954 ff, Vol. 33, p.254 and Vol. 40, p.50). There is some variation in Mss. with respect to the use of these terms. The variant *mtqyymʾ* (i.e. *itpaʿʿal*) for *mtwqmʾ* in Ms. Oxford b. 1 for Ker. 4b should especially be noted. This is the oldest dated Ms. of the Talmud existing (1123 CE).

[57] According to the version of Rav Saʿadia Gaon (*Siddur R. Saadja Gaon*, ed. I. Davidson, S. Assaf and B.I. Joel, Jerusalem 1978, p. 138).

8.331 Mishna Qiddushin ch. IV begins with the words: עשרה יחסים עלו מבבל, "Ten genealogical stocks *went up/came up* from Babylon".

In the discussion of this Mishna in the Gemara (bT 69b) we read: אביי אמר: עלו מאיליהם תנן. ורבא אמר: העלום תנן, "Abaye said: The interpretation we learned of the Mishna is - they *came up of their own accord*. Raba said: We learned - he (Ezra) *brought them up* (against their will[58])".

The Mishna as it stands is ambiguous and the verb can be construed as a simple *qal*, as in the interpretation of Abaye, or as the passive of *hifʿil*, as does Raba.

8.332 In bT Shabbat 20a, in a discussion of Mishna I:11 כדי שיצת האור ברובן "(there must be) enough time for the fire *to be enkindled* in the greater part of them" a *Baraita*[59] is cited in support of the interpretation that it means that the fire should be burning strongly enough of its own accord that it requires no stoking: כדי שתהא שלהבת עולה מאיליה ולא תהא שלהבת עולה על ידי דבר אחר, "enough time so that the flame should *burn* (lit.: ascend) *of its own accord* and not *be made to burn* (ascend) *by means of something else*[60].

8.333 סלק

In the Scroll of Fasting (ed. B. Lurie, Jerusalem 1964, p.15) we find the infinitive of סלק used in early Jewish Palestinian Aramaic in a similar fashion: בעשרין ושבעה ביה תבת סלתא למסק על מדבחא, "On the twenty-seventh of it (Marḥeshvan) choice flour was again *offered up* (lit.: returned to go up) on the altar." (Cf. note 24)

8.34 עמד

An enigmatic Mishna (Nazir II:2) speaks of a person projecting a vow on a cow and employs the verb עומדת "will stand up" twice in reference to this cow. It would seem that the discussion in bT 10a-b pivots on whether one interprets the morphosemantically ambiguous verb עומדת as a simple *qal* or as an anti-causative, i.e. on whether the cow stood up of its own accord ( עמדה מאיליה ) or whether the person involved made it stand up ( אוקמה בידיה).

[58] According to the commentary of Rashi: *ʿl krḥm*.

[59] Cf. the commentary of Rashi and *Sifra*, *Emor*, parasha 13,7 (ed. Weiss, p. 103c). Observe that the latter is a midrash on Lev. 24:2 *lhʿlt nr tmyd* "to have a lamp burning continuously". The LXX in the parallel verse Ex. 27:20 reflects the same exegesis as this *Baraita*: *ἵνα κάηται* "in order that it (the lamp) be burning (continuously)" (=Vulgate: *ut ardeat*) and may reflect a variant *lʿlt* (*qal*) but the matter requires further study. Cf. also Shabbat 21a.

[60] For further examples in MH with both the verbs *ʿlh* and *yrd*, see Mishna Zebaḥim IX: 1-5 and Tosefta Para III:5.

8.35 עבר

Mishna Pesaḥim ch. III opens with the words: ואלו עוברים בפסח, "And the following things *must be removed* (lit.: pass away) on Passover". Cf. the commentary of Ch. Albeck: מעבירים אותם, "one must remove them"[61].

8.36 קרב

The most frequent use of the *qal* of קרב in MH is to serve as the passive of הקריב, i.e. "to offer up" (a sacrifice)→ "to be offered up". Cf. Zebaḥim XIV:10: קורבנות היחיד שהוקדשו למשכן יקרבו במשכן. ואם הקריבן בבמה פטור[62], "the sacrifices of individuals which were consecrated for the tabernacle *must be offered up* (lit. draw near) in the tabernacle; but if he *offered* them on a high-place - he is not liable".

8.361 The corresponding use of *qal* of this root in its normal meaning is comparatively rare in MH. Cf. Sanhedrin III:8 קרבו, "draw near (pl.)"[63].

9.0 Non-Jewish Middle Aramaic dialects

The following are but two examples from non-translational texts in other MA dialects:

9.1 אתא

9.11 Samaritan Aramaic

In Samaritan Aramaic the *pe'al* of אתא is used in the sense "to be created, formed" and serves as the passive of אנדה "create, form (lit.: bring)".

Cf. the liturgical poem Marqa XVI, line 140: דאתא בה עלמה, "by which the world *was created, formed*" and in line 152 יהוה רבה דאנדה עלמה, "the great 'Name' that *created* the world"[64].

9.12 Syriac

---

[61] Ch. Albeck, *Shisha Sidre Mishna*, Jerusalem 1958, Vol. II Moed, p.149. [P.S. Cf. also the commentary of E. Baneth on this Mishna (*Mischnajot: Die sechs Ordnungen der Mischna*, Teil II - Moëd, ed. A. Sammter, Berlin 1926, p. 180): "Das Intransitiv für das Passivum des Transitivs ist bei Verben der Bewegung nicht selten." He lists several other examples.]

[62] Ms. Kaufmann vocalizes *yqrbw* as *nif'al*: *yiqqārebū*; likewise VIII:5 (2x) but VIII:2 (sing), 8 as *qal*. This is apparently a secondary reinterpretation since *nif'al* forms with *nun* for this verb do not appear in the Mishna, the past being always *qārāḇ* and the participle *qāreḇ*.

[63] [P.S. Cf. the examples listed for the root *'ll* in M. Sokoloff's new dictionary (note 53), p. 409, meaning 4, "to be brought in".]

[64] Ed. Z. Ben-Ḥayyim, *The Literary and Oral Tradition of Hebrew and Aramaic amongst the Samaritans*, Vol III, Part II, Jerusalem 1967, p. 236-7.

In his commentary on Gen 3:8-9 Ephrem the Syrian attempts to explain the reason the Lord called out to Adam after he sinned[65]: *kd dyn lʾ mn twḥrth wlʾ mn qlʾ dʾštdr qdmwhy ʾtw lmtḥzyw lh byd tkšptʾ ...*, "Now when neither through His delay (in acting) nor through the sound (of His feet) which was sent forth before Him, they could be *induced/brought* (lit.: came)[66] to reveal themselves to Him by imploring (Him)...".

10.0 Although I have limited myself in this article to a discussion of the basic verbs of motion, nevertheless I might point out that the use of *qal/peʿal* as the passive of *hifʿil/afʿel* is not restricted to intransitive verbs as such[67]. A few examples must suffice.

10.1 שתה - השקה / אשקי

In addition to its basic meaning "to drink" the *qal/peʿal* of שתה serves as the passive of its suppletive causative השקה / אשקי in the sense "to be made to drink, to be irrigated" in MH and MA.

10.11 Mishnaic Hebrew

Cf. Mishna Moed Qatan I:3 זרעים שלא שתו לפני המועד לא ישקום במועד, "Seeds that *have* not *been watered* (lit.: drank) before the mid-festival days, *may* not *be watered* (lit.: one may not water them) during the mid-festival days".

10.12 Syriac

1 Corinthians 12:13 "and we *have* all *been made to drink* (ἐποτίσθημεν) of one Spirit". Pesh: *ʾštyn* — the *peʿal* form.

10.2 חמה, "to see" ↔ חווי / חזי, "to show"

Ms. Neophyti of the PT translates the three occurences of the *hofʿal* of ראה in the Pentateuch with the simple *peʿal* חמה, i.e. Ex. 25;40; 26:30 and Dt. 4:35 (in the last verse the reading with *peʿal* appears in the margin)[68].

11.0 Conclusion

Several questions remain unresolved:

---

[65] Ed. R.M. Tonneau, *Sancti Ephraem Syri in Genesim et in Exodum Commentarii*, Louvain 1955, p. 40, lines 7-8.

[66] Note that this is actually the passive of a double causative: "to be caused - to make (cause) - oneself - seen". Such constructions, although common in modern European languages such as English, seem to be rare in Semitic and deserve further study.

[67] It *is* probably limited, by definition, to non-factitive verbs.

[68] For a similar example with *ḥzʾ* in the Old Syriac version of the NT, see Joosten, *The Syriac Language*, p. 275, 2.1.2 (Math. 2:22).

1. Are the morphosyntactic alternates *hif'il/af'el* plus object versus anti-causative simply stylistic variants or is there an inherent opposition between the two (apart from the constraint mentioned in section 1.0 on page 3)? In other words, what is the difference between יצא and הוציאוהו ?

2. What is the precise relation between a) יצא as anti-causative b) יצא מאיליו / מעצמו and c) יצא לו — i.e. a verb of motion and the so-called *dativus ethicus*? If the example cited above in 7.1. from 2 Peter 1:17,18 is indeed an anti-causative, then a and c are not necessarily mutually exclusive, as are a and b. The relation between these three syntagms and the *ittaf'al* likewise warrants further investigation[69].

---

[69] A further question is the relation of these syntagmes to the use of *hof'al* as a substitute for *qal* in verbs of motion *inter alia*, in liturgical poetry of the Byzantine period; cf. J. Yahalom, "The Passive in Liturgical Poetry: Verbal Themes in Poetry and Prose", in *Leshonenu* 45 (1980), pp. 17-31. Particularly suggestive is the example quoted on page 27 from a poem of Yannai: *ḥlp 'šr m'ydh hwqm/ḥwq brytw l'dtw qm*, "As recompense (for the fact) that he (Pinchas) *arose* from the assembly (an allusion to Num. 25:7 *wyqm mtwk h'dh*) the enactment of a covenant with him *was established* for his clan (descendants)" (i.e. his descendants were awarded an eternal, inherited priesthood). In other words, *qm* "was established" in stich B clearly serves as an anti-causative, i.e. as the passive of *hqym* (BH *hwqm*) whereas *hwqm* "he arose" in stich A would seem to be a learned calque of either *qm lw* (*'md lw*) or *qm m'ylyw* (*'md m'ylyw*). (Note that this is the reading in one of the most ancient Mss. of the *piyyuṭim* in existence, whereas in later Mss. of the same work the two verbs have been switched so that *qm* appears in the first stich and *hwqm* in the second, in accordance with BH (and Modern Hebrew) usage.) Note also that the four examples from verbs of motion cited on page 26 of the article (*hwrṣ, hwb', ywb', khwb'*) are all predicated of persons. Are these forms simply learned variants of *rṣ lw* (= *brḥ lw*), *b' lw, ybw' lw* and *kšb' lw* respectively?

# Die Partikel אז im biblischen Hebräisch

Martin Jan Mulder, Leiden

In diesem zu Ehren meines Kollegen und Freundes Hoftijzer verfassten Artikel wollen wir uns mit dem adverbialen, konjunktionalen und interjektionellen Aspekt der Partikel אז beschäftigen. Zu diesem Entschluss hat uns eine Bemerkung in einem gediegenen und einleuchtenden Aufsatz über das hebräische *pronomen demonstrativum* als hinweisende Interjektion von der Hand von Kollegen A.S. van der Woude veranlasst[1]. Im genannten Beitrag befasst sich van der Woude hauptsächlich mit dem Wort זה usw., aber "anhangsweise" bemerkt er dann, "dass auch das mit זה verwandte hebräische Demonstrativadverb אז zuweilen die ursprüngliche interjektionelle Natur bewahrt hat und manchmal sogar als Konjunktion verwendet wird"[2]. Als "hervorhebende Interjektion" möchte er אז etwa in Gen. 49:4; Jos. 22:31; Richt. 5:19; Jes. 41:1 usw. betrachten, als Konjunktion scheint die Partikel, seiner Meinung nach, in Micha 3:4 verwendet zu sein: "Wenn sie zu Jahwe schreien, wird Er sie nicht erhören..."[3].

Im Alten Testament findet אז sich 122 mal[4], dazu 18 mal מאז[5]; einmal מן־אז (Jer. 44:18), und dreimal die Form אזי (Ps. 124:3ff.)[6]. Die Verteilung von אז ohne מ[ן] über die einzelnen Bücher ergibt: Pentateuch 17 mal (Gen.: 5; Ex.: 5; Lev.: 4; Num.: 1; Deut.: 2); Frühere Propheten 41 mal (Jos.: 9; Richt.: 7; 1 Sam.: 2; 2 Sam.: 8; 1 Kön.: 8; 2 Kön.: 7); Spätere Propheten 22 mal (Jes.: 8; Jer.: 7; Zeph.: 2; Ez., Hos., Mich., Hab., und Mal. je 1); Schriften (Hagiographen) 42

---

[1] A.S. van der Woude, "Das hebräische Pronomen Demonstrativum als hinweisende Interjektion", *JEOL* 18 (1964), 307-313. Herrn Kollegen Prof. Dr. B. Hartmann, Zürich, danke ich für die Korrektur meines Manuskriptes.

[2] A.S. van der Woude, a.a.O., 312.

[3] A.S. van der Woude, a.a.O., 312f.

[4] Nach $KBL^3$ 130 mal. Auch E. Jenni, Art. *ywm*, *THAT* 1, 715 scheint dieser Angabe zu folgen.

[5] Gen. 39:5; Ex. 4:10; 5:23; 9:24; Jos. 14:10; 2 Sam. 15:34; Jes. 14:8; 16:13; 44:8; 45:21; 48:3, 5, 7f.; Ps. 76:8; 93:2; Spr. 8:22; Ruth 2:7. Überdies ist diese Form auch in einem Lachisch-Ostrakon attestiert: *KAI* 193, 7; vgl. *DISO* , 7 s.v. *ʾz ii*.

[6] Wohl als eine dialektische (*BDB* (1968),23), oder archaistische Form ($GB^{17}$,20), oder Nebenform (*HAHAT* [= *Hebräisches und Aramäisches Handwörterbuch über das Altes Testament* 18, (Herausg. R. Meyer - H. Donner], Berlin usw. 1987, 29) betrachtet. Ebenfalls im Aramäischen gibt es die Formen *ʾz* und *ʾzy*; siehe *KAI* 214,7; 215,9 und 233, 6.14.

mal (Ps.: 13; Spr.: 5; Hiob: 8; 1 Chr.: 8; 2 Chr.: 6; Hld., und Koh. je 1). Wie öfter, gibt es vor allem zwischen Chr. einerseits und Sam. und Kön. andererseits parallele Texte (etwa 1 Chr. 11:16 mit 2 Sam. 23:14; 1 Chr. 20: 4 mit 2 Sam. 21: 18 usw.). Im Allgemeinen kann man sagen, dass אז in der jüngeren nicht mehr als in der älteren Literatur vorkommt[7]. Am meisten findet sich die Partikel, einschliesslich אזי, im Buch der Psalmen.

Verwandtschaft mit der biblischen Form אז begegnet auch in vielen anderen semitischen Sprachen, etwa im Ugaritischen *idk*[8]; im Arabischen *ʾiḏ, ʾiḏā, ʾḏan, ʾiḏḏāka*; und im Biblisch-Aramäischen אדין usw.[9]. Vielleicht handelt es sich bei der Etymologie der Partikel um das "ursemitische Demonstrativ" ז, "dieser", mit demonstrativem א[10]. Aber diese Herleitung ist doch unsicher[11]. Bereits W. Gesenius zeigte dies in seinem *Thesaurus* , obwohl er אז unter der Radix אזה erörterte[12]. Neuere hebräische Wörterbücher sind ebenfalls unsicher. So hält das Wörterbuch von Brown, Driver, und Briggs das Wort *wahrscheinlich* für ein Substantiv "time"[13], während sowohl GB[17] als auch das neue Wörterbuch von Gesenius-Meyer-Donner nur melden, dass es sich

[7] In Richt. 5 (: 8, 11, 13, 19, 22) schon 5 mal, in Tritojesaja jedoch dreimal (58: 8, 9, 14), gegen Deuterojesaja nur einmal (41: 1).

[8] Vgl. u.a. J. Aistleitner, *Wörterbuch der ugaritischen Sprache*, Berlin 1963, 7 (Nr. 81); C. H. Gordon, *Ugaritic Textbook*, Rome 1965, 351 (§19.79); J. C. L. Gibson, *Canaanite Myths and Legends*, Edinburgh 1977, 142 s.v. *id*.

[9] Siehe W. Baumgartner, *KBL*[1], 1048, für weitere semitische Parallelen.

[10] Siehe J. Barth, *Die Pronominalbildung in den semitischen Sprachen*[2], Hildesheim 1967, 103f. und 74ff.; vgl. dazu auch F. Böttcher, *Ausführliches Lehrbuch der hebräischen Sprache* , I, Leipzig 1866, 335f. (§529); H. Ewald, *Ausführliches Lehrbuch der hebräischen Sprache des alten Bundes*[8], Göttingen 1870, 263 (§104[e]); weiter F. E. König, *Lehrgebäude der hebräischen Sprache* , II.1, Leipzig 1895, 249 (§111.I.6), der *ʾz* als Deutelaut-Adverbium der Zeit bezeichnet (apokopiertes *zh*), von dem *ʾzy* "die urspr. Gestalt jenes Ausdrucks zu enthalten (scheint)". Vgl. auch sein *Hebräisches und aramäisches Wörterbuch zum Alten Testament*[3.4], Leipzig 1922, 9f.*s.v.* *ʾz* ("Demonstrativgebilde aus *z* + *ʾ*"). Im Punischen ist *ʾz* mitunter als Demonstrativpronomen verwendet, G. Garbini, "Considerazioni sull' iscrizione punica di Pyrgi", *OrAnt* 4 (1965), 37f.; G. Levi Della Vida, a.a.O., 51; G. Garbini, "Note di epigrafia punica II", *RSO* 42 (1967), 1-13; KAI 277,2; J. Friedrich, *Phönizisch - Punische Grammatik* , Roma 1951, §113.

[11] So auch bereits J. Olshausen, *Lehrbuch der hebräischen Sprache* , Braunschweig 1861, 423 (§222e).

[12] G. Gesenius, *Thesaurus Philologicus Criticus Linguae Hebraeae et Chaldaeae Veteris Testamenti* , Lipsiae 1829, I, 58f. Auch andere und ältere Wörterbücher zeigten *ʾz* so an, etwa E. Scheidius (- J.J. Groenewoud), *Lexicon Hebraicum et Chaldaicum Manuale in Codicem Sacrum Veteris Testamenti* , I, Trajecti ad Rhenum/ Lugd. Batavorum 1805, 10. Das damals auch sehr bekannte Wörterbuch von G. B. Winer, *Lexicon Manuale Hebraicum et Chaldaicum in Veteris Testamenti Libros* 4, Lipsiae 1928, 39, fragte sich, ob *ʾz* eine "vox primitiva" sei (gegen Schultens ad Spr. 8:22).

[13] *BDB*, 23.

um ein Adverb (der Zeit) handelt[14].

In Grammatiken und Wörterbüchern wird öfter der adverbiale Charakter der Partikel hervorgehoben. So meint die 28. Auflage der hebräischen Grammatik von W. Gesenius, umgearbeitet von E. Kautzsch: "Als *Adverbia primitiva* sind wohl eine Anzahl von Bildungen zu betrachten, die in engster Verwandtschaft mit dem *Pronomen demonstr.* stehen, indem sie direkt aus einer Verbindung sogenannter *Deutelaute* hervorgegangen sind. Zum Teil haben dieselben nachträglich starke Verstümmelungen erlitten; doch ist der Umfang der letzteren fast nirgends mehr mit Sicherheit zu ermitteln"[15]. Als erstes Beispiel wird dann אז erwähnt. Die bekannte Grammatik von Joüon spricht ebenfalls über "l'adverbe אז"[16]. Und Wörterbücher, wie von Gesenius-Buhl und ihren Nachfolgern Meyer-Donner[17], bezeichnen אז an erster Stelle als Adverb. Andere Wörterbücher sind, wohl mit Recht, mehr zurückhaltend, wie KBL[3] und das Lexikon von Zorell[18], der אז nur als "particula (temporalis)" andeutet.

Schon Ibn Ezra, in seinem Kommentar zu Ex. 15: 1 אז ישיר משה, bemerkt zur Funktion der Partikel אז: "Es ist Gebrauch der heiligen Sprache beim Wörtchen אז das Futur anstatt des Präteritums zu verwenden". Nachdem er einige Beispiele vorgeführt hat, fährt er fort: "So ist es auch in der ismaelitischen (= arabischen) Sprache"[19]. Gerade der *funktionelle* Aspekt der Partikel lenkte die Aufmerksamkeit auf sich, und hat manchen Versuch zur Deutung ausgelöst. Es fällt dabei auf, dass man ab und zu die Interpretation der sogenannten "verbalen Zeit" von der Bedeutung von אז abhängig machte. So etwa noch Gesenius

---

[14] *GB*[17], 20; *HAHAT*, 28; vgl. auch F. Zorell, *Lexicon Hebraicum Veteris Testamenti* , Roma 1984, 26.

[15] W. Gesenius - E. Kautzsch, *Hebräische Grammatik*[28], Leipzig 1909, 306 (§100i); vgl. auch F. Böttcher, a.a.O., 330 (§524); B. Stade, *Lehrbuch der hebräischen Grammatik*, I, Leipzig 1879, 221 (§369), und 128 (§171a); R. Meyer, *Hebräische Grammatik*, II, Berlin 1969, 172 (§86.2).

[16] P. Joüon, *Grammaire de l' Hébreu Biblique*[2], Rome 1947, 304 (§113i). Auch C. Brockelmann, *Hebräische Syntax*, Neukirchen 1956, 120 (§122k), spricht über "Adverbium".

[17] W. Gesenius - F. Buhl, *Hebräisches und Aramäisches Handwörterbuch über das Alte Testament*[17], Leipzig 1921, *s.v.* ; *HAHAT, s.v.*.

[18] F. Zorell, a.a.O, *s.v.*.

[19] Der Herausgabe der *Miqra'ōt Gedolōt* aus Wien (5619), Nachdruck Schocken (5697), z. St., entnommen; vgl. auch schon Mechilta zu Ex. 15:1 (34a), und dazu W. Bacher, *Die Anfänge der hebräischen Grammatik*, Amsterdam 1974 (= *ZDMG* 49 (1895), 3. Ibn Ezra wird öfter zitiert, etwa durch Sal. Glassius, *Philologiae Sacrae ... libri quinque* , Amstelaedami 1711, lib.III, tract.III, Canon xlix.1 (p.417). S. Abramson, "Biblical Explanations based on Medieval Exegesis", *BetM* 32 (1986/87), 355ff., teilt mit, dass nach etwa Ibn Ezra und David Kimchi *šm* auch "dann" bedeuten kann. Er stellt vor, danach *'z* in Gen. 12:6; 13:7; 49:4 und Richt. 5:11 durch "dort" zu übersetzen.

in seinem übrigens grundlegenden *Lehrgebäude*: "Für die *Vergangenheit* steht das *Futurum* a) bey einigen auf Vergangenheit hindeutenden Partikeln $\alpha$) אז *damals* ..." Und nach einigen Beispielen fährt er fort: "Wenn אז *dann* bedeutet, bleibt die Bedeutung des *Futuri* ..."[20]. Richtiger allerdings wäre es, in der Übersetzung die Bedeutung von אז vom Kontext abhängig zu machen, und nicht von vornherein "Zeit", "Aspekt", oder "Aktionsart" des Verbs durch die Bedeutung von אז bedingen zu wollen. Heutzutage konstatiert man, etwa in der Beschreibung der Tempusübergänge, oft nur, dass nach den Partikeln אז und טרם "häufig auch in erzählendem Kontext das Imperfekt" steht, und dass "אז am Satzanfang ... das Tempus-Morphem '*wa*' (ersetzt)", und überdies, dass es sich "oft in einleitenden oder überleitenden Sätzen der Erzählung" findet[21].

Es ist angebracht, hervorzuheben, dass die Partikel אז im biblischen Hebräisch, wenigstens bei der übertragung in unsere modernen Sprachen, multifunktionell ist, wie sich leicht aus den Wörterbüchern herauslesen lässt. So wird אז völlig selbständig in einem Nominalsatz verwendet, etwa

Gen. 12:6 (vgl. 13:7): והכנעני אז בארץ, "zu dieser Zeit (wohnten) die Kanaaniter im Lande";

Jos. 14:11: ככחי אז וככחי עתה, "ich bin jetzt so stark wie damals";

2 Sam. 23:14: ודוד אז במצודה ומצב פלשתים אז ביתלחם, "David war damals in der Bergfeste, während die Wache der Philister in Bethlehem war" (= 1 Chr. 11:16);

Jer. 22:15f.: אז טוב [לו], "damals ging es [ihm] gut";

Hos. 2:9: כי טוב לי אז מעתה, "denn damals ging es mir besser als jetzt".

Es sei jedoch zu den letztgenannten Beispielen bemerkt, dass טוב hier auch als 3. Person sing. masc. qal des Verbs fungieren kann, sodass nicht ganz sicher ist, ob diese Formen den nominalen Sätzen einzureihen sind[22].

Die Funktion der Partikel ist in genannten Beispielen deutlich temporal andeutend, dazu auch anaphorisch (rückwärts) verweisend. Diese beiden semantischen Aspekte der Partikel (temporal und anaphorisch) werden sich auch fast immer in den anderen Funktionen der Partikel

---

[20] W. Gesenius, *Lehrgebäude der hebräischen Sprache mit Vergleichung der verwandten Dialekte* , Leipzig 1817, 773 (§206.4).

[21] W. Schneider, *Grammatik des biblischen Hebräisch*[2], München 1976, 198 (§§48.4.3.4; 48.4.3.41).

[22] Zorell, a.a.O., 281; KBL[3], 354f.; vgl. dazu auch H. Bauer - P. Leander, *Historische Grammatik der hebräischen Sprache des Alten Testamentes*, Halle 1922, 392y; G. Bergsträsser, *Hebräische Grammatik*, II, Leipzig 1929, §28b.

erweisen[23]. Wohl fragt man sich, ob man in den angeführten Beispielen אז auch schon als "hervorhebende Interjektion" bezeichnen kann[24]. Wenn es diesen Aspekt der Partikel überhaupt geben möchte, ist er doch wohl genauer als "Aufmerksamkeitserreger" einzustufen, weil man bei der grammatischen Bezeichnung "Interjektion" geneigt ist, eher an Wörter zum Ausdruck der Freude, des Schmerzes, und anderer Empfindungen zu denken. Ich möchte also die Wörter "Interjektion" und "interjektionell" zur Bezeichnung gewisser Funktionen unserer Partikel lieber vermeiden, weil אז sich auch in seiner primitivsten Form m. E. gar nicht auf Empfindungen bezieht.

Weithin am häufigsten kommt אז vor einer konjungierten verbalen Form, das heisst, vor einem — traditionell so genanntem — Perfekt oder Imperfekt, vor. Die Fälle, in denen אזmit einem Partizip verbunden ist, sind nur sehr selten, und sie sind wohl als Nominalsatz einzustufen, etwa

Gen. 13:7: והכנעני והפרזי אז ישב בארץ, "damals wohnten die Kanaaniter und Perisiter im Lande",

eine Konstruktion *ad sententiam*, für die der hebräische Pentateuch der Samaritaner ישבים liest[25];

Jer. 32:2: ואז חיל מלך בבל צרים על־ירושלם, "damals belagerte das Heer des Königs von Babel Jerusalem".

Von den 122 Belegstellen der Partikel אז im biblischen Hebräisch sind 37 mit einem Perfekt (abgesehen von den oben genannten Versen Jer. 22:15f. und Hos. 2:9 mit der Form טוב), und 71 mit einem Imperfekt konstruiert. Wenden wir uns zuerst den Perfektkonstruktionen zu, dann fällt es auf, dass die Konstruktion von אז mit Perfekt etwas häufiger als die Konstruktion mit dem Imperfekt in den allgemein als ältere Stufe der hebräischen Sprache betrachteten Teilen des Alten Testaments vorkommt, etwa Richt. 5:11.13.19.22. Freilich macht die Form ירד in 5:13 einige Schwierigkeiten; aber statt dieser Form für ein nur hier vorkommendes, apokopiertes Imperfekt des Piʿel der Radix רדה zu halten, wie man früher oft tat[26], ist es besser mit den neueren

[23] Nicht ganz deutlich ist die Funktion von *ʾz* in Nominalsätzen wie Richt. 5: 8 und Pred. 2:15, weil es sich hier möglicherweise um korrupte Texte handelt, s. textkrit. Apparat in *BHS* und *HAHAT*, z.St.; zu Richt. 5:8 zudem R.G. Boling, *Judges* (Anchor Bible), Garden City 1975, 110, der *lḥm* als 3. Person plur. Perf. lesen will; P. C. Craigie, *VT* 22 (1972), 350f., der den Text in: *ʾz lḥmš ʿrym* , "then was there for five cities ..." ändern will, wie auch etwa J. A. Soggin, *Judges* (OTL), London 1981, 86, nach ihm.

[24] Siehe A. S. van der Woude, a.a.O., 312f.

[25] Siehe A. von Gall, *Der hebräische Pentateuch der Samaritaner*, Giessen 1918, z.St.

[26] Siehe etwa J. Buxtorf, *Lexicon Hebraicum et Chaldaicum complectens*$^{3}$, Basileae 1621, 709 (*s.v. rdh*); S. Amama, in: *Critici sacri* , II, Amstelaedami 1698, z.St. (Sp.

Wörterbüchern diese Form als Perfekt des Qal von ירד zu lesen[27].

In vielen Fällen ist אז mit dem Perfekt als blosses Adverb der Zeit zu betrachten, welche eine Vergangenheit zum Ausdruck bringt, etwa: Gen. 4:26: אז הוחל לקרא בשם יהוה, "zu dieser Zeit fing man an, den Namen des JHWH anzurufen",
wo man, aufgrund der Lesungen von LXX und Vulgata, אז auch wohl durch זה ersetzen will[28]. Auch nach einer sogenannten Petucha (פ) oder Setuma (ס) kommt אז mit Perfekt öfter vor, so
Jos. 10:33: אז עלה הרם מלך גזר לעזר את־לכיש, "zu dieser Zeit zog Horam, der König von Geser, hinauf, um Lachisch zu helfen";

1 Kön 8:12 (2 Chr. 6:1): אז אמר שלמה, "zu dieser Zeit sprach Salomo";
2 Kön. 14:8: אז שלח אמציה מלאכים אל־יהואש, "zu dieser Zeit sandte Amazja Boten zu Joahas";
2 Chr. 8:17 (vgl. 1 Kön. 9:26): אז הלך שלמה, "zu dieser Zeit ging Salomo".
In diesen und ähnlichen Fällen wird durch das Vorangehen der adverbialen Partikel den übrigens nicht genau definierten Zeitaspekt näher betont [29]. Überdies hat אזauch hier immer eine anaphorische Funktion, weil die Partikel auf etwas Vorangegangenes zurückgreift.

Neben diesen Fällen, die ziemlich genau abzugrenzen sind, gibt es Fälle, in denen es nicht so deutlich ist, ob es sich um ein Adverb zum Ausdruck der Vergangenheit handelt, oder eher um eine Konjunktion. In Ex. 4:26 nimmt man heute fast immer und mit Recht an, dass unmittelbar nach וירף ממנו, "da liess er von ihm ab", die Worte אז אמרה, "damals sagte sie" einen neuen Satz einleiten. LXX aber liest hier ein kausales *διότι εἶπεν*, und die Vulgata eine temporale Konjunktion: *(et dimisit eum) postquam dixerat*[30]. W. H. Schmidt führt in seinem Kommentar zur Stelle G. Schneemann an, der darauf hinweist, dass אז mit einem Verb des Redens "ein liturgisches Stück vermutlich

598), der mitunter auch die Übersetzung der Vulgata kritisiert; I. H. Michaelis, *Biblia Hebraica ... Brevesque Adnotationes*, Halae Magdeburgicae 1720, z.St; dazu auch C. F. Burney, *The Book of Judges*, London 1930, 130ff.

[27] *GB*[17], 316b; *BDB*, 432b; *KBL*[1], 401b; *KBL*[3], 415; R. G. Boling, a.a.O., 111; vgl. noch *GK* §69g.

[28] Vgl. *BHS* , tekstkr. Apparat z.St.

[29] Vgl. für den nicht genau zu datierenden Zeitaspekt der Partikel auch J. A. Montgomery, "Archival Data in the Book of Kings", *JBL* 53 (1934), 49, der betont, dass ʾz "in the original record" "appears to replace some definite date or circumstance"... "or it may be the equivalent of such indifinite temporal phrases".

[30] Vgl. auch Targum Onqelos (Herausgabe von A. Sperber, *The Bible in Aramaic*, I, Leiden 1959): *bkyn ʾmrt*; vgl. Peschitta (Herausgabe *The Old Testament in Syriac*, Leiden 1977) z. St.: *hayden*.

alter Tradition" einleiten kann, wobei oft "nicht an einen einmaligen Akt, sondern eher an eine Sitte oder einen Brauch gedacht zu sein" scheint[31].

Als ein die Vergangenheit anzeigendes Adverb, und wohl nicht als Konjunktion, ist אז in Gen. 49:4; Ex. 15:15[32]; Richt. 5: 11,13,19, 22; 8:3; 13:21; 21:17f; 1 Kön. 9:24[33]; 22:50; Jes. 33:23[34]; Jer. 11:18[35]; Hab. 1:11; Mal. 3:16; Ps. 40:8; 89:20; Hiob 28:27[36]; Hld. 8:10; 1 Chr. 15:2 und 16:7 zu betrachten. 1 Chr. 16:7 ist interessant, weil hier die Zeit, auf die die adverbiale Partikel sich (anaphorisch) bezieht, näher durch ביום ההוא definiert ist, falls man nicht annehmen muss, dass diese Wörter überflüssig sind[37]. In 2 Sam. 2:27 trägt אז einen temporalen Charakter, durch מהבקר, "heute morgen", näher bestimmt. Die Partikel bekommt in diesem Kontext in der deutschen Übersetzung meistens die Bedeutung "schon", weil sie als Konjunktion betrachtet wird, und es eine Beziehung gibt zwischen לולא und אז[38].

Nur in den folgenden Fällen scheint אז, konstruiert mit nachfolgendem Perfekt, als reine Konjunktion zu fungieren. In Jos. 22:31 sagt Pinhas zu den Rubenitern usw.: "heute erkennen wir, dass JHWH unter uns ist: weil (אשר) ihr euch nicht an JHWH versündigt habt mit dieser Tat,

---

[31] W. H. Schmidt, *Exodus* (BK II/1), Neukirchen-Vluyn 1988, 231f. Es handelt sich um die Dissertation von G. Schneemann, *Deutung und Bedeutung der Beschneidung nach Ex 4, 24-26*, Prag 1979. Vgl. noch B. S. Childs, *Exodus*, London 1974, 99, der auch die kausal-konjunktionelle Funktion der Partikel an dieser Stelle zurückweist: "rather the clause in v.26b is an editorial reference by the story's narrator to her words in v. 25b"; so auch etwa C. Houtman, *Exodus* (COT), I, Kampen 1986, 413.

[32] Weniger der korrekten Bedeutung nach übersetzen hier etwa Childs ("indeed"), und Houtman ("ja") z.St. Richtig hingegen *HAHAT* ("damals"). Es sei jedoch bemerkt, dass bereits P. Ruben, "The Song of Deborah", *JQR* 10 (1897/8), 544, hinsichtlich der Bedeutung von *'z* in Richt. 5:8 der Meinung war: "*'z* is by no means "then", but "yea", "nay", wobei er auch Gen. 49:4; Richt. 5:19; Jer. 11:18; Hgl.8:10; Ps. 96:12; Hiob 28:27 anführte.

[33] Vgl. hierzu die Version der LXX zu 2:35f, wo *'z* ... *'k* des hebräischen Textes als *οὕτως* ... *τότε* gefasst ist.

[34] Wir halten hier den masoretischen Text an, vgl. textkr. Appar. in *BHS* z.St., dazu etwa H. Wildberger, *Jesaja* (BK X/3), Neukirchen-Vluyn 1982, 1311f.

[35] Auch hier gibt es Textschwierigkeiten, die jedoch die Position und die Funktion von *'z* nicht zu beeinflussen brauchen; vgl. hierzu auch R. P. Carroll, *Jeremiah* (OTL), London 1986, 275.

[36] In *HAHAT*, z. St., versehentlich verzeichnet unter Imperf.

[37] LXX (Herausgabe von H. B. Swete, *The Old Testament in Greek*, II, Cambridge 1922) zieht *bywm hhw'* zum vorhergehenden Vers; die Handausgabe von A. Rahlfs (1935) aber nicht: s. etwa J.W. Rothstein - J. Hänel, *Kommentar zum ersten Buch der Chronik* (KAT XVIII/2), Leipzig 1927, 290; hingegen auch W. Rudolph, *Chronikbücher* (HAT 21), Tübingen 1955, 120.

[38] C. Brockelmann, a.a.O., §176b.

אָז הִצַּלְתֶּם אֶת־בְּנֵי יִשְׂרָאֵל [מִיַּד יהוה], "da habt ihr die Israeliten (aus der Hand JHWHs) gerettet"[39].

In 2 Kön. 13:19 sagt ein zorniger Gottesmann zum König: אָז הִכִּיתָ אֶת־אֲרָם [לְהַכּוֹת חָמֵשׁ אוֹ־שֵׁשׁ פְּעָמִים], "(Hättest du fünf oder sechsmal geschlagen,) so hättest du Aram geschlagen[40].

In Ps. 119:92 wird gesagt: [לוּלֵי תוֹרָתְךָ שַׁעֲשֻׁעָי] אָז אָבַדְתִּי בְעָנְיִי", "(Wäre dein Gesetz nicht mein Trost gewesen,) so wäre ich in meinem Elend verkommen".

Es ergibt sich, dass אָז in diesen Fällen als eine konditionale Konjunktion im Nachsatz betrachtet wird. Aber auch in diesen doch wohl sehr wenigen Fällen, hat die Partikel sowohl seinen zeitlichen, als seinen anaphorischen Aspekt beibehalten. Es wäre nämlich nicht unmöglich, "so" oder "da" in diesen Nebensätzen ohne Schwierigkeiten durch "in diesem Zeitpunkt" zu ersetzen.

In den 71 Fällen, in denen אָז mit einer Imperfektform konstruiert ist, findet man eine Anzahl Fälle, in denen dieses Imperfekt in einem präterativen Kontext vorkommt. Viel ist hierüber schon in Grammatiken usw. geschrieben worden. Wir möchten jetzt stillschweigend darüber hinweggehen[41]. Neuerdings hat Rabinowitz[42] jedoch zu zeigen versucht, dass in diesen Fällen (er verzeichnet Ex. 15:1; Num. 21:17; Deut. 4:41; Jos. 8:30; 10:12; 22:1; 1 Kön. 3:16; 8:1 (= 2 Chr. 5:2); 9:11; 11:7; 16:21; 2 Kön. 8:22 (= 2 Chr. 21:10); 12:18; 15:16 und 16:5) אָז mit einer Imperfektform nie, wie bei אָז mit einer Perfektform der Fall ist, eine blosse Nachfolge anzeigt. Er betont hingegen, dass "ʾaz + an imperfect verbform in a preterite context is a redactional stylistic device used to introduce a body of textual material as a temporally non-successive addition to what has previously been narrated"[43]. Ausführlich demonstriert er diese Hypothese an 1 Kön. 16: 15-22, in-

---

[39] Schon A. Knobel, *Das Buch Josua* (KEHAT 13), Leipzig 1861, 480, weist auf die Bedeutung "da" für ʾz vor Nachsätzen hin; vgl. auch etwa Boling, a.a.O., 504, der die Partikel im Nachsatz nicht übersetzt: "Because you have not committed this treachery against Yahweh, you have rescued the Bene Israel from Yahwe's hand". Besser jedoch T. C. Butler, *Joshuah* (World Bibl. Commentary 7), Waco (Texas) 1983, 239: "In that way, you have delivered..." etc.

[40] Vgl. *GK*, §159dd.

[41] Nebenbei sei hier die Untersuchung von W. von Soden, "Tempus und Modus im Semitischen" (in: *Bibel und Alter Orient*. Altorientalische Beiträge zum Alten Testament von Wolfram von Soden [Herausg. H.-P. Müller, *BZAW* 162], Berlin/New York 1985), 33, erwähnt, der darauf hinweist, dass die Gegenwartsformen des Verbs auch gebraucht werden "in den vor allem akk. und arab. Zustandssätzen, zu denen auch die hebr. Impf.-Sätze nach *āz* "damals" zu stellen sind".

[42] I. Rabinowitz, "ʾAz Followed by Imperfect Verbform in Preterite Contexts: A Redactional Device in Biblical Hebrew", *VT* 34 (1984), 53-62; vgl. noch J. Dus, "Gibeon", *VT* 10 (1960), 358 Anm. 1.

[43] Rabinowitz, a.a.O., 56.

dem er nachzuweisen versucht, dass die Verse 21 und 22 "is definitely regarded as prior to 16-18 in sequence of time. This dispositional post-placement yet temporal priority is signalled and expressed by *ʾaz* + the imperfect verbform at the outset of *v.* 21"[44]. Wie dem auch sei, in all diesen Fällen kann man אז wieder als ein Adverb zum Ausdruck der (schon vergangenen) Zeit auffassen.

Auch in den folgenden Fällen kann man אז als ein temporelles Adverb betrachten: Ex. 12:44, wo es sich um einen gekauften Sklave handelt, den man hinsichtlich des Passafestes beschneiden soll, אז יאכל בו, "dann darf er davon essen". Hier ist אז, "dann", deutlich temporell bedingt. Ähnliche Fälle liegen vor in Gen. 24:41[45] ; Ex. 12:48; Lev. 26:34 (2x), 41 (2x)[46]; Deut. 29:19; Jos. 1:8 (2x); 20:6; 1 Sam. 6:3; 20:12; 2 Sam. 5:24; Jes. 35:5f.; 41:1; 58:8f, 14; 60:5; Jer. 22:22; 31:13; Ez. 32:14; Micha 3:4[47]; Zeph. 3:9, 11; Ps. 2:5; 19:14; 51:21 (2x); 56:10; 96:12 (= 1 Chr. 16:33)[48]; 119:6; 126:2 (2x); Spr. 1:28; 2:5, 9; 3:23; 20:14; Hiob 3:13; 9:31; 11:15; 13:20; 22:26; 33:16; 38:21; 1 Chr. 14:15 (vgl. 2 Sam. 5:24), und in 1 Chr. 22:13.

In all diesen Fällen deutet אז immer auf anaphorische Weise eine Zeit an, welche eintritt oder eintreten wird, wenn die Voraussetzungen oder die begleitenden Umstände erfüllt sind, seien diese Voraussetzungen und Umstände nun imaginär oder real, präsentisch oder futurisch.

In den eben angeführten Fällen gibt es jedoch Texte, in denen man אז auch als Konjunktion im Nachsatz von konditionellen Fügungen betrachten kann, wie Jes. 58:13f.: "Wenn [אם] du am Sabbath deinen Fuss zurückhältst...",
אז תתענג על־יהוה, "dann wirst du an JHWH deine Lust haben"; Hiob 9: 30f.: "Wenn [אם] ich mich wüsche...",
אז בשחת תטבלני, "dann würdest du mich in die Grube eintauchen". Dies ist vor allem nach (oder vor) der Partikel אם der Fall; ebenso Spr. 2:5; Hiob 11: (13), 15; 22: (23), 26. Daneben gibt es Fälle, in denen man אז als Konjunktion in konditionellen Konstruktionen betrachten kann. So sagt in 2 Kön. 5:3 ein israelitisches Mädchen zu ihrer syrischen Herrin: "Ach (אחלי), wenn nur mein Herr bei dem samaritanischen Propheten wäre",

---

44 Rabinowitz, a.a.O., 54ff. (Zitat: 56).

45 Vgl. auch *GK* [28], §107c Anm.3.

46 Das erste *ʾw-ʾz* liest LXX: τότε; vgl. Peschitta: *whjdjn*.

47 Wie schon oben (S. 132) mitgeteilt, betrachtet Van der Woude *ʾz* an dieser Stelle als Konjunktion "wenn".

48 Es wäre auch möglich *ʾz* hier als Konjunktion zu fassen, und zu übersetzen: "das Feld sei fröhlich und alles, was darauf ist, *wenn* alle Bäume im Walde jauchzen". H. Gunkel, *Die Psalmen*[5], Göttingen 1968, 423, ändert *ʾz* in *ʾp*, aber ohne textkritische Veranlassung. Vgl. auch das parallele 1 Chr. 16:33, wo *ʾz* noch deutlicher als temporelles Adverb hervorgehoben ist.

אז יאסף אתו מצרעתו, "dann würde er ihn von seinem Aussatz heilen".
Ps. 119:5 fängt auch mit אחלי an: "Ach, wenn meine Gänge doch fest wären, deine Gebote zu halten", worauf Vers 6 fortfährt:
אז לא־אבוש, "dann werde ich nicht zuschanden (wenn ich auf all deine Gebote schaue)".

In Ps. 69:5 ist schliesslich die temporelle Funktion der Partikel אז schwer zu bestimmen. Es wird gesagt, dass diejenigen mächtig sind, "die mich verderben, die mich grundlos anfeinden". Und dann fährt der Vers fort:
אשר לא־גזלתי אז אשיב, "was ich nicht geraubt habe, soll ich ... erstatten". Viele Übersetzungen übertragen hier אז nicht. Die Partikel ist an dieser Stelle jedoch textkritisch gesichert, wie etwa auch die alten Versionen, wie LXX (*τότε*) und Vulgata (*tunc*) zeigen. Gunkel meint, dass אז, "damals gab ich es zurück" oder "soll ich alsdann zurückgeben" aus זאת verderbt ist. Er übersetzt also: "das soll ich erstatten!"[49]. Er weist überdies auf den auch durch uns schon erwähnten Artikel von Ruben hin, der אז aus dem phönizischen אז=זה erklärt[50]. Auch Dahood pflichtet Ruben bei, indem er schreibt: "Progress in the study of Northwest Semitic dialects and their interrelationships confirms Paul Ruben's identification ... of *ʾaz* with the Phoenician demonstrative pronoun *ʾz* ..."[51]. Seine Übersetzung des Hemistichiums ist aber bemerkenswert: "What I did not steal, this must I restore?"[52]. Er betrachtet die zweite Hälfte folglich als eine Frage. Wenn diese Erwägung richtig ist, dann ist es ebenfalls möglich die Partikel als ein Adverb der Zeit zu betrachten, und zu übertragen: "was ich nicht geraubt habe, kann ich es zu gegebener Zeit zurückgeben?".

In dem neuen Wörterbuch von Wilhelm Gesenius, durch R. Meyer und H. Donner im Jahre 1987 in einer ersten Lieferung vorgelegt, wird אז auch als Konjunktion zur Verstärkung bei poetischen Wiederhohlungen (Gen. 49:4; Jer. 11:8), oder zur Hervorhebung (Ps. 56:10; 69:5) angezeigt[53]. In dem etwas älteren Wörterbuch von Koehler-Baumgartner-Hartmann-Kutscher jedoch vermeidet man bei der Partikel explizit über Konjunktion zu sprechen[54]. Unsere Untersuchung hat gezeigt, dass die Partikel grammatisch jedenfalls auf andere Weise gedeutet und gewürdigt werden kann. Auch wenn man mitunter in eini-

[49] H. Gunkel, a.a.O., 298.

[50] P. Ruben, a.a.O., 544 Anm. 2. Nach ihm ist dies auch in Spr. 20:14 und Pred. 2:15 der Fall.

[51] M. Dahood, *Psalms II. 51-100* (Anchor Bible), Garden City (NY) 1968, 157.

[52] Dahood, a.a.O., 153.

[53] *HAHAT*, 29.

[54] *KBL*$^3$, 26.

gen doch recht wenigen Fällen auf eine Funktion von אז als Konjunktion, oder als verstärkende oder hervorhebende Partikel schliessen kann, dann spielt das Faktum, dass die Partikel grundsätzlich eine (bestimmte oder unbestimmte) Zeitangabe darstellt so mit, dass es nicht unmöglich ist auch in genannten Fällen אז als Adverb zum Ausdruck der Zeit zu betrachten.

Ergebnis dieser kurzen Übersicht über Vorkommen und Verwendung der Partikel אזim biblischen Hebräisch ist, dass die Partikel nicht nur anfänglich, sondern auch späterhin nur als Zeitadverb fungierte. In den wenigen Fällen, in denen אז als Konjuntion oder auch als "Aufmerksamkeitserreger" zu betrachten ist, ist dies vor allem Folge der Übertragung der Partikel in unsere modernen auf Hypotaxe eingestellten Sprachen.

# The Biblical Hebrew Nominal Clause with a Prepositional Phrase

Takamitsu Muraoka, Melbourne

This short study, which is respectfully dedicated to the distinguished scholar whose own contributions on the complex nature of the Hebrew nominal clause have been a source of inspiration and stimulation to us[1], is concerned with a particular kind of Hebrew nominal clause one constituent of which is a prepositional phrase with locative or existential signification. Examples of nominal clauses with a preposition such as Kaf of comparison are rather rare. We shall not deal with three member nominal clauses such as Gn.43:43 כֹּל אֲשֶׁר־אַתָּה רֹאֶה לִי הוּא *all that you see is mine*; clauses of this type are also infrequent.

Our study is based on a systematic reading of the entire books of Genesis and Judges. Besides, results obtained through our recent study on the Hebrew nominal clause in Late Biblical Hebrew, Qumran Hebrew, and Early Rabbinic Hebrew will also be drawn upon[2].

The peculiarity of this particular type of nominal clause has been already noted by some scholars.

Joüon says that the prepositional phrase generally precedes[3], which is contrary to his observation that the word-order in the nominal clause is normally Subject-Predicate[4]. Unlike in other types of deviation from this norm, Joüon does not explain why the prepositional phrase causes

---

[1] See his "The nominal clause reconsidered", *VT* 23 (1973) 446-510, which is a most extensive review article on F.I. Andersen, *The Hebrew Verbless Clause in the Pentateuch* (Nashville/New York, 1970); "Philological-grammatical notes on 1 Kings xi 14" *Oudtestamentische Studiën* 25 (1989) 29-37.

[2] T. Muraoka, "The nominal clause in Late Biblical Hebrew and Rabbinic Hebrew" [Heb.] to appear shortly in a volme of studies by members of an international team of scholars who worked in 1987-88 at the Institute for Advanced Studies of the Hebrew University in Jerusalem on Mishnaic Hebrew grammar under the leadership of Prof. M. Bar-Asher. The corpus of this study comprised Chronicles, Ezra, Nehemia (excluding those passages with parallel in Samuel and Kings), The Temple Scroll from Qumran, the Mishna tractates Berakoth and Shabbath according to the Codex Kaufman, parts of the midrashim Mechilta d'Rabbi Ishmael and Sifré Devarim.

[3] P. Joüon, *Grammaire de l'hébreu biblique* (Rome, 1923), §154 *f*.

[4] Op. cit., ib.

such deviation. His examples are: Ps. 31:16 בְּיָדְךָ עִתֹּתָי *my destiny is in your hands*; Hg 2:8 לִי הַכֶּסֶף *the silver is mine*; 1Sm 1:2 וְלוֹ שְׁתֵּי נָשִׁים *and he had two wives*; also 1Sm 25:36; Ps 24:1.

We ourselves observed that a prepositional phrase in the first slot tends to be emphatic, mostly in the sense of "identificatory"[5]. For example, Lv 25:23 לִי הָאָרֶץ *the earth is mine*; 1Sm 17:47 כִּי לַיהוה הַמִּלְחָמָה *for the battle is the Lord's*. As we shall see below, we believe that circumstantial clauses such as 1 Sm 1:2 quoted by Joüon ought to be treated as a category of its own.

Andersen finds himself unable to lay down any clear rules for the distribution of the two sequences, S–P and P–S, when P is a prepositional phrase. To illustrate this ambiguity he cites, for instance, Lv 13:46 אֲשֶׁר הַנֶּגַע בּוֹ // 13:45 אשר־בו הנגע; Gn 32:7 וְאַרְבַּע־מֵאוֹת אִישׁ עִמּוֹ // 33.1 ועמו ארבע מאות איש[6]. In our view, this ambiguity is largely a function of Andersen's definition and understanding of the concept of "identification". According to him, most Hebrew verbless clauses can be either classificatory or identificatory, the latter when there is total semantic overlap between the entities indicated by the S and P as in שָׂרָה אֵשֶׁת אַבְרָהָם *Sarah is Abraham's wife*. A prepositional phrase, by definition, does not refer to an entity, so that there can be no overlap between the two entities. By contrast, the way we understand "identification" is perfectly applicable to a clause such as 1Ch 5:22 מֵהָאֱלֹהִים הַמִּלְחָמָה *it was with God that the war originated*, i.e. it was not of human origin. See also 2Ch 20:15 כִּי לֹא לָכֶם הַמִּלְחָמָה כִּי אִם לֵאלֹהִים *for the war is not yours, but God's*; cf. 20:17 לֹא לָכֶם לְהִלָּחֵם בָּזֹאת *it is not up to you to fight in this case*.

Recently D. Cohen has stated that the nominal clause with a prepositional phrase as one of its principal constituents display the word-order

Prep.-N + Nid
OR
Nd + Prep.-N

In other words, he observes that whether the noun is determinate or indeterminate plays a decisive role. He goes on to claim that this is most

---

[5] T. Muraoka, "Emphasis in Biblical Hebrew", Ph.D. Diss. (Jerusalem, 1969), p. 9: see now our *Emphatic Words and Stuctures in Biblical Hebrew* (Jerusalem/Leiden, 1985), pp. 14f. On our understanding of "identificatory" or "identification", which deviates from the normal usage, see *Emphatic*, pp. 7-9.

[6] Andersen, *Verbless*, pp. 49f.

likely a language universal. The validity of this law in respect of Semitic languages is shown by Cohen with an example from Classical Arabic: *fi-l-bayti rajulun "there is a man in the house"* as against *ʾar-rajlu fi-l-bayti "the man is in the house"*[7]. We shall see however that this is a rather sweeping generalisation which, at least as far as Classical Hebrew is concerned[8], does not accord terribly well with actual data. On the other hand, there is no doubt that the determinate or indeterminate nature of the noun is of crucial importance to our consideration[9].

We first indicate an overall distribution pattern of the two sequences:

| | Nd-prep. | Prep.-Nd | Nid-prep | Prep.-Nid |
|---|---|---|---|---|
| Genesis | 26 | 11 | 24 | 13 |
| Judges | 18 | 7 | 19 | 3 |
| LBH[10] | 28 | 39 | 14 | 52 |
| Temple Scroll | 1 | 0 | 7 | 12 |
| Mishnah | 0 | 0 | 6 | 0 |
| Mechilta | 15 | 0 | 23 | 1 |
| Sifré Deut. | 0 | 0 | 1 | 2 |

A few general observations can be made with confidence on the basis of the above statistics.

1. In terms of the general frequency of the two sequences, namely whether the prepositional phrase follows or precedes, LBH and the Hebrew of the Temple Scroll stand together in that the pattern in which the prepositional phrase precedes is markedly more frequent than in the rest of the corpus examined in this study.

2. *Pace* Cohen there are too many examples which do not conform with the rule formulated by him (see above). To cite only a few such examples:

---

[7] D. Cohen, *La Phrase nominale et l'évolution du système verbal en sémitique. Études de syntaxe historique* (Paris, 1984), pp. 38-40. Nd = determinate noun or noun phrase; Nid = indeterminate noun or noun phrase.

[8] Even in Japanese, from which Cohen cites an example to argue his case for the universality of the syntax, *koko ni naifu wa aru* is quite as natural as *naifu wa koko ni aru* for "the knife is here", though as a reply to the question "Where is the knife?" the latter is more idiomatic.

[9] This feature was duly noted by us: Muraoka, "Emphasis", pp. 5f. et passim; idem *Emphatic*, pp. 8f. et passim. Andersen went further by attempting to establish a gradated scale of determinateness: Andersen, *Verbless*, pp. 32, 46f., and Table 1 on p. 109. In Hoftijzer's scheme also is this feature accorded centrality: see, e.g., "N.C. reconsidered", pp. 466ff., 471ff., 486f.

[10] LBH = Late Biblical Hebrew.

Nid-prep.: Gn 8:9 כִּי־מַיִם עַל־פְּנֵי כָל־הָאָרֶץ *for there was water on the entire surface of the earth*; 11:6 הֵן עַם אֶחָד וְשָׂפָה אַחַת לְכֻלָּם *indeed it is one nation and they have a common language*; 24:25 גַּם־תֶּבֶן גַּם־מִסְפּוֹא רַב עִמָּנוּ *we have plentiful supply of both straw and provender*; 29:6 הֲשָׁלוֹם לוֹ *Is he well?*; Jdg. 7:20 חֶרֶב לַיהוה וּלְגִדְעוֹן *The Lord and Gideon have a sword*; 1Ch 12:41 כִּי שִׂמְחָה בְּיִשְׂרָאֵל *for there is joy in Israel.*

Prep.-Nd: 2Ch 13:12 וְהִנֵּה עִמָּנוּ בָרֹאשׁ האלהים *and behold God is with us at our head*; 17:9 וְעִמָּהֶם סֵפֶר תּוֹרַת יהוה *and they had the book of the law of the Lord with them*. See also Josh. 1:9 כִּי עִמְּךָ יהוה אֱלֹהֶיךָ *for the Lord your God is with you*; 22:31 ... כִּי־בְתוֹכֵנוּ יהוה *for the Lord is amongst us*; 1Kg 4:13 לוֹ חַוֹּת יָאִיר *he has the village of Yair.*

3. Joüon's position does not seem to be verified by this study except perhaps in respect of LBH and the Hebrew of the Temple Scroll; even there, in purely statistic terms, one can hardly claim that the prepositional phrase *generally* precedes.

A closer look at the data allows us to make further observations.

4. The relatively few examples of the pattern Prep.-Nd comprise the following types.

a) Nd = personal pronoun: Gn 26:24 כִּי אִתְּךָ אָנֹכִי *for I am with you*; 30:2 הֲתַחַת אֱלֹהִים אָנֹכִי *can I take the place of God?*; similarly in 50:9; Jdg 14:4 מֵיהוה הִיא *it was from the Lord*; 19:18 מִשָּׁם אָנֹכִי *I am from there*; Ezr. 2:59, Ne 7:61 אִם מִיִּשְׂרָאֵל הֵם *if they are part of Israel*; Ne 9:37 וּבְצָרָה גְדוֹלָה אֲנָחְנוּ *we are in dire straits*. This is in keeping with our understanding that the personal pronoun tends to occupy the unobtrusive, second slot, unless it is to be accorded some special prominence or focus, and it can be seen that in these cases the focus is rather on the preceding prepositional phrase. Examples of the opposite sequence are far and few between: 1Ch 12:1 וְהֵמָּה בַּגִּבּוֹרִים עֹזְרֵי הַמִּלְחָמָה *they are the warriors who helped him at the time of the battle*, where a group of men are singled out to be commemorated; Ezr 10:4 אֲנַחְנוּ עִמָּךְ *we are with you*, where the clause immediately follows עָלֶיךָ הַדָּבָר, thus the position of אנחנוappears to be due to contrast or juxtaposition of the two parties involved; 9:7 מִימֵי אֲבֹתֵינוּ אֲנַחְנוּ בְּאַשְׁמָה גדולה הַיּוֹם הַזֶּה *since the time of our forefathers we have been exceedingly sinful up to this day*, where the pronoun occupies the second slot, thus conforming with the rule formulated by A. Bendavid[11]. See also Gn 31:38 זֶה עֶשְׂרִים שָׁנָה אָנֹכִי עִמָּךְ *Already twenty years I have been with you*. Cf. Ct 2:16 דּוֹדִי לִי וַאֲנִי לוֹ *my love is mine and I am his*; 6:3 אני לדודי ודודי לי *I am my love's and my love is mine*, where the focus on the *I – he* relationship is fittingly expressed by the word-order chosen, whereas the opposite sequence would highlight one's attachment to the other and the intimacy of the relationship.

b) We have included here cases in which the first slot is occupied by an interrogative: Gn 29:4 מֵאַיִן אַתֶּם ... מֵחָרָן אֲנָחְנוּ *where are you from? We are from Haran*; 32:18 לְמִי אַתָּה *whose are you?*; Jdg 6:13 וְאַיֵּה כָל־נִפְלְאֹתָיו ... *and where are all his wonders?*; also 8:18. An interrogative of any kind commonly occupies the first slot.

c) In the remaining cases it is possible to recognise a greater or lesser degree of prominence given to the preceding prepositional phrase by the way of contrast, identification, emphasis and the like. Thus Gn 3:16 וְאֶל־אִישֵׁךְ תְּשׁוּקָתֵךְ וְהוּא יִמְשָׁל־בָּךְ *it shall be your husband that you will yearn for, and he is going to be your master*; similarly at 4:7 אֵלֶיךָ תְּשׁוּקָתוֹ וְאַתָּה תִּמְשָׁל־בּוֹ; 26:20 לָנוּ הַמָּיִם *the water is ours*; 27:13 עָלַי קִלְלָתְךָ *Let the curse fall on me*; Jdg 6:37 וְעַל־כָּל־הָאָרֶץ חֹרֶב *and driness on all the ground* in contrast to the immediately preceding אִם טַל יִהְיֶה עַל־הַגִּזָּה לְבַדָּהּ *if there is dew on the fleece alone* and the position of על כל הארץ probably due to attraction to the preceding locative phrase; 1Ch 29:1 כִּי לֹא לְאָדָם הַבִּירָה כִּי ליהוה אלהים *for the palace will not be for man, but for the Lord God*, a passage replete with acknowledgements of God's uniqueness, so in vs. 11 לְךָ יהוה הַגְּדֻלָּה וְהַגְּבוּרָה וְהַתִּפְאֶרֶת וְהַנֵּצַח וְהַהוֹד כִּי־כֹל בַּשָּׁמַיִם וּבָאָרֶץ לְךָ יהוה הַמַּמְלָכָה ... *Thine, O Lord, is the greatness, and the strength, and the glory, and the victory, and the majesty; for all that is in heavens and earth is thine (?); thine is the kingdom, O Lord...*; in vs. 12 וְהָעֹשֶׁר וְהַכָּבוֹד מִלְּפָנֶיךָ וְאַתָּה מוֹשֵׁל בַּכֹּל וּבְיָדְךָ כֹּחַ וּגְבוּרָה ... *and the riches and the honour proceed from thee, and thou rulest all, and in thy hand reside power and strength*; vs. 14 כִּי מִמְּךָ הַכֹּל וּמִיָּדְךָ נָתַנּוּ לָךְ *for everything comes from thee, and of thy own have we given thee*; vs. 16 כֹּל הֶהָמוֹן הַזֶּה ... מִיָּדְךָ הִיא וּלְךָ הַכֹּל *all this abundance*

[11] See A. Bendavid, *Biblical Hebrew and Mishnaic Hebrew*, vol. 2 [Heb], (Tel Aviv, 1971), pp. 701, 817f., 821, 828.

... *comes from thy hand and all belongs to you*[12]. In a rather similar context we find 2Ch 20:12 עָלֶיךָ עֵינֵינוּ *our eyes are upon thee*. Cf. also 2Ch 20:15,17 cited above. Contrast is clearly marked in 2Ch 32:8 עִמּוֹ זְרוֹעַ בָּשָׂר וְעִמָּנוּ יהוה אֱלֹהֵינוּ לְעָזְרֵנוּ *he has an arm of flesh, whereas we have the Lord our God to help us*. In Jdg. 16:27*b* וְשָׁמָּה כֹּל סַרְנֵי פְלִשְׁתִּים *all the lords of the Philistines were there* the preceding adverb, being of anaphoric force referring back to הבית in 16:27a וְהַבַּיִת מָלֵא הָאֲנָשִׁים וְהַנָּשִׁים *and the house was full of men and women*, can be said to have found its natural position[13]. See also Jdg 20:27.

d) In addition, we find in Ch a series of clauses of the pattern Prep.-Nd, most of them in a register or list, which makes one wonder whether we are dealing here with genuine nominal clauses or not: e.g. 1Ch 27:2 עַל הַמַּחֲלֹקֶת הָרִאשׁוֹנָה ... יָשָׁבְעָם *Jashobeam was in charge of the first division*, where it is not certain, either, that ישׁ־בעם should be treated as Nd, for although it is a personal name, it could be glossed as "a man by the name of Jashobeam"; 27:25 וְעַל אֹצְרוֹת הַמֶּלֶךְ עַזְמָוֶת *Over the royal treasury was Azmaveth*; similarly 26:12, 27:26,27,28,29,30,31,34: 2Ch 17:15,16,18; 31:15; Ezr 8:33. One might say that in this "database" the field of the area of responsibility is highlighted over against the field of the personnel assigned to the area. However, a measure of caution is in order in view of the above-quoted 1Ch 29:12 וְהָעֹשֶׁר וְהַכָּבוֹד מִלְּפָנֶיךָ *and the riches and honour proceed from thee*, in which the sequence Nd-Prep. is remarkable, since all the parallel clauses in the immediate context show the opposite sequence. Thus it appears more than likely that the intended prominence could have been signalled by some unique intonation pattern, and not necessarily by means of word-order differentiation, for there is no other instance in which the prepositional phrase in the sequence Nd-Prep. is given prominence. We may conclude, however, that, if some prominence was to be accorded to the prepositional phrase, one would normally have chosen the sequence Prep-Nd.

5. In Gn and Jdg. the sequence Prep.-Nd is well-nigh confined to circumstantial clauses: e.g. Gn 16:1 וְלָהּ שִׁפְחָה מִצְרִית *and she had an Egyptian handmaid*; 24:29 וּלְרִבְקָה אָח *and Rebekah had a brother*; Jdg. 3:16 וְלָהּ שְׁנֵי פֵיוֹת *and it had two blades*; 16:27 וְעַל־הַגָּג כִּשְׁלֹשֶׁת אֲלָפִים אִישׁ וְאִשָּׁה הָרֹאִים בִּשְׂחוֹק שִׁמְשׁוֹן *and on the*

[12] On the function of the pronoun *hy'* in vs. 16, see P. Joüon (translated and revised by T. Muraoka), *A Grammar of Biblical Hebrew* (forthcoming), §154 *i*.

[13] See Joüon (Muraoka), §155 *pa*.

*roof there were about three thousand men and women watching Samson's show*. However, it does not follow that this is a typical sequence for the circumstantial clause; in fact, such a clause is generally believed to put the subject first[14]. In Jdg. 19:10 we find both patterns side by side: וְעִמּוֹ צֶמֶד חֲמוֹרִים חֲבוּשִׁים וּפִילַגְשׁוֹ עִמּוֹ *and he had with him a couple of saddled asses and his concubine was with him*; add the remarkable pair (Gn 32:7 and 33:1) noted by Andersen (see above). See also Gn 1:2 וְחֹשֶׁךְ עַל פְּנֵי תְהוֹם *and the darkness was upon the surface of the deep*; Jdg 3:27 וְהוּא לִפְנֵיהֶם *and he was ahead of them*. The Chronicler, however, uses the same sequence in clauses other than circumstantial as well, and again in lists: 2Ch 17:14 וְאֵלֶּה פְקֻדָּתָם לְבֵית אֲבוֹתֵיהֶם לִיהוּדָה שָׂרֵי אֲלָפִים עַדְנָה הַשָּׂר וְעִמּוֹ גִּבּוֹרֵי חַיִל שְׁלֹשׁ מֵאוֹת אָלֶף׃ וְעַל־יָדוֹ יְהוֹחָנָן הַשָּׂר וְעִמּוֹ מָאתַיִם וּשְׁמוֹנִים׃ *This was the muster of them by fathers' houses: Of Judah, the commanders of thousands: Adnah the commander, with three thousand mighty men of valour,* [15]*and next to him Jehohanan the commander with two hundred and eighty thousand*; similarly in vss. 17,18. On 2Ch 20:6 וּבְיָדְךָ כֹּחַ וּגְבוּרָה *the power and strength are in your hands*, and 26:18 לֹא־לְךָ עֻזִּיָּהוּ לְהַקְטִיר לַיהוה כִּי לַכֹּהֲנִים בְּנֵי־אַהֲרֹן *it is not up to you, O Uzziah, to burn incense to the Lord, but up to the priests the sons of Aaron*, see our discussion above on 2Ch 29:11ff. Note that בידך כח וגבורה at 2Ch 20:6 is immediately preceded by הֲלֹא אַתָּה־הוּא אֱלֹהִים בַּשָּׁמַיִם וְאַתָּה מוֹשֵׁל בְּכֹל מַמְלְכוֹת הַגּוֹיִם *Art thou not God in heaven? Doest thou not rule over all the kingdoms of the nations?*

6. A great proportion of clauses of the sequence Nd-prep. (and to a lesser extent, Nid-prep.) are of one of the following three categories:

a) Circumstantial clause: e.g. Gn 12:6 וְהַכְּנַעֲנִי אָז בָּאָרֶץ *and the Canaanites were in the land at the time*; 24:15,45 וְכַדָּהּ עַל שִׁכְמָהּ *with her pitcher on her shoulder*; Jdg 4:22 וְהַיָּתֵד בְּרַקָּתוֹ *with the tent-pig in his temple*; 2Ch 13:13 וְהַמַּאְרָב מֵאַחֲרֵיהֶם *and the ambush was behind them*; Gn 24:22 וּשְׁנֵי צְמִידִים עַל יָדֶיהָ *with two bracelets on her arms*; Jdg 7:16 וְלַפִּדִים בְּתוֹךְ הַכַּדִּים *with torches inside the jars*.

b) Introduced by the presentative הנה: Gn 20:15 הִנֵּה אַרְצִי

---

[14] See Muraoka, *Emphatic*, p. 14; Andersen, *Verbless*, p. 45, Rule 5; idem, *The Sentence in Biblical Hebrew* (The Hague/Paris, 1974), p. 78.

[15] On the possible theological motivation in matters of grammar, see Joüon (Muraoka), *Grammar*, §155 *ne*.

לְפָנֶיךָ *behold my land is before you*; 24:51 הִנֵּה רִבְקָה לְפָנֶיךָ *behold Rebekah is before you*; Jdg 17:2 הִנֵּה הַכֶּסֶף אִתִּי *behold the silver is with me*; Gn 8:11 הִנֵּה עֲלֵה זַיִת טָרָף בְּפִיהָ *behold there was a freshly plucked olive leaf in its mouth*; Jdg 14:8 וְהִנֵּה עֲדַת דְּבוֹרִים בִּגְוִיַּת הָאַרְיֵה וּדְבָשׁ *and behold there was a swarm of bees inside the cadavre of the lion, and honey.*

c) Introduced by a reference to the God of Israel or the like (cf. note 15): Gn 21:22 אֱלֹהִים עִמְּךָ בְּכֹל אֲשֶׁר אַתָּה עֹשֶׂה *God is with you in whatever you do*; 39:3 וַיַּרְא אֲדֹנָיו כִּי יהוה אִתּוֹ *and his master noted that the Lord was with him*; similarly 39:23; Jdg 6:12 יהוה עִמְּךָ *the Lord is with you*; 1:22 וַיהוה עִמָּם *and the Lord was with them* (also circumstantial); 2Ch 15:2 יהוה עִמָּכֶם בִּהְיוֹתְכֶם עִמּוֹ *the Lord is with you, while you are with him*; 15:9 כִּי יהוה אֱלֹהָיו עִמּוֹ *that the Lord his God was with him*; 20:9 כִּי שִׁמְךָ בַּבַּיִת הַזֶּה *for thy name is in this house*; Ezr 8:22 יַד אֱלֹהֵינוּ עַל כָּל־מְבַקְשָׁיו לְטוֹבָה וְעֻזּוֹ וְאַפּוֹ עַל כָּל־עֹזְבָיו *the hand of our God is for good upon all those who seek him, and his might and wrath are upon all those who forsake him*. See also 1Ch 21:29, 22:18, 28:20, 2Ch 1:1, 20:17, and cf. Ne 11:23 כִּי מִצְוַת הַמֶּלֶךְ עֲלֵיהֶם *for the royal decree is incumbent upon them.*

7. Further to the point made above under 1. it needs to be stressed that, in a straight nominal clause indicating the existence of a certain person or object the normal sequence is Nid-prep.: Gn 25:23 שְׁנֵי גֹיִים בְּבִטְנֵךְ *two nations are in your stomach*; 29:6 הֲשָׁלוֹם לוֹ *Is he well?*; 41:29 שָׂבָע גָּדוֹל בְּכָל־אֶרֶץ מִצְרָיִם *there will be great plenty in all the land of Egypt*; 43:28 שָׁלוֹם לְעַבְדְּךָ *your servant is well*; Jdg 3:19 דְּבַר־סֵתֶר לִי אֵלֶיךָ *I have something to speak to you in confidence*; similarly 3:20; 16:9,12,14,20 פְּלִשְׁתִּים עָלֶיךָ שִׁמְשׁוֹן *Philistines are upon you, Samson*; 19:20 שָׁלוֹם לְךָ *Peace be to you*; 21:17; 1Ch 12:19 שָׁלוֹם לְךָ וְשָׁלוֹם לְעֹזְרֶךָ *Peace be to you and peace be to your helper*. We have excluded from our consideration here those clauses introduced by הִנֵּה and circumstantial clauses, though we should perhaps include those introduced by כִּי such as Gn 25:28 כִּי צַיִד בְּפִיו *for game agreed with his taste*; Jdg 8:24 כִּי נִזְמֵי זָהָב לָהֶם *for they had golden earrings* — cf. 8:30 כִּי נָשִׁים רַבּוֹת הָיוּ לוֹ *for he had many wives*; 1:19 כִּי־רֶכֶב בַּרְזֶל לָהֶם *for they had iron chariots*; sim. 4:3; 4:17 כִּי שָׁלוֹם בֵּין יָבִין מֶלֶךְ־חָצוֹר וּבֵין בֵּית חֶבֶר *for there was peace between Jabin the king of Hazor and*

*the house of Heber*; 1Ch 4:41 כִּי מִרְעֶה לְצֹאנָם שָׁם *for they had a grazing ground for their flock there*; 12:41 כִּי שִׂמְחָה בְּיִשְׂרָאֵל *for there was joy in Israel*; 2Ch 15:5 כִּי מְהוּמֹת רַבּוֹת עַל כָּל־יוֹשְׁבֵי הָאֲרָצוֹת *for there were many disturbances inflicted on the inhabitants of the lands*.

8. Having regard to a large number of cases of Prep.-Nd which appear in lists and also a considerable number of clauses of the same sequence in which the prepositional phrase occupies the firts slot on account of some measure of prominence accorded to it (see 6. above), we are led to the conclusion that the normal sequence for the type of nominal clause under consideration in this study, a sequence which is neutral in respect of the prominence to be given to either of the two principal constituents, is N-Prep., on condition that the first slot is not a personal pronoun. As indicated above a few times, the intonation can presumably override this rule of thumb.

# Word Order in Different Clause Types in Deuteronomy 1-30

L.J. de Regt, Amsterdam

In this article I will attempt to relate word order to clause types in the corpus of Deuteronomy 1-30. It is of interest to see to what extent word order in principal clauses is different from the order in subordinate clauses. I will show that the traditional distinction between principal clause and subordinate clause is difficult to maintain for Deuteronomy 1-30 as far as word order is concerned. On the whole, word order does not suffice as a criterion for that distinction.

With a view to my doctoral dissertation, I set up a system of registration in which grammatical categories have been recorded for each clause in Deuteronomy 1-30. In the dissertation, patterns were deduced from the frequencies of those categories and of their interrelationships. The registered data of the corpus constituted the direct input for frequency tables by means of SAS-procedures [1]. Firstly, of each parameter

[1] SAS was used to get the registered data of Deuteronomy 1-30 into a data set, after which SAS procedures were used to analyze the data in the data set.

In the data step, SAS was asked to create a data set, and programming statements (infile and input statements) were included that perform the processes necessary to build the data set. Details can be found in the SAS User's Guide (1985), chapter 3 "Introduction to the Data Step", p. 25-38. Further details on the statements are found in chapter 4 "SAS Statements Used in the Data Step", p. 99-100, 130-134. It is possible to print the observations of a SAS data set, i.c. the registered data of Deuteronomy 1-30, by means of the Print procedure. Relevant details can be found in chapter 43, p. 1007-1008.

Tables were sometimes based on a restricted corpus rather than the complete corpus. An example of this is the table on order in clauses without certain elements that might have a conditioning effect on order (see section 2 of this article). For a table to be based on a specific subset of clauses, a subsetting If statement in the data step caused SAS to process only those observations that met the condition specified in the If statement (SAS Guide, chapter 4, p. 98; chapter 5 "SAS Expressions", p. 223-225). The resulting data set therefore contained a subset of the original complete data set. Thus, the subsetting If statement in the present example excludes clauses with certain order-conditioning elements from the data subset on which the table is based. A subsetting If statement is always preceded by a Set statement (chapter 3, p. 27; chapter 4, p. 205, 208-209).

The frequency tables were produced by means of the Freq procedure. A Tables statement specified the parameter(s) in question and what table was wanted. Details (e.g. verb form, subject, order, clause type) the categories were listed with their frequencies and percentages. Secondly, in cross-tabulation tables the frequencies of the categories of one parameter were subdivided according to the categories of another parameter. For instance, the parameters verb form and order were thus related one to another. This was also done with the parameters verb form and clause type. In this article I will relate the parameters order and clause type.

More analysis of grammatical constructions in a textual corpus can provide us with interesting quantitative data. Research on Hebrew grammar should be more comprehensive and less selective. As Claassen points out, this is often a motive for turning to computer-assisted methods (Claassen 1988, p. 290-291). After carrying out comprehensive and quantitative research on complete corpuses in biblical Hebrew, the different corpuses can be compared. Apart from such factors as textual character and style, computer-assisted research on syntax would thus contribute to our knowledge of diachronic processes in biblical Hebrew syntax and of the relative antiquity of the corpuses (Hardmeier 1970, p. 179).

Before interpreting the cross-tabulation table of order and clause type, I will briefly discuss the two parameters separately, as I have done more extensively in the dissertation (de Regt 1988, p. 24-25, 34-43, 68-71, 74). Allowance is made for the rounding off of percentages.

## 1. The Clause Type Parameter

The categories of the clause type parameter are not formally recognizable in clauses. Principal clauses are divided into conditional apodosis clauses, adversative clauses, parenthetical main clauses and (other) main clauses. The division of subordinate clause types has been made on some broad semantic groupings but I am fully aware that other groupings are also possible. I will now give examples of clause type categories. At the end of this section, I will briefly discuss the frequency table on clause types.

In the corpus four main clauses within another clause are found, one of which is 4:48d.

4:48 d *hwʾ ḥrmwn*
that Hermon
[... as far as Mount Sirion] – that is Hermon – [and all the

---

are found in chapter 37, p. 945-952.

A Label statement specified the names of the parameters (chapter 4, p. 150). To specify the names of parameter categories, Format statements and Value statements were used with the Format procedure (chapter 9, p. 340-341; chapter 35, p. 913-919, 924- 927).

plain ...]

For such clauses, the term *parenthetical* is used in Nida (1957, p. 180).

An *adversative clause* is a principal clause that contrasts with (indicates the alternative to what is said in) another principal clause which closely precedes the adversative clause. As is illustrated by 15:23b and 15:6f, adversative clauses are not necessarily marked as such by a (specific) conjunction.

15:23 a *rq ʾt-dmw lʾ tʾkl*
only its blood not you eat
b *ʿl-hʾrṣ tšpknw kmym*
on the ground you pour out it like water
a Only its blood you shall not eat;
b you shall pour it out on the ground like water.

15:6 e *wmšlt bgwym rbym*
and you rule over nations many
f *wbk lʾ ymšlnw*
and over you not they rule
e And you will rule over many nations,
f but they will not rule over you.

An interesting example of an *object clause* is found in 4:26b. In 4:26, a is a main clause and b is the object clause. At the same time a prepositional direct object occurs in a. Thus, in this example, the main clause to which the object clause is connected also has an object among its own elements.

4:26 a *hʿydty bkm hywm ʾt-hšmym wʾt-hʾrṣ*
I call to witness against you today the heavens and the earth (PDO)
b *ky ʾbd tʾbdwn mhr mʿl hʾrṣ*
that perish you perish quickly from off the land
a I call heaven and earth to witness against you today
b that you will soon utterly perish from the land.

An object clause is regarded as an element in the order formula of the main clause. The order formula of 4:26a is V - DPO OCL.

An *exceptive clause* is found in 15:4a [2].

15:4 a *ʾps ky lʾ yhyh bk ʾbywn*
save that not he is with you poor

[2] Joüon remarks on this clause: "Pour introduire une exception après une proposition positive on emploie surtout *ʾps ky* excepté que ..." (Joüon §173a, transcription mine).

However, there will be no poor among you

A *specifying clause* gives more information about the way in which the action in the preceding clause is executed. An example is 22:21e.

22:21 d *ky-ʿ nblh bysrʾl*
for she did folly in Israel
e *lznwt byt ʾbyh*
play the harlot house of her father
d because she has wrought folly
e by playing the harlot in her father's house

A *circumstantial clause* makes mention of a circumstance under which the action/situation in another clause takes place. An example is 22:6b.

22:6 a *ky yqrʾ qn-ṣpwr lpnyk ... ʾprḥym ʾw byṣym*
if it is met nest of bird before you ... young ones or eggs
b *whʾm rbṣt ʿl-hʾprḥym ʾw ʿl-hbyṣym*
and the mother sitting on the young ones or on the eggs
a If you chance to come upon a bird's nest ... with young ones or eggs
b and the mother is sitting on the young ones or on the eggs

A *temporal clause*, although similar to a circumstantial clause, particularly provides information about the point or period of time to which another clause is temporally related. Examples are 2:14d and 29:21d.

2:14 a *whymym ... šlšym wšmnh šnh*
and the days thirty and eight year
d *ʿd- tm kl-hdwr ʾnšy hmlḥmh*
until perish all the generation men of the war
*mqrb hmlḥmh*
from the camp
a And the time ... was 38 years
d until the entire generation, the men of war, had perished from the camp.

29:21 a *wʾmr hdwr hʾḥrwn bnykm*
and say the generation the next your children
*... whnkry*
... and the stranger
d *wrʾw ʾt-mkwt hʾrṣ hhwʾ wʾt-thlʾyh*
and they see plagues of the land that and its sicknesses
a And the generation to come, your children ... and the stranger ... will say

d when they see the plagues of that land and its sicknesses

The only *concessive clauses* are found in 28:62b and 29:18f.

29:18 e *šlwm yhyh-ly*
peace it is to me
f *ky bšrrt lby ʾlk*
though in stubbornness of my heart I go
e I shall have peace
f though I walk in the stubbornness of my heart

A *subject clause* is treated as an element in the order formula of the clause to which it is connected. The examples are 21:1f and 27:26b.

27:26 a *ʾrwr*
cursed
b *ʾšr lʾ- yqym ʾt-dbry htwrh-hzʾt*
who not carries out the words of this law
a Cursed be
b (he) who does not carry out the words of this law.

*Elliptical clauses* are defined as constructions in which no element of the order parameter occurs (see section 2). An example is 4:17a.

4:16 b ... *tbnyt kl-bhmh*
...likeness of all beast
17 a *ʾšr bʾrṣ*
which on the earth
16 b ...the likeness of any beast
17 a that is on the earth

Clauses may continue the clause type category of a preceding clause. In the following example two *causal clauses* occur. The conjunction *ky* occurs in the first one only.

16:19 c *wlʾ tqḥ šḥd*
and not you take reward
d *ky hšḥd yʿwr ʿyny ḥkmym*
for the reward it blinds eyes of wise
e *wyslp dbry ṣdqym*
and it twists words of righteous
c and you shall not take a bribe
d for a bribe blinds the eyes of the wise
e and twists the words of the righteous

In this example, a specific conjunction still occurred in the first causal clause. In other instances however, no conjunction specifically indicates the clause type category. 29:21d above is one of those examples. As Andersen points out, the relationships between clauses are often sufficiently indicated by the content of the clauses that are joined. The special subordinating conjunctions can then be replaced by w without loss of clarity (Andersen 1974, p. 117-118).

It is thus hard to draw a boundary line of a syntactic nature between coordination and subordination of clauses, when one looks at conjunctions. The frequencies and percentages of the clause type parameter categories are shown in table 1.

| clause types | frequency | percentage |
|---|---|---|
| main | 1256 | 40.0 |
| relative | 526 | 16.8 |
| final | 330 | 10.5 |
| conditional protasis | 219 | 7.0 |
| cond. apodosis | 190 | 6.1 |
| object | 162 | 5.2 |
| causal | 151 | 4.8 |
| temporal | 77 | 2.4 |
| elliptical | 64 | 2.0 |
| adversative | 52 | 1.7 |
| comparative | 51 | 1.6 |
| specifying | 32 | 1.0 |
| circumstantial | 16 | 0.5 |
| exceptive | 6 | 0.2 |
| parenthetical main | 4 | 0.1 |
| concessive | 2 | 0.1 |
| subject | 2 | 0.1 |
| total | 3140 | |

Table 1: *Clause Types in Deuteronomy 1-30*

Main clauses number 1256 (40.0%). Conditional apodosis clause, adversative clause and parenthetical main clause are categories which together number 246 (7.8%). When these figures are put together, it is shown that almost half of the clauses could be treated as a principal clause (47.8%). More than half of the clauses in the corpus are subordinate.

2. The Order Parameter

Of certain elements in clauses the order has been registered. These clause elements are the following: direct object without preposition (DO), prepositional direct object (PDO), indirect object without preposition (IO), prepositional indirect object (PIO), object clause (OCL), subject (S), subject clause (SCL), nominal predicate (P), verb (V). Of a prepositional object, the nota objecti is the first element.

Order elements may be discontinuous. Their components are not always contiguous (Pike & Pike 1980, p. 245). This is illustrated by the direct object in 30:19b.

30:19 b *hḥyym whmwt* *ntty* *lpnyk* *hbrkh*
the life and the death (DO) I set (V) before you the blessing
*whqllh*
and the curse (DO)
life and death have I set before you, blessing and curse

There may be elements in a clause that are not part of the order parameter. When one or more of such elements (adjuncts, prepositional phrases and vocatives) occur between order elements, this is indicated by a dash. Thus the order formula for 30:19b is DO V - DO.

The nominal predicate only occurs in nominal clauses and in verbal clauses in which the lexical stem of the verb is *hyh* or *ḥšb*.

7:26 b *whyyt* *ḥrm* *kmhw*
and you are (V) curse (P) like it
and you become accursed like it

2:20 a *ʾrṣ-* *rpʾym* *tḥšb* *ʾp-hwʾ*
land of Rephaites (P) it is accounted (V) also that (S)
That also was accounted a land of the Rephaites.

Many participles and infinitive constructs have been treated as verbs. Consequently, they appear as verbs in the order parameter and the (partial) clauses in which they occur have been treated as verbal clauses. An example of such a partial clause is 22:21e in section 1.

Subject clauses and object clauses are clauses in their own right and are thus categories of the clause type parameter. On the other hand, they are also elements in another clause. When a subject or object consists of more than one word, this is no reason to regard it as more than one subject or object. Similarly, when a subject clause or object clause is in fact a series of subject clauses or object clauses, it is still regarded as one subject clause or object clause in the order of the clause to which it belongs. Hence, SCL stands for subject clause (series) and OCL stands for object clause (series). In this connection, 4:21 provides a good example.

4:21 b *wyšbʿ*
and he swore
c *lblty ʿbry ʾt-hyrdn*
to not cross me the Jordan
d *wlblty bʾ ʾl-hʾrṣ hṭ wbh*
and to not come to the land the good
b and he swore
c that I should not cross the Jordan
d and that I should not enter the good land

c and d are a series of two object clauses to the main clause b. The order formulas for these clauses are as follows: b V OCL; c V S PDO; d V.
Like any parameter, the order parameter has its categories. Each different order formula that has been registered constitutes a category of this parameter. The table on order in the whole corpus of Deuteronomy 1-30 would require too much space if every order formula were to be mentioned separately. Instead, a summary of this table is given.

| | before the verb | after the verb |
|---|---|---|
| S | 268 (incl. S - V - S) | 620 |
| DO | 79 (incl. DO V - DO) | 624 |
| PDO | 30 | 396 |
| IO | 0 | 74 |
| PIO | 5 | 41 |

These figures also include order categories in which subject, verb, as well as object (DO or PDO) occur. Such order categories can be grouped according to the respective order of verb, subject and object: VSO 86; VOS 75; SVO 56; OVS 8; OSV 4; SOV 0. In 979 clauses V is the only order element.
The only S - V - S instance occurs in 2:10.
In every case of VOS order, the object is a pronominal suffix attached to the verb or to the nota objecti. The exceptions are 14:7b, 14:8a (two causal clauses) and 21:15d which is part of a conditional protasis and the only example of V - DO S.
21:15 d *wyldw- lw bnym hʾhwbh whśnwʾh*
and they bear him sons the loved and the hated
and they have both born him sons, both the loved and the hated

An OVS example is 18:15a, the only DO V - S instance in the corpus.

18:15 a *nby᾽* *mqrbk* *m᾽ḥyk* *kmny*
prophet from the midst of thee of your brothers like me (DO)
18:15 a he will raise up (V) for you the Lord your God (S)
*yqym* *lk* *yhwh* *᾽lhyk*
he will raise up (V) for you the Lord your God (S)
A prophet from among you, of your brothers, like me,
will the Lord your God raise up for you.

The verbs in the four OSV cases are all participles. In one case the object is an interrogative pronoun (10:12a). The remaining instances are the main clauses of 4:12bc and 24:6b, a causal clause.

24:6 b *ky-npš hw᾽ḥbl*
for life he take in pledge
for he would be taking life in pledge

Table 2 is based on a selection from the corpus. It takes into account only those clauses in which certain elements that might have a conditioning effect on order do not occur.

For instance, the conjunction *w* conditions the verb to be order-initial if this conjunction is "part" of the verb form in question. This applies to the narrative, the perfect consecutive and other verb forms in which *w* occurs. Thus, VS order is to be considered regular only if there are clauses to be found "die mit einem Verbum finitum beginnen, ohne dass diesem eine Partikel wie *wa* vorangeht" (Schlesinger 1953, p. 382).

Table 2 is based on the clauses without preposition, interrogative particle, conjunction, interjection, negation, casus pendens, preverbal vocative, preverbal phrase/adjunct. It can be summarized as follows.

| | before the verb | after the verb |
|---|---|---|
| S | 51 | 71 |
| DO | 38 (incl. DO V - DO in 30:19b) | 60 |
| PDO | 9 | 53 |
| IO | 0 | 5 |
| PIO | 1 | 4 |

These figures include order categories in which subject and verb, as well as object (DO or PDO) occur: SVO 15; VSO 12; VOS 6; OVS 6; OSV 1; SOV 0. In 125 clauses V is the only order element.

The OSV instance is found in 4:12b.

| order | freq. | % | order | freq. | % |
|---|---|---|---|---|---|
| DO - V IO | 1 | | V | 125 | 28.50 |
| DO S V | 1 | | V - DO | 9 | 2.1 |
| DO V | 30 | 6.8 | V - PDO | 9 | 2.1 |
| DO V - DO | 1 | | V - PDO OCL | 1 | |
| DO V - S | 1 | | V - OCL | 4 | 0.9 |
| DO V S | 4 | 0.9 | V - S | 1 | |
| PDO V | 8 | 1.8 | V DO | 36 | 8.2 |
| PDO V S | 1 | | V DO S | 6 | 1.4 |
| PIO V OCL | 1 | | V PDO | 22 | 5.0 |
| OCL V | 1 | | V IO | 1 | |
| P | 19 | 4.3 | V IO DO | 1 | |
| P - S | 2 | 0.5 | V IO PDO | 1 | |
| P S | 8 | 1.8 | V PIO DO | 1 | |
| P V | 4 | 0.9 | V OCL | 10 | 2.3 |
| P V - S | 2 | 0.5 | V SCL | 1 | |
| S | 5 | 1.1 | V S | 41 | 9.4 |
| S P | 15 | 3.4 | V S - DO - DO | 1 | |
| S V | 33 | 7.5 | V S PDO | 6 | 1.4 |
| S V - DO | 2 | 0.5 | V S DO | 1 | |
| S V - PDO | 4 | 0.9 | V S PDO | 4 | 0.9 |
| S V DO | 3 | 0.7 | V S PIO | 1 | |
| S V PDO | 6 | 1.4 | V S PIO OCL | 1 | |
| S V IO | 1 | | V S OCL | 1 | |
| S V PIO | 1 | | | | |

Table 2: *Clauses in Deuteronomy 1-30 without preposition, interrogative particle, conjunction, interjection, negation, casus pendens, preverbal vocative, preverbal phrase/adjunct*

4:12 b *qwl dbrym ʾtm šmʿym*
sound of words you hear
you heard the sound of words

The preverbal prepositional indirect object is found in 26:17a[3].

26:17 a *ʾt-yhwh hʾmrt hywm*

[3] It does not go without saying that *ʾt-yhwh* is a PIO rather than a PDO. However, the two participants which have been called double direct objects (Joüon §125u; Gesenius §117cc) are not of the same rank. One of them is always slightly more actively involved in causing the event to happen (Cohen 1975, p. 21). "... in an act of asking, the person asked is more important in precipitating the asking - more agent-like - than the thing requested ..." (Cohen p. 13). In this connection, the discussions of three-place causative constructions in Lyons (1968, p. 368-370, section 8.2.14) and in Comrie (1989, p. 168-183) are illuminating.

the Lord you have caused to say today
b *lhywt lk* *l'lhym*
to be to you to God
a You have caused the Lord to declare today
b that he is your God

An OVS instance is found in 5:22a.

5:22 a *'t-hdbrym h'lh dbr yhwh*
the words these spoke the Lord...
these words the Lord spoke...

One of the instances of S order is found in 4:3a.

4:3 a *ʿynykm*
your eyes
b *hr't*
seeing
c *'t 'šr ʿ yhwh bbʿl pʿr*
what he did the Lord at Baal Peor
a It is your eyes
b that have seen
c what the Lord did at Baal Peor.

3a cannot be connected to another (partial) clause and is thus treated as a nominal clause consisting of one element only (Meyer 1972, p. 9, §90.6a; Talstra 1987, p. 105).

An example of P order is found in 3:26d. Again, P is the only element in this nominal clause that is part of the order parameter (Meyer p. 9).

3:26 d *rb- lk*
enough (P) to you
Let it be enough to you.

Of the 122 subjects in a verbal clause, 58.2% (71) occur after the verb whereas not less than 41.8% (51) occur before the verb. (In the complete corpus, 30.1% (267) of the 888 subjects in verbal clauses occur before the verb.)

Of the 98 DO and 62 PDO objects, 38.8% (38) and 14.5% (9) occur before the verb. (In the complete corpus, these percentages are much lower: 11.2% (79) and 7.0% (30).) Taken together, 29.4% (47) of the (P)DO objects are preverbal (against only 9.7% (109) in the complete corpus).

It is shown, then, that in the restricted corpus subjects and direct objects (especially DO objects) occur more often before the verb than is the case in the complete corpus, proportionally speaking. When clauses with elements that might have a conditioning effect on order are excluded, VS and VO are still to be considered regular. It is, however, less clear that classical Hebrew (in Deuteronomy 1-30) is a VS/VO language.

In this connection Greenberg's Universal 6 should be mentioned: "All languages with dominant VSO order have SVO as an alternative or as the only alternative basic order." (Greenberg 1963, p. 79). Table 2 and the above summaries, which are based on the corpus (complete and restricted), seem to show that its dominant order is VSO, with SVO and to a lesser degree VOS as alternative basic orders.

## 3. Order in Relation to Clause Types

In this section the order parameter will be set off against the opposition between principal and subordinate clause. Table 3 on the clause type and order parameters is based on the complete corpus, with the exception of the 64 elliptical clauses. In such clauses no element of the order parameter occurs. The total number of cases in the table is 3076.

The order categories, i.e. the order formulas, are given in the rows and the clause type categories in the columns. The total numbers of row category instances are given on the right of each row whereas the total numbers of column category instances have been mentioned in table 1.

Of order categories with a frequency of more than ten, the principal clause percentage is mentioned in the first column. This figure shows what percentage of the row category instances are attested in principal clauses. For example, 90.8% (59) of the 65 DO V instances are found in a principal clause.

The clause type categories of table 1 are abbreviated as follows: main, rel, fin, prot, apod, obj, caus, temp, adv, cpr, spec, circ, exc, -main-, ccs and subj, respectively.

We have seen that almost half of the clauses (47.8%) in the complete corpus can be treated as a principal clause. We are now in a position to see whether for clauses with a certain order the percentage of principal clauses is higher or lower than 47.8%. Differences between order in principal clauses and order in subordinate clauses can thus be observed.

Of clauses in which a subject precedes a nominal predicate (SP and S-P), 61.5% (40) are a principal clause, whereas of clauses with the subject after the nominal predicate (PS and P-S), the principal clause percentage is only 33.3% (21). In 27.2% (41) of the causal clauses a subject and a nominal predicate occur. For the other clause types, the proportion of instances with a subject and a nominal predicate is much lower.

The principal clause percentage of the 1020 clauses with a postverbal DO/PDO (excluding the two DO V - DO instances) amounts to 50.1% (511). Of the 109 clauses with a preverbal DO/PDO (including the DO V - DO instances), this percentage is much higher: 91.7% (100). In other words, almost half of the postverbal objects (509) are found in subordinate clauses. Only 9 preverbal objects, however, occur in subordinate clauses, four of which are causal clauses. Or to put it another way, almost half (518) of the DO/PDO objects are found in subordinate clauses. Only 9 (1.7%) of them are preverbal, whereas of the 611 objects in a principal clause not less than 100 (16.4%) occur before the verb. Most preverbal objects, then, are found in principal clauses.

On a very small scale, this can be illustrated by the frequencies of conditional protasis and apodosis clauses with a preverbal DO/PDO. There are 4 DO V apodosis clauses but there are only one DO V and one DO V IO protasis in the corpus. The protasis instances are found in 19:18c and 20:11b, respectively.

20:11 b *ʾm- šlwm t‘nk*
if peace it answers to you
if its answer to you is peace

2 PDO V apodosis clauses are attested whereas no protasis with a preverbal PDO is found in the corpus.

Of all 120 indirect objects (IO/PIO), 32.5% (39) are found in a principal clause. Only 5 indirect objects (PIO) occur before a verb. Four of these are found in a main clause, of which 26:17a in section 2 is an example. The remaining instance is found in 4:10h, a final clause.

4:10 h *wʾt-bnyhm ylmdwn*
and their children they teach
and that they may teach their children so

More than half (494) of the subjects in a verbal clause are found in subordinate clauses. 29.1% (144) of them occur before the verb, and of these 105 are found in relative clauses. Of the 394 subjects in a verbal principal clause, 123 occur before the verb, which is proportionally only slightly more (31.2%).

Proportionally, there are more preverbal subjects in adversative clauses than in main clauses. Among adversative clauses, 9 preverbal subjects are attested against 5 postverbal subjects. Of the subjects in main clauses, however, only 31.5% (108) are preverbal. One of the SV adversative clauses is found in 28:12e.

28:12 d *whlwyt* *gwym* *rbym*
and you lend nations many
e *w᾽tm* *l᾽* *tlwh*
and you not you borrow
d and you shall lend to many nations
e but you shall not borrow

The table shows that only in relative clauses (as in adversative and circumstantial clauses) do preverbal subjects outnumber postverbal subjects. Postverbal subjects occur in 97 relative clauses whereas preverbal subjects occur in 105 relative clauses. In all these 105 instances the verb is a participle, except for two perfects in 9:2ab.

9:2 ... *bny* *ʿnqym*
children of Anakites
a *᾽šr* *᾽th* *ydʿt*
whom you know
b *w᾽th* *šmʿt*
and you hear
Anakites, whom you know and of whom you have heard

It should be remembered that not only in relative clauses with a participle but also in the other participle clauses subjects occur before the verb (45 times), with the exception of only 9 instances, e.g. 13:4b.

13:4 b *ky mnsh* *yhwh* *᾽lhykm* *᾽tkm*
for testing (V) the Lord your God (S) you (PDO)
for the Lord your God is testing you

Subjects mostly occur before, rather than after participles, irrespective of the clause type. In relative clauses with a participle, subjects are thus only expected to occur before the verb.

In other subordinate clauses, most subjects occur after the verb. However, not less than 17 (31.5%) of the subjects in causal clauses occur before the verb. As has been mentioned above, the percentage of subjects that are preverbal is virtually the same in principal clauses (31.2%).

As has been mentioned at the beginning of this section, the above observations are all based on the complete corpus. Among them, observations with regard to preverbal subjects and objects play an important part. These results, however, may have been influenced by order-conditioning elements. They might be different if the table on order and clause type were to be based on the restricted corpus from which certain elements that may have a conditioning effect on order are excluded.

The summary below shows the frequencies of subjects and objects (DO/PDO) in principal and subordinate clauses in the restricted corpus.

| | principal clauses | subordinate clauses |
|---|---|---|
| subjects | 100 | 22 |
| preverbal subjects | 44 (44.0%) | 7 (31.8%) |
| objects (DO/PDO) | 118 | 41 |
| preverbal objects (DO/PDO) | 45 (38.1%) | 2 (4.9%) |

As has been pointed out in section 2, the proportions of preverbal subjects and direct objects as against postverbal ones in the restricted corpus are higher than in the complete corpus. Also, the principal clause percentage in the restricted corpus is higher than in the complete corpus. However, this does not imply that in the restricted corpus proportionally less preverbal subjects and objects are found in subordinate clauses. Rather, the proportions of preverbal subjects and preverbal objects (DO/PDO) in subordinate clauses as against principal clauses are approximately the same in both corpuses. It would thus seem that these proportions are hardly influenced by the order-conditioning elements.

In the restricted corpus, the percentage of direct objects in a subordinate clause that are preverbal (4.9%) is 7.8 times smaller than the percentage of such objects in a principal clause (38.1%). This proportion is approximately the same in the complete corpus, in which the percentage of direct objects in a subordinate clause that are preverbal (1.7%) is 9.6 times smaller than the percentage of such objects in a principal clause (16.4%). Preverbal direct objects in subordinate clauses, when compared to such objects in principal clauses, are thus proportionally as few in the restricted corpus as in the complete corpus.

In the restricted corpus, the percentage of subjects in a subordinate clause that are preverbal (31.8%) is 1.4 times smaller than the percentage of such subjects in a principal clause (44.0%). This proportion is approximately the same in the complete corpus, in which the percentage of subjects in a subordinate clause that are preverbal (29.1%) is 1.1 times smaller than the percentage of such subjects in a principal clause (31.2%). Preverbal subjects in subordinate clauses, when compared to such subjects in principal clauses, are thus proportionally as few in the restricted corpus as in the complete corpus.

As has been mentioned, a high proportion (105) of the 144 preverbal subjects in subordinate clauses in the complete corpus are found in a relative clause. This also applies to the restricted corpus, in which 5 out of 7 preverbal subjects in subordinate clauses occur in a relative clause.

After excluding the order-influencing elements from the corpus, the proportions of preverbal subjects and preverbal objects (DO/PDO) in subordinate clauses as against principal clauses change only slightly.

## 4. Conclusions

A number of observations have already been made in the previous sections.

It seems that in Deuteronomy 1-30 the traditional distinction between principal and subordinate clause is only partly reflected in the word order. On the whole, order is not a decisive criterion by which to draw that distinction for the corpus.

Still, in clauses with a subject and a nominal predicate, the subject is more often found before the predicate when the clause is a principal clause. And most preverbal direct and indirect objects are found in a principal clause.

Only slightly more preverbal subjects are found in principal than in subordinate clauses. Among subordinate clauses, however, most preverbal subjects are found in a relative or causal clause. In the other subordinate verbal clauses, only 10.6% (22) of the 207 subjects occur before the verb. As far as preverbal subjects are concerned, relative and causal clauses are rather like principal clauses. Relative and causal clauses apart, it can be observed that very few preverbal subjects occur in subordinate clauses whereas most of them are found in principal clauses.

The relative and causal clauses illustrate that it is instructive to differentiate between subordinate clause types.

The proportions of preverbal subjects and preverbal direct objects in subordinate clauses as against principal clauses are hardly influenced by certain elements that might condition order. These elements do not by definition alter the relation between order and clause type.

| princ.cl. | % | main | apod | adv | -main- | rel | fin | prot |
|---|---|---|---|---|---|---|---|---|
| DO - V | | 1 | | | | | | |
| DO - V IO | | 1 | | | | | | |
| DO S V | | 3 | | | | | | |
| DO V | 90.8 | 52 | 4 | 3 | | 1 | 1 | 1 |
| DO V - DO | | 2 | | | | | | |
| DO V - S | | 1 | | | | | | |
| DO V IO | | | | | | | | 1 |
| DO V S | | 4 | | | | | | |
| PDO V | 96.2 | 22 | 2 | 1 | | | | |
| PDO V OCL | | 1 | | | | | | |
| PDO V S | | 3 | | | | | | |
| PIO V | | 2 | | | | | 1 | |
| PIO V OCL | | 1 | | | | | | |
| PIO V S OCL | | 1 | | | | | | |
| OCL V | | 1 | | | | | | |
| OCL V IO | | 1 | | | | | | |
| P | 14.3 | 3 | | | | 18 | | |
| P - S | | 2 | | 1 | | | 2 | |
| P S | 31.6 | 18 | | | | 6 | | 4 |
| P S P | | | | | | | | |
| P V | 36.4 | 3 | 1 | | | | | |
| P V - S | | 2 | | | | | | |
| P V S | | | | | | | | 1 |
| S | 39.1 | 8 | 1 | | | 1 | 1 | 2 |
| S - P | | 1 | | | | | | |
| S P | 60.9 | 34 | 1 | 1 | 3 | 4 | | |
| S - V | | 1 | | 1 | | 1 | | |
| S - V - S | | 1 | | | | | | |
| S - V DO | | 1 | | | | | | |
| S V | 47.5 | 65 | 5 | 5 | | 64 | 3 | 4 |
| S V - DO | | 2 | | | | 1 | | |
| S V - PDO | | 5 | 1 | | | 1 | | |
| S V DO | 58.3 | 12 | | 2 | | | 3 | |
| S V DO PIO | | | | | | | | |
| S V PDO | 52.9 | 9 | | | | 5 | 1 | |
| S V IO | 17.4 | 3 | | 1 | | 19 | | |
| S V IO PDO | | 1 | | | | | | |
| S V IO - OCL | | | | | | 1 | | |
| S V IO OCL | | 4 | | | | | | |
| S V PIO | 0 | | | | | 12 | | |
| S V PIO PDO | | | | | | | | |
| S V PIO OCL | | | | | | 1 | | |
| S V OCL | | 1 | | | | | | |
| S V P | | 1 | | | | | | |

| obj | caus | temp | cpr | spec | circ | exc | ccs | subj | total |
|---|---|---|---|---|---|---|---|---|---|
| | | | | | | | | | 1 |
| | | | | | | | | | 1 |
| | 1 | | | | | | | | 4 |
| 1 | 2 | | | | | | | | 65 |
| | | | | | | | | | 2 |
| | | | | | | | | | 1 |
| | | | | | | | | | 1 |
| | | | | | | | | | 4 |
| | 1 | | | | | | | | 26 |
| | | | | | | | | | 1 |
| | | | | | | | | | 3 |
| | | | | | | | | | 3 |
| | | | | | | | | | 1 |
| | | | | | | | | | 1 |
| | | | | | | | | | 1 |
| | | | | | | | | | 1 |
| | | | | | | | | | 21 |
| | 1 | | | | | | | | 6 |
| 1 | 26 | | | | 2 | | | | 57 |
| | 1 | | | | | | | | 1 |
| 5 | 2 | | | | | | | | 11 |
| | | | | | | | | | 2 |
| | | | | | | | | | 1 |
| 2 | 5 | | | | 3 | | | | 23 |
| | | | | | | | | | 1 |
| 5 | 13 | | | | 3 | | | | 64 |
| | 1 | | | | | | | | 4 |
| | | | | | | | | | 1 |
| | | | | | | | | | 1 |
| 1 | 5 | | | | 6 | | | | 158 |
| | | | | | | | | | 3 |
| 1 | | | | | | | | | 8 |
| 2 | 4 | | | | | | | 1 | 24 |
| | 1 | | | | | | | | 1 |
| | 2 | | | | | | | | 17 |
| | | | | | | | | | 23 |
| | | | | | | | | | 1 |
| | 1 | | | | | | | | 2 |
| | | | | | | | | | 4 |
| | | | | | | | | | 12 |
| | 1 | | | | | | | | 1 |
| | | | | | | | | | 1 |
| | 1 | | | | | | | | 2 |
| | | | | | | | | | 1 |

| princ.cl. | % | main | apod | adv | -main- | rel | fin | prot |
|---|---|---|---|---|---|---|---|---|
| V | 47.9 | 385 | 70 | 14 | | 204 | 105 | 84 |
| V - DO | 52.4 | 30 | 3 | | | 6 | 6 | 8 |
| V - DO - DO | | 1 | | | | | | |
| V - DO S | | | | | | | | 1 |
| V - PDO | 33.3 | 19 | 2 | | | 1 | 7 | 1 |
| V - PDO - PDO | | 1 | | | | | | |
| V - DO - OCL | | 1 | | | | | | |
| V - OCL | 63.6 | 6 | 2 | | | 3 | | |
| V - P | | 3 | 1 | | | | | |
| V - S | 39.3 | 15 | 6 | 1 | | 7 | 7 | 14 |
| V - S PDO | | | | | | 1 | | |
| V DO | 47.5 | 158 | 32 | 13 | | 42 | 100 | 31 |
| V DO - DO | | 2 | 1 | | | | | 1 |
| V DO S | 44.4 | 24 | 8 | | | 10 | 4 | 8 |
| V PDO | 49.0 | 97 | 24 | 3 | | 15 | 47 | 12 |
| V PDO - PDO | | | 2 | | | | | |
| V PDO PIO | | 1 | | | | | | |
| V PDO OCL | | | | | | 1 | | |
| V PDO S | | 1 | | | | 1 | | |
| V IO | 16.7 | 3 | | | | 9 | 3 | |
| V IO DO | | | | | | 1 | | |
| V IO PDO | | 6 | | | | | | |
| V IO OCL | | | | | | 1 | 1 | |
| V IO S | | | | | | 4 | | 1 |
| V IO S PDO | | 1 | | | | | | |
| V IO S OCL | | 2 | | | | 1 | | |
| V PIO | | 4 | | 1 | | | | |
| V PIO DO | | 3 | | | | | | |
| V PIO - PDO | | 1 | | | | | | |
| V PIO PDO | | | | | | | 1 | |
| V PIO OCL | | | | | | 1 | 1 | |
| V OCL | 62.5 | 38 | 5 | 1 | 1 | 9 | 10 | 5 |
| V P | | | 1 | | | 1 | 1 | |
| V SCL | | 1 | | | | | | 1 |
| V S | 42.1 | 128 | 13 | 1 | | 55 | 23 | 28 |
| V S - DO | | 3 | 1 | 1 | | | | |
| V S - DO - DO | | 1 | | | | | | |
| V S PDO | | 9 | | | | | | |
| V S - OCL | | | | | | 5 | | |
| V S - S | | 1 | | | | | 1 | |
| V S DO | 50.0 | 7 | | | | 1 | | 4 |
| V S PDO | 40.7 | 17 | 3 | 2 | | 4 | 1 | 5 |
| V S PIO | | 2 | | | | 4 | | |
| V S PIO OCL | | | | | | 2 | | |
| V S OCL | 50.0 | 9 | 1 | | | 2 | | 2 |
| V S P | | 3 | | | | | | |

| obj | caus | temp | cpr | spec | circ | exc | ccs | subj | total |
|---|---|---|---|---|---|---|---|---|---|
| 64 | 16 | 2 | 19 | 11 | 2 | 1 | 2 | | 979 |
| 5 | 2 | | | 3 | | | | | 63 |
| | | | | | | | | | 1 |
| | | | | | | | | | 1 |
| 2 | 1 | | | | | | | | 33 |
| | | | | | | | | | 1 |
| | | | | | | | | | 1 |
| | | | | | | | | | 11 |
| | | | | | | | | | 4 |
| 1 | 2 | 1 | 1 | | | 1 | | | 56 |
| | | 1 | | | | | | | 2 |
| 27 | 17 | | | 7 | | | | | 427 |
| | | | | | | | | | 4 |
| 4 | 12 | 1 | 1 | | | | | | 72 |
| 28 | 9 | 3 | | 10 | | 1 | | 1 | 253 |
| | | | | | | | | | 2 |
| | | | | | | | | | 1 |
| | | | | | | | | | 1 |
| | | | | | | | | | 2 |
| | | | 3 | | | | | | 18 |
| | | | 1 | | | | | | 2 |
| | | | | | | | | | 6 |
| | | | | | | | | | 2 |
| | | | 5 | | | | | | 10 |
| | | | | | | | | | 1 |
| | | | | | | | | | 3 |
| 1 | | | | | | | | | 6 |
| 1 | | | | | | | | | 4 |
| | | | | | | | | | 1 |
| 1 | | | | | | | | | 2 |
| | | | | | | | | | 2 |
| | 1 | | 1 | 1 | | | | | 72 |
| | | | | | | | | | 3 |
| | | | | | | | | | 2 |
| 8 | 11 | 54 | 16 | | | | | | 337 |
| | | | | | | | | | 5 |
| | | | | | | | | | 1 |
| | | | | | | | | | 9 |
| | | | | | | | | | 5 |
| | | | | | | | | | 2 |
| | 1 | | 1 | | | | | | 14 |
| 1 | 6 | 14 | 1 | | | | | | 54 |
| | | | 2 | | | | | | 8 |
| | | | | | | | | | 2 |
| | 5 | 1 | | | | | | | 20 |
| 1 | | | | | | | | | 4 |

References

F.I. Andersen, *The Sentence in Biblical Hebrew*, The Hague/Paris 1974.

W.T. Claassen, "Computer-Assisted Methods and the Text and Language of the Old Testament - An Overview", in W. Claassen (ed.), *Text and Context: Old Testament and Semitic Studies for F.C. Fensham* (Journal for the Study of the Old Testament, Supplement Series, 48), 1988, p. 283-299.

D.R. Cohen, "Subject and Topic in Biblical Aramaic: A Functional Approach Based on Form-Content Analysis", in *Afroasiatic Linguistics* 2 (1975), p. 1-23.

B. Comrie, *Language Universals and Linguistic Typology: Syntax and Morphology*, 2nd ed., Oxford 1989.

W. Gesenius, *Gesenius' Hebrew Grammar*, ed. E. Kautzsch, 2nd English ed. A.E. Cowley, Oxford 1910, [15]1980.

J.H. Greenberg, "Some Universals of Grammar with Particular Reference to the Order of Meaningful Elements", in: J.H. Greenberg (ed.), *Universals of Language*, 2nd ed., New York 1963, p. 73-113.

Ch. Hardmeier, "Die Verwendung von elektronischen Datenverarbeitungsanlagen in der alttestamentlichen Wissenschaft", in *Zeitschrift für die alttestamentliche Wissenschaft* 82 (1970), p. 175-185.

P. Joüon, *Grammaire de l' hébreu biblique*, Rome 1923 (reprint 1965).

J. Lyons, *Introduction to Theoretical Linguistics*, Cambridge 1968 (reprint 1979).

R. Meyer, *Hebräische Grammatik, Band III: Satzlehre*, Berlin [3]1972.

E.A. Nida, *Learning a Foreign Language*, New York 1957.

K.L. Pike & E.G. Pike, *Grammatical Analysis* (Summer Institute of Linguistics Publications in Linguistics, 53), Dallas 1977, [2]1980.

L.J. de Regt, *A Parametric Model for Syntactic Studies of a Textual Corpus, Demonstrated on the Hebrew of Deuteronomy 1-30* (Studia Semitica Neerlandica, 24), Assen/Maastricht 1988.

*SAS User's Guide: Basics*, Version 5 ed., SAS Institute Inc., Cary, North Carolina 1985.

K. Schlesinger, "Zur Wortfolge im Hebräischen Verbalsatz", in *Vetus Testamentum* 3 (1953), p. 381-390.

E. Talstra, "Towards a Distributional Definition of Clauses in Classical Hebrew: A Computer-Assisted Description of Clauses and Clause Types in Deut 4, 3-8", in *Ephemerides Theologicae Lovanienses* 63 (1987), p. 95-105.

# Nominal Sentence Negation in Biblical Hebrew: The Grammatical Status of אין*

P. Swiggers, Leuven

Nominal sentences are a well-known feature of Semitic languages.[1] Their pervasiveness in Semitic can be correlated with
(a) a higher degree of predicativity of nominal elements - a feature which receives confirmation from the extension of participial forms into (finite) verbal paradigms (cf. static verbs in Biblical Hebrew, or the evolution of the verbal system in Syriac and Modern Aramaic);
(b) the aspect-boundedness of the copulative verb;
(c) a neater distinction between rhematic and thematic elements, mostly in terms of position of segments[2].

Authors of Biblical Hebrew grammars have mostly taken for granted the existence of nominal sentences, without bothering to define them. It seems that two possible approaches can be conceived, viz.
(1) to define a nominal sentence in terms of non-congruence (or the non-necessity of congruence) between a subject term and a predicate term;

---

* This study is dedicated to Professor Jacob Hoftijzer, on his 65th birthday. The subject matter of this article has close ties with Prof. Hoftijzer's interest in the status of grammatical morphemes bearing a particular syntactic function, such as the *h* locale or *ʾt*, on which he has given us two model studies: J. Hoftijzer, "Remarks Concerning the Use of the Particle *ʾt* in Classical Hebrew", in *Oudtestamentische Studiën* 14 (1965), p. 1-99 and *A Search for Method: A Study in the Syntactic Use of the h-locale in Classical Hebrew*, Leiden 1981.

[1] For a general survey, see D. Cohen, *La phrase nominale et l'évolution du système verbal en sémitique. Etudes de syntaxe historique*, Paris 1984, with further references. For a study of nominal sentences in Biblical Hebrew, see F.I. Andersen, *The Hebrew Verbless Clause in the Pentateuch*, Nashville 1970 and id., *The Sentence in Biblical Hebrew*, The Hague 1974 (passim); neither of these works deals explicitly with negation in nominal sentences in Biblical Hebrew. Andersen's 1970 book has been thoroughly – and in my view adequately – criticized by J. Hoftijzer, "The Nominal Clause Reconsidered", in *Vetus Testamentum* 23 (1973), p. 446-510 (this article includes no discussion of *ʾyn*).

[2] The latter characteristic receives confirmation from "agreement" patterns which indicate the relative autonomy of the thematic and rhematic portions: in (a) the verb agrees with the suffix on the subject term.
a. *qwly ʾl-yhwh ʾqrʾ*
my voice - to YHWH - I call
"My voice call[s] to YHWH" (Ps. 3:5).

(2) to define a nominal sentence in terms of morphological opposition with non-nominal sentences.

The first approach is viable to some extent only. As a matter of fact, given its morphosyntactic focus, it presupposes (a) the possibility of identifying, for each sentence, a subject term, and (b) a straightforward application of congruence patterns in non-nominal sentences. Both (a) and (b) are problematical assumptions. First, subject marking is in principle a matter of correlating a verbal ending with a sentential subject. In sentences (1) and (2) this sentential subject is either formally or contextually recoverable.

1. וַיַּעַשׂ אֱלֹהִים אֶת־הָרָקִיעַ
"and God made the firmament" (Gen. 1:7).
2. כְּתֹב זֹאת זִכָּרוֹן בַּסֵּפֶר
"Write this up for a memorial in a book" (Ex. 17:14).

But in (3) the subject marking (second person singular) is semantically deviant from the intended impersonal meaning:

3. לֹא־תָבוֹא שָׁמָּה
there - you shall come - not [glosses are to be read from right to left]
"There shall not come thither (the fear of briers and thorns)" (Is. 7:25).

Moreover in (4), where a passive construction is used, we have a void reference to a third person singular subject, whereas the "deep" meaning of the sentence presupposes an impersonal unspecified agent:

4. לֹא־יֵעָשֶׂה כֵן בְּיִשְׂרָאֵל
in Israel - thus - it is done - not
"No such thing ought to be done in Israel" (2 Sam. 13:12).

The difficulties with (b) lie in the fact (see note 2) that congruence in verbal sentences can be not with the head of the "subject term" but with one of its satellites; to this one must add the cases of non-obligatory congruence (in number, gender and person) between subject term and verbal ending:

5. יֹאכְלוּ עוֹף הַשָּׁמָיִם
of the heavens - the fowl (sing.) - they will eat
"The birds of the heavens shall eat" (1 Ki. 14:11).
6. יָשָׁר מִשְׁפָּטֶיךָ
your commandments - is just
"Upright are your commandments" (Ps. 119:137).

In view of this it seems preferable to define a nominal sentence in terms of morphological characteristics, and more specifically as negatively marked with respect to verbal sentences: a nominal sentence is characterized by the absence of a finite verb[3].

Nominal sentences are parallel to verbal sentences in that they can be subject to full or restricted negation. In verbal sentences negation is expressed as a rule by לֹא, which can fulfill the functions of a full or restricted negation.

7. וְלֹא תַצְלִיחִי לָהֶם
"You shall not prosper in them" (Jer. 2:37).

8. כִּי לֹא אֶעֱזָבְךָ עַד אֲשֶׁר אִם־עָשִׂיתִי אֵת אֲשֶׁר־דִּבַּרְתִּי לָךְ
"I will not leave you until I have done that which I have spoken of to you" (Gen. 28:15).

Verbal sentences and nominal sentences contrast at least in two ways with respect to negation:

(1) verbal sentences do not show the negation marker אין

(2) in nominal sentences the distinction between total and restricted negation is marked by the opposition between אין and לא[4].

The opposition between verbal and nominal sentences is clear from contrastive pairs such as

9. לֹא יָדְעוּ ... אֵינָם יֹדְעִים

[3] Some authors (e.g., J.P. Lettinga, *Grammatica van het Bijbels Hebreeuws*, Leiden 1978[8], p. 156) have posited "compound nominal sentences", such as (b) and (c):

b. *whnhr hrbyʿy hwʾ prt*

"The fourth river - (it is) the Euphrates" (Gen. 2:14).

c. *hmt ... yʾklw hklbym*

"The dying man - dogs will eat him" (1 Ki. 21:24).

However, constructions such as (b) and (c) are not compound but unipredicative, nor are they nominal, as example (c) shows. It rather seems that this type of construction involves extraposition of the thematic element, which can stand in relation with whatever case, and which can even be introduced by a relativizer, as in example (f):

d. *yhwh bswph wbśʿrh drkw*

"YHWH, in the whirlwind and in the storm is his path" (Nah. 1:3).

e. *ʾt-kl-hʾrṣ ʾšr ʾth rʾh lk ʾtnnh*

"All the land that you see, I will give it to you" (Gen. 13:15).

f. *ʾšr-ykh ʾt-qryt-spr wlkdh wntty lw ʾt-ʿksh bty lʾšh*

"He who will defeat Qiryat-Sefer and take it, I will give him my daughter Aksa as wife" (Judg. 1:12).

[4] See, e.g., for negation with *lʾ*, cases such as

g. *lʾ ʾyš ʾl*

"God is not a man (is a non-human)" (Num. 23:19).

h. *lʾ-kn ʿbdy mšh*

"My servant Moses is not so" (Num. 12:7).

"They do not know (the manners of the God of the land) ... they are not knowing" (2 Ki. 17:26a-b)

10. אֵין־עָיֵף וְאֵין־כּוֹשֵׁל בּוֹ לֹא יָנוּם וְלֹא יִישָׁן

"There is no one who is weary, no one who stumbles on it, no one dozes, no one slumbers" (Is. 5:27).

Total vs. restricted negation in nominal sentences is clear from examples (11)-(14), with (11)-(12) illustrating total negation, and (13)-(14) restricted negation:

11. אֵין יוֹצֵא וְאֵין בָּא

"There was none who went out or came in" (Josh. 6: 1)[5].

12. וְאִם־אֵינְךָ מְשַׁלֵּחַ

"If you will not be sending" (Gen. 43:5).

13. וּמִן־הַבְּהֵמָה אֲשֶׁר לֹא טְהֹרָה הִוא

"And among the animals that are not clean" (Gen. 7:2).

14. לֹא לְמַעַנְכֶם אֲנִי־עֹשֶׂה

"It is not because of you that I do this" (Ez. 36:32).

In the remainder we will be concerned with the negator אין. The status of this form has hardly received sufficient attention in grammars of Biblical Hebrew[6], which as a general rule consider the form to be an adverb or a particle. It should be noted, however, that אין can serve as an "internal" negator in nominal compounds:

15. אֵין־קֵץ

"endless" (literally "not-end", i.e. without end) (Is. 9:6).

16. אֵין־מִסְפָּר

"innumerable" (literally "not-number", i.e. numberless) (Jer. 2:32; 1 Chron. 22:4).

---

[5] As B.K. Waltke - M. O' Connor, *An Introduction to Biblical Hebrew Syntax*, Winona Lake 1990, p. 623 rightly point out, *ʾyn* contrasts with *yš* as a predicator of non-existence in nominal sentences; cf.

i. *yš mpzr*

"There is one who scatters" (Prov. 11:24).

[6] J. Carmignac, "L'emploi de la négation *ʾyn* dans la Bible et à Qumran", in *Revue de Qumran* 8 (1972-1975), p. 407-413, mainly deals with the position of *ʾyn* relative to its "complement", with almost exclusive focus on the Qumran materials. An excellent survey of syntagmatic patterns involving *ʾyn* can be found in T. Muraoka, *Emphatic Words and Structures in Biblical Hebrew*, Jerusalem - Leiden 1985, p. 102-111. I am, however, reluctant to accept the author's semantic interpretation (see p. 77-82) of *ʾyn*.

In addition, the form אין manifests three characteristics the combination of which[7] suggests that the form cannot be considered a mere particle or adverb.
(A) אין can easily take suffixes, as shown in (17) and (18):

17. אֵינֶנִּי נֹתֵן לָכֶם תֶּבֶן
"I am not giving you straw" (Ex. 5:10).
18. קוֹל דְּבָרִים אַתֶּם שֹׁמְעִים וּתְמוּנָה אֵינְכֶם רֹאִים
"You heard a sound of words, but you didn't see a similitude" (Deut. 4:12).

(B) אין occurs in a status constructus combination with nouns, as shown in examples (19) and (20).

19. אֵין־יוֹסֵף בַּבּוֹר
"Joseph was not in the pit" (Gen. 37:29).
20. אַל־תַּעֲלוּ כִּי אֵין יהוה בְּקִרְבְּכֶם
"Don't attack! For YHWH is not in your midst!" (Num. 14:42).

The construct form אֵין can in some cases be contrasted with the absolute form אַיִן, which is much rarer:

21. אֵין־בּוֹ מְתֹם
"There is no health in it!" (Is. 1:6).
22. וְכֹחַ אַיִן לְלֵדָה
"There is no strength to give birth!" (Is. 37:3).

(C) אין occurs as the predicative nucleus[8], as is clear from examples such as

23. וְאֵינֵךְ עַד־עוֹלָם
"And you shall never be any more" (Ez. 27:36).
24. וּשְׁכַבְתֶּם וְאֵין מַחֲרִיד
"You shall lie down and there will be no one to terrorize (you)" (Lev. 26:6).

---

[7] None of the features is on itself a sufficient indication. As a matter of fact, in Biblical Hebrew some particles take suffixes (e.g. *ʾt*, *ʿwd*, *lbd* etc.), some adverbs occur in a status constructus form (e.g., *dēy* status constructus of *day*), and some particles occur as full predicates (e.g., *yš*).

[8] It can also occur as a propositional negator (in coordinative structures), as in the following example:
j. *wʾm-ʾyn mth ʾnky*
"and if not so, I am dead" (Gen. 30:1).

These three characteristics suggest, as a minimal hypothesis, that אין can be regarded as a nominal element, which has been more or less fossilized in its status of negator[9]. The nominal origin of אין[10] would explain (a) its general occurrence in a status constructus form (אין must be regarded as the head of the predicate, the complement of which is constituted by the term to which the negation applies), and (b) its combination with *l* + infinitive construct, as in (25)[11]:

25. וְאֵין עִמְּךָ לְהִתְיַצֵּב
"And no one is able to stand against you" (2 Chron. 20:6).
26. עָלָיו אֵין לְהוֹסִיף וּמִמֶּנּוּ אֵין לִגְרֹעַ
"Nothing can be added to it and nothing can be taken from it" (Qoh. 3:14).

The nominal origin of אין would also explain its rôle in terms of positional slots. As a matter of fact, אין can occur in contrastive positions, as shown in (27) and (28):

27. מֶלֶךְ אֵין בְּיִשְׂרָאֵל
"(It was in those days) - a king, there was none in Israel" (Judg. 19:1).
28. אֵין מֶלֶךְ בְּיִשְׂרָאֵל
"There was no king in Israel (in those days)" (Judg. 17:6).

It seems that as a general rule אין occurs before the rheme (or, better, before the content-part of the rheme, given that אין can be considered the "modal" part of the rheme). This is clear from examples (21), (22) and (26) for instance. It must be observed, however,

---

[9] Another interesting case of fossilization in Biblical Hebrew is the frozen nominal *ʾšry* (in the plural construct), used in exclamatory sentences; e.g.
k. *ʾšry hʾyš ʾšr lʾ hlk bʿṣt ršʿym*
"Enviable is the man who does not walk in the counsel of the ungodly" (Ps. 1:1).
l. *ʾšryk yśrʾl*
"You are to be envied, Israel" (Deut. 33:29).
On this form, see W. Janzen, "*ʾšry* in the Old Testament", in *Harvard Theological Review* 58 (1965), p. 213-226.

[10] It is not clear what kind of basic meaning should be given to *ʾyn*: "absence (of)" (= non-presence), "non-existence" or "non-occurrence"? As a predicate in nominal sentences it should be translated as "there is not" or "is absent/not present".

[11] In this function *ʾyn* followed by *l* + infinitive construct parallels constructions with noun + *l* + infinitive construct, such as
m. *wʾm rʿ bʿynykm lʿbd ʾt-yhwh*
"It is evil in your eyes to worship YHWH" (Josh. 24:15).
One can, e.g., compare example (22) with the following sentence:
n. *ky hwʾ hntn lk kḥ lʿśwt ḥyl*
"For it is he who gives you the strength to produce wealth" (Deut. 8:18).

that the theme/rheme distinction applies only straightforwardly in sentences which do not involve the speaker and/or his audience. The reference to the speaker and/or to the audience in fact cuts through the theme/rheme distinction, since the communicative deixis is itself rhematic, although it is (partially) implied as a situational theme. In the case of אין used in sentences involving such a deixis, it seems that the latter is primarily treated as rhematic in Biblical Hebrew, given that אין precedes the deictic element referring to the speaker and/or to his audience, as can be seen in examples (29)-(31):

29. וְאֵין־אֶתְכֶם אֵלַי
"You, yourselves, did not turn to me" (Hag. 2:17).
30. וְאֵין־לָנוּ אִישׁ לְהָמִית בְּיִשְׂרָאֵל
"None of us shall kill an Israelite" (2 Sam. 21:4).
31. כִּי אֵין זוּלָתְךָ לִגְאוֹל
"And none except you has the right to redeem it" (Ruth 4:4).

In conclusion, the analysis of the combinatory and syntagmatic properties of אין does not support the view that this form should be treated as a particle or as an adverb. On the contrary, it suggests that אין should be described as a (strongly fossilized) nominal element, functioning as the head of a negative predication.

# Hebrew Syntax: Clause Types and Clause Hierarchy*

E. Talstra, Amsterdam

## 1. *Form and Function*

Offering a volume on Hebrew and Aramaic *Syntax* to professor Hoftijzer is more than appropriate. On the first pages of his inaugural address *Verbale Vragen*[1] Professor Hoftijzer mentioned the need for more research on the syntax of classical Hebrew. He also discussed there the problem of the relationship between "form" and "function" with respect to the Hebrew verbal system. In his lengthy review of Francis Andersen's study of the Hebrew verbless clauses[2] Hoftijzer argued in favor of an inventory of linguistic forms to be used as the basis of the study of Hebrew syntactical studies. His approach not only invites the reader to pay more attention to the central role to be played by syntax in linguistic and exegetical studies, but also confronts one with a choice for a clear order in linguistic argumentation: a registration of forms precedes the conclusion of functions.

When applied at the level of syntactic analysis Hoftijzer's proposal requires a rather intensive type of grammatical research as the size of his review of Andersen itself suggests. In my experience, however, the method proposed by Hoftijzer concords well with the type of computer-assisted text linguistic analysis, several aspects of which I present below.

First, once a well organized database of Hebrew is available, the contribution of computer programs in collecting sets of grammatical data

* I thank drs. J.W. Dyk for the corrections of my English text.

1 J. Hoftijzer, *Verbale Vragen. Rede uitgesproken bij de aanvaarding van het ambt van gewoon hoogleraar in het Hebreeuws, de Israëlitische oudheden en het Ugaritisch aan de Rijksuniversiteit te Leiden op 10 mei 1974*, Leiden, 1974.

2 J. Hoftijzer, "The nominal clause reconsidered", *Vetus Testamentum* 23 (1973) p. 446 - 520. See for recent examples of the functional type of Hebrew syntactical analysis for instance: K.F. Lowery, *Toward a discourse grammar of Biblical Hebrew* (University of California Dissertation), Los Angelos, 1985; Th. J. Finley, "The Proposal in Biblical Hebrew: Preliminary Studies Using a Deep structure Model", *Zeitschrift für Althebraistik* 2 (1989) p. 1-13.

arranged according to various distributional features makes it substantially easier to meet the demands of form-based syntactic research.

Second, of greater importance is the fact that the creation of such a database is in itself a contribution to the form-based research of Hebrew syntax. It is this second point that constitutes the theme of the present article.

In using computer programming to build up a database of grammatically analyzed Hebrew text, one soon encounters various aspects of the problem Hoftijzer referred to, i.e. the relationship between the 'form" and the "function" of linguistic elements. When preparing a text database one has to make a choice: either flag all elements of the computer text with labels that are indicators of grammatical functions, or let a computer program grammatically analyze all elements of the text on the basis of form and distribution and let the machine store the outcome of such analysis. The first mentioned alternative is basically the model of the database used in the work of Lowery[3] and others employing functional grammar as a model. The second procedure requires a clear theory both on the variation in type and on the hierarchical structure of linguistic data. What linguistic material should one accept as data: surface text, morphemes, grammatical word functions, clauses or even clause connections? And on what grounds? For instance, is the information *"construct state"* regarding the noun יום in the phrase יום יהוה equally clear as it is with the noun יום in the phrase כל ימי חייך ? Should a label *"consecutive perfect"* simply be added in the computer text to all occurrences of, e.g., the form ונתן, where this seems to be the correct interpretation of that form? (cf. I Ki. 13:3 and I Ki. 22:12,15). Such an interpretative addition would imply the creation of a database with priority given to "function" rather than to "form".

Doubting the value of an computer-assisted linguistic research based on function labels of an *ad hoc* and interpretative nature, I would argue in favor of the reverse approach: register forms and try to let a computer program propose function labels. A program is capable of doing so, if it is allowed to combine the observation of *forms* with, on the one hand, the application of a set of combinatory morpho-syntactic *rules*, and with, on the other hand, information on the part of speech of non-flecting lexemes to be derived from a *lexicon*. This will make it possible for a program to observe linguistic forms and propose function labels at various linguistic levels. Sometimes a morpheme is sufficient indication of *"construct state"*; sometimes one needs the entire phrase to be able to conclude to *"state"*. On many occasions a combination of morphemes is sufficient to draw a conclusion as to the function label of

[3] Op. cit., Chapter II, p. 54ff.

verbal tense (e.g. *imperfect*); on other occasions, however, one will need to be aware of the presence of a complex construction, e.g.: "imper. Clause ⇒ W-Qatal Clause"[4] to be able to conclude that the traditional function label *"consecutive perfect"* is applicable[5].

As the examples mentioned indicate, the discussion on "form" and "function" is one of great importance in the field of computer-assisted grammatical research and the production of text databases. The choice in favor of registering simple and complex linguistic forms implies a choice for the longer and more complicated way. Nevertheless this way is in my experience a more rewarding one, because it contributes directly to syntactic research. The task to be performed is the establishment of a hierarchy of grammatically analyzing programs, that firstly describe words according to their morpheme structure and their part of speech, secondly construct phrases from the individual words and thirdly put markers of clause boundaries between the phrases in the text.

Therefore, the building of a grammatically analyzed textcorpus is a field of research in itself. On other occasions I have reported on this work as far as word level, phrase level and clause level data are concerned[6]. In this article I will report on part of the work of data analysis on clause level and text level, thus emphasizing the value of the argumentation promoted by Hoftijzer: analysis of forms should have priority over analysis of functions. In my opinion this also holds true for the analysis of complex forms at higher linguistic levels, i.e. clause types and clause hierarchy.

## 2. *I Kings 2: 8-9*

To study the balance of formal and functional argumentation, I have chosen a segment from the last words of king David to Solomon: I Ki.

---

[4] See the analysis made by: M. Vervenne, 'Hebrew Verbform and Function. A syntactic Case Study with Reference to a Linguistic Data Base', in: *Actes du Second Colloque International Bible et Informatique: Méthode, outils, résultats. Jérusalem, 9-13 juin 1988*, Paris - Genève, 1989, p. 605-640.

[5] Though I see the value of looking for other than the traditional grammatical terminology, I will continue to use this terminology in the context of this article, because it is helpful to emphasize the difference between formal description and functional labeling.

[6] E. Talstra, "An hierarchically structured data base of Biblical Hebrew Texts. The relationship of grammar and encoding", in: *Colloque "Bible et Informatique: le Texte", Louvain-la-Neuve, 2-3-4 sept. 1985*, Genève, 1986, p. 337-349; E. Talstra, "Towards a Distributional definition of Clauses in Classical Hebrew: A Computer-Assisted Description of Clauses and Clause Types in Deut 4,3-8", *Ephemerides Theologicae Lovanienses*, 63 (1987) p. 95 -105; C. Hardmeier - E. Talstra, "Sprachgestalt und Sinngehalt. Wege zu neuen Instrumenten der computer-gestützten Textwahrnehmung", *Zeitschrift für die alttestamentliche Wissenschaft*, 101 (1989) p. 408 - 428.

2:8-9, the passage about Shimei. Among exegetes and translators, a variety of opinions exists about the interpretation and translation of the last line of verse 9. Is the clause of line 6 (והורדת) intended as a clause with function of finality, an expression of confidence or as a direct order? From existing translations one can conclude that at least four different types of syntactical hierarchy are constructed by exegetes in verse 9 upon which to base their translation.

These hierarchies are listed below together with some examples of the translations that result from them. The hierarchies are constructed with the help of a computer program that reproduces a text with a system of indentations to indicate for all clauses on what foregoing clauses they are dependent. The reader should notice that clauses with an identical number of tabulations do not necessarily belong to an identical textual level, e.g. verse 8 line 6 and verse 9 line 3. Such is only the case when two clauses have an identical tabulation *and* no other clauses, or only clauses of an embedded level are found in between, e.g. verse 8, line 2 and 4. The system of indentation, therefore, is indicative of clause hierarchy only, not of a system of fixed textual levels. The program used to produce these clause hierarchies is not a textprocessing facility, but a research tool used to calculate morphological and syntactical correspondances between clauses. It is being developed in order to search for which clause parameters (conjunctions, verbal tense forms, etc.) are decisive in determining a clause relationship. The more succesful this research is, the more the program will "learn" Hebrew syntax and be able to predict clause hierarchies in other texts. Further I will describe the textual interpretation that comes along with the respective types of syntactical hierarchy of I Ki. 2:9 in more or less traditional terminology in order to clarify at which grammatical or semantic points the translators have made decisions. In section 3 of the article a look is taken at what kind of grammatical calculations a computer program would need to make in order to conclude that one out of the four syntactical hierarchies constructed by exegetes is to be seen as the best option. Clearly this is not meant to suggest that a grammatical choice made by computer-aided calculation for that reason now should be beyond dispute. The case presented here should serve as a test for the possiblities of computer-assisted studies in form-based syntax of Biblical Hebrew. The text of I Ki. 2:9 has been chosen because it is one of the many cases that demanded special attention in the course of a running research project in textgrammar: to establish all clauses and clause relationships in the books of Kings.

SYNTACTICAL HIERARCHIES OF THE TEXT OF I KINGS 2:8-9

a. line 6 (of vs. 9) is dependent on line 5.

| | | |
|---|---|---|
| והנה עמך שמעי בן גרא בן הימיני מבחרים | IKi02,08 | 1 |
| . והוא קללני קללה נמרצת ביום | IKi02,08 | 2 |
| . . . לכתי מחנים | IKi02,08 | 3 |
| . והוא ירד | IKi02,08 | 4 |
| . . . לקראתי הירדן | IKi02,08 | 5 |
| . . ואשבע לו ביהוה | IKi02,08 | 6 |
| . . . לאמר | IKi02,08 | 7 |
| . . . . . אם אמיתך בחרב | IKi02,08 | 8 |
| ועתה | IKi02,09 | 1 |
| . אל תנקהו | IKi02,09 | 2 |
| . . כי איש חכם אתה | IKi02,09 | 3 |
| . . . וידעת | IKi02,09 | 4 |
| . . . . . את אשר תעשה לו | IKi02,09 | 5 |
| . . . . . והורדת את | IKi02,09 | 6 |
| שבתו בדם שאול | ,, | ,, |

*Buber*[7]

1 Jetzt aber:
2 - nimmer darfst du ihn ungestraft lassen,
3 - du bist ja ein weiser Mann,
4 du wirst wissen,
5 was du mit ihm tun musst
6 dass du sein Greisentum mit Blut ins Gruftreich niedersteigen lassest.

*NBG*[8]

1 Maar nu
2 - moet gij hem niet ongestraft laten,
3 - want gij zijt een wijs man
4 en weet wel,
5 wat gij doen moet
6 om zijn grijze haar met bloed in het dodenrijk te doen nederdalen.

---

[7] M. Buber, F. Rosenzweig, *Die Bücher der Geschichte, verdeutscht von Martin Buber gemeinsam mit Franz Rosenzweig*, Köln, 1965.

[8] *Bijbel. Vertaling in opdracht van het Nederlands Bijbelgenootschap*, Amsterdam, 1951.

*Würthwein (ATD)*[9]

1 Du aber
2 - sollst ihn nicht ungestraft lassen,
3 - den du bist ein kluger Mann
4 und weisst,
5 was du ihm tun wirst,
6 dass du sein graues Haupt blutbefleckt
in die Unterwelt hinabfahren lässest.

These translations consider line 6 to be a dependent clause with function of finality. The connection with line 5 is supported by functional correspondences of the two verbs: 2 masc. sing. The W-Qatal of line 6 derives in this schema its final function from the modal functioning yiqtol + אשר of line 5. This function of line 5 seems to be accepted by all translators: "You (will) know what you *should* do". Comparable constructions can be found e.g. in Ex. 4:1 and Deut. 1:18[10]. One may doubt, however, whether the translations of line 6 proposed in this context are correct. The translation: "to bring down his head ..." could equally well have been given for a Hebrew construction with an infinitive: להוריד (cf. Gen. 37:25). So one has to explain why a W-Qatal can take the same function here. Moreover, other cases of a sequence: W-Qatal אשר+yiqtol - W-Qatal exist, where it is impossible to combine the last W-Qatal with the preceding yiqtol, even when the two tenses are congruent in person, gender and number (cf. Gen. 42:38).

b. line 6 is dependent on line 4.

| | | |
|---|---|---|
| ועתה | IKi02,09 | 1 |
| . אל תנקהו | IKi02,09 | 2 |
| . . כי איש חכם אתה | IKi02,09 | 3 |
| . . . וידעת | IKi02,09 | 4 |
| . . . . את אשר תעשה לו | IKi02,09 | 5 |
| . . . והורדת את שיבתו בדם | IKi02,09 | 6 |
| שאול | ,, | ,, |

*RSV*[11]

1 Now
2 - therefore hold him not guiltless
3 - for you are a wise man:
4 you will know

[9] E. Würthwein, *Die Bücher der Könige. 1.Köninge 1 - 16*, (Altes Testament Deutsch 11,1), Göttingen, 1985$^{2}$.

[10] P. Joüon, *Grammaire de l'Hébreu Biblique*, Rome, 1923 (1965), §113.m terms this the "nuance de devoir".

5 what you ought do to him
6 and you shall bring his grey hear down with blood to Sheol.

*Gray*(OTL)[12]

1 But
2 - do not you (reading: ואתה) hold him guiltless,
3 - for you are an astute man.
4 So take note
5 how you deal with him,
6 and bring his grey hair with blood down to Sheol.

According to this schema the W-Qatal of line 6 is read parallel to the W-Qatal of line 4. Though the translation by Gray, using two commands, is the most clear one in this respect, the RSV in my opinion is not a principally different one. The translations use two comparable tense forms connected by "and". This implies that the effect of a W-Qatal used after a Nominal Clause[13] (such as in Deut. 4:30 6:1-3 22,2) is considered to be continued in the W- Qatal of line 6. The majority of translations, even when they choose a different syntactical schema as underlying structure, see the function of W-Qatal in line 4 as a modal one, translating: "you will know", "you know well" or "you should know". Exceptions are the translations given by Würthwein (a) and Rehm (d).

c. line 6 is dependent on line 3.

| | | |
|---|---|---|
| ועתה | IKi02,09 | 1 |
| . אל תנקהו | IKi02,09 | 2 |
| . . כי איש חכם אתה | IKi02,09 | 3 |
| . . . וידעת | IKi02,09 | 4 |
| . . . . את אשר תעשה לו | IKi02,09 | 5 |
| . . והורדת את שיבתו בדם שאול | IKi02,09 | 6 |

*Noth* (BKAT)[14]

1 Nun aber
2 - Lass ihn nicht ungestraft;
3 - denn du bist ein weiser Mann

[11] *The Revised Standard Version*, 1952

[12] J. Gray, *I & II Kings*, (Old Testament Library), London, $1977^{3}$.

[13] W. Gesenius - E. Kautzsch, *Hebräische Grammatik*, Leipzig, $1909^{28}$, §112.t and Joüon, *op. cit.*, §119.h.n.r. only mention the use of W-Qatal after a clause with a participle. Only Joüon, §119.v. has a short remark on W-Qatal after a *"proposition nominale du passé"*.

4 und weisst wohl,
5 was du ihn tun sollst,
6 und du wirst seine grauen Haare mit Blut in die Unterwelt hinabfahren lassen.

*Mulder* (COT)[15]

1 Maar nu,
2 - houd hem niet voor onschuldig.
3 - Je bent immers een wijs man,
4 je weet toch
5 wat je te doen staat.
6 Je zult zijn grijze haar bebloed in de onderwereld doen afdalen.

Here the commentaries seem to have accepted a functional difference between the two W-Qatals of line 4 and 6. They translate both lines as dependent on the nominal clause of line 3, nevertheless the two lines are not seen as functional parallels. This is the main difference between schema b and c. After the descriptive statement of line 3, the W-Qatal in line 4 is seen as having a slightly modal function, expressing David's confidence that Solomon will find some way to deal with Shimei, referred to by *"wohl"* or by *"toch"*: "you do know what to do with him." Line 6, however, is seen as a direct hint: "no doubt you will bring down ... ." Noth emphasizes the difference between line 4 and line 6 by re-introducing the subject "du" in combination with a change of tense: *"du wirst"*. Mulder also differentiates by changing the tense forms. Probably this functional difference is due to the fact that the translators see the W-Qatal of ידע (Q) as more static or descriptive than the W-Qatal of ירד (Hif.) because of the different numbers of actants involved.

d. line 6 is dependent on line 2.

| | | |
|---|---|---|
| ועתה | IKi02,09 | 1 |
| . אל תנקהו | IKi02,09 | 2 |
| . . כי איש חכם אתה | IKi02,09 | 3 |
| . . . וידעת | IKi02,09 | 4 |
| . . . . את אשר תעשׂה לו | IKi02,09 | 5 |
| . והורדת את שׂיבתו בדם שׁאול | IKi02,09 | 6 |

[14] M. Noth, *Könige 1* (Biblischer Kommentar Altes Testament IX.1), Neukirchen-Vluyn, 1968.

[15] M.J. Mulder, Koningen Deel I (I Koningen 1-7), (Commentaar op het Oude Testament), Kampen, 1987.

*NEB*[16]

1 But you (reading: ואתה)
2 - do not need to let him go unpunished now;
3 - you are a wise man
4 and you will know
5 how to deal with him;
6 bring down his grey hairs in blood to the grave!

*Rehm*[17]

1 Nun aber
2 - lass ihn nicht ungestraft!
3 - Du bist ein kluger Mann
4 und weisst,
5 was du mit ihm tun sollst.
6 Lass sein graues Haar mit Blut in die Unterwelt kommen!

These translators also seem to have felt a semantic tension between the W-Qatal forms of line 4 and 6. They have chosen to solve it by postulating a different syntactical relationship for each of these lines. The W-Qatal of line 4 depends on the Nominal Clause of line 3, whereas the W-Qatal of line 6 is made dependent on the prohibitive of line 2, to the effect that line 6 now has a direct command: bring down ...!

### 3. *A Proposal: grammatical calculations*

From this survey of clause hierarchies and the various translations based on them, one may ask now: what is decisive here - observation of forms, grammatical functions, semantic considerations, deep structure, or textual interpretation? A better way of putting the question might be to try to define a hierarchy of methods. Where do we start? With "forms" or with "functions"? Should we postulate a deep structure connection between the clauses of the text and then describe what different syntactic forms can be used to represent a deep structure?

To postulate a deep structure[18] underlying the connection of line 6 with a foregoing clause would help little, for what the various translators already have done is establish what kind of expression line 6 is and fix that interpretation by means of a translation suggesting a syntactic hierarchy. Thus we have as many proposals with respect to deep structure here as we have different types of translation. Moreover, the fact

---

16 *The New English Bible*, 1970.
17 M. Rehm, *Das erste Buch der Könige. Ein Kommentar*, Würzburg, 1979
18 Cf. Th. J. Finley, *op. cit.*, see ftn. 2.

that different syntactic interpretations can be represented graphically as shown above may even lead to the conclusion that the concept of deep structure does not contribute anything to *syntax* that could not equally well be contributed to it by means of a description of complex forms.

For this reason I would propose to follow the suggestions made by Hoftijzer and make an inventory of *forms* first, establishing the relationships between clauses based on morphological correspondences and clause types and describing the semantic effects of the words used in the clauses of this syntactical hierarchy thereafter.

Computer programming presents us with a possibility of isolating and marking the total number of clauses in a text corpus (i.e. for this test: the books of Kings), as well as establishing the different types represented by these clauses and calculating the frequency of the relations that exist between the clauses of the various types. Clearly all this is not a matter of mere registration and counting[19]. One works with preliminary definitions of clauses and phrases, which are open to modification by the results of the first versions of the program. The demarcation of clauses is a complex procedure be it done with or without computer-aided formal procedures[20].

Clauses can be isolated partly automatically, e.g. the sequence *pronoun -conjunction - verb* implies that with the conjunction a new clause begins (I Ki. 2, vs. 9, line 3). For the remainder it is still a matter of linguistic classification. For instance, *participle* and *infinitive* are regarded as opening separate clauses if a NP and/or a PP are dependent on them (I Ki. 2, vs. 8, line 3).

Another difficulty is that also computer-aided procedures cannot escape the circularity which one finds in more traditional syntactic studies. Actually one is using the same textual corpus twice: first to registrate and to categorize observations of forms, second to apply the statistics of these categories in order to decide upon the more complex cases in the corpus. This means that one cannot pretend to decide upon cases of grammatical discussion by using computer technique. It should be used to test the consistency of a grammatical theory.

As I have tried to show in the preceding section, the four schema's of syntactical hierarchy underlying the different translations of I Ki. 2:8-9 represent implicit theories of Hebrew syntax on several functions of W-Qatal. The question is now whether it would be possible to discover criteria with which to test whether one of the four schemas is likely to

---

[19] See the results of a similar research project on Deuteronomy in: L.J. de Regt, *A parametric Model for Syntactic Studies of a Textual Corpus, Demonstrated on the Hebrew of Deuteronomy 1 - 30* (University of Leiden Dissertation), Assen, 1988.

[20] Cf. E. Talstra, "Towards a Distributional definition of Clauses", see ftn. 6.

be the best choice.

The computerprogram that is being constructed now to establish clause hierarchies and to contribute to syntactic research is in many respects still in an experimental stage. At the moment it performs the following actions:

**1** While reading the text of the books of Kings the program registrates the *opening type* of each clause. With opening type I mean the row of words or phrases from the beginning of the clause up to and including the verb. If no verb is being used, the words or phrases until the encountering of a NP and/or a PP are registered. For example:

| | | | | | |
|---|---|---|---|---|---|
| כי | + | - | - | - | Qatal |
| ו | + | לא | +- | - | Yiqtol |
| - | - | לא | +כן | NP | - |

In the books of Kings 380 different types of clause openings were registered. This preliminary figure will no doubt change somewhat once the clause demarcation has been critically revised.

**2** Secondly, these clause opening types are classified under labels of a more traditional type, such as Wayyiqtol-Clauses, W-X-Qatal-Clauses, Nominal Clauses, etc. This implies that the program is able to produce statistics of the data both in terms of the observed syntactic forms and in terms of more general type labels dependent on syntactical theory. I reproduce here only the more compact matrix of clause relationships according to their type labels. The form-based matrix is a much larger one. The following should be read according to the formula:

Clause type: *row(y,x)* is connected to a preceding Clause type: column **n** times.

For example, Type 8 (infinitive) is connected to Type 0 (narrative) 225 times.

| type | 0 | 1 | 2 | 3 | 4 | 5 | 6 | 7 | 8 | 9 | Totals |
|---|---|---|---|---|---|---|---|---|---|---|---|
| | Narr | Qat | W-X | W-Q | Yiq | Imp | WeY | W-X | Inf | NC | |
| 0. Narr. | 1872 | 142 | 75 | 19 | 19 | 4 | 3 | 2 | 7 | 64 | 2207 |
| 1. ..Qatal | 325 | 248 | 39 | 40 | 48 | 32 | 7 | 3 | 86 | 136 | 964 |
| 2. W-X-Qatal | 72 | 25 | 25 | 1 | 2 | 1 | 0 | 0 | 1 | 31 | 158 |
| 3. W-Qatal | 34 | 42 | 4 | 118 | 58 | 24 | 2 | 13 | 11 | 28 | 334 |
| 4. ..Yiqtol | 65 | 57 | 5 | 47 | 115 | 32 | 6 | 9 | 48 | 89 | 473 |
| 5. Imper. | 129 | 23 | 3 | 5 | 10 | 107 | 0 | 1 | 33 | 32 | 343 |
| 6. We-Yiqtol | 4 | 5 | 0 | 2 | 13 | 30 | 17 | 1 | 1 | 5 | 78 |
| 7. W-X-Yiqtol | 2 | 6 | 2 | 12 | 18 | 5 | 2 | 9 | 4 | 8 | 68 |
| 8. Infin. | 225 | 129 | 19 | 28 | 36 | 16 | 4 | 6 | 64 | 49 | 576 |
| 9. N. Clause | 373 | 144 | 43 | 41 | 43 | 44 | 9 | 4 | 53 | 349 | 1103 |
| Totals | 3101 | 821 | 215 | 313 | 362 | 295 | 50 | 48 | 308 | 791 | 6304 |

Table 1: *Preliminary table of all clause relations in the books of Kings*

| | cl. connect. | distance | morphol. corresp. | frq. of conn. (in Kings) | score |
|---|---|---|---|---|---|
| a. | 6 ⇒ 5<br>*ʾšr* + yiqtol<br>⇒ W-Qatal | 1:<br><br><br>(4) | 3: person<br>gender<br>number<br>of verb (2) | 58:<br>(yiqtol +<br>W-Qatal)<br>(3) | 9 |
| b. | 6 ⇒ 4<br>W-Qatal ⇒<br>W-Qatal | 2:<br><br><br><br>(3) | 4: ident. tense<br>form;<br>person,gender,<br>number<br>of verb (4) | 118:<br><br><br><br>(4) | 11 |
| c. | 6 ⇒ 3<br>Nominal Cl.<br>⇒ W-Qatal | 3:<br><br><br>(2) | 1: pronoun =<br>person,gender,<br>number<br>of verb (1) | 28:<br><br><br>(1) | 4 |
| d. | 6 ⇒ 2<br>*ʾl* + yiqtol<br>⇒ W-Qatal | 4:<br><br><br><br>(1) | 4: verbal sfx =<br>noun sfx;<br>person,gender<br>number<br>of verb (3) | 58:<br>(yiqtol +<br>W-Qatal)<br><br>(3) | 7 |

Table 2: *Table of clause parameters (I Ki. 2:9, line 6)*

**3** From this information the program is able to "learn" a little Hebrew syntax. When used for the first time the program will, for each clause of a text, ask the user to mention the foregoing[21] clause to which the present one has some syntactical connection. Once a connection has been indicated at by the user, the existence of a relationship between the two clause types involved (e.g. between a Noun Clause and a W-Qatal Clause: I Ki. 2:9 line 3 and 4) will be stored and the morphological correspondences between both clauses will be calculated (in this case: person, gender and number of the verb ידע are congruent with person, gender and number of the pronoun אתה). The next time a similar pair of clauses appears in a text, the program is able to make a proposal. This proposal will be based on three calculations:

- the frequency of occurrences of the same clause connection in the text corpus established so far,
- the number of morphological correspondences between the two clauses being dealt with,
- the distance between the two clauses.

**4** The experiments with this program are now being directed to the most complex of tasks, i.e. the increase of the number of correct syntactical hierarchies proposed. Thus far the following procedure is

[21] The concept of the foregoer has been discussed with L.J. de Regt (see ftn. 19) during his research in the syntax of the book of Deuteronomy. It appeared to be a useful parameter to base the description of clause connections and functions upon.

used: For each clause of a text the program proposes first a number of possible syntactical hierarchies, comparable to the four schema's of I Ki. 2:9 as found in the existing translations. Next it calculates which textual hierarchy should be preferred from the point of view of a form-based syntax. To do so, the program constructs for each clause a table containing the possible clause connections and their parameters.

In the case of I Ki. 2:9 line 6 the result is a table as reproduced above.

The Table demonstrates the scores of each of the four possible clause connections (a - d) on the parameters: "distance" between the two clauses involved, number of "morphological correspondences" of the two clauses and the "frequency" of the same clause connection occurring in the book of Kings. The figures between brackets show the relative order of the four possible clause connections in terms of highest to lowest score. The column "score" is the sum of the three relative scores. Clause hierarchy b appears to obtain the highest score.

Based on the formal correspondences observed I would suggest that the schema b is the best option to accept. The W-Qatal of line 6 is dependent on the W-Qatal of line 4. Both lines constitute a parallel construction dependent on the nominal clause of line 3. This means that both line 4 and line 6 adopt the modal function of a W-Qatal clause in such a position. In terms of a communicative or semantic point of view one could translate both clauses as representing a strong confidence of David, not a direct command or another type of instruction:

.... For you are a wise man.
(I am sure) you will know what to do with him.
(I am sure) you will bring him down ...

The research has to be continued from this point presently. The use of the clause parameters has to be refined. To mention some details:

**1** It does not seem to be obvious that "distance" should be regarded as equally important for each type of clause connection. Narrative clauses can be connected even with a large number of direct speech lines in between, while infinitive or אשר- constructions cannot.

**2** Similarly not all morphological correspondences should be regarded as of identical weight. The syntactical hierarchies of type b and d show an equal number of morphological correspondances, i.e. 4. However, the identity of tense form in type b is evaluated here (by the present author, not yet by the program) as having more weight than identity of suffixes as in type d. For that reason the relative score of type b (4) is higher than the relative score of type d (3).

**3** Clause connections can be based on clause opening types only, without further morphological correspondances, e.g. לא + verb ⇒ כי

אם. This type of connection also needs to rank among the other parameters. Therefore, the calculation of frequencies of clause connections which until now was using the general classification of the "foregoer" (cf. column 4 , the hierarchies of type a and d in the Table of clause parameters) has to be refined.

4. *Conclusions*

It is difficult to tell where exactly the form-based syntactical study will lead us eventually. The present article may have demonstrated that the choice in favor of the registration of forms as proposed by Hoftijzer is a good option, both theoretically and practically. I expect this approach to become a helpful tool for Bible translators and a good instrument to develop and test theories of syntax and textgrammar for semitists.

Computer-assisted research of a textgrammatical type will provide the exegete with a tool to construct the syntactic framework of a textual composition, without being too much dependent on *ad hoc* textual interpretation. As a result exegetical discussion will gain more profit from grammatical argumentation both in stilistic and in literary critical textual analysis.

# Process and Result and the Hebrew Infinitive: A Study in Linguistic Isomorphism

Yishai Tobin, Be'er Sheva and Tel-Aviv

## 1. Introduction

As Saussure so aptly put it: *"c'est le point de vue qui crée l'objet"*. Indeed, the choice of the *linguistic sign* as the unit of linguistic analysis necessitates the adoption of the "isomorphism hypothesis" or the principle of "one-form/one meaning" which —by definition— implies the interface of phonoloy-morphology-syntax-semantics, or, the theoretical and methodological search for a single set of principles which can be equally applied to all levels of language.

This Saussurian dictum advocating isomorphism was previously overlooked by most traditional grammarians and has not found much more than superficial support among modern post-Saussurian neo-traditional grammarians all of whom consistently continue to classify and categorise "problematic", "irregular", or "exceptional" forms and form-classes according to the supposedly separate, independent and autonomous levels of language.

A classic example of a particular class of "problematic", or "exceptional" forms or form-classes which has been classified and categorised according to phonetic or phonological criteria only is the "defective" *I-Nun* class of Hebrew verbs. The theoretical and methodological "calling card" of these verbs is that the first consonant of their triconsonantal (CCC) root is a *nun* /*n*/ which often is "assimilated", "disappears", or "falls out" in specific linguistic environments:

**(i)** in the first (*kal/paal*) conjugation of the paradigmatic verb conjugation system (in the "imperfective" in Biblical Hebrew or "future" tense in Modern Hebrew);

**(ii)** in the imperative forms;

**(iii)** in certain infinitives.

What is particularly interesting regarding the *I-Nun* class, however, is that the *n*-Deletion rule (as presented by Bolozky 1978:18-19) is considered to be only a "minor rule" due to its limited distribution in the verb paradigm. Even when the extension of the distribution of the *n*-Deletion rule to other conjugation patterns (*nifal, hifil*) has been postulated (Barkai 1975 and Scharzwald 1973), it was still considered to be quite a "minor" phonological rule. Furthermore, even when this "minor" rule works, it does not work without exceptions. Indeed, the exceptions to the rule greatly outnumber the very limited cases where it works! Thus, Bolozky does not consider the minor *n*-Deletion rule to be a particularly productive one. Even worse, neither he nor anyone else has explored the possibility that there may be additional semantic factors which motivate what may appear to be the arbitrary limited distribution of *n*-Deletion in the verb system[1].

Theoretically speaking, the most interesting result of "the case of the missing *nun /n/*" is that it has produced two alternative infinitive forms for a selected sub-class of verbs (among which is a further sub-class within those verbs whose third consonant in the triconsonantal (CCC) root is a pharyngeal or laryngeal consonant *ayin* /ʿ/ or *aleph* /ʾ/: where one infinitive form "retains" the initial *nun/n/* whilst the other infinitive form "loses" or "drops" the initial *nun/n/*, e.g.:

(a) *liNGo*ʿa or *laGa*ʿ*at* = "to touch"
(b) *liNTo*ʿa or *laTa*ʿ*at* = "to plant".

This phenomenon of alternative infinitive forms is but a "minor" rule and certainly not a "productive" one, since it, too, does not work all the time. In fact, like the *n*-Deletion rule, it only holds for a very limited number of cases. Once again, one could consider the possibility that there may be additional semantic factors which might motivate the limited distribution of this particular morphophonemic phenomenon as well.

Due to the fact that the classification of these "irregular" or "defective" forms has only been phonologically based, it has generally been accepted that:

**(i)** those roots which have alternative infinitive forms may be viewed as phonetically predictable;

[1] I will not discuss here the distribution of the "*nun-less*" forms in the various paradigms. It is most interesting to note, however, that the phonetically defective form has been appealed to by various scholars as a linguistic means to explain linguistic distribution, particularly with regard to the alternative imperative-future alternation in Modern Hebrew (e.g. Berman 1981a:269, 1981b:616-617, Yaeger-Dror and Sister 1987:1137-1138).

(ii) the resulting alternative infinitive forms may be viewed as allomorphs;

(iii) if these alternative infinitive forms are allomorphs they are, therefore, "synonymous";

(iv) if they are, indeed, "synonyms" then the choice of one infinitive form over the other might be a question of "syntax", "style", "register", "diachrony", or "diglossia".

## II. The Problem

Hebrew might be considered to be rather unique because it has sets of alternative infinitive forms that have been viewed as "doublets" or allomorphs: i.e. there are two familiar and common ways of forming infinitive forms from a subset of the same triconsonantal roots. This traditional view of alternative infinitival allomorphs can be found in most monolingual Hebrew dictionaries (e.g. Even-Shoshan 1974, Gur 1947, Medan 1964). The same holds true for most bilingual Hebrew-English, English-Hebrew dictionaries as well (e.g. Alcalay 1965, Ben-Yehuda and Weinstein 1968, Wittenberg 1974).

Previous to this study, none of the major linguistic analyses of Modern Hebrew — be they transformational-generative or similarly inspired (e.g. Berman 1978, Gliner 1989), structural (e.g. Rosén 1977), traditional or prescriptive (e.g. Bahat and Ron 1976, Sivan 1979) — has presented an adequate explanation of why Hebrew speakers may choose one member of this familiar infinitive pair as opposed to the other in spoken and written discourse. Thus, they have either inherently accepted the traditional view that the members of this infinitive doublet are, indeed, synonomous, or they have not viewed this question as being a problem at all or certainly not one which was worthy of their attention.

Indeed, Hebraists, philologists, linguists, and, consequently, language teachers and translators, of all theoretical persuasions, generally appeal to certain familiar categorical axioms which fairly accurately describe the favoured versus the disfavoured uses of these infinitive forms, but do not really explain why speakers and writers choose one form over the other.

The most prevalent and popular "explanations" of the favoured versus the disfavoured distribution of these particular forms include the following:

(a) The "syntactic" explanation: the most time-honoured way of "explaining" the distribution of alternative linguistic forms is by listing their different syntactic functions within a sentence, (usually employing the traditional grammatical categories of "parts of speech"). However, since both these alternative forms in Hebrew function as infinitives, the listing of this and other syntactic categories may, at best, accurately serve to designate and categorise their syntactic function in sentences. It must be remembered, however, that syntactic labels do not explain why speakers and writers will choose one infinitive form over the other in spoken and written discourse.

**(b)** The "historical" or "diachronic" explanation: one of the two alternative forms is found to be older than the other. In case of the alternative infinitive forms under discussion here, both alternative infinitive forms have been found in Biblical Hebrew, e.g. *liNGo*ʿa (Gen. 20:6, Jos. 9:19, Job 6:7) versus *laGa*ʿ*at* (2 Sam. 14:10)/*liNTo*ʿa (Jes. 51:16. Jer. 1:10. 31:28(27), 18:9) versus *laTa*ʿ*at* (Eccl. 3:2) (Mandelkern 1978:720, 742), and have remained in the language system to the present. Often times, one of the forms is considered to be the more "correct" form (*laGa*ʿ*at*), but since both forms appear in the Bible, and Biblical Hebrew is usually the source of most normative claims, this "prescriptive" claim will not hold either.

**(c)** The "stylistic" explanation: one of the two alternative forms is considered to be either more "formal" or "informal" than the other, and, therefore, is reserved for specific "formal" and/or "informal" contexts. Yet, even a cursory collection of data clearly indicates that both infinitive forms can and do appear in the same text, passage paragraph and sentence in both "formal" and "informal" linguistic contexts, thus making the appeal to a "stylistic" explanation both incorrect and unfeasible. Indeed, different native speakers do not always agree which of the alternative infinitive forms is more "formal" than the other. Furthermore, both forms appear in literary as well as journalistic texts of all styles and registers and neither can be considered to be a "style marker" (i.e. an indicator of a specific syle or register) in the sense of Enkvist (1973).

**(d)** The "diglossia" explanation: one of the two alternative forms is considered to belong to the "spoken" language while the other to the "written" language. Once again, even a cursory collection of data clearly reveals that both infinitive forms can and do appear in both spoken as well as written Hebrew, thus making the appeal to "diglossia" as an explanation for the distribution of these forms inadequate and unreasonable.

(e) The "synonyms" explanation: (a), (b), (c) and (d) above are all implicitly based on the notion that these alternative infinitive forms are "synonyms" (i.e. "mean the same thing") and are chosen arbitrarily according to their syntactic function, and/or degree of formality and/or the specific mode of communication. It appears, however, that these forms may not always be interchangeable, and a subtle semantic distinction may indeed exist between them. Therefore, this appeal to synonymy (and by definition, all the other synonymy-based explanations above) is, at best, incomplete.

These familiar syntactic, diachronic, stylistic and diglossic explanations are so firmly entrenched within theoretical and applied linguistic research, that they virtually have become the ready-made, automatic replies invariably used to explain the distribution of these "synonymous" infinitive pairs in Hebrew discourse. Indeed, both in essence and in practice, they have been transformed into axiomatic and unquestioned categorical and convenient theoretical and methodological tools. And no wonder! On the surface, at least, these "explanations" usually appear "to work". Most of the time, they seem to successfully categorise and describe the most frequent and favoured functions and occurrences of the linguistic forms in question.

Unfortunately, these "explanations", like so many other "convenient tools", have also turned into "tools of convenience". In other words, they have allowed researchers to disregard or ignore those cases where the data do not fit their preconceived categories. Thus, the disfavoured, less frequent, or special uses of these forms have been swept under theoretical and methodological rugs and subsequently placed in a kind of theoretical limbo. In short, the problematic data have generally been isolated and classified as "exceptional cases" doomed to remain in the purgatory of a theoretical vacuum without much hope of being understood or explained.

## III. The Analysis

We will present an alternative analysis which will show that each phonologically distinct infinitive form has a different invariant meaning based on a marked distinctive semantic feature which systematically distinguishes it from its so-called synonymous allomorph. Furthermore, we will also claim that it is this difference in meaning which motivates the distribution of each infinitive form in the language. In other words, we are proposing that what were formerly considered phonetically motivated, synonymous, allomorphs are indeed two distinct linguistic signs which can be systematically opposed to each other. Our alternative analysis will be based on the sign-orientated notions of invariance, markedness and isomorphism[2].

Specifically, our analysis is based on the following six principles:

1. We agree with the fundamental assumption that both alternative infinitive forms share a common semantic domain which is signalled by the triconsonantal (CCC) root they share.

2. We further maintain, however, that the alternative infinitive forms are not "synonyms"; but rather each possesses a single invariant meaning which: (a) distinguishes it from the other, and (b) will motivate its distribution in the language.

3. We further believe that these invariant meanings are in a marked versus unmarked relationship revolving around the notions of *process* versus *result*.

4. The notions of *process* versus *result* may show how language may reflect two fundamental ways of viewing action/states/event: either as focussing on the *process* involved in the action/state/event, or, alternatively, from the point of view of the *result* (outcome, final point or goal)[3].

5. According to our proposed analysis, one member of the infinitive pair (*laGa*ʿ*at/laTa*ʿ*at*), the "phonetically irregular, defective or *marked* form", will also be *marked* for the semantic feature *Result*: i.e. making a specific claim that an action/state/event is to be perceived from the point of view of its result, (outcome, final point, destination, goal, etc.) whilst the other member of the pair (*liNGo*ʿ*a/liNTo*ʿ*a*), the phonetically "regular" or *unmarked*

[2]The semiotic linguistic orientation underlying this analysis has been further discussed in Tobin (1985, 1987, 1988a, 1989a, 1990a, in prep. a,b). Similar sign-orientated analyses for Modern Hebrew may be found in Tobin 1981, 1982, 1984, 1986, 1986/1988b-d, 1989b,c, 1990b.

[3]The concept of *process-result* as a fundamental and primary theoretical principle in language — worthy of a book-length study on its own (Tobin (in prep.b)) — has not been given its proper due in linguistic research. There are several reasons for this anomaly: *Process-Result* generally has been viewed as a secondary principle of categorisation within the realm of verbal aspect which has primarily focused on the traditional concept of "perfective" versus "imperfective" or "complete" versus "incomplete" actions. Limiting the concept of *process-result* to a mere pragmatic implication of "perfectiveness" within the highly problematic category of verbal aspect has not allowed linguists to recognise it as a fundamental semantic distinctive feature which cuts across almost all traditional and modern categorisations.

form, is also *unmarked* or *neutral* semantically: i.e. it either may be viewed as a process or as a result.

6. This particular marked/unmarked relationship may be stated here as part of an invariant meaning in the form of discourse instructions:

   **(a)** the unmarked member of the pair (*liNGoʿa/liNToʿa*), makes no claim with regard to *process* versus *result*. It means: THE ACTION/STATE/EVENT MAY EITHER BE VIEWED AS A PROCESS OR AS A RESULT.

   **(b)** the marked member of the pair (*laGaʿat/laTaʿat*), on the other hand, makes a specific claim regarding *process* versus *result*. It means: THE ACTION/STATE/EVENT MUST BE VIEWED AS A RESULT.

This semantic system may be presented schematically in the following way (figure 1):

| Semantic Substance | Form | Meaning |
|---|---|---|
| The manner an action-state-event may be viewed | *liNGoʿa/liNToʿa* | UNMARKED FOR PROCESS/RESULT |
| | *laGaʿat/laTaʿat* | MARKED FOR RESULT |

Figure 1: The *PROCESS-RESULT* System

The markedness relationship may be schematized in the following way (figure 2):

UNMARKED -
*liNGoʿa/liNToʿa*
MARKED -
*laGaʿat/laTaʿat*
UNMARKED -
*liNGoʿa/liNToʿa*

Figure 2: The *UNMARKED-MARKED* Relationship

Thus the unmarked member of the pair making no claim to *process* versus *result*, is the more flexible, neutral and open-ended of the two. It allows for any and all views of an action/state/event either as a process or result. Therefore it may be used in any and all linguistic and situational contexts and modes of communication. The marked member of the pair making a claim that the action/state/event must be viewed from the point of view of result, is generally more limited in its distribution. It is reserved for those linguistic and situational contexts where a "resultative" point of view is both necessary and appropriate. In short, this paper is based on the assumption that the choice of one infinitive form versus the other is not determined arbitrarily, but is motivated by the markedness relationship of its invariant meaning.

IV. The Data

We will first examine the distribution of the alternative infinitive forms in various linguistic contexts. The *liNGo*ʿ*a* versus *laGa*ʿ*at* ("to touch") opposition is probably the one most frequently used in the language. Our claim is that the use of the marked form *laGa*ʿ*at* makes a claim for the feature "Result": i.e. stresses the action/state/event from the point of view of its outcome, final point, destination, goal, etc. Indeed, the Biblical use of *laGa*ʿ*at* (2 Sam. 14:10) or *ke-Ga*ʿ*at* (Ez. 17:10) both clearly stress the end point or the result of the action of "touching", namely death or utter destruction:

1. *we-lo*ʾ *yosif* ʿ*od laGa*ʿ*at bax* ...(2 Sam.14:10)

   "he shall not *touch* thee anymore ..."

   Context: The famous story of the woman of Tekoa who is sent by Joab to speak to King David after Absalom's fleeing and death. The woman, disguised as a mourner, tendentiously relates to the King all the woes of the losses of her husband, the slaying of her one son by the other, the violent reaction of the rest of the family seeking revenge by wanting to kill the remaining son and heir, in short, we are being presented with a series of violent acts whose result is being emphasized and stressed. The King then takes charge of the woman using the marked form *laGa*ʿ*at* giving further force and credence to his pledge to protect her.

2. *ha-lo*ʾ *xe-Ga*ʿ*at bah ruax ha-qadim* ...(Ez. 17:10)

   "when the east wind *toucheth* it ..."

   Context: A famous parable of Ezekiel spoken unto the house of Israel in the name of the Lord about the planting, prospering and possible ultimate *withering* of a vine where the marked form is used to specify the possible withering or the death of the vine after being touched by the east wind with an emphasis on the *result*:

"Yea behold, being planted, shall it prosper?
Shall it not *utterly wither*, when the east wind *toucheth* it?
In beds where it grew it shall *wither*." (Ez. 17:10)

The Biblical uses of *liNGo*ʿa, the unmarked form, on the other hand, present the concept of "touching" in the sense of "approaching", "hurting", "touching" in a "negative" or "unrealised" context: i.e. a "touch" not being consummated, finished or completed:

3. *lo*ʾ *netatixa liNGo*ʿ*a* ʾ*eleyha* (Gen. 20:6)
   "Therefore, suffered I thee *not to touch* her."

4. *we-*ʿ*ata lo*ʾ *nuxal liNGo*ʿ*a bahem* (Jos. 9:19)
   "...now, therefore *we may not touch* them."

5. *me*ʾ*anah liNGo*ʿ*a nafši* (Job 6:7)
   "My soul *refuseth to touch* them."

In each case, the *process* message is being directly implied while the *result* message may also — but not necessarily — be inferred. This more open-ended process-orientated "negative", "unrealised", or unconsummated message is more suitable to the neutral or unmarked form rather than the marked form making a specific claim for *Result*.

A similar difference in distribution can also be found in Modern Hebrew. Both in spoken and written Hebrew of all stylistic registers when the literal *physical* touching of an object is being focused on and/or being forbidden, the marked form *laGa*ʿ*at* is invariably used. In signs found both in museums and universities on the one hand, a well as in neighbourhood groceries or in the marketplace (*šuk*) on the other, when any object (a painting, sculpture, computer or bread, fruit, or vegetables) is being forbidden to be touched, the use of the marked form is used both verbally or in written signs:

6. *lo laGa*ʿ*at*! or *al Ga*ʿ*at*!
   "Do Not Touch!", "Hands off!"

The marked form, not unsurprisingly, also adds a certain "force" to an utterance both in spoken and written discourse:

(a) In the headline of a newspaper article dealing with the problems between psychiatrists and patients:

   7. *ha-metapel muxan lekabel al atsmo mexir šel kaas we-tiskul mi-tsad ha-metupal keivan še-ha-kaas yaazor lo laGa*ʿ*at be-mašehu xašuv be-xayav* (*Ha-Aretz* 2 June 1987)

"The analist is ready to take on himself the price of the anger and frustration of the patient since the anger will help him *to touch* ("reach", "uncover") something important in his life."

(b) From recorded conversations:

8. *yeš lo pensia gdola, ax hu lo rotse laGa'at ba*
"He has a large pension, but he refuses *to touch* it."
Context: A woman complaining about her elderly father wo insists on living with her despite the fact that she knows he has money of his own. The use of the marked form emphasizes her frustration.

9. *asur laGa'at ba-et šeli!*
"It's forbidden *to touch* my pen!"
Context: An older brother admonishing his little brother for touching his new expensive Parker pen.

(c) From radio interviews:

10. *omdim ba-tor kedei laGa'at be-Adam...*
"They stand on line in order *to touch* Adam."
Context: A description of the hysterical behaviour of the teenage fans of Adam, a very handsome pop singer.

In all the above examples the *result* of the "touching" is being emphasized and stressed by the speakers or writers who have, most appropriately, chosen the marked form over the unmarked form.

I have also found one example where both the marked and unmarked forms were used in the same utterance in a radio interview:

11. *ratsiti liNGo'a be-kama nosim aval lo aspik laGa'at be-kulam*

"I wanted *to touch on* (*liNGo'a*) several subjects, but I won't have time *to touch*(*laGa'at*) ("deal with", "arrive at") all of them.

A similar distribution can also be found for the *liNTo'a* or *laTa'at* ("to plant") opposition as well. When either the *process* and/or the *result* of a planting might be inferred, the neutral or unmarked form is used, but when the planting *takes root* or the *result* of the planting is being emphasized, the marked form is used both in Biblical as well as Modern Hebrew.

The unmarked infinitive appears three times in the book of Jeremiah in the expression *livnot we-liNTo'a* ("to build and to plant") as part of series of actions where either the *process* and/or the *result* might be inferred:

12. *livnot we-liNTo*ʿa (Jer. 1:10, 31:28, 18:9)

"See, I have this day set thee over the nations
and over the kingdoms,
To root out and to pull down,
And to destroy and to overthrow;
To build, and *to plant*." (Jer.1:10)

"And it shall come to pass that like as I have watched over them to pluck up and to break down, and to overthrow and to destroy, and to afflict; so will I watch over them to build and *to plant*, saith the Lord." (Jer. 31:28)

"And at one instant I may speak concerning a nation, and concerning a kingdom, to build and *to plant* it ..." (Jer.18:9)

The above *liNTo*ʿa examples were all part of a list of deeds God says he will do through the words of a prophet. But when the *roots* or the *result* of the planting is being emphasized, we get the marked form:

13. *ʿet laTaʿat we-ʿet laʿaqor natu*ʿa ((Eccl. 3:2)

"A time *to plant* (root!) (Y.T.) and a time to pluck up (uproot) (Y.T.) *that which is planted*" (i.e. that which has already taken root!) (Y.T.)

The same markedness opposition also holds true in Modern Hebrew where one can either *liNTo*ʿa or *laTaʿat etsim* ("plant trees") but one can only *laTaʿat šorašim* ("plant roots").

This markedness relation also holds true when the act of planting is being used in a "metaphorical" sense. In the book of Isaiah we have the metaphorical "planting of the heavens" (*liNTo*ʿa *šamayim*) as part of a series of acts to be performed by God presented through the words of a prophet:

14. "And I have put My words in thy mouth,
And have covered thee in the shadow of my hand,
That I *may plant* the heavens ..." (Jes. 31:16)

However, when a metaphorical "planting of roots" is being emphasized, the marked form is preferred, (in this case in Modern Hebrew):

15. *lo hitslaxnu laTaʿat šorašim be-xevra ha-mitsrit* (*Ha-Aretz* 21 November 1987)

"We didn't succeed in *planting roots* in Egyptian society."

Context: An interview with the first Israeli Ambassador to Egypt.

Let us now list all the other roots with the alternative infinitive forms in the *I-NUN* class and classify them according to the marked-unmarked relationship regarding the semantic features of *process* and *result*:

16. *li(N)so›* or *laSe›t* - "to carry, bear, lift, raise; to transfer, to take;, to contain; to pardon; to forgive; to suffer, endure" (Alcalay 1965:1694)[4]

Example 16 fits the phonological subclass of alternative infinitives formed from *I-NUN* roots whose third root consonant is a pharyngeal or laryngeal. In this case the unmarked form is used for the first set of dictionary meanings "to carry, bear, lift, raise", which are the more *process-orientated* ones while the marked form is restricted to the other dictionary meaning which are the more "performative" speech act verbs marked for *result*. Indeed, we can create the following minimal pair:

17. *ani lo yaxol linso› oto* — "I can't 'carry/bear/lift/raise' it

versus:

18. *ani lo yaxol lase›t oto* — "I can't 'take/suffer/endure/stand' him

It is particularly interesting to note that there are other triconsonantal roots in this same class *I-NUN*/Pharyngeal/Laryngeal) that do not have alternative infinitive forms. One might view this as evidence of a "non-productive, minor rule" or one might point out that all of these particular roots (which either delete their I-*nun* or not) only appear with the unmarked infinitive and may be viewed as being either neutral containing both kinds of meaning or as *process-orientated* verbs *par excellence*:

19. *linboaḥ* - "to bark"

20. *linvo‹a* - "to flow, gush, (pour, sprout) forth"; "to result, issue, derive from"

21. *lingoha* - "to shine, glitter, brighten, illuminate, shed light"

22. *linso‹a* - "to travel, journey, move, migrate"[5].

[4]It should also be noted that the marked infinitive *laSe›t* also appears with the second conjugation (*piel*) with the meaning "to marry", a "performative" speech act or *result-orientated* verb *par excellence*.

[5]In Israeli Hebrew this infinitive appears both with and without a *nun*, but *never* with the marked infinitive ending *-a‹at*.

23. *linqo'a* - "to be dislocated"[6].

Indeed, if we carry our sign-orientated analysis even further we might even postulate the /*a'at*/ suffix for the marked infinitive as a possible linguistic sign in its own right meaning MARKED FOR RESULT since there are other irregular of defective infinitives ending with /*a'at*/ that:

**(i)** may or may not belong to a particular phonetically inspired form-class (e.g. *I-YOD*);

**(ii)** may or may not have an unmarked alternative infinitive form;

and all of which signify *result* verbs *par excellence*:

24. *laDa'at* - "to know" (*Y-D-'*)

25. *laQaXat* - "to take" (*L-Q-X*)

Furthermore, the /*t*/ itself appears as an irregular infinite ending on other sub-classes of irregular or defective verbs under the rubric of (i) and (ii) above all of which are also *result* verbs *par excellence*:

26. *laLeDet* - "to give birth" (*Y-L-D*)

27. *laTS'et* - "to go out, come out, go away, emerge, depart, leave; to appear, rise, expire, fail; to be exempt; to empty one's bowels, defecate" (*Y-TS-'*)

28. *laTSeQet* - "to pour (in, out), cast (metal)" (*Y-TS-Q*)

29. *laReDet* - "to come (go) down, descend, decrease, diminish" (*Y-R-D*)

30. *laševet* - "to sit, dwell, live, stay, reside, abide, settle" (*Y-Š-V*)

31. *laTet* - "to give, hand over, grant, yield,; to allow, permit, let; to put, place, establish, appoint, to make, render" (*N-T-N*)[7]

32. *laLeXet* - "to go, walk, step, wander, travel, go away, depart, disappear, vanish, pass away, proceed, continue" which is in opposition to the purely *process orientated leHaleX* - "to walk about, stroll, promenade" both of which are derived from the root (*H-L-X*).

---

[6]In Israeli Hebrew the marked form *laQa'at* can also be heard in expressions such as "to sprain one's ankle", etc. when the result of the dislocation or sprain is specifically mentioned and being emphasized.

[7]Some of these infinitives have alternative forms (e.g. *liTen* "to give" often found in legal contracts where the *process of giving* is at issue) which we will not deal with here.

It may also be possible that the suffix *-ot* - the "irregular" suffix for the *III-HEH* class may also belong to this *process* versus *result* markedness relationship. Indeed, it may very well be that what has previously been considered to be purely phonologically determined irregularities in Hebrew and other languages (e.g. "irregular", ablaut, or strong verbs in the Germanic languages and alternative infinitive endings in the Romance languages) may have a fundamental semantic and, therfore, isomorphic explanation as well.

## V. Conclusion

In this paper we have offered a solution to a specific linguistic problem employing the sign-orientated theoretical and methodological approach based on the concepts of invariance, markedness and distinctive feature theory as part of a larger holistic and isomorphic view of language. We have postulated the *process-result* dichotomy as a primary principle to explain different "form-classes" within the classification of Hebrew infinitives composed of "defective" roots, although it could also be applied to nouns, infinitives, gerunds, adjectives and possible other "parts of speech" or other morphological, syntactic or semantic categories within and across languages. Thus, the isomorphic principles of invariance and markedness might be viewed as an alternative means to discover new insights into previously unexplained and problematic linguistic data. This paper could, therefore provide an argument for a more natural and holistic analysis of language as part of a larger semiotic system used by human beings to communicate.

## References

R. Alcalay, *The Complete English-Hebrew, Hebrew-English Dictionary*, Tel-Aviv 1965.

M. Barkai, "On phonological representations, rules and opacity", *Lingua* 37 (1975) p.363-376.

J. Bahat and M. Ron, *ve-dayek!* Tel-Aviv 1976.

E. Ben-Yehuda, and D. Weinstein, *Ben-Yehuda's Pocket English-Hebrew Hebrew-English Dictionary*, New-York 1968.

R. Berman, *Modern Hebrew Structure*, Tel-Aviv 1978.

R. Berman, "Regularity and Anomaly: the Acquisition of Hebrew Inflectional Morphology", *Journal of Child Language* 8 (1981a), p.265-282.

R. Berman, "Language Development and Language Knowledge: Evidence From the Acquisition of Hebrew Morphophonology", *Journal of Child Language* 8 (1981b), p.609-626.

S. Bolozky, "Chapter two: Some aspects of Modern Hebrew phonology", in Berman (1978), p.11-67.

N. Enkvist, *Linguistic Stylistics*, The Hague 1973.

A. Even Shoshan, *ha-milon ha-ivri ha-merukaz*, Jerusalem, 1974.

L. Glinert, *The Grammar of Modern Hebrew*, Cambridge 1989.

Y. Gur, *milon ivri*, Tel-Aviv 1947.

S. Mandelkern, *Konkordantsia le-tanax*, Jerusalem and Tel-Aviv, 1978.

D. Medan, *me-aleph ad tav: milon ivri šimuši*, Jerusalem 1964.

H. Rosén, *Contemporary Hebrew*, The Hague 1977.

O. Scharzwald, *Lexical Representations, Phonological Processes and Morphological Processes in Hebrew*, University of Texas, Austin Phd dissertation.

R. Sivan, *leksikon le-šippur ha-lašon*, Tel-Aviv 1979.

Y. Tobin, "Participation systems, prepositions and deep structure case as decoding devices for Modern Hebrew", *ITL Review of Applied Linguistics* 54 (1981), p.45-63.

Y. Tobin, "Asserting one's existence in Modern Hebrew: A Saussurian based analysis of the domain of attention in selected 'existentials' ", *Lingua* 58 (1982), p.341-368.

Y. Tobin, "Language teachers should rush in where good translators fear to tread", *ITL Review of Applied Linguistics* 65 (1984), p.79-91.

Y. Tobin, "Two aspects of sign theory", *Bulletin CILA* 41 (1985), p.120-141.

Y. Tobin, "Discourse variation in the use of selected 'contrastive conjuctions' in Modern Hebrew: Theoretical hypotheses and practical application", in J. House-Edmonson and S. Blum-Kulka (eds.), *Interlingual and Intercultural Communication*, Tübingen 1986, p.259-277.

Y. Tobin, "Aspectual markers in Modern Hebrew: A sign-oriented approach", in D. Assaf (ed.) *Proceedings of the Ninth World Congress of Jewish Studies: Hebrew and Jewish languages*, vol.1, 1986, 53-60. Reprinted in S. Morag (ed.), *Studies on Contemporary Hebrew*, vol.2, Jerusalem 1988, p.584-92.

Y. Tobin, "Three sign-oriented linguistic theories: A contrastive approach", in H. Bluhme and G. Hammarström (eds.) *Descriptio Linguistica*, Tübingen 1987, p.51-75.

Y. Tobin, (ed.) *The Prague School and Its Legacy* (Linguistic and Literary Studies in Eastern Europe, 27), Amsterdam and Philadelphia 1988a.

Y. Tobin, "Modern Hebrew tense: A study of the interface of objective and subjective spatio-temporal and perceptual deictic relations", in V. Ehrich and H. Vater (eds.) *Temporalsemantik*, Tübingen 1988b, p.52-80.

Y. Tobin, "The dual number in Modern Hebrew: A sign-oriented approach", *Journal of Literary Semantics* 12 (1988c), 176-201.

Y. Tobin, "A semantic analysis of the Modern Hebrew interrogatives *eix* and *keitsad* = HOW", *General Linguistics* 28 (1988d), p.183-219.

Y. Tobin, (ed.), *From Sign to Text: A Semiotic View of Communication* (Foundation of Semiotics 20), Amsterdam and Philadelphia 1989a.

Y. Tobin, "Space, time and point of view in the Modern Hebrew Verb", in Y. Tobin (ed.) (1989a), (1989b), p.61-92.

Y. Tobin, "The ayin-dalet system in Modern Hebrew: a sign-oriented approach", in H. Weydt (ed.) *Sprechen mit Partikeln*, Amsterdam and New York 1989c, p.391-402.

Y. Tobin, *Semiotics and Linguistics* (London Linguistics Library), London and New York 1990a.

Y. Tobin, "Invariant meaning: alternative variations on an invariant theme", in L. Waugh and S. Rudy (eds.) *New Vistas in Grammar: Invariance and Variation*, Amsterdam and Philadelphia 1990b, p.42-64.

Y. Tobin, *Invariance, Markedness and Distinctive Feature Analysis: A Contrastive Study of the Semantic Systems of Hebrew and English* (Current Issues in Linguistic Theory). Amsterdam and Philadelphia, (in prep. a)

Y. Tobin, *Process and Result in Language: A study of Aspect in the English Verb* (Longman Linguistics Library), London and New York (in prep. b).

M. Wittenberg, *milon ivri angli rav-hekafi*, Jerusalem 1974.

M. Yaeger-Dror and E. Sister. " 'Scuse me, waitaminute!': directive use in Israeli Hebrew." *Linguistics* 25 (1987), p.1127-1163.

# Some Reflections on the Use of Post-Predicative *hwā* in Classical Syriac

Lucas Van Rompay, Leiden

Like many other Semitic languages, Aramaic, in the course of its history, has witnessed the gradual introduction of verbal functions and verbal forms into the nominal sentence.[1] The present article aims at studying some aspects of this development in Classical Syriac, an Aramaic language known to us from a large number of literary texts dating from the third century C.E. onwards.

The basic pattern of the nominal sentence in Classical Syriac consists of the predicate and an enclitic personal pronoun, which expresses the subject,[2] e.g. *šanyā (h)w* "he is a madman" ["a madman - he"] (W-Yoh. 9,13)[3]. This pattern may be extended with the expression of the subject (nominal or pronominal) outside the basic nexus-complex. In such cases the pronominal subject within the nexus-complex constitutes a "lesser subject" (s), juxtaposed to the "subject" (S) outside the complex. The possibilities are either S-[P-s] or [P-s]-S.[4]. E.g. *ʾenā w-(ʾ)āb(y) ḥad (ḥ)nan* "I and the Father are one" ["I and the Father, one - we"] (W-Yoh. 7,8 = Peshitta John 10,30) and *šarrirāʾit rab (h)u ʾAlāhā hānā* "Verily great is this God" ["... great - he, this God"] (W-Yoh. 30,20 - 31,1).

In addition to these patterns, Classical Syriac has developed a conjugated form of *ʾit*, i.e. the particle *ʾit* expanded with pronominal suffixes, which has the function of a copula: *ʾitay* "I am", *ʾitayk* "you are" etc. The position of this copula appears to be free.[5]

---

[1] For a general survey and an analysis of several of these languages, see D. Cohen, *La phrase nominale et l'évolution du système verbal en sémitique. Etudes de syntaxe historique*, Paris 1984.

[2] G. Goldenberg, "On Syriac Sentence Structure", in M. Sokoloff (ed.), *Arameans, Aramaic and the Aramaic Literary Tradition*, Ramat-Gan 1983, 98-100.

[3] The abbreviations used in the course of the article are explained at the end.

[4] *Ibid.*, 102-104. For some remarks on the status of the enclitic personal pronoun in this structure, see J. Joosten, *The Syriac Language of the Peshitta and Old Syriac Versions of Matthew. Syntactic Structure, Translation Technique and Inner Syriac Developments*, Ph. D. thesis, Hebrew University, Jerusalem 1988, 146-148.

[5] Cf. T. Muraoka, "On the Syriac Particle *it*", *Bibliotheca Orientalis* 34 (1977), 21-22; Goldenberg, *art. cit.*, 126-128.

Whereas the basic nominal sentence is neutral with regard to aspect and tense, the introduction of a verbal copula is needed when "non-present" markings are desired.[6] In Syriac the verb *hwā* "to become, to be" is used for this purpose. Because of the marking of tense inherent in this verb form, Nöldeke does not regard it as a copula.[7] The question may be raised, however, whether this strict distinction need be maintained. As a matter of fact, it appears that in some languages verbs meaning "to be" have been reduced to the status of a verbal copula (or auxiliary verb).[8] This might well be the case for Syriac *hwā*. In the following I intend to describe some of the conditions under which *hwā* appears, without trying to solve the difficult question of its exact status.[9]

As a full verb, *hwā* continues to be used throughout the period of Classical Syriac, with the meaning "to become". As to its position in the sentence, it enjoys the same freedom as all other verbs. In its reduced status, as a perfect form and placed after the predicate, *hwā* is used to mark the past tense in the nominal sentence.[10] Moreover, by virtue of its postposition, the first consonant (*h*) is lost in pronunciation. To indicate this, the *mbaṭṭlānā* ("linea occultans") is used, a horizontal stroke written above or under the *h*. It should be stressed, however, that the *mbaṭṭlānā* does not occur in ancient manuscripts.[11] For this reason, it is sometimes impossible to distinguish between the use of *hwā* as a full verb (which can take any position in the sentence) and the use of the reduced, enclitic form.

The postposition of *hwā* as well as its enclitic nature point to a certain analogy with the use of the personal pronoun in the pure nominal sentence.[12] There seems, indeed, to be a parallelism between e.g. *makkik (h)u* "he is humble" ["humble - he"] and *makkik (h)wā* "he was humble" [humble - he was"]. In both cases there is a fixed word order

[6] Cf. J.B. Callender, *Studies in the Nominal Sentence in Egyptian and Coptic*, Berkeley - Los Angeles - London 1984, 5.

[7] T. Nöldeke, *Kurzgefasste syrische Grammatik*, 2nd ed., Leipzig 1898, 238: "... während *hwā* keine eigentliche Copula darstellt, da es immer eine wirkliche Tempusform ist."

[8] Cohen, *op. cit.*, 210-211 (where the situation in Geʿez is discussed).

[9] The present description is based on an analysis of a limited corpus of early Syriac texts, most of which have not been translated from another language.

[10] In many cases the explicit marking of the past tense is not needed in nominal sentences and is understood from the context. E.g. *d-ʾāp lā methazyā (h)wāt Teqlā ʾen ʿartellāyā (h)y* (W-Thec. 159,6) "so that Thecla could not be seen (to descry) whether she was naked" [... "whether naked - she"].

[11] Cf. R. Duval, *Traité de grammaire syriaque*, Paris 1881, 130-131 and 318-323.

[12] Cf. G. Khan, *Studies in Semitic Syntax*, Oxford 1988, 143: "The enclitic resumptive pronoun in such constructions is distributionally equivalent to the verbal copula *hwā*." However, the example given here is weak: it contains the imperfect form *nehwē*, which is never enclitic and enjoys a free position in the sentence.

and the second term is enclitic. How far does the analogy go? What are the limitations of the enclitic, post-predicative use of *hwā*?

The most common use of post-predicative *hwā* (in its perfect form) is the one found in combination with the active participle (*kāteb*, *mkatteb*, *makteb*). This structure is mainly used for "an on-going, repeated or habitual action in the past".[13] Its history throughout various phases of Aramaic has been analyzed in great detail by D. Cohen.[14] Whereas in earlier phases of Aramaic the perfect form *hwā* may occur either before or after the participle, its position in Syriac is after the participle.[15] Although the participial sentence has much in common with the nominal sentence, it should be noted that for the third person the opposition normally is not between *kāteb (h)wā* and **kāteb (h)u*, but between *kāteb (h)wā* "he wrote / he was writing" ["writing - he was"] and *kāteb* "he writes / he is writing" ["writing - (he)"]. For the other persons, however, the enclitic personal pronoun normally is required, e.g. *kāteb (h)wēt* "I wrote" vs. *kāteb (ʾ)nā* "I write". The use of the pure participle, without the enclitic pronoun for the third person, may be seen as marking a step towards the inclusion of the participle within the verbal system.[16] Under those circumstances the enclitic *hwā* obtains the status of an auxiliary verb, marking the past tense and the durative (or repetitive) aspect.

The use of *hwā* after participles is comparable with its use after *ʾit*, either in its unsuffixed or suffixed form.[17] The combination of *ʾit* and

[13] T. Muraoka, *Classical Syriac for Hebraists*, Wiesbaden 1987, 46. The functions of *hwā* in this combination are different, therefore, from the functions of *hwā* as an independent verbal form.

[14] D. Cohen, *op. cit.*, 335-591. Classical Syriac has not been included in Cohen's study.

[15] For Imperial Aramaic, see M.Z. Kaddari, "The Existential Verb HWH in Imperial Aramaic", in M. Sokoloff (ed.), *Arameans, Aramaic and the Aramaic Literary Tradition*, Ramat-Gan 1983, 43-46.

[16] Goldenberg, *art. cit.*, 112-117. Not only the active participle of the *peʿal*, but all other participial forms as well may be used without the enclitic pronoun. An example of the passive participle *peʿal* is: *meṭṭol mānā ʾaḥid tarʿā d-ballānā* (W-Yoh. 22,10-11) "Why is the door of the bath closed?". The passive participle may, therefore, take over the meaning of the perfect of the internal passive, e.g. *ʾAḥiqar sāprā qṭil* "Ahikar the scribe is killed" (ed. F.C. Conybeare e.a., *The Story of Ahikar*, London 1898, 54,1), where the participle is the equivalent of the passive perfect of Imperial Aramaic: *ʾḥyqr spr*ʾ ... *qṭyl* (ed. A. Cowley, *Aramaic Papyri of the Fifth Century B.C.*, Oxford 1923, 214, col. V,70-71). For cases where the predicative adjective is used without the enclitic pronoun and where the adjective may be considered to have been "verbalized", see Goldenberg, *art. cit.*, 116, as well as Joosten, *The Syriac Language*, 129, note 8.

[17] For the various meanings of *ʾit*, see Muraoka, "On the Syriac Particle *it*", and Goldenberg, *art. cit.*, esp. 130-131. For the combination *ʾit – (h)wā*, see E. Beck, "Grammatisch-syntaktische Studien zur Sprache Ephräms des Syrers (Schluss)", in *Oriens Christianus* 69 (1985), 3, as well as Joosten, *The Syriac Language*, 158.

*hwā* indicates a state in the past, not a process.[18]

The situation is slightly different for the passive participle *ktib*, which by its nature indicates the past. The enclitic *hwā* is sometimes used for the pluperfect.

When we consider the use of *hwā* after nominal predicates, it appears that, apart from the combination with participles, the largest number of occurrences is after adjectives, mostly – but not exclusively – in the absolute state.[19] This phenomenon lends support to Goldenberg's thesis that "in the domain of syntax the category of participles should be considered as also comprising the participial adjectives".[20] To this category belong, besides the participles, the forms *qṭel*, *qaṭṭil*, and to a lesser degree, *qaṭṭāl* and possibly *qṭol*. Some examples are (nos. 1-9):

1. *kad makkik (h)wā ᵓetmakkak* (K-Sim. 730,23) "while he was humble, he humiliated himself"

2. *d-lā p(ᵓ)ē (h)wā d-nahmē mennan ᵓAlāhā* (K-Sim. 790,3-4) "that it was not (or: had not been) right that God abandoned us"

3. *d-raḥḥiqā (h)wāt menhon rhibutā* (K-Sim. 926,21-22) "for terror was far from them"

4. *w-ᶜeddānā zᶜor (h)wā w-laḥmā layt (h)wā* (W-Yoh. 38,10) "and the time was short, and there was no bread"

5. *w-saggiᵓā (h)wāt karyutā* (W-Thec. 137,3) "and great was the grief"

6. *nemrā ḥad d-ṭāb biš (h)wā* (W-Thec. 156,12) "a leopard which was very savage"

7. *meṭṭol d-ḥabbib (h)wā ᶜlēh Pawlos* (W-Thec. 164,6) "because Paul was dear unto her"

8. *d-šahyā (h)wāt w-ṣadyā* (T-Ephr. 9,14) "that it (i.e. the earth) was waste and desolate"[21]

---

[18] Muraoka, *Classical Syriac*, 66.

[19] The distinction between the use of the absolute and emphatic state for the predicate is still somewhat problematic, cf. Goldenberg, *art. cit.*, 99, note 5 and 115-116, as well as J. Joosten, "The Predicative Adjective in the *Status Emphaticus* in Syriac", in *Bibliotheca Orientalis* 46 (1989), 18-24.

[20] Goldenberg, *art. cit.*, 115.

[21] Pesh. Gen. 1,2 has *ᵓarᶜā hwāt toh w-boh*. In his explanation Ephrem first replaces the verb form *hwāt* by *ᵓitēh (h)wāt*: *d-(ᵓ)itēh (h)wāt toh w-boh* and subsequently gives the two adjectives with *hwāt* in postposition.

9. *hānā dēn puqdānā qallīlā (h)wā* (T-Ephr. 30,7) "this commandment was an easy one"[22]

There can be no doubt that in most of these cases *hwā* after the predicate is used for the expression of a state in the past. Post-predicative *hwā* apparently alternates with *ʾitaw(hy) (h)wā*. One has to do with a general, unspecified past.

However, there does not seem to be a complete overlap between post-predicative *hwā* and *ʾitaw(h)y (h)wā*. Whereas *ʾitaw(h)y (h)wā* by its nature does not allow any distinction or fixation in time, post-predicative *hwā* may be required when specification in time is needed or when the pure notion of a "general past" does not suffice. The following passage may illustrate this (no. 10):

10. *d-hānā da-(ʾ)ḥrāyā (h)wā la-ḥšabt(y)* [to be read: *l-maḥšabt(y)*?] *hwā leh qadmāyā l-ṣebyān(y). w-hānā d-nukrāyā (h)wā la-ʿbāday hwā leh baytāyā l-suʿrān(y). w-hānā d-raḥḥiqā (h)wā la-šrār(y) hwā leh qarribā l-haymānut(y). w-hānā d-nappiqā (h)wā l-ḥeššokā hwā leh smikā b-meštutā* (K-Sim 759,4-10 and nearly identical in 898,11-17) "for the one who had been the last for my thought has become the first for my will, and the one who had been estranged from my deeds has become the intimate for my act, and the one who had been removed from my truth has become familiar to my faith, and the one who had been expelled into the darkness has become the guest at my wedding-feast"

In each of the main clauses *hwā*, as a full verb, means "has become". The state described in each of the subordinate clauses is not simultaneous with the processes mentioned in the main clauses. Rather, there appears to be a temporal opposition between them, in that the subordinate clauses express anteriority. In the subordinate clauses a situation is described which used to exist, but has been interrupted or changed into another, different situation. The perfect form *hwā*, following the predicate, apparently serves to mark this opposition. As a result, the combination of the predicate with *hwā* here does not parallel a participle + *hwā*, but rather a perfect form.[23] As a matter of fact, this is proved by the following sentence in the text, which has the perfect form twice: *w-hānā da-šdāy(hy) ṣebyāneh ... ʾaʿʿelteh mawdyānuteh* (K-Sim. 759,11-12 and 898,17-19) "and the one whose will had expelled him ... his confession has introduced him ...".

[22] A superlative meaning would fit here very well: "this commandment was the easiest one (or: the easiest possible)", cp. *ibid.*, 36,22 *meṭṭol da-zʿorā (h)wā* "because it was the smallest possible". Cf. Joosten, *art. cit.*, 21-22.

[23] For the use of the Syriac perfect with a pluperfect meaning, see Nöldeke, *Kurzgefasste syrische Grammatik*, 194, §257.

It appears, therefore, that apart from its use for the unspecified past (with *hwā* as a general past tense marker), the combination of a participial adjective with *hwā* may in some cases retain functions that are inherent in the perfect form of *hwā*.[24]

A closer examination of the passages where *hwā* follows a substantive predicate – much less numerous than those where *hwā* follows a participle or an adjective – will reveal that in a number of these cases *hwā* is used with the function described above (nos. 11-15).

11. (a man was sitting there who had an important position) *wa-kristyānā (h)wā w-beh b-hānā rdupyā ʾet(ʾ)eleṣ (h)wā wa-sged l-šemšā* (K-Sim. 750,20-21) "and he had been (or: used to be) a Christian and in this same persecution he had been forced and had worshipped the sun"

12. *ʾen Šemʿon d-ḥabbib(y) (h)wā w-rāḥm(y) hānā kuleh rgez ʿlay* (K-Sim. 750,26-751,1) "If Simon, who had been (or: used to be) my beloved and my friend (i.e. before my apostasy), has become so angry with me ..."

13. *hālēn gdayyā (h)waw dil(y) ... hāšā dēn breh d-(ʾ)abā ... dbar ʾennon* (W-Yoh. 40,19-41,1) "These were my kids ... but now the Son of the Father ... has taken them "

14. *ʾit gēr d-zannāyē (h)waw w-rawwāyē w-kad mṭāt lwāthon marduṭā d-melkē ṭābē hwaw nakpē wa-msaybrānē* (N- Bard. 563,4-6) "For there are (people) who had been (or: used to be) fornicators and drunkards and after the instruction of good advisers had come to them, they became chaste and abstinent"

15. *d-(ʾ)āpen ʿdammā d-y(h)abtāh l-baʿlāh ʾamtāh (h)wāt, ʾellā yawmānā ʿarrtāh (h)i* (T-Ephr. 72,15) "for although until (the moment) she had given her to her husband she had been her servant, however on this day she was her rival"

Thus it seems that for a number of cases where post-predicative *hwā* occurs after a substantive, the perfect form *hwā* is used with a more specific tense marking than when it is used in combination with participles or participial adjectives. The latter structure mostly indicates a general, unspecified past, whereas in the above examples *hwā* following a substantive marks a state or a process which in some way or another is limited in time or which involves a time setting distinct from the context. It certainly cannot be excluded that this specific tense marking

---

[24] For the use of *hwā* after a participle to express "a durative action anterior to an action in the past", see Joosten, *The Syriac Language*, 203-204 and 208.

has determined the choice of a post-predicative *hwā* structure, rather than the structure *ʾitaw(hy) (h)wā*.

Specific tense marking does not, however, seem to be the overall explanation for the use of *hwā* after substantives. Other factors may be at work as well. One of them is related to the use of perfect forms in conditional sentences.[25] In some types of conditional sentences, especially when the protasis contains an irrealis, introduced by *ʾellu* (rarely *ʾen*) "if", the use of *hwā*, both in the protasis and in the apodosis, is frequent,[26] even after a substantive predicate. Some examples are (nos. 16-19):

16. *d-(ʾ)ellu ʿaynā lā nahhirā (h)wāt, ḥšaḥteh dēn d-nuhrā d-šemšā yattirtā (h)wāt* (K-Sim. 911,12-13) "for if the eye would not have been luminous, the use of the light of the sun would have been superfluous"

17. *ʾellu ʿbid (h)wā hākannā barnāšā hu l-napšeh lā ʾitaw(hy) (h)wā ʾellā mānā (h)wā d-haw man da-mziʿ leh* (N-Bard. 543,24-544,1) "If man would have been made such, he would not have been autonomous [lit. "to himself"], but he would have been an instrument of the one who makes him move"[27]

18. *ʾellu gēr kulmeddem meškḥin (h)wayn l-meʿbad ḥnan hāwēn*[28] *kul w-(ʾ)en meddem lā māṭē (h)wā b-(ʾ)idayn l-meʿbad mānē (h)wayn da-(ʾ)ḥrānē* (N-Bard. 608,22- 25) "For if we would have been able to do everything, we would have been everything, and if it would not have belonged to our abilities to do anything, we would have been instruments of others"

19. *ʾellu gēr šabrē (h)waw ... lā ʾāmar (h)wā* (T-Ephr. 33,2-3) "If they would have been children, ... he would not have said ..."

The analysis given above suggests that the use of *hwā* after a substantive predicate may be governed by certain conditions, which do

---

[25] Nöldeke, *Kurzgefasste syrische Grammatik*, 195-196, §259.

[26] *Ibid.*, 299-301, §375. See also E. Beck, "Die konditionale Periode in der Sprache Ephräms des Syrers", in *Oriens Christianus* 64 (1980), 21-31, where the use of the participle with *hwā* is discussed, mainly in the apodosis after a protasis with *ʾellu*. As for the use of *hwā* after a substantive or an adjective, Beck argues: "Syntaktisch ändert sich wenig, wenn bei diesem Ausdruck an die Stelle des Partizips ein Adjektiv oder ein Substantiv oder auch ein īt (layt) tritt", *ibid.*, 27.

[27] In the first part of the sentence, after a prepositional predicate (*l-napšeh* "to himself"), *ʾitaw(hy) (h)wā* is used. In the second part, after a substantive (*mānā*), *hwā* is used. Compare also example no. 18.

[28] This form precedes the predicate. Although Nau reads it as a participle *(hāwēn)*, a perfect form (*hwayn*) would not be impossible.

not apply to post-predicative use of *hwā* after participles or adjectives. Among these we have pointed to the pluperfect meaning of the structure with *hwā* as well as to its use in conditional sentences after *ʾellu*. In addition, there may be other factors determining the occurrence of this structure.

Post-predicative *hwā* occurs after substantives in some identificatory sentences (nos. 20-23).

20. *yawmā dēn ʿrubtā (h)wāt* (K-Sim. 919,21) "The day was a Friday"[29]

21. *ʿeddānā (h)wā gēr d-(ʾ)etbaryat beh Ḥawwā* (T-Ephr. 36,2) "for it was the moment at which Eve was created"

22. *meṯṯol d-(ʾ)arʿā (h)wāt d-Qaʾin* (T-Ephr. 52,20-21) "because it was the land of Cain"

23. *dāmyā dēn d-(ʾ)araʿ ʾApamya (h)wāt* (T-Ephr. 116,4) "It is likely that it was the land of Apamea"

It is difficult to ascertain for each of these cases why post-predicative *hwā* was chosen instead of *ʾitaw(hy) (h)wā* or other structures. One reason may be that when *hwā* is used the predicate is immediately recognisable as such. This marking cannot be obtained by using *ʾitaw(hy) (h)wā*, which enjoys a free position in the sentence.

A structure of a somewhat different nature is the combination *šmeh (h)wā N* "his name was N" or *N šmeh (h)wā* "N was his name". It is problematic whether *šmeh* in this construction is subject or predicate.[30] Among the many available examples the following have been selected (nos. 24-26):

24. (two priests) *da-šmeh (h)wā l-ḥad ʿBedhayklā* (K-Sim. 739,25) "(of whom) the name of one was ʿB."[31]

25. *d-haw rēšhon da-šmeh (h)wā ʾApollo* (W-Yoh. 57,19) "of that chief of theirs, whose name was Apollo"[32]

26. *ḥad dēn gabrā ʾAnsipros šmeh (h)wā* (W-Thec. 129,4-5) "a man, Onesiphorus was his name"[33]

---

[29] Comp. however K-Sim. 887,11: *ʾitaw(hy) (h)wā dēn yawmā ḥamšā b-šabbā* "The day was a Thursday".

[30] For some remarks on the syntax of this structure, see Goldenberg, *art. cit.*, 132-133. For parallel structures in Hebrew, see J. Hoftijzer, "The Nominal Clause Reconsidered", in *Vetus Testamentum* 23 (1973), 470–471.

[31] Similar constructions occur in K-Sim. 750,18-19; 774,23-24; 954,15-16 and 19.

[32] Similarly W-Yoh. 21,13.

[33] Similarly W-Thec. 149,3.

In addition to the occurrences of *hwā* after a substantive predicate, *hwā* may also be found after an adverbial or prepositional predicate. It is difficult to ascertain whether *hwā* in such cases has the status of an enclitic.[34] The structure with *hwā* alternates with *ʾitaw(hy) (h)wā*. A distinction between the two structures cannot easily be established. Some examples are provided (nos. 27-29).

27. *b-puqdān mawhpāṭā rabbā d-tammān (h)wā b-dukkat šarrirā* (K-Sim. 955,4-5) "by the order of the great mobed who was there instead of the commissioner"

28. *wa-d-ʿammeh (h)wā breh d-(ʾ)Alāhā* (W-Yoh. 36,19-20) "and that the Son of God was with Him"

29. *d-hi msarhbuteh d-ḥewyā luqbal ḥewyā (h)wāt* (T-Ephr. 36,2) "for the very hastiness of the serpent was against the serpent"[35]

As some of the above examples have already shown, the status of *hwā* is not always clear. There can be no doubt that when the Syriac literary language was being established, the functions and meanings of *hwā* constituted a complex situation, which was only partly subject to the strict rules of the classical language. The gradual reduction of the verbal form *hwā* to a status comparable with that of a copula reveals itself in the post-predicative position of *hwā* as well as in its enclitic status and in its loss of some of the verbal functions (the verb instead being used as a pure past tense marker).[36] Not only was the reduction restricted to the perfect form *hwā*,[37] but even for this form it did not take place indiscriminately. Whereas it reached its furthest stage in the combination of the participle and the adjective with *hwā*, it was much less radical in the combination with substantives. As was shown above, in these combinations post-predicative *hwā* could only be used when certain conditions were met.[38] These conditions are partly linked with verbal functions of the perfect form (the expression of the pluperfect

[34] In T-Ephr. 39,30-31 *w-(ʾ)āp kad hi meštawḥrānuteh meṭṭol hādē hwāt (h)wāt* "even when his delay occurred for this very reason" the composite verbal form, *hwāt (h)wāt*, retains its full verbal function.

[35] Comp. however T-Ephr. 98,20: *ḥzā tub la-lbuš Yawsep d-luqbal Yawsep ʾitaw(hy) (h)wā* "Furthermore he saw the garment of Joseph, which was against Joseph".

[36] It should be noted that the combination *lā (h)wā* (or: *lā hwā*) is mainly used for the present tense. This structure has not been considered here. Cf. Nöldeke, *Kurzgefasste syrische Grammatik*, 228 as well as 255-256.

[37] A similar development did not take place for the imperfect form (*nehwē*), nor for the participle (*hāwē*).

[38] Nöldeke's examples of post-predicative *hwā* following a substantive are taken from the Old Testament Peshitta, esp. *hu kumrā (h)wā d-(ʾ)Alāhā mrayymā* (Gen. 14,18) "he was priest of God Most High" (*Kurzgefasste syrische Grammatik*, 228). It should be noted that Ephrem, after having quoted this verse in his commentary

and the use of the perfect form in conditional sentences) and may partly be related to other factors of a syntactic nature.

Finally, it should be stressed that the present investigation is based on a limited corpus of texts. In order to reach firmer conclusions, a more comprehensive study will be needed, which will have to take into account not only the possibility of historical developments, but also eventual distinctions between literary genres.[39]

Abbreviations

K-Sim. = *Martyrium Beati Simeonis bar Sabbaʿe* and *Narratio de Beato Simeone bar Sabbaʿe*, ed. M. Kmosko, *Patrologia Syriaca* I,2, Paris 1907, col. 715-959.

N-Bard. = *Bardesanes. Liber legum regionum*, ed. F. Nau, *Patrologia Syriaca* I,2, Paris 1907, col. 536-611.

T-Ephr. = *Sancti Ephraem Syri in Genesim et in Exodum Commentarii*, ed. R.M. Tonneau, (Corpus Scriptorum Christianorum Orientalium 152/Syr. 71), Louvain 1955.

W-Thec. = *The History of Thecla, the Disciple of Paul the Apostle*, ed. W. Wright, *Apocryphal Acts of the Apostles*, London 1871, p. 128-169.

W-Yoh. = *The History of John, the Son of Zebedee, the Apostle and Evangelist*, and *An Account of the Decease of Saint John, the Apostle and Evangelist*, ed. W. Wright, *op.cit.*, p. 4-72.

(T-Ephr. 68,23-24), uses a different construction in his paraphrase: *w-kumrā ṭub ʾitaw(hy) (h)wā* (T-Ephr. 68,28-29) "and furthermore he was a priest". This change may indicate that for Ephrem the construction with post-predicative *hwā* was not the obvious one. Similar hesitations as to the use of this construction may have existed among the Syriac translators of the New Testament, see Joosten, *The Syriac language*, 236 (Mt. 1,19) and 282 (Mt. 4,18).

[39] Whereas the evidence drawn from the hagiographic texts in our corpus seems to present a quite homogeneous picture with regard to language and style, Ephrem's Commentary on Genesis stands apart in many respects. The artistic and highly sophisticated language of this Commentary needs an independent investigation.